When the Lions R...
The story of the famous Wembley Speedway ...

Peter Lush and John Chaplin

London League Publications Ltd

When the Lions Roared
The story of the famous Wembley Speedway team
Peter Lush and John Chaplin

© Peter Lush and John Chaplin. Foreword © Bert Harkins. Introduction © John Chaplin.

The moral right of Peter Lush and John Chaplin to be identified as the authors has been asserted.

Cover design © Stephen McCarthy.

Cover photos: Front cover based on Wembley Lions programme from 1946.
Back: Freddie Williams (top left) Wembley Lions 1970 (JSC – top right), Tommy Price with the British Riders Championship trophy in 1946 (bottom right).

All photographs are as credited to the photographer or provider of the photo. No copyright has been intentionally breached; please contact London League Publications Ltd if you believe there has been a breach of copyright.

The photo credits are as follows: JSC: John Somerville Collection, including photos from Wright Wood, Alf Weedon, Mike Patrick, Peter Morrish and John Jarvis; JCA & MKC: John Chaplin Archive and Mike Kemp Collection; any uncredited photos are from Peter Lush's private collection. Wembley Speedway programmes from the 1940s and 1950s courtesy Wembley National Stadium Ltd.

This book is copyright under the Berne Convention. All rights are reserved. It is sold subject to the condition that it shall not, by way of trade or otherwise, be lent, resold, hired out or otherwise circulated without the publisher's prior consent in any form of binding or cover other than that in which it is published and without a similar condition being imposed on the subsequent purchaser.

A CIP catalogue record for this book is available from the British Library.

First published in Great Britain in October 2016 by London League Publications Ltd,
PO Box 65784, London NW2 9NS

ISBN: 978-1-909885-11-0

Cover design by Stephen McCarthy Graphic Design, 46, Clarence Road, London N15 5BB

Editing and layout by Peter Lush

Printed and bound in Great Britain by Charlesworth Press, Wakefield

This book is dedicated to the memory of Horatio Nelson 'Bronco' Wilson, the only Wembley Lions rider killed in a track accident after the Second World War. He died after a meeting at Harringay in August 1947.

Foreword

'Wembley'. No matter what sport you follow, the name 'Wembley' always adds an extra bit of magic and glamour to the occasion. This book by Peter Lush and John Chaplin traces the history of our sport, Speedway, at the famous Empire Stadium and the riders who rode there for the Lions from the pre-war days through the post-war years until 1971.

As a schoolboy Speedway fan in Glasgow – I was a Glasgow Tigers fan then but when I began riding Speedway as a novice, it was at Old Meadowbank, home of their rivals, Edinburgh Monarchs – I followed Speedway through the *Speedway Star* and the earlier *Speedway Gazette*. I read about Wembley legends, Freddie Williams, Bill Kitchen, Split Waterman, Trevor Redmond and other Lions' stars, and never thought that I would eventually meet up with them, but I did. Freddie was the new team manager when the Lions returned to the track in 1970, Bill was the ACU Machine and Track Examiner and good ol' T.R. was the promoter at Wembley along with businessman, Bernard Cottrell.

I also met the legendary 'Split' Waterman in 2015 when Ove Fundin and I rodeto Spain on our motorcycles to visit the former world finalist and his wife, Avril in Nerja, near Malaga.

In the 1970s at Wembley, we also had BBC DJs, David Hamilton and Ed Stewart as our meeting presenters and they often gave Saturday night Wembley Speedway a plug on their radio shows, so Speedway got a lot of publicity in those days.

As a young fan, my introduction to Wembley was travelling down from Glasgow on the overnight bus with some friends to watch the World Final at that famous stadium. A long, tiring journey, but well worth the discomfort just to watch that amazing event. Riders in polished shiny black leathers, JAP (J.A. Prestwich, British bikes) Speedway machines with their chrome frames, handlebars and rear mudguards sparkling under the floodlights and the roar of the huge crowd for heat one when all the lights in the stadium and centre green went out, apart from that ribbon of floodlights illuminating the race track ... very impressive.

My connections with Wembley went back to when my school and Cycle Speedway friend, Peter Christie wrote to Wembley and they sent us a complete set of Lions body colours for our Glasgow League Cycle Speedway team, the Mansewood Lions. We were the best turned-out team in Scotland! Little did I know that many years later, I would go from captain of the Mansewood Lions to captain of the 'real' Wembley Lions Speedway team.

I had been racing in Australia in the winter of 1969 when I was told that my team, Coatbridge Monarchs, had closed and that I and some of my team mates, Reider Eide, Wayne Briggs and Brian Collins were being transferred to Wembley. It was a big move, but the opportunity to ride with Scandinavian stars, Ove Fundin, Gote Nordin, Sverre Harrfeldt and race at the famous Empire Stadium, was too good to miss. We only lasted two years at the stadium before the Football Association put paid to league Speedway racing, but we built up a great following and riding for Wembley played a very big part in my Speedway career.

Riders such as World Finalist, Dave Jessup rode for Wembley in his teenage years and even the 19-year-old Tommy Jansson rode a few meetings for us. Although not yet a heat leader, his potential was very clear and I was disappointed when he was released after three meetings. Later, he became a crowd favourite when he rode for Wimbledon. We rode together in Australia. It was a great loss for his fans, family and friends when he lost his life in a track accident in Sweden in 1976.

So, with the famous Twin Towers demolished and no plans for Speedway at the new Wembley Stadium, we can sit back, read this book and say: 'Thanks for the memories'.

Bert Harkins

Introduction

WEMBLEY. Everything that is magical and majestic about sporting endeavour is contained in the name. The theatre of glorious triumph, and at once the boulevard of broken dreams.

The Empire Stadium ... it has a certain uncompromising dignity about it. It has, since its opening in 1923 – by a strange coincidence the same year speedway gestated at West Maitland – been revered, envied indeed, the world over and throughout the entire sporting community.

It has been the scene, since 1929, of so much speedway hope and glory, yet its importance to Wembley on occasions has been served in miserly fashion by Wembley's backroom administrators. Speedway was largely confined 'below stairs' to the servants' quarters ... except by one man.

His name: Arthur James Elvin, born in 1899, described as 'sports promoter'. The son of a Norwich policeman, he left school at 14, became first a soap salesman and then a First World War Observer in the Royal Flying Corps. Shot down and made a prisoner of war, an escape attempt failed because he couldn't swim, which instilled in him a determination to construct a public swimming pool.

Not long after the war he was destitute. By 1924 he had run out of money and, as a distressed officer, a charity offered him a job in a cigarette kiosk at the grand British Empire Exhibition at Wembley Park. It changed his life.

After the show was over the centrepiece of the Exhibition, the magnificent Empire Stadium, had gone into liquidation as 'financially unviable' and was about to be demolished. But by way of astute dealings with a near bankrupt gambler named James White in 1927, Elvin offered White £122,500 for the stadium, using a £12,000 down payment and the balance plus interest payable over 10 years. White accepted, but almost immediately committed suicide. Elvin raised £150,000 in two weeks to buy the place outright and he became chairman.

The boy from the provinces in the fullness of time also became a Knight of the Realm and universally renowned as the martinet owner who ran Wembley, which eventually included his public swimming pool – the marvellous Empire Pool.

Elvin was the sport's "greatest and most powerful friend". The words are those of the distinguished and legendary chronicler of the dirt-track art, Basil Storey, as part of an Elvin eulogy in the old *Speedway Star & News* on 23 February 1957, just a few days after the great man's death.

Those of us long enough in the speedway tooth to recall the glory days of the Wembley Lions will know that meetings there began with the Lions' famous signature tune, *Entry of the Gladiators*. Storey described Sir Arthur as Wembley's "Gladiator in Chief". His power lay in his dynamic drive and a personality that, wrote Storey, "virtually ruled the sport".

"Indeed," went on Basil, "it is impossible for anyone to even attempt to describe in cold print how much Sir Arthur Elvin meant to speedway. He is completely, tragically, irreplaceable."

Soon after Sir Arthur died, when speedway's light had become exceedingly dimmed in the sporting firmament, Storey wrote that "much drivel has been written ... concerning the alleged harmful influence of Wembley's power in speedway. Drivel, believe me, is the operative word, for Wembley has been the beacon of hope to which a near-dying sport has clung these last three years or more."

Had it not been for the weekly crowds Elvin's speedway team had attracted to his sporting emporium, Wembley would surely have gone to the knacker's yard long ago.

At the time, tracks had been sinking to the right of us, and tracks had been sinking to the left of us – in London and the provinces – like ships in a storm. But, for the struggling survivors in the speedway lifeboats, there was always the friendly, encouraging gleam of the Wembley beacon piercing the tempest.

And, if you have ever had a *deja vu* experience – the distinct impression that something has happened before – then you have one right there. Honestly, don't you find an ominous echo of that same situation today?

And here's another one. Basil was at pains to point out: "As a senior speedway reporter [he covered the sport for the *Daily Express* at the time], I'm prepared to confess right now that, but for Sir Arthur Elvin's continued association with the sport, it would probably have been next to impossible to 'sell' speedway to the national press.

The national press has been burying speedway for years. But the fact that Elvin of Wembley, through thick and thin, remained actively connected with the game, stayed the Fleet Street voice from declaring the last Amen. You could see it in an editor's eyes – 'Elvin's in it ... it can't be so bad!'" Well, Elvin has gone, and so has Wembley as we of speedway knew it. The spiritual home of speedway has gone to the devil ... a devil called football.

But even though speedway at Wembley may be dead, it doesn't have to be buried, thanks to an enthusiast, writer and publisher Peter Lush. Peter had the mesmerizing experience of watching the Lions as a 15-year-old when they were briefly reincarnated in 1970, and it inspired him to write this book.

Peter says: "Wembley introduced me to speedway and wanting to write about 'my team' is the motivation for this book. The Lions are very interesting historically and an important and often overlooked part in the Wembley Stadium story. I have enjoyed doing it and may well do another speedway book in the future."

Peter has applied himself meticulously and diligently to the task of writing the Wembley speedway story from when the Lions first took to their less than perfect track again after the Second World War in 1946, chronically recording their rip-roaring achievements – the triumphs, the tragedies and the star-spangled glossy personalities – year-by-year until the lid of the coffin was finally closed on what by any imagination has to be a wonderful, unique and – if we are honest – an all too brief, but indelible, mark in any sphere of sport.

My introduction to Wembley was much more traumatic than Peter's. I was captivated by the sport as a 12-year-old when watching the sport at the old Alexander Sports Stadium, Perry Barr in Birmingham in 1946. We were in the Northern League (Second Division). It was by no means a championship winning team: it was known as the Team of Trailers, but they were fantastic to watch.

Wembley were National League (First Division) and, as such, out-of-reach demigods, with a team of icons whose amazing exploits we could only marvel at by reading about them every week in the speedway Press. They were the days when speedway's big knockout contest, the *Daily Mail* National Trophy, was run on FA Cup lines. They threw in the minnows with the big boys. We qualified with fellow Second Division side Sheffield for the First Round Proper – that's the First Division round. And we drew ... Wembley. The Lions took us to the cleaners, 157–58 over two legs. But at least we got to actually ride at the Empire Stadium, losing 80–27 at their place and 31–77 at Perry Barr.

Two years later I was privileged to be among the 90,000 crowd in the spine-tingling atmosphere of Wembley on a really big night, the 1948 British Riders Championship Final won by the incredible Australian Vic Duggan. I have never forgotten that first experience of being part of the great cliff of sound that magic night. I think I walked around in a state of intoxication for some days afterwards, such was the impression with which it left me.

This book has long been necessary to do proper justice to the Wembley Lions' story from 1946 onwards. I am pleased to be able to contribute the story from 1929 until the outbreak of war. All speedway fans, whatever their nationality or persuasion, will find the story of the Lions' lost glory as enthralling and thrilling as anything Elvin's Gladiators served up on those magic nights at Wembley.

John Chaplin
August 2016

Thank you

I would like to thank: John Chaplin for his support and expertise – it has been a pleasure and great learning experience to work with John; John Somerville for his help with providing photos for the book – his work in developing an archive of the sport's photos is very important in maintaining its history; John Chaplin and Mike Kemp for providing photos from their collections; Matt Jackson for providing his profiles of the Wembley riders from 1946 to 1956 and the statistics for that part of the book, saving hours of work; Bert Harkins for writing the foreword and Mark Lewisohn for recalling his time as a young Wembley fan; Wembley National Stadium Ltd for allowing us to reproduce covers of Wembley Speedway programmes; the staff at the British Library in St Pancras, the Brent Local History archive in Willesden and the London Metropolitan Archives; Tony and Susie McDonald of Retro Speedway for their support; and finally my partner, Rosemary, for her ongoing support and patience – she's starting to enjoy our annual outing to Cardiff and is now an Antonio Lindback fan.

Peter Lush
August 2016

London League Publications Ltd would like to thank Steve McCarthy for designing the cover and the staff of Charlesworth Press for printing the book.

About this book

I always thought that someone else would write the post-war history of the Wembley Lions. A book was published on the pre-war period, and there seemed to be plenty of speedway authors working on the history of the sport. But nobody stepped up to the plate…

One of the advantages of co-owning a sports publishing company is that it gives me the opportunity to write about the teams and sports that are important to me. Mainly this has been in rugby league, but I also co-authored the history of Hendon Football Club, which gave me the chance to meet and reminisce with my childhood football heroes.

I was put in contact with John Chaplin by John Somerville. I met John at Cardiff in June 2016, and we agreed that he would contribute chapters to the book on Wembley pre-War. While these do not cover the team in the same level of detail as the post-war section, they make the book more complete and put the post-war period in context. John contributed to the rest of the manuscript, which I wrote.

My original plan was to base the book on local newspaper coverage. But the *Wembley Observer* had little about Speedway in the post-war period, although I found out later that the *Wembley News* may have been a better source, but too late to use any material from that paper except for attendances in 1970 and 1971, so my main research was done using the *Speedway News*, *Speedway Gazette* and *Speedway Star*, along with *Backtrack* and *Classic Speedway*. Other publications used are listed in the bibliography. Pen names were used in some speedway magazines in the 1940s and 1950s, credits are given to the name of the author used with the article.

Peter Lush

The passing of 'Bronco' Wilson

The Chairman and Directors of Wembley Stadium Limited wish to place on record the deep sorrow they feel at the tragic death of Lion 'Bronco' Wilson. They also wish to express their sincere sympathy to his wife and parents. Sincere condolences are also tendered by Bronco's team mates, the whole of the staff at Wembley, and every member of the Wembley Speedway Supporters Club.

Alec Jackson writes: This is a very unhappy day at Wembley. The passing of Bronco Wilson has been a terrible shock to all of us, and the sport of speedway racing is a great deal poorer by his death.

He earned the respect of everyone with whom he came in contact. He was a great trier, never knowing when he was beaten, and if ever a Speedway rider had a heart of a Lion, it was Bronco.

I feel his departure rather deeply because I spent much time with Bronco since his release from the Army (Bronco's real name was Nelson – I was responsible for giving him the name Bronco) putting him through his paces at our Rye House training track.

All of you, our supporters, will remember how Bronco started at Wembley in 1946, full of determination, and after a season's riding he was one of the most improved riders in speedway racing.

Bronco was a nice, quiet sort of fellow; he never had anything wrong to say about anyone. He had a secret ambition which we at times talked about – he wanted to live in the country with a few acres of land which he could work – he did not like town life.

Only a few days ago, he walked into my office full of smiles, having just returned from Newcastle (his home town). He and Split had done a northern trip – Newcastle and Glasgow – where between them they had won everything.

In the passing of Bronco, we have lost a true and gallant sportsman in the widest sense. The many thousands of you whom Bronco has thrilled and given endless joy will join me in saying: Rest in peace Bronco old boy, you will never be forgotten.

The management also wish to thank the hundreds of supporters who have written, telephoned or sent telegrams expressing condolences and sympathy. As it is impossible to answer them individually, it is hoped those supporters will accept this acknowledgement.

* * * * * *

This book is dedicated to the memory of Horatio Nelson 'Bronco' Wilson, the only Wembley Lions rider in the post-Second World War period to be killed in a track accident. A tribute was made to him in the Wembley programme on 21 August 1947, which is reproduced above, along with a photo of him. Further information on his career with the Lions is included in chapter 24.

About the authors

Peter Lush grew up in London, where he still lives. He has always been interested in sport. He first went to a speedway meeting in 1970 when a friend took him to a Wembley Lions meeting. He quickly got hooked, and went to most of the Wembley home meetings after that. In 1971 he went to every home meeting, including the one against Belle Vue at Newport. When Wembley closed, not wanting to support one of their London rivals, he became an Ipswich fan. He watched them on-and-off until he drifted away from the sport in the mid-1980s. He rediscovered speedway about 20 years later and started watching again on television. He finally decided to go to a live meeting at Rye House, only to find it was rained off when he got there. He now watches regularly on television, goes to Cardiff each year and two or three other meetings. He has a great interest in the sport's history, and reads *Backtrack* and *Classic Speedway* regularly. He also contributed to the *British Speedway Memories* book produced by Retro Speedway, writing mainly about how wonderful the Wembley Lions were.

He started watching rugby league at Fulham in October 1980 with Dave Farrar. In 1995, with Michael O'Hare, they wrote *Touch and Go – A history of professional rugby league in London*, and Peter and Dave set up London League Publications Ltd. The company has now published over 80 books, mainly on rugby league. Peter often has to work on book development and design, but other books he has written or edited include *I wouldn't start from here, Tries in the Valleys, From Fulham to Wembley, The Rugby League Grounds Guide, Rugby League Review 2007, Rugby League Review Number 2,* (all with Dave Farrar), *Trevor Foster* (with Simon Foster and Robert Gate) *Peter Fox – The Players' Coach* (with Graham Williams), *Hendon Football Club* (with David Ballheimer), *Big Jim* (with Maurice Bamford), *Tries and Conversions – South African rugby league players* (with Hendrik Snyders), *Rugby Football: A United Game* (an historical novel) and two cricket grounds guides. He was also joint editor of the national rugby league magazine *Our Game*, and has written for various magazines, journals and newspapers on the game and other sports. In real life he is the director of Training Link, a charity providing basic skills training to help people find work, in central London.

John Chaplin, a career Fleet Street journalist, is generally acknowledged throughout the speedway world to be the leading authority on the history of the sport. An author and broadcaster, his pedigree goes back 60 years to when he first saw speedway racing at Perry Barr, Birmingham in 1946 and he claims to be a lifelong Birmingham fan. He founded and edited his own hugely successful *Vintage Speedway Magazine* and is a regular contributor to *Speedway Star* magazine and *Classic Speedway*.

John's previous publications include: *Wings and Space: A History of Aviation, Speedway: The Story of the World Championship, John Chaplin's Speedway Special: The Classic Legends, Ove Fundin – Speedway Superstar, Tom Farndon: The Greatest Speedway Rider of Them All* (with Norman Jacobs), *Ivan Mauger: The Man Behind the Myth, Speedway Superheroes* (with John Somerville), *Speedway: The Greatest Moments* (with John Somerville), *Main Dane: My Story* by Hans Neilsen (Edit, production, design), *History of the Speedway Hoskins* by Ian Hoskins (Edit, production, design), *A Fistful of Twistgrip* and *Speedway Legends* (with John Somerville).

Contents

Part One: Wembley Speedway 1929 to 1939
1. 1929 to 1930: Launching the Lions ... 1
2. The 1930s and the real Wembley Lions ... 9
3. Wembley and the World Championship ... 19
4. Wembley and women in speedway ... 27

Part Two: 1946 to 1956
5. The Lions return ... 31
6. 1946: Champions ... 35
7. 1947: Champions again ... 47
8. 1948: A year in exile ... 57
9. 1949: Back home and another title ... 71
10. 1950: Arrival and departure ... 81
11. 1951: Another title and the London Cup ... 91
12. 1952: A sixth title but no Cups ... 99
13. 1953: Champions for the last time ... 107
14. 1954: Two Cups ... 117
15. 1955: No trophies! ... 127
16. 1956: The last season ... 137
17. Mister Wembley ... 143
18. The Lions leave speedway ... 147

Part Three: 1970 and 1971
19. The Lions reborn ... 153
20. 1970: Back on track ... 157
21. 1971: The Lions rampant ... 167
22. Memories of the Wembley Lions by Mark Lewisohn ... 173
23. The end ... 177

Part Four: The riders
24. The Lions' riders 1946 to 1956 ... 181
25. The Lions' riders 1970 and 1971 ... 219

Appendix 1: Statistics and Records ... 232
Appendix 2: Wembley Lions results ... 234

Bibliography ... 253

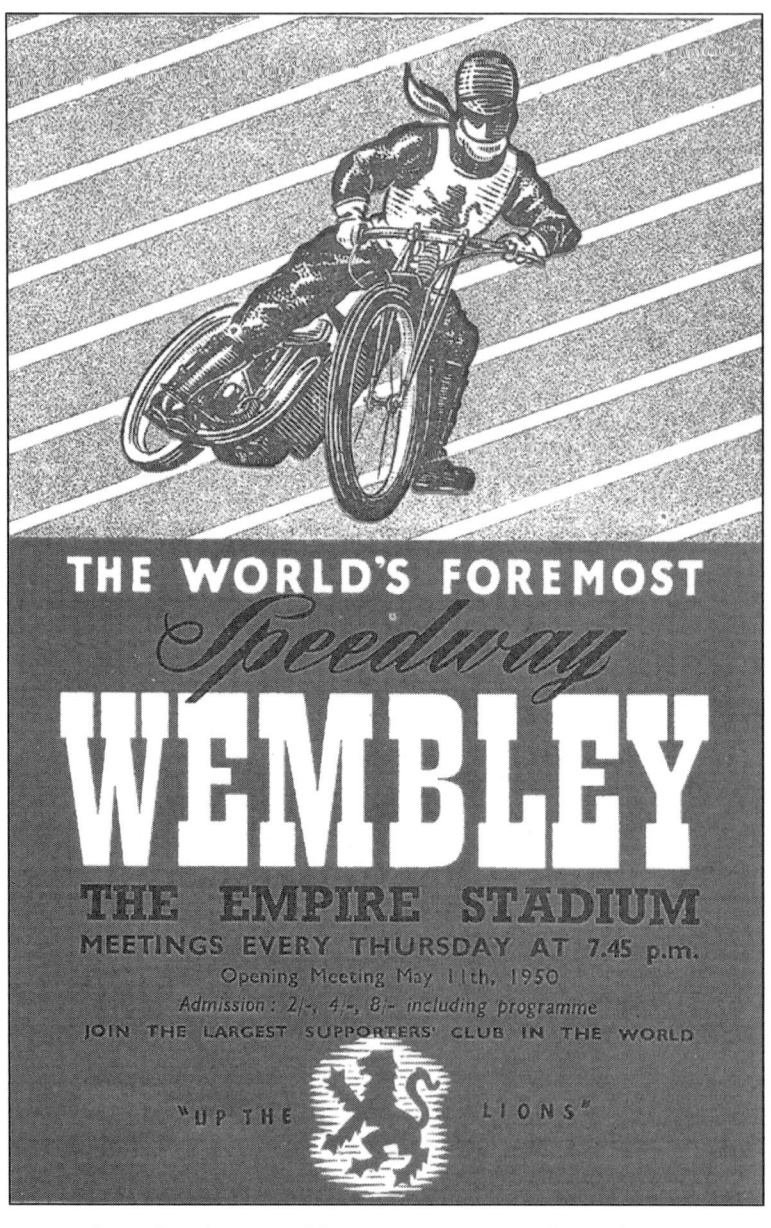

An advert for the Wembley Lions meetings from the 1950s.

Part One: Wembley Speedway 1929 to 1939

This part of the book is based on a series of articles that John Chaplin wrote for the *Speedway Star* at the time that the original Wembley Stadium was to be demolished. They have been edited by Peter Lush for use in this book, to give readers some historical background on the development of the pre-war Wembley Lions. It is not the intention of the authors for these chapters to provide a comprehensive history of the Lions for this period.

1. 1929 to 1930: Launching the Lions

Sir Arthur Elvin first introduced speedway to the Empire Stadium in May 1929, after the launch of the sport in England in 1928. However, he was boycotted by the other tracks who refused to allow the top riders, most of whom were under the control of International Speedways, to appear for their hated rival.

The one exception was the pioneer star Cyclone Billy Lamont, known the speedway world over as The Man with a Month to Live because no one with such a reckless track technique as his could possibly survive longer. He told the bosses to whom he was contracted that they could do what they liked, he was going to ride at Wembley's opening meeting.

He did so because Sir Arthur had called in the leading speedway spin doctor of the day, Johnnie S. Hoskins, the man who had invented the sport six years earlier in West Maitland, New South Wales, and Roarin' John it was who had given Billy his first rides.

Elvin gave Johnnie the task of putting together for him a Lions team that would not only be up and running, but up and winning. Johnnie scoured the north for likely talent and uncovered a gold mine. Jack Ormston, Harry Whitfield, Arthur Atkinson, Gordon Byers, HR Ginger Lees and Frank Charles, who became some of England's greatest stars.

And so began the mighty cavalcade of other famous Lions: Buster Frogley, Colin Watson, George Greenwood, speedway's first official World Champion Lionel Van Praag, Tommy Price, Bill Kitchen, the Williams brothers, Fred and Eric, Split Waterman, Bruce Abernethy, Bill Gilbert, Brian Crutcher ... and in the brief revival of 1970 to 1971, Ove Fundin, Dave Jessup, Gote Nordin, Sverre Harrfeldt, not forgetting Bert Harkins and lots, lots more.

Sir Arthur had missed the start of the 1928 mushrooming speedway phenomenon because, ever the businessman, he was occupied in introducing greyhound racing to the Empire Stadium; anything to keep the cash customers coming through the turnstiles. He had to make Wembley pay.

By the time 1929 came round, and Elvin decided that speedway racing, the new rage of the age, would be an asset to Wembley. Two things had happened: all the big star riders – the real crowd-pullers of the game – were under contract to the other established tracks, principally International Speedways which controlled circuits in London and the provinces; and league racing had been introduced.

Elvin's Wembley didn't have a team. And none of his rivals felt disposed to assist him in finding one. Not only that, they jealously guarded their stars and would not release any to ride at Wembley, not even in a demonstration race.

Then, a lunch date between Elvin and Lionel Wills, the man whose despatches from Australia about the new dirt-track sport had inspired its introduction to Britain, resulted in the creation of, at the time, speedway's most dynamic partnership. Wills told Elvin that, obviously, the man to help him out of his predicament was John S. Hoskins, the very creator the sport in West Maitland six years earlier, who had spent the previous year in Britain virtually as an itinerant track doctor, and who at that very moment was languishing in a rented Wembley house wondering where his next penny was coming from. Talk about fate.

Johnnie's efforts at team-building resulted in 50 riders being given contracts. Yes, 50. According to the Stenner's booklet, *Wembley Lions 1929–47*, no expense was spared to find the right men for the Lions. Johnnie's character decreed that he would be profligate with someone else's money.

There is a picture of him, a smug smile on his face, with his 1929 Lions. They included Bert Fairweather, an 18-year-old mechanic-turned-rider, Ron Hieatt, a capture from Swindon, Len Reeve, Crawley Rous, Australians Jack Jackson and Stan Catlett, Art Warren, Charlie Barrett from Newcastle, Harry Whitfield and 19-year-old Jack Ormston from Middlesbrough, two men who were to become stars eventually, and Wally 'Nobby' Key, later to distinguish himself at New Cross and Wimbledon.

They were all captained by the one name on Wembley's books, Arthur 'Buster' Frogley, a Hertfordshire farmer and aviation enthusiast who, with his brother Roger, was among the first English riders to challenge the supremacy of the visiting Australian crack riders.

Though Hoskins was given his head to pursue riding talent, Elvin's unique influence was felt by the performers from the start. It is said he insisted that sportsmanship must rank above all else with his riders, and no matter how good a man was, he must play fair, on and off the track.

The Elvin brand of morality was demonstrated further a couple of years later when it was announced that there was to be a grand Wembley Garden Party in aid of the Wembley and West Ham Riders Benevolent Fund. Wembley also ran West Ham at the time. Officials and riders were giving their services free and there was also to be a fund-raising dance in the Wembley restaurant at which Mr JS Hoskins was to conduct an auction, again to raise funds.

The snag was, it was to be held on a Sunday, which attracted fierce opposition from a body called The Lord's Day Observance Society (LDOS) which, until not too long ago, always raised objections to anyone intending in any way to enjoy themselves on a Sunday, and also various local Christian organisations.

Elvin wrote a letter to the LDOS pointing out that his intention was to benefit riders 'who might be unable to follow their occupation through injury or any other cause'. Nevertheless, he wrote: "I have decided to cancel the event in question, although no exception has been taken by members of the General Public to the proposed charitable event. It is not my wish, however, that anything should be carried on at the Empire Stadium, recognised as it is as the Nation's Great Sports Centre, to disturb in any way the susceptibilities of even a small section of the community."

Elvin went on, tellingly: "Whilst I have no doubt that this decision will give pleasure to those Local Christian Workers who have seen fit to protest, it will cause great disappointment amongst the thousands of our Speedway Supporters ... I have therefore decided instead to hold a special speedway meeting here on Friday, 9th October, when the whole receipts will be handed over to the Benevolent Fund. I have no doubt that those Local Residents who have seen fit to protest against the holding of Sunday's proposed event, will show their appreciation of my action in a practical manner by supporting such a worthy cause." He had a way with him.

But in 1929 such was the animosity towards Wembley by the hugely successful International Speedways, that no mention was made in *Speedway News,* a magazine also controlled by the International Speedways organisation, of the first meeting to be held at 'the nation's great sports centre'.

It took place on 16 May, and Wembley spent £25,000 (£743,000 now) on the forthcoming show. The football pitch had to be cut away on the straights and the bends to shape a track, which was surfaced with 5,000 tons of cinders. It was 378 yards round, 30 feet wide on the straights and 45 feet wide on the bends, with large grey cabinet-style loudspeakers standing on the Wembley turf and nearly a million candlepower of lighting. There were even flowers adorning the flagpoles, another of those touches of Elvin perfection.

The stage was set for a crowd of Cup Final proportions. After all, the nearby White City speedway had attracted a crowd of 78,000, so Wembley, with a capacity of more than 100,000, should be fine for at least that. Rival promoters scoffed. Wembley, they said, was too far out of London. Fans would not make the effort to get there. They weren't wrong.

At 8pm on the big night, a bugler announced the entry of the riders from the famous tunnel ... but only 5,000 people were in the stadium to welcome them. Those who did turn up saw an open meeting in which Roger Frogley won the Empire Stadium Shield from his brother Buster. Roger also won, by two races to one, a match race against the one really big star who did grace the occasion, The Cyclone, Billy Lamont.

The Wembley Cup, a handicap event, went to Alf Foulds, who had been at that first historic meeting in February the previous year at High Beech when dirt-track racing was officially launched in England.

The very next night, the Wembley Lions rode their first league match, at White City. They lost 25–17. In the Wembley side was an early Briggo, Charlie Briggs, Nobby Key, Bert Fairweather, Crawley Rous, Len Reeve, Ron (billed as Bern) Hieatt and Buster Frogley. The White City side was Eddie Green, Del Forster, Hilary Buchanan, Dank Ewen, Jack Bishop, Clem Cort and H. Crook. The result was one of nine defeats in the Lions' first 11 matches.

Such was the attraction of speedway all over London that celebrities from the world of show business and literature, war heroes, politicians, foreign potentates, diplomats, sporting heroes and heroines, aristocrats and even royalty were to be seen among the excited throng and even presented trophies.

Top personalities snapped at the speedways included racing motorists Sir Alan Cobham and Sir Henry Segrave, actresses Gladys Cooper and Peggy O'Neil, author Edgar Wallace, assorted titled personages led by Colonel the Master of Semphill, Under-Secretary of State for War Lord de la Warr, aviatrix Amy Johnson, King Alphonso of Spain, the Maharajah of Tikari, Princess Ingrid of Sweden and Prince George Duke of Kent.

The Wembley management had decided to follow their rivals and ride the immense popularity of dirt-track racing by putting on two meetings a week. But the average speedway attendance at the Empire Stadium for the first six meetings was a mere 2,786, who were lost amid the vast terraces of the arena. By the end of June, Elvin had abandoned one of his weekly meetings.

It was a disaster of immense proportions, and many a promoter would have cut his losses and quit the sport. Not so Arthur Elvin. He had opened Wembley speedway in the face of daunting difficulties, but his high hopes seemed doomed.

Then, just when it seemed that neither the Hoskins ability for staging crowd-pulling stunts and finding new riding talent, or the faith of Arthur Elvin, could save speedway at Wembley, something happened which changed the whole picture virtually overnight.

The Cyclone: Spectacular Billy Lamont, the big name who defied his bosses to keep faith with his Wembley pal Johnnie Hoskins. (MKC & JCA)

A-List celebrities were attracted to the new sporting phenomenon: Novelist Edgar Wallace presents a trophy to Frank Arthur. (MKC & JCA)

Elvin's army puts Wembley back together after the 1929 speedway season: Relaying turf for the stadium's football pitch. (MKC & JCA)

Speedway catches on: The Wembley car park fills up with people anxious to see the new rage of the age. (MKC & JCA)

There was a simple solution. And it was Elvin who found it. He started a football-style supporters club – something at the time that was new to speedway clubs. By offering privileges to members, including reduced prices of admission, the Wembley Speedway Supporters Club grew rapidly. The Empire Stadium, with its enormous spectator capacity, was in a unique position to offer generous inducements to paying customers which would have been ruinous to smaller and less fortunate tracks.

A massive advertising campaign began, and soon everyone was talking about Wembley speedway. The club quickly enrolled 10,000 members, and by the end of the season the number had grown to 15,000.

In mid-season the Lions started winning matches and began to climb the Southern League table. They strung together nine successive victories which lifted them from the bottom position to a final fifth place. The meagre support that had been producing a loss of £500 (almost £15,000 at today's valuation) a meeting at the start of the season, turned into an average of 10,000 spectators a meeting. Wembley speedway had begun to make a profit.

The amazing turnaround in Wembley's fortunes was studiously ignored by Elvin's miffed rivals at International Speedways. The company's mouthpiece, *Speedway News* magazine, conspicuously failed to carry either advertisements for Wembley speedway, or reports of league matches in which Wembley was engaged, except when the Lions were beaten by one of International Speedways' sides.

Hoskins, not to be outdone entirely by his boss, came up with the idea of staging a £200 (practically £6,000 today) championship meeting, creating a great deal of much-needed publicity. It produced a record speedway crowd at the Empire Stadium, 41,600, more than double the previous best attendance. And the fans kept clamouring for more, so much so that Wembley's season stretched until November 28. It couldn't happen today, of course, the BSPA would not allow it.

The Lions' concluding matches, mostly against northern clubs, served an important purpose. They provided another opportunity for Hoskins to give out-of-town talent the once-over. His foraging resulted in the signing of Arthur Atkinson and George Greenwood from Leeds, Charlie Barrett from Newcastle and Charlie Shelton from Nottingham.

The emphasis that Wembley placed on making the main part of its programme the inter-team contest, rather than the individual scratch, handicap and match racing as other tracks did, lifted the profile of dirt-track racing. It enabled the sport to shed its image of being little better than a fairground stunt and gave it the status of a genuine sport. Soon other managements followed Wembley's lead.

In 1930, Elvin's dreams of turning Wembley into speedway's premier club began to come true. The Lions swept to the Southern League title. They lost only three matches, won 20 and drew one. There was no integrated national league then, but a Northern and Southern League, each with 13 teams. Wembley also won the sport's first knockout competition, the London Cup, by beating Stamford Bridge in the home-and-away final by an aggregate of 105-86. Wembley had so many good riders in 1930 that a second team took to the track, called the Cubs, which rode friendly matches.

New Zealand champion Wally Kilmister joined the Lions and Norman Evans and Cliff Parkinson came south from Middlesbrough. But the big capture of the season was Colin Watson from Harringay, a major star, who took over the captaincy of the senior side from Buster Frogley. The Harry Whitfield-George Greenwood partnership earned a formidable reputation by introducing and perfecting the art of team riding.

Along with the team success, Elvin ensured that his 'Ascot of the Speedways' was not short of additional attractions in the name of entertainment. Team matches were peppered with such meetings as the Wembley Gold Cup, the Wembley Grand Prix, Wembley Cubs versus Spain, the Wembley Junior Championship and the famous and enduring 'Cinders', in which star visiting riders were invited to make attempts on the Wembley one-lap flying start track record. Success brought a handsome silver plaque.

There was another innovation, too. Whit Monday saw the first appearance of Wembley's first team mascot, Johnnie Hoskins's six-year old son Ian, later to become a distinguished speedway promoter in his own right. Ian made his debut by leading the grand parade on a miniature motorcycle dressed in special leathers and wearing a crash helmet painted half red and half white, the team colours, with the word Wembley emblazoned on the front. He was later to establish a mascot's track record of 86.8 seconds for a two lap rolling start.

It was the year when England versus Australia internationals were introduced, and Wembley staged the fifth and final test in a rainstorm on 26 September. Colin Watson and Jack Ormston were in the England side, which also included Jack Parker, Frank Varey, Squib Burton, Frank Charles, Gus Kuhn and Roger Frogley. Australia was represented by Vic Huxley, Dick Case, Max Grosskreutz, Ron Johnson, Bluey Wilkinson, Jack Chapman, Charlie Spinks, Arnie Hansen and Bill Lamont.

England's 49–45 victory clinched the series 4–1 for the home country. In the individual contest for the Empire Cup that followed, Vic Huxley beat Bill Lamont and Colin Watson in the final. He received his trophy from Lady Ryrie, wife of the Australian High Commissioner.

Wembley had at last become accepted by the so-called speedway establishment. Not only did *Speedway News* carry advertisements for meetings at the Empire Stadium, but also regular reports of the meetings. The Lions were on a roll. Their boss, the exacting Elvin, demanded the best. And as speedway racing began to be accepted as a serious national sport, his Lions delivered. At the start of the 1930s they had become champions of the Southern League for the first time and won the London Cup again.

But almost unnoticed was a significant triumph right at the end of the season over the Cocks of the North, Belle Vue, the side that was to become Wembley's most formidable opponent as the 1930s progressed. The country was still divided into north and south, and the Aces had won the Northern League title decisively, drawing one and losing only one of their 21 matches, a marginally better record than Wembley's, who had lost three and drawn one of their 24 matches.

A hardly reported challenge match between the two sides to decide The Champions of England resulted in home and away wins for the Lions. Under the headline 'Another Wembley Triumph', the *News* reported: "Wembley accomplished what no other side has managed to do this season when they went to Manchester last Wednesday week and defeated the greatly strengthened Belle Vue team on its own track."

The score at Manchester was Belle Vue 23 Wembley 29.5. At Wembley the score had been Wembley 27 Belle Vue 20. The *News* reported: 'Wembley ... not only won, on aggregate points, the title of British Champions for the season, but had the unique record for 1930 of a double at Belle Vue's expense.

Wembley 1931: From left: Norman Evans, George Greenwood, Jack Ormston, Col Stewart, Wally Kilmister, Johnnie Hoskins on Colin Watson's shoulders, Lionel Van Praag, Buster Frogley behind Harry Whitfield, Charlie Shelton, Jack Jackson. In front Cliff Parkinson, Ian Hoskins (mascot). (MKC & JCA)

Showing off the silverware: The Lions 1930, standing from the left: George Greenwood, Wally Kilmister, Stan Catlett, Norman Evans. Front: Harry Whitfield, Buster Frogley, Johnnie Hoskins, Ian Hoskins (mascot), Colin Watson and Jack Ormston. (MKC & JCA)

2. The 1930s and the real Wembley Lions

Arthur Elvin's Empire Stadium continued to bask in the sweet smell of success in 1931 with a second league championship. The team, although they had the London Cup snatched from them by Crystal Palace, also became the first winners of the new National Speedway Trophy.

It was a magnificent trophy, sponsored by a leading national newspaper, the *Daily Mail*, whose support of the new sport not only conveyed upon it respectability, but also ensured it would be given the widest possible exposure to the public.

And ominously, Belle Vue emulated the Lions' Southern League double by posting their name at the top of the Northern League for a second successive year. But the signs were there that a national league was not far off. In the north the table was reduced to six teams: Belle Vue, Leeds, Sheffield, Leicester Super, Preston and Glasgow, but the fixtures were not completed. And a Belle Vue reserve team appeared in eighth place in the 10-strong Southern League, having taken over from Harringay.

The Aces, the team of all the talents, were to dominate the National League for much of the decade, winning four consecutive titles from 1933 after Wembley's success in 1932, the year that north and south finally got together to form the National League.

The Lions had to settle for second place in the league, twice to Belle Vue in 1934 and 1936 and once to West Ham in 1937. As compensation they took the National Trophy in 1932, making it a league and trophy double, and the London Cup in 1932 and 1933. In the next six years they were losing National Trophy finalists three times, twice to the old enemy from Manchester.

But if by 1931 the Lions as a team had established themselves among speedway's undisputed elite, a position that Elvin considered was no more than Wembley's due, other significant events were happening individually and within Wembley's administration.

Since 1929 the major individual event of the season, a championship sponsored by the leading London evening newspaper, *The Star*, had taken place. The first competition, split into an Overseas Final and a British Final because the riders from Australia and America were considered too good for the Britons, was a series of match races.

The Overseas final was between Australia's 'Wizard' Frank Arthur and 'Broadside' Vic Huxley. Arthur won in two straight runs at Wimbledon and Harringay. There was drama aplenty in the British Final, in which Roger Frogley of Crystal Palace met Jack Parker of Coventry. The final had to be held in London, presumably, because the contest was sponsored by a metropolitan newspaper.

They raced one round at Crystal Palace and one round at Lea Bridge, these two races constituting one meeting of the two men, and one round at Wimbledon. If a decider was necessary, a coin was to have been tossed to determine where it should take place.

Frogley, an aviation enthusiast, not only crashed at Crystal Palace he also crashed his plane making a landing. Not seriously injured, he defeated Parker in four straight runs. The complication at Wimbledon was that the pair raced in fog "so bad", reported the *News*, "that one could have but a vague idea of what was going forward on the far side of the track, and under the circumstances the riders as a whole kept the riding up to an astonishingly high standard."

The weather conditions flummoxed the reporter, who described one race where Frogley was seen to be in the lead from Parker: "He took Jack some little distance out from the grass

... gaining a couple of lengths ... Just what happened on the back straight was shrouded in mystery, but when they appeared again on the second corner, Frogley had increased his lead."

Confusingly, the winners of the two competitions were not given their trophies on the night. Arthur received his, plus a £100 (almost £3,000 today) cheque, from author Edgar Wallace at White City, and Frogley was presented with his at Harringay. In 1930 the final of this prestigious event was moved to Wembley. It was the first step along the road that was to establish the Empire Stadium as speedway's premier stage.

A year later a 'World's Championship' competition made a brief - a very brief - appearance. And an aggressive, abrasive and talented Australian named Lionel Van Praag joined the Lions.

Johnnie Hoskins had scooped rival promoters for Van Praag's signature. The young man's reputation had gone before him. He had paid his own fare to England and representatives from most of the major tracks were waiting at the dockside to meet his ship.

But his old friend Hoskins, the man who had given him his first chances in Australia, spirited him away and the pair left for Southampton where the Lions were riding where Johnnie secured his name on a Wembley contract.

On 4 June 1931, Van Praag rode in the Wembley reserve team against a German side. Within weeks he was in the Lions' senior team. Before the month was out it was being reported: "Lionel Van Praag ... who has been watched as anxiously as any rider who ever came to England, is slowly but surely improving on our tracks, and would now make a perfectly good second string, even on smaller tracks."

By July he was in the big time, included in the Australian team for the second test at Leicester. It was a sensational international debut. Partnered by the experienced Dick Case, Van Praag top scored for the Australians with nine points in the 16 heat match which Australia won by a single point, 47–46, though England lost both Squib Burton and Wal Phillips in accidents.

In the 'World's Championship', yet another match race competition, Wembley's captain Colin Watson, who was now also the England skipper, was chosen to challenge Australian number one Vic Huxley of Wimbledon, who had been nominated as the first holder of the title. Norman Pritchard, editor of the *News*, wrote: "That he (Colin) will succeed in depriving Vic of his new official title I do not believe." Note, if you will, the use of the word 'official'.

The first round took place, on a scorchingly beautiful day, at, amazingly, West Ham. Huxley won. Both riders were mounted on the new JAP engines. The second round took place at Stamford Bridge, where Watson, to the surprise of the critics, levelled the score, beating Huxley in two straight runs. The decider, was set bizarrely for Watson's home track, Wembley.

In an incident-packed match, that was beset by falls and mechanical problems, Huxley won by two runs to one. 'Huxley Still World Champion' screamed the headlines.

Big attraction: An advertisement from the *Speedway News* proclaiming the final round of the 'World's Championship' at Wembley in 1931, which also included a league match v Belle Vue and community singing. Note the prices. (MKC & JCA)

Top left: The final of the early major individual competition was sponsored by the *Star* newspaper and split into the Overseas Final and the British Final because the Australians were considered superior. Here Frank Arthur (left) meets Vic Huxley before the 1929 Overseas Final. Arthur won. (MKC & JCA)

Top right and below: Battling for the title: Colin Watson and Vic Huxley (outside in the race) in their 1931 match for the 'World's Championship' at Stamford Bridge (MKC & JCA)

That was in June. Injuries to the competitors in the eliminators meant that it was not until October that Huxley was challenged again; Jack Parker finally won the right to a tilt at the title. Parker won the first match on his home track at Southampton, and Huxley won the second leg at Wimbledon. But, curiously, though the competition had been liberally billed all season as an 'official' world title, suddenly an editorial in the *News* commented: "We cannot agree with the claim that the competition ... is a World Championship. Other riders in other countries may object, and with good reason, that on their own tracks they might beat either Huxley or Parker. There was held in Paris, as recently as last Sunday, a competition designated the Championship of the World, which was won by Billy Lamont, with Ray Tauser runner-up. As neither Huxley nor Parker was present, it is obvious that the advertised title is absurd. In point of fact, Huxley and Parker are contending for the British Open Championship."

Parker duly took the title from Huxley in the decider at Wimbledon, but the reports of the meeting carefully avoided calling it the World Championship. The headline read: "Jack Parker Champion". And the report referred to 'the Championship title'. The word 'World' was studiously absent.

The *News* pointed out that there were four riders present who could claim to be World Champions – America's Ray Tauser, who had won the World's Speedway Derby in Australia, Bill Lamont who had won the Paris World Championship, Vic Huxley the holder of what was described as the 'official' World Championship, and Parker who had just relieved him of the title.

"And the Australians," said the *News,* "are highly incensed at all this, declaring that Tommy Benstead could beat the lot of them!"

Well ...

And so it was that the World Championship suddenly became the British Open Championship, and much later the Golden Helmet British Match Race Championship. But it would not be long before Wembley, Lionel Van Praag and World Championship – 'official' - would be forever immortalised in speedway legend.

With the virtual collapse of the Northern League and the formation of the National League, HR 'Ginger' Lees was snapped up from Preston. He proved to be world class and was one of Wembley and England's finest. Reg Bounds also arrived from West Ham.

Behind the scenes, it came to Elvin's notice that West Ham was doing less than good business. The Wembley chief decided the sport would be robbed of keen competition if the home of the Hammers closed down, so he took over and started a Wembley-style supporters club. Johnnie Hoskins found himself managing West Ham and Wembley, but after a single season of never working so hard in his life, he gave up West Ham to concentrate on Wembley once again. Alec Jackson, one of the early northern English pioneers at Salford and Belle Vue, whose racing career had been cut short by injury, was installed at West Ham in Johnnie's place in 1932.

The following year, the pair crossed over, Hoskins moved to West Ham and Jackson took over at Wembley. It proved to be beneficial to both. Hoskins achieved legendary status as the Hammers' boss and Jackson proved to be the dynamic that carried Wembley to undreamed of success right into the 1950s. He believed in encouraging youth, particularly English youth, and not only mechanical excellence through specialised club workshops, but also physical excellence. His riders were encouraged to take part in weekly keep-fit sessions with a professional trainer.

Victorious Lions on parade: Winners of the first *Daily Mail* National Trophy in 1931, captain Colin Watson holds the magnificent trophy. Members of the team behind him include, Jack Ormston Harry Whitfield, Wally Kilmister and Charlie Shelton. (MKC & JCA)

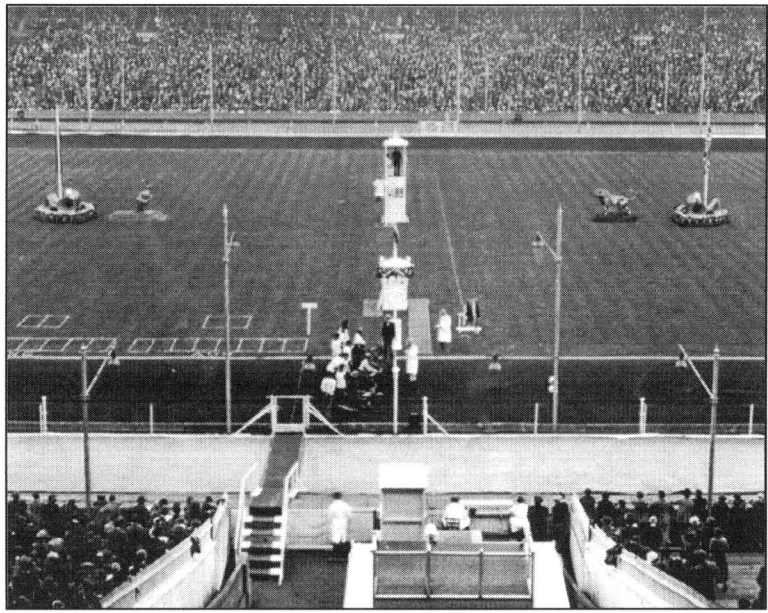

Packed Wembley terraces for the first Test in June 1934. As the Lions and the Kangaroos face each other at the starting gate, Elvin had arranged for the figures of a lion and a kangaroo to face one another on the centre green. Australia won 69–38. (MKC & JCA)

Speedway was hugely popular. By the mid-1930s the Wembley Supporters Club membership had risen to 25,000 'Britain's biggest' and West Ham had more than 11,500 members. New Cross supporters hired 23 coaches to take them on their annual outing, many more travelling in their own vehicles. More than 2,600,000 people paid to watch the sport in 1934, up more than a quarter of a million on the previous year. Elvin and Wembley's faith in speedway racing had at last paid off handsomely.

The final parting of the ways between Wembley and John S. Hoskins came in the winter of 1932–33. Now why would Johnnie, or any man with any sense, want to give up managing the Wembley Lions? They were his boys, the speedway team he had taken as a bunch of no-hopers and never-was-ers and lovingly stolen, fashioned, cajoled and welded them into probably the most formidable combination of cinder track heroes in the country, with the possible exception of the Belle Vue Aces.

They had been league champions three times, National Trophy winners twice, London Cup winners twice, and Jack Ormston had been London Riders Champion. In addition, the major national individual tournament, the Star Championship Final, was by then a regular event at the Empire Stadium. In four seasons, Hoskins had put Wembley on the crest of the speedway waves.

But let Johnnie explain in his own words. In his book, *Speedway Walkabout*, he wrote: "Foreign riders were beginning to find their way to England. Our riders began to visit Australia and New Zealand during the winter months, and to compete on the Continent. I had long had the desire to tour Australia, but lacked the capital, so when riders like Frank Arthur and Jack Parker came to me and suggested a tour of the best English riders and all the top Australians, I fell for the idea.

By cable I made arrangements with the managements of the principal stadiums in five Australian states. It was as simple as that. We applied to the ACU for official sanction. AJ Elvin blocked it. He didn't like the idea of so many of his top riders going to Australia."

Johnnie's boss, the indomitable, implacable, irascible Arthur Elvin, had put the mockers on the Hoskins grand plan. "'We went anyway," said Johnnie.

What Johnnie didn't say was that included in his star-spangled touring party were nearly all Arthur Elvin's Wembley Lions. In another book that Johnnie had written many years before, the amusing little tome *We Do Have Fun*, he listed them: Jack Ormston, Gordon Byers, Harry Whitfield, George Greenwood, Norman Evans, Wally Lloyd, Cliff Parkinson, almost an entire Wembley team. No wonder Elvin was not amused.

"I hankered after a little adventure again," confessed Roarin' John.

His troupe was certainly adventurous. Apart from Jack Parker, there were also the top Australians, Vic Huxley, Frank Arthur, Max Grosskreutz, Bluey Wilkinson and, in Lionel Van Praag and Stan Catlett, yet more Wembley Lions. There was, however, a little more to it all than sheer adventure, and cussedness on behalf of the Old Warhorse. The key to it all was in those three little words "I ... lacked the capital". Money, of course.

As had happened to him so often in his turbulent life, and would indeed befall him again on numerous occasions in the future, Johnnie was strapped for cash. His son Ian said: "There was a conflict of interests between Johnnie and Elvin. My father felt that, for the crowds the speedway was bringing in, he was being paid peanuts. Elvin of course was the ultra-conservative, and Johnnie was completely the opposite. And, to be truthful, he was a little in awe of Elvin."

As far as Johnnie was concerned, he was acting solely in the interests of the sport, you understand. He wrote: "If ever a tour deserved official backing, it was the one which sailed from London at the close of the season in 1932. We didn't get any help, so Wembley and I parted company."

Unfortunately, Johnnie's adventure turned into a nightmare. Though the Australian enterprise was a huge success and, according to Johnnie, "put Australia back on the speedway map", he made the mistake of trying his luck in America on the return trip to Britain.

"We felt that with such star performers as Jack Ormston, George Greenwood, Frank Arthur and Billy Lamont, and the American Ray Tauser, we could not go wrong," he recalled.

It was the height of the depression in America. He could find no one willing to finance the enterprise, except gangsters, and Johnnie, being an honest man, would have nothing to do with them. Johnnie's versions of how it all turned out are – shall we say – somewhat conflicting. But Ian is convinced that in the end, those who entrusted their fates to his entrepreneurial skills almost certainly had to pay for their own passages home.

Johnnie's fate, though, lay with West Ham. "And it made him, of course," said Ian. Hoskins became the darling of the Docklands crowds at Custom House, and the East Enders adored his brash promotional talents. He was to prove the only other speedway boss, apart from Elvin, to entice a high-profile Royal, the Duchess of Kent, to present trophies at a speedway meeting. The Duke of Edinburgh was the other, at Wembley in 1948 for the Speedway Riders Championship Final, which temporarily replaced the World Championship immediately after the Second World War.

Wembley, being Wembley, had to be the best at everything. It was fundamental to the gospel according to Elvin – once, of course, he had confounded those of his rivals who were both envious and jealous of his entertainment emporium.

Sir Arthur could not bear to think that someone had got the better of him. It was the driving force that had seen him persevere with speedway racing when all the signs were that it was destined to be a resounding disaster under his famous twin towers.

It is true that, over the years, very few of his undertakings did not enjoy the Midas touch of the Middlesex martinet. Most things that Elvin cared to dabble in invariably did turn to gold, which is why this Wembley tale tickles my fancy so much. Because it was one Elvin enterprise that went hopelessly and deliciously wrong. It is the story of the search for the REAL Wembley Lions. It began one day in 1937 when the great man sent for his then speedway manager Alec Jackson. Arthur Elvin had decided that the time had come to teach his great rival across North London at Harringay, Tom Bradbury-Pratt, a salutary lesson.

Bradbury-Pratt was always making a big song and dance about how good his Tigers were, but apart from the stitched emblem that adorned the blue and gold Harringay team jerseys, he had been able to find only a stuffed life-sized tiger to be his side's mascot. Elvin decided he would go one better and obtain some real-live breathing tribute to the spirit that ruled Wembley.

"Alec," commanded Elvin. "Go out and find me a lion!"

Now, it just so happened that one of Alec's old friends, Frank Copeman of the old Leicester Super days, heard of the quest and advised Alec that there were some lions at Leicester, kept by Chapman's Circus.

Alec and one of Wembley's mechanical wizards, Cyril Spinks - some years later to be instrumental in Tommy Price's and Freddie Williams's World Championship successes – duly presented themselves at the circus and negotiated for a lion cub which, they were assured, was "so tame as to be really affectionate. Just like a well-trained puppy."

Top left: Mr and Mrs Van Praag with Wembley's lion cubs pictured in a page from Speedway News
Top right: Prelude to disaster: Gwen Van Praag with the twin real Wembley Lions, all cuddly and docile, before they had to be returned to the circus (Both pictures: MKC & JCA)

By the time the troop arrived back at the Empire Stadium, according to Alec: "The little chap was a lifelong pal, fawning all over us as sweet-natured as a fireside moggy."

The Big Chief was a bit startled. "How old is he, Alec?" inquired Elvin.

"Nine months," replied Alec.

"Hmmm," sniffed Elvin. "I suppose you know that they kill at twelve."

"Not this one," said Alec, and promptly swung the wee beastie across his shoulders in confident fashion and waltzed off to Wembley's racing pits where lots of super publicity pictures were taken.

The real Wembley Lion was snapped quite happily with pretty girls, one of whom was the wife of Wembley's captain Lionel Van Praag, and everything was lovely. Until the next morning, when Cyril Spinks, who had been appointed keeper of the real Wembley Lion, arrived at the stadium to find the little fellow had gone berserk during the night and all but demolished the makeshift kennel home that Cyril had so painstakingly constructed.

Confronted with the wildest, most ferocious lion cub in the world, Alec sought advice from London Zoo. It turned out that what had upset the real Wembley Lion was being parted from its twin sister. And she was back at the circus in Leicester.

So, with the aid of a lump of raw meat, the cub was enticed into a crate, and the intrepid Alec and Cyril set off to reunite the cub with its sister. Sure enough, as soon as the two mini-man-eaters clapped eyes on each other Alec's half of the gruesome twosome became, once again, all docile and palsy-walsy. Alec and Cyril pointed themselves in the direction of Wembley once more, this time with two real Wembley Lions instead of one.

And to be on the safe side, the resident circus lion-tamer had given them a crash course in lion-taming so that they would be able to deal with any future emergencies that might arise. But which wouldn't - if you see what I mean.

Alec remembered it like this: they were bowling along quite happily at about 50 mph when one of the car's door locks – evidently disturbed by one of the cubs tugging at it on its chain – burst and the door flew open.

Cyril gallantly sprang into the back of the car to try and salvage the situation. In doing so he inadvertently stepped on the tail of one of the lion cubs. The injured animal took the only revenge it knew, it buried its teeth in Cyril's leg.

Somehow, Alec was able to bring the whole crazy caboodle to a safe halt and knock up a local chemist in order to dress Cyril's wounded leg. And eventually they made it back to Wembley, real Wembley Lions and all.

There the cubs took to Alec and Cyril in an astonishing way. But only to Alec and Cyril. Anyone else who approached them was greeted with the most blood-curdling growls. So, it was reluctantly agreed, the real Wembley Lions would have to be returned to the circus permanently.

And Alec added a poignant footnote to the whole sorry episode. He said: "Do you know, when I came to say goodbye to them, I knelt down and they both kissed me. Cyril too."

Who am I, my friends, to doubt him?

Catching them young – supporters, that is: An enthusiastic fan receives some basic instructions on machine preparation from her heroes, Reg Bounds (left) Arthur Atkinson (centre) and Gordon Byers.
(MKC & JCA)

3. Wembley and the World Championship

We have seen how there came into being an 'official' World Championship that never was. In 1931, when the 'official' tag was mysteriously, but undoubtedly justifiably, done away with at the conclusion of the season.

By 1936, the World Championship monster had once again reared its ugly head. The 'conservative' Arthur Elvin was definitely against it because he thought it would not be a money-spinner, even though he had been staging 'world championship' type meetings for the *Star* newspaper's tournament since 1930.

Elvin was nothing if not meticulously precise. Just how much so was revealed when he released the crowd figures for Wembley for the 1936 season. For the first time more than two million customers had paid to see speedway at Wembley. The exact figure was 2,085,048 – the odd 48 being cited as evidence of how precise Elvin was in anything he did.

During the year, his war with his hated North London rivals at Harringay had rumbled on. The Lions visited Harringay in a league match in September, and lost by the unlikely score of 45–26; a disaster for Wembley. Manager Alec Jackson forbade any of his riders to compete in the second half of the programme in protest at the state of the Harringay track which, he said, was too wet.

The headlines screamed: "Wembley Walk Out! Sensational Action at Harringay."

The speedway press was shocked. An editorial in the *News* proclaimed: "Mr Jackson ... the Wembley manager has always impressed by his keen sportsmanship and level-headedness, and it seems he must have had some good reason for his action ... though his action was unconventional."

Incensed, the towering Harringay boss, Tom Bradbury-Pratt, demanded a full Control Board inquiry – and the squabble brought an unprecedented amount of post into the *News* office. The editor threatened the Control Board that if it persisted in keeping the matter *sub judice,* it would print "some of the more rabid letters".

The whole thing resulted in a Control Board adjudication that "a breach of the regulations had been committed [by Wembley] and the riders should each be fined £10. The Wembley manager, Mr Alec Jackson was also fined £25."

The verdict was that "the track was fit to ride on ... but it has not been maintained as originally approved and must be brought up to the Board's requirements before a track licence can be renewed for the 1937 season."

The *News* printed the names of the riders involved: Frank Charles, Eric Gregory, Ginger Lees, Wally Kilmister, George Greenwood, Gordon Byers and Wally Lloyd – and noted that if the trouble resulted in better track surfaces "it has been cheaply bought at the price of the fines - £95."

Right at the beginning of the 1936 season the first official World Championship competition was announced: "There will be held ... instead of the British Individual Championship and the National Riders Championship, the first official World's Speedway Championship in which riders from upwards of 10 countries will compete. So ambitious is the scale ... that the total prize money involved will approximate to the enormous sum of £4,000." (£135,000 today).

The ultimate winner was to receive a magnificent trophy, £500 (£16,000) in cash in addition to his start and points money which could bring his total to £675 (£23,000). The runner-up would receive a gold medal and £250 (£8,500) in cash, the third man will receive a silver medal and £100 (£3,375), and the fourth will receive a bronze medal and £50 (£1,700). There was also to be "A trophy for the best performance by an overseas rider not domiciled in the British Empire", an obvious sop to the sub-standard other nationalities that might compete.

And here was the killer. The public was informed: "This final will differ from last year's National League Riders Championship Final in that instead of starting at zero, each finalist will take the field (or track?) credited with bonus points calculated on his percentage performance .... in his qualifying rounds."

It was incredibly complicated. And it meant, of course, that the World Final was based on a handicap principle. Reporter John Harrison of the *Star* newspaper, under the headline "The World's Championship Scheme Is Bad!" was moved to observe, damningly: "I have worked in close company with the Union [the Auto-Cycle Union] for the past 19 years and I have never known them to use the most common sense and direct method.

I can only, therefore, thank Heaven that I am not this year the poor unfortunate official who has to keep the riders' score charts up-to-date. He is going to have a rough time!"

When the FIM met to seek approval for the new world title, it was at first opposed "by certain countries. It was afterwards realised ... that the inauguration of this championship should help considerably in popularising speedway racing throughout the world ..."

Maybe Johnnie Hoskins was still feeling put out after his parting-of-the-ways with Wembley, but he later reported: "When the World Championship was introduced, promoters all jumped at the idea with delight and enthusiasm, except the Wembley chief, who nearly had a spasm. The crowds were pouring through his Wembley turnstiles and he was doing fine. Everyone else wanted a World Final, but Arthur Elvin wouldn't fall in line. He treated the idea with derision. He said that the national press would scorn the idea. 'And besides', he asked, 'supposing the crowds don't turn up, who is to pay for all the losses?'

For fully three months the arguments went on, and finally we agreed a £50 (£1,700) guarantee from each promoter. The Press gave reams of publicity. Everybody fell for the ballyhoo, except the riders. To them, it was only another meeting like scores that had gone before, and they couldn't see much glamour in being World Champion.

At last the big night came round, and I sat up in the Royal Box with the directors and members of the Control Board. We watched the crowds assemble from a thousand different places to fill the stadium with a near-capacity crowd. The guarantors paid no guarantees, nor did they expect any profit. But we set the ball rolling on its way down the years."

In the event, 66,000, or 75,000, (the reported figures varied), saw Frank Charles (England & Wembley) win Heat one of the first official World Speedway Championship Final from Dick Case (Australia & Hackney), Wal Phillips (England & Wimbledon) and George Newton (England & New Cross), with a new track record of 73.6 seconds.

If Johnnie Hoskins was in the Royal Box, Arthur Elvin was at the starting gate directing operations at what was the forerunner of the most memorable speedway events in the sport's history, and of course the most emotional and dramatic experiences that millions of speedway fans would witness.

And that night, Thursday 10th September 1936, was not short of drama. Those who were there saw Frank Charles turn out in a new pair of boots worn specially for the occasion, speed king Sir Malcolm Campbell present the winner's trophy and West Ham's Australian star Arthur 'Bluey' Wilkinson score a 15 point maximum ... and not be crowned the first Speedway Champion of the World.

Speedway's grandest moment ended in farce because of the infamous bonus point system. The *News* reported: "A fortnight ago we expressed the wish that someone should win all his heats at Wembley and yet fail to gain the championship. Wilkinson has obliged. He has beaten all his opponents in turn. He accomplished the seemingly impossible feat of beating (Eric) Langton (13 bonus points), and (Lionel) Van Praag (12 bonus points), the joint favourites, in successive races, with scarcely a moment's breathing space in between. If that is not the work of a champion, what is?"

Yes, the man who went through the meeting unbeaten ended up in third place. Wembley's Australian captain, Van Praag, was immortalised by becoming champion after a run-off with Langton (England & Belle Vue).

What that vast crowd did not know, and neither did Elvin, or he would surely have been apoplectic, was that there had been a conspiracy between Langton and Van Praag over the run-off for the title, and Langton, who lost, would for the rest of his life harbour a grudge against the Australian who he felt had reneged on their agreement. He would also feel shame that he had agreed to the deal in the first place.

The agreement had been, according to him, that whoever was in the lead at the end of the first lap would be left unchallenged to win. The other would collect the prize money. Langton had led until the last bend, when Van Praag had swept past him.

There had also almost certainly been some sort of agreement between Van Praag and Wilkinson. The idea was to make the maximum amount of money from the meeting. Hadn't Hoskins written that the riders thought 'it was only another meeting ... and they couldn't see much glamour in being World Champion'?

In spite of it all, the *News* acclaimed the new World Champion. He had, said the *News*, all the qualities of a champion: confidence, ability, study of the game and his opponents, the right temperament, mechanical skill and "the physique to withstand the exacting demands of six hard races in a single night. We are the more pleased at his success because he has been the conscientious leader of the Wembley team in spite of his interest in the individual competition." Their headline was: "Well Done, Van Praag!"

Left One of the greatest: Frank Charles in his Wembley colours at the Empire Stadium.
Right: Lionel Van Praag: Johnnie Hoskins signed him for Wembley. (Both photos: MKC & JCA).

A night to remember: Riders at the start of the first official World Final. From the left they are Wal Phillips (England), George Newton (England), Dick Case (Australia) and Frank Charles (England). To the right, in the suit and hat is Arthur Elvin. Frank Charles won the race in a new track record time of 73.6 seconds in front of 65,000 fans at Wembley. (MKC & JCA)

Left: History makers: Eric Langton (left) doesn't look happy after being defeated by Lionel Van Praag who, though being presented with the World Championship trophy by speed king Malcolm Campbell, appears as though he can't quite believe it.

Below: The cinder-stained first three at the first official World Championship Final in 1936. Winner Lionel Van Praag holds the gleaming trophy, runner-up Eric Langton is on the right and Bluey Wilkinson, third, on the left.
(Both photos: MKC & JCA)

The 1936 Lions at Belle Vue in their 'away' race jackets which did not have the rampant lion: From the left, back row Wally Lloyd, Eric Gregory, Frank Charles, Alec Jackson, R.H. Ginger Lees, Gordon Byers, George Greenwood. Front. Cliff Parkinson, Lionel Van Praag. (MKC & JCA)

They had to be the best ... on and off the track: The Lions limber up: From the left Colin Watson, George Greenwood, Harry Whitfield, H.R. Ginger Lees, Hal Herbert, Lionel Van Praag, Gordon Byers and Norman Evans. (MKC & JCA)

The 1938 Lions in their distinctive sweaters: From left Alec Jackson, Wally Kilmister, Tommy Price, Lionel Van Praag, Eric Gregory, George Wilks, Cliff Parkinson, Frank Charles, Malcolm Craven.

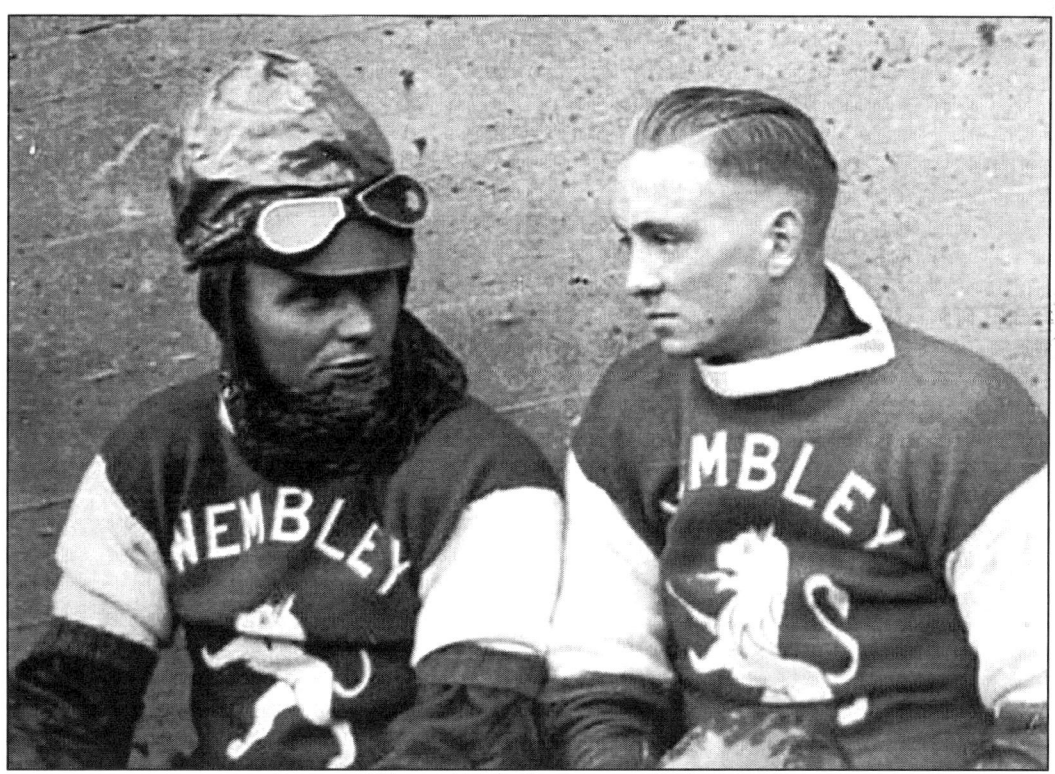

George Wilks and Malcolm Craven. (MKC & JCA)

Packing them in: The Wembley crowd experiences the thrill of action from the 1936 Test v Australia, with Dicky Smythe leading from Vic Huxley, Jack Parker and Eric Langton. (MKC & JCA)

4. Wembley and women in speedway

The vexed question of women on the speedways inevitably reared its head at Wembley. Johnnie Hoskins hated them. His antipathy towards girls and the cinders was well known, and it persisted for years – though the old devil was at pains to conceal his dislike of the female of the species when it suited him.

He raised the subject of the battle of the sexes when he felt he could capitalise on his views or they would bring him a decent amount of publicity. He welcomed the girls into the ranks of his supporters clubs, that was fine, but he once went public to insist that riders' wives and girlfriends should be banned from the tracks, which brought the wrath of the ladies down upon his head.

"Women and Speed Don't Mix, Says Johnnie Hoskins", was the headline, above the dissertation: "Women - women – that's the trouble with half the fellows in this game. One eye on a blonde in the grandstand, the other on the prize sheet, and not a thought for the team. Why the devil speedway riders want women cluttering up their cars, and taking their minds of the job of racing, I'll be blowed if I can understand.

This is a he-man's game. If you must have a girl, marry her, drown her, tie her up [hardly acceptable then, let alone today], but keep her away from the speedway. Some of those streamlined models of irresistible charm and glorious glamour ... don't know the mischief they're doing to a teams' chances," he went on. "Gimme the hard-boiled, steel-booted, ambitious youngster whose fingers prefer to glide over a piece of high-revving mechanism and whose thoughts are one hundred per cent on speed. And now, girls, I'm feeling so much better and I hope it leaves you the same," concluded the Old Warhorse. It didn't, of course.

Instead, a cartoon appeared in the speedway press of damsels pelting him with saucepans, brooms and other household objects, much, no doubt, to Roarin' John's amusement. It had attracted controversial publicity, Johnnie's staple diet. And they had spelled his name right. So that was all right.

His philosophy for dealing with the gentlemen of the press, he admitted, was: "I long ago found it pays to tell the truth ... if it sounds interesting enough."

All of which is a mere prelude to the subject of this instalment of the saga of Wembley, speedway's spiritual home. A convenient peg on which to hang the story of the part that women played in it.

Ah, the ladies. During a stroll down Empire Way to view for positively the last time those famous twin towers, one of the names you may have noticed is that of Fay Taylour, probably the most famous woman rider to appear at Wembley.

Actually, if you had blinked you would probably have missed the previous mention of Fay. She was on a list of the holders of The Cinders, the legendary traditional competition held weekly by Arthur Elvin for stars of the day to have a go at lowering the one lap flying start track record.

It went on from the very earliest of days of speedway at Wembley, and among the top names to have held The Cinders were: Ray Tauser, Max Grosskreutz, Jack Ormston, 'Smiling' Jim Kempster, England's first speedway Test captain, George Greenwood, and many more.

Tauser was the first holder of the record, on 16 May 1929, with a time of 21 seconds for a single flaying lap, which represented a speed of 36.82 mph. Fay was next. She lowered Tauser's time to 20.8 seconds on 6 June with a speed of 37.18 mph.

The names of Fay and her great rival, Eva Askquith, appear prominently in the list of match race results for that first year of speedway at Wembley. Eva beat Fay 2–0 on 4 June, Fay beat Eva 2–1 on 27 June, Art Warren beat Eva 1–0 on 8 August, Eva beat another top lady rider, Sunny Somerset 1–0 on 29 August and Geoff Taylor beat Eva 1–0 on 7 November. The girls didn't just have a go among themselves, they took on the men, and occasionally beat them.

According to Johnnie, few people realised the importance played by Fay and Eva in the early years of the sport. After the First World War, motorcycles were available comparatively cheaply. Motorcycle sport, such as hill climbs, grass track racing and cross-country events attracted thousands of enthusiasts, among them a few women. The girls asked for, and were given, no favours. They rode against the best on equal terms and they progressed, according to their skill, with their male opponents.

Fay and Eva emerged as two girls of outstanding ability. Fay was Irish. Eva, a product of riding and hunting, from Yorkshire.

"Fay", said Johnnie, "had personality and winning ways. We called her the lass with the blue Irish eyes and she was the equal of any but the very topmost performers in any branch of motorcycle or car racing. Eva was the opposite, but also a brilliant rider. They gave added interest to the sport at a time it badly needed publicity. They rode against the men at tracks up and down the country, but it was when they met in opposition to each other that the sparks began to fly.

Even the star riders leaned over the pit gates to see Fay and Eva hefting their big Douglas machines and racing with utter abandon to the finishing flag. Fay would hold up the start of a race while she adjusted her hair, applied a little lipstick or exchanged a few words with officials on the line." *[Fay vehemently denies this narcissism. 'I seldom, if ever, indulged in that old-fashioned custom of powdering one's nose.']*

Eva never worried about such trivialities. She sat watching and waiting for the starter's gun. "I never could", quoth the Old Rascal, "make up my mind which was the better rider of the two."

Both had victories over men to their name. Fay had been inspired to try her luck on the cinders after seeing racing at Stamford Bridge. Indulged by Fred Mockford at Crystal Palace she had beaten Joe Francis but, increasingly frustrated at the initial lack of opportunities for women riders in Britain, she spent a winter in Australia. She was the first British speedway rider to race in Australia where among her scalps was the pioneer Sig Schlam in Perth.

Eva beat riders such as Gordon Byers, later to become a top Wembley Lion, and had the distinction of riding at reserve for the victorious Leeds team against Sheffield at Owlerton in July 1929. In one of her two rides she came second in the fastest race of the night.

Fay was on the boat sailing back to England following yet another successful trip to Australia and New Zealand, when she heard that women had been banned forever from taking part in speedway racing. The ban, which was to last for a full half century, was the result of an 'incident' at the Empire Stadium. A material witness to that incident was a lovely lady named Jessie Hole [nee Ennis]. In addition to her speedway skills, Jessie was a top stunt rider, and entertained the crowds with her daring by crashing through panes of plate glass and hoops of fire. She and her brother George were also part of a motorcycle acrobatic team, so she was not unfamiliar with powerful bikes.

Indeed, Jessie startled the assembled company at the presentation of the Millennium Man trophy to six times World Champion Ivan Mauger at Beaulieu by asking the great man if he ever rode motorcycles other than speedway bikes.

Left: Girls on top: Fay Taylour (left) and Eva Askquith before a match race at Wembley. They were of outstanding ability. (MKC & JCA)
Right: Parade leader: Jessie Hole was leading the ladies before their special race when Billie Smith went over her handlebars ... and women were banned from speedway for 50 years (MKC & JCA)

When he confessed he had not done so recently, she told him that a week before she had been lapping the Donnington Park road racing circuit on her New Imperial at something like 107mph. Jessie was 92 at the time.

She had watched her brother on the dirt-track at Stamford Bridge, and like Fay was inspired to try it for herself. George had taught her to ride and maintain a motorcycle, and her parents had bought her a Scott bike. She said: "My parents really wanted me to learn the piano, but in the end they gave up and bought me the bike instead. The boys at The Bridge used to let me practice with them, and they would lend me a Dirt-Track Douglas."

"The Boys", said Jessie, "didn't like Fay Taylour at all. She used to beat them occasionally, of course."

It was at Wembley on Thursday 15 May 1930 that Jessie got her big chance to take part in a special race for women riders at the Empire Stadium. The *Glasgow Evening News* carried a picture of Jessie and her opponents, Mrs Billie Smith and Sunny Somerset, claiming, wrongly, that it was the first time such a contest had been staged at Wembley.

Disaster awaited on the historic parade. The contest was billed in *Speedway News* as a Novel Match Race and, significantly, what happened was not reported by the magazine.

Jessie said: "I was leading the parade. The stadium was packed. I was in front of the other two and going quite fast. I didn't actually see what happened because they were all behind me, but I was told later that one of the boys cut across in front of Billie, she shut off and went over her handlebars, breaking a collar bone. They announced over the loudspeakers that the women's race would not now take place, and at the end of the meeting they announced that the accident had been reported to the ACU which had ruled that women were to be banned from ever again taking part in dirt-track racing in England."

Not unnaturally, there are other versions of what happened, and other speculation on the reason for the ban. The Hoskins version is this: "Five lady riders had been booked in at the Empire Stadium to boost the publicity and the attendance. Among them was a married women competitor (that was Billie Smith) who fainted on the line in front of a huge crowd. That was too much for the strict disciplinarian Arthur Elvin, managing director and supreme authority.

'Get them out of here. All of them. I never want to see women racing here again. I'll bring in legislation to have them stopped,' he thundered. As a powerful member of the Speedway Control Board he did all that he threatened."

Blame it all on Elvin. Well, you pays your money and you takes your choice.

Fay's version appears to corroborate Jessie's: "The promoters, finding their crowds dwindling, and searching for ways to get extra publicity, decided to stage a women's race and then announce a ban on women riders ..."

Was it all a put up job? The mystery deepens.

Fay continued: "Apart from Eva, the few women some promoters had used occasionally were too slow to interest spectators, and it was a race between such riders that was now staged as a forerunner to the announcement of the ban.

Conveniently, one rider fell on the approach to the ramp before reaching the track and broke a collar bone. Next morning came the big announcement: 'Women Banned from Speedway Racing'. It gave the promoters headlines. They'd put women on the tracks to get publicity, now they were banning them for the same purposes."

Fay never forgave the sport for that ban on women riders. In recording her career she was highly indignant about the treatment she and her contemporaries received. Claiming to have been responsible for the first newspaper trophy to be awarded to speedway racing, she recalled how she had persuaded Lord Riddell, who was married to one of her mother's cousins, to go and see her race at Crystal Palace.

"In those days," she said, "we took the bends in a streamlined slide, the left leg trailing in line with the bike to the back wheel, while our bodies lay forward over the long wheel-based machines. It was pretty to watch."

Overwhelmed at the spectacle Lord Riddell had said he would send his reporters to a meeting. "He donated the *News of the World* Trophy," said Fay. "I'd hoped he might buy me a speedway bike after what he'd seen, but all he produced was lunch at the Savoy. Perhaps he thought it no game for a woman."

Photo: Winning combination: Eva Askquith and her mechanic (MKC & JCA)

Part Two: 1946 to 1956

5. The Lions return

After an absence of almost seven years, speedway returned to Wembley on 9 May 1946, when Belle Vue were the visitors for a National League match. It was appropriate that the famous Manchester club should be the opposition. They had kept the sport alive during the war, regularly hosting meetings on a Saturday night, and the Aces and the Lions were arguably the sport's two 'glamour' clubs.

In the 1930s the Lions had been one of the sport's top clubs. Their involvement in the sport, with that of the then Mr Arthur Elvin, gave the new sport credibility, particularly with the press. The Lions had struggled initially in 1929, the first season of league racing. But they recruited new riders, and by the end of the season 60,000 attended their match against Stamford Bridge. In 1930 the Lions won the league, a feat they repeated in 1931 and 1932. But after that they were runners-up three times, in 1934, 1936 and 1937 – the first two to Belle Vue and the third to West Ham. Speedway was also an important regular income stream for the Empire Stadium, along with greyhound racing. In 1939, the season had been abandoned with the start of the Second World War.

During the War, John Chaplin says that "Though speedway racing ceased at the Empire Stadium, Wembley certainly took part in the war effort. Football continued to be played there, servicemen and women in uniform were admitted free to the skating and ice hockey events at the Empire Pool. Starting in 1942, the restaurant was thrown open on Christmas morning and Sir Arthur's organisation dispensed traditional yuletide turkey dinners to thousands, that year and throughout the conflict. In 1944 the BBC broadcast a Wembley coming-of-age programme to mark its 21st anniversary.

When peace finally came, a great thanksgiving service was held, at which was revived the famous crowd community singing, begun by Thomas Radcliffe, the man dressed in white who became familiar to millions at FA Cup Finals when he led the stadium in the traditional *Abide With Me*.

The stadium saw its share of action. A doodlebug flying bomb had zoomed between the towers and exploded in the grounds, blowing one greyhound kennel to bits – but only two of the 150 valuable dogs within it were casualties, and they were only slightly hurt.

At the end of the war in August 1945, Elvin's speedway manager, Alec Jackson, had only a few months to get the Empire Stadium geared up and ready to continue the Wembley Lions success story."

After VE day in May 1945, the sport slowly returned to action. Belle Vue ran a complete season, and Wembley's Tommy Price made regular appearances in the mixture of team and individual meetings. Eric Gregory and Wally Lloyd, who had both ridden for the Lions before the War, rode in some of the early meetings. Towards the end of the season Malcolm Craven, another pre-war Wembley rider, also appeared in Manchester. Bill Kitchen had ridden regularly from 1940 to 1943, but then had a break until his returning to track action in June 1945. Both Kitchen and Tommy Price had some success in 1945. The former won the British Championship Final, while the latter won the Star Riders Championship.

Bradford staged their first post-war meeting on 23 June, with riders competing for the AJ Elvin Cup. Exeter, Glasgow, Middlesbrough, Newcastle, Rye House and Sheffield all saw speedway return before the end of the season. There was no possibility of organising a league, so the sport's fans eagerly awaited the start of the 1946 season.

The sport was re-establishing itself in a country that had come through over six years of war. Thousands of men were still in the Armed Forces; there was still rationing and a huge housing crisis, particularly in the cities which had been heavily bombed. It was a time of austerity, but also a time of hope and optimism, with people looking for change reflected in the election of a majority Labour government for the first time, on a programme of reform and modernisation.

But it was also a country looking to move beyond the deprivations of war, and the drab existence that millions of people had endured. People were desperate for entertainment, with sports events seeing huge crowds, as well as enormous attendances at the cinema and in dance halls.

The 1946 season offered speedway an enormous opportunity, but the sport also faced problems. Unlike football or cricket, which had relatively stable structures, the sport had a record of teams coming and going. In 1939, three teams, Middlesbrough, Stoke and Crystal Palace, had all withdrawn from league competition. That season, the National League Division One had seven teams: Belle Vue, Wimbledon, Wembley, West Ham, Harringay, Southampton and New Cross. A further six teams, including Belle Vue Reserves competed in the Second Division, while Edinburgh and Glasgow had competed in the Union Cup.

Of the seven pre-war Division One teams, Wembley, Wimbledon, Belle Vue New Cross and West Ham returned. They were joined by Odsal, who had run a successful series of meetings in 1945, and were based at the massive Bradford Northern Rugby League Odsal Stadium.

The Northern League – to all intents and purposes the Second Division – also consisted of six teams: Middlesbrough, Sheffield, Norwich, Birmingham, Newcastle and Glasgow. All the teams entered the National Trophy, and for the London teams the London Cup made a welcome reappearance.

Speedway and Ice News [The *News*] said in an editorial on 10 April that the new season was the most important in speedway's history, after the absence of league racing for six years. They were confident of the sport's popularity, but the promoters faced team building problems. Australians and Americans were not available due to transport problems, and "the passage of time has thinned the ranks of the British riders." It was important for the promoters to get new blood.

A pooling system was adopted by the Speedway Control Board (SCB), linked to a grading system for riders, with differential pay rates. The grading system only lasted a couple of months, and was removed in early June after pressure from the Speedway Riders Association (SRA).

The initial pooling of riders for the National League was done on 7 March. Most teams were given six or seven riders, but Wembley only took four: Bill Kitchen – from Belle Vue, Tommy Price and George Wilks, who had been pre-War Lions, and Bob Wells. The Lions said that they would complete their team from novices found at their training school at Rye House. The *News* reported that there was 'mild surprise' that Belle Vue had chosen Jack Parker ahead of Bill Kitchen, although apparently those 'behind the scenes' knew that Parker was brilliant on the Belle Vue track, while Kitchen was looking for a change.

Each team was allocated one 'Grade One' rider, and Kitchen was first choice for the Lions as theirs, and became team captain. Tommy Price was initially a Grade Two rider, but was promoted to Grade One in May.

The *Speedway Gazette* [The *Gazette*] reported a couple of weeks later that Kitchen had a 'long cherished ambition' to ride for the Lions. Remarkably, he did not move to London in his first season at Wembley, but kept his home in Morecambe, where he ran an engineering business with his brother. He would often take a late train home after meetings at Wembley, arriving in the early hours of the morning.

Of course, many of the established riders were now in their mid to late 30s, and the 'novices' were often in their mid-20s, mostly having been in the Armed Forces, unlike today when a novice is usually aged 16 or 17.

The training school at Rye House was a very important part of Wembley's post war development. Wembley's manager, Alec Jackson, was one of the best developers of young talent in the sport, and had been a Major in the Signals Corp during the war, so was aware of many talented young motorcycle riders in the Army. The *News* reported that his three months training school at Rye House the previous summer had produced 12 riders with the potential to become stars, although very few had previous speedway experience. The report named Australian Bluey Thorpe, Jim Kemp – who held records on two tracks in Italy, Frank Taylor, Gunner Bennett, Craftsman Snatchfold, and two riders from the RAF: Bill Gilbert and Sergeant Roy Craighead. Jackson had a two year option on the Rye House track, but offered it to other London clubs one day a week for novices to practice. Realising there were only so many team places at Wembley, he had already transferred WS Rogers to West Ham.

There is little doubt that Alec Jackson's development of young riders was crucial to the success of the Lions. In 1950, in a contribution to *Tommy Price's Speedway Mixture,* published in 1950, he outlined how he recruited young riders. By the time he wrote this article, he had four years success to reflect on.

He said that he received hundreds of letters from prospective riders, and had developed a form for them to complete. He liked former Army boys, especially despatch riders or those who had ridden on the cinder tracks set up by soldiers overseas. He believed that Army life bred discipline. He didn't like 'boasters', but favoured 'listeners' who wanted to learn.

He explained how the bikes worked to the novices, and said they should go quietly at first. This would get rid of the 'wobblers' and he would then send the ones who could handle a bike out in fours. He would tell them not to race. When he had chosen the more promising riders, he would put three at the gate and the best one a quarter of a lap behind. He would tell the three at the gate not to let the backmarker through.

H said that when he started the sessions, three 12 machines they supplied to the riders would rarely survive a morning session intact. But since then things had improved and there was less damage. His advice was to look on speedway as a pleasurable sport. Tommy Price's simple comment was that the novices should be enthusiastic.

Improvements had been made to speedway facilities at Wembley before the war, both to the track, the lighting and the stands. Alec Jackson, worked with Sir Arthur Elvin, Wembley's legendary chairman & managing director to provide the best possible facilities for the riders. For the riders they had a fitness trainer, Tommy Barnett, a former Watford footballer who was appointed at the beginning of June and use of the gym facilities at the Empire Pool. For the bikes there was a workshop and team of mechanics to support them.

Wembley had developed the idea of a mass membership Supporters Club before the war, and this was continued in 1946. Three administrators were employed to manage the service for the fans. Members were given cheap admission, there were dances and social events, and an annual outing to the seaside. There were also local branches, often organising social activities as well as trips to the Lions meetings, and for those further away from the Empire Stadium, weekly coach trips to the Lions meetings. This was particularly important at a time of limited car ownership.

The *Gazette* reported on 22 April that the Lions were confident about the forthcoming season. Bill Kitchen had already won trophies at Newcastle and Glasgow, which Alec Jackson said was a sample of big things to come. Jackson mentioned Alf Bottoms as another promising youngster from the Rye House training school.

So everything was set for the launch of the new season. In 1938, an aggregate of 539,376 fans had been to speedway at Wembley. This had dropped to 251,573 in the foreshortened 1939 season. The 1946 season was very important. There was no floodlit football at this time, and for most working people, county cricket was unavailable to them except on Saturdays because it was played during the working day. Television was restricted to a tiny audience around London, and only greyhound racing offered any rivalry to speedway in evening sports entertainment, although it was not really a family sport in the way that speedway was, and did not offer the 'glamour', excitement and human endeavour that speedway could. But could the sport take advantage of the opportunities that were opening up for it?

6. 1946: Champions

Speedway opened in London for the new season at New Cross on 17 April. Tommy Price was included in 'The Rest' team that raced against the home team. The Lions' first match was at West Ham on Good Friday, two days later, when 57,000 saw them win an exciting Challenge match 42–41. A young Freddie Williams had been named at reserve before the meeting, but in the event did not ride. Of the newcomers who did, Bob Wells (who had been on the Lions' books pre-war but had not ridden in a National League match), Alf Bottoms and Bill Gilbert were in the team, with Roy Craighead and Bronco Wilson at reserve. Wells was the most impressive. He won the match for the Lions in the last heat. Bill Gilbert had been excluded, and Wells, riding Bill Kitchen's bike after his had developed problems just before the start, beat the Hammers' Geary and Lawrence.

The Lions raced two more matches, a 47–34 defeat at Wimbledon against a combined Wimbledon-New Cross team and a 49–34 win at Belle Vue in the league before their home meetings started. The Lions had a convincing victory in Manchester. Tommy Price was in brilliant form on a track he had ridden regularly during the War, and Bob Wells also impressed. Wells had been a Prisoner of War for five years and since coming home had been working in the skate-hire section of the Empire Pool. After the Belle Vue meeting, home star Jack Parker had reported that his bike had been stolen. It turned up the next day; the Wembley riders had put it on their lorry by mistake.

The Lions' home meetings began at Wembley on 9 May. Their home meetings usually began in the second week of May, after the FA Cup and Rugby League Challenge Cup Finals had taken place. Parts of the football pitch had to be taken up so that the speedway track could be put in place.

For their first home meeting, the management only had five days to get the Stadium ready after the Rugby League Challenge Cup Final on 4 May. They were preparing for a crowd of 80,000. The sides of the football pitch had to be taken up, and 250 tons of specially prepared cinders put down. The 40 track lighting posts had to be put up, along with the starting gate, the phones and everything else needed to run a speedway meeting.

Sir Arthur Elvin was clerk of the course, a position he relinquished during the season. The *News* said that "Speedway racing is one of the sports that 'gets' this man of all sports. He likes to be in the thick of it and the smooth running of a Wembley meeting is due to [his] quick appreciation of the smallest details.

The Lions' opponents were Belle Vue. In his programme notes, Alec Jackson welcomed Bill Kitchen to the team, and said that he had always wanted to sign him for Wembley. He also said how pleased he was to keep Tommy Price, George Wilks and Bob Wells. He introduced the new riders: Alf Bottoms, Bill Gilbert, Roy Craighead and Bronco Wilson. Bottoms was a poultry farmer in Middlesex with grass track racing experience, but had never ridden speedway until going to the Rye House training school. Gilbert and Craighead had trials at West Ham and Dagenham before the War, and had been training with the Lions. Gilbert had recently been demobbed from the RAF, while Craighead was still serving. Wilson had been a despatch rider in the RASC, and ridden in Italy. He was from Newcastle, was six feet tall and had a special machine built to carry his 14 stones weight. He had turned up at Rye House for a trial just with a pair of gloves, and had borrowed some leathers and a bike.

Jackson said that "We are the only team in the league using four permanent team riders who before the War did not hold a speedway riders agreement. Undoubtedly it will take a little time before the newcomers really settle down, due to the very simple fact that they have not raced, or in fact, ever seen some of the tracks... My policy is a long-term one. Using old speedway riders of a low calibre won't get us very far in the long run – but youngsters who have the ability and the keenness, will eventually come out on top."

'Only' 50,000 supporters came to watch the Lions beat Belle Vue 50–32 in what the *Gazette* reported as a series of processions. Given that none of the riders had ridden at Wembley for almost seven years, and some never, maybe that is not surprising. One noticeable point was Bill Kitchen 'nursing' home some of the Wembley newcomers, something that was to be common during the season. Kitchen had been nominated as the holder of the Match Race Championship, but lost both legs to New Cross star Ron Johnson. Wimbledon's Norman Parker had been the original nomination to challenge Kitchen, but had withdrawn through injury.

The Supporters' Page in the programme talked about the "very heavy" entertainment tax imposed on the sport, which is why the club could not offer any substantial admission concessions to supporters, although there were reductions for children. Coaches were available to take supporters to away meetings. During the interval, the band of the Irish Guards had entertained the crowd, along with Robbie Hayhurst, who gave a demonstration of motor-cycle trick riding.

After the meeting, supporters in the 7/6 enclosure could go dancing in the stadium restaurant for free. But, because of the limited space, people from the 3/6 and 1/6 enclosures had to pay 1/-, although this was reduced to 6d if they were wearing a Wembley badge! (NB The average weekly wage in 1946 was £7/6/8.)

But the Lions were back at home. The *News* reported that it was a "Gloriously fine evening, Wembley looked as only Wembley can: brilliant with colour, fresh, bright and emanating an air of supressed excitement."

Wembley dominated the league in 1946. But that did not look likely two days after the opening meeting at the Empire Stadium. The Lions travelled to Bradford, and went down by 20 points to Odsal in front of 28,000 fans. Bill Kitchen broke the track record and was the Lions' only race winner. But on the following Monday, Wembley went to Wimbledon, and a 5–1 in the last heat from Bob Wells and Bill Gilbert saw the Lions home. In the return match, Wembley won more comfortably, with Kitchen, Price and Wilks all in good form, and the 'novices making a favourable impression' according to the *Gazette*.

By the end of the month the Lions had won seven of eight National League matches. The crowd against Wimbledon had fallen to 43,000 – probably because it was a horrible wet evening, and of course most of Wembley's standing accommodation had no roof at this time. But 65,000, a record crowd for a league match, were there to see an injury-hit New Cross side beaten by 30 points, with Bill Kitchen recording his first maximum of the season. West Ham put up more resistance to give the Lions their hardest home match of the season so far, and 70,000 saw the Lions win 47–36. The former Wembley captain from the 1930s, Colin Watson, was riding for West Ham.

June saw more variety in the Lions' fixtures. A narrow challenge match defeat to 'The Rest' at Odsal was followed by two easy National Trophy wins against Birmingham, home league wins against Odsal and Belle Vue, and three ACU Cup matches.

But had Wembley exceeded their manager's expectations? In the *Gazette*, renowned speedway journalist Basil Storey said that Alec Jackson had been prepared for Wembley to lose many matches this season, until the novices got more experience. However, the obvious all-round strength of Wembley team and consistency of each member of team must have shaken him. Then there was the brilliant captaincy of Bill Kitchen, combined with the unselfishness of Kitchen, Price and Wilks; their inspired prompting and aptitude to learn of their less experienced colleagues are some of reasons for Wembley's success. He concluded that Jackson's Lions were making history on their merits.

In the *News*, Bill Kitchen wrote about Wembley's campaign so far, and the pressures this produced. He said that the "Lions are top of ladder, but, believe me, it is going to be a darned sight more difficult to keep there than it was to reach the exalted pedestal. Being league leaders brings many headaches. First of all, your team becomes the Aunt Sally of all – critics, rival supporters, and, on occasions, your own followers vent their feelings in no uncertain manner. Every match becomes a knock—out tie. ... One defeat is magnified and it is no use offering excuses. There is a strain about the whole business of keeping at the top, a nervousness that is reflected only in the manager's office and in the pits.

Fortunately, while with Belle Vue, I have gone through the trying experience of keeping at the top. Now I am leading the Lions in their bid for the crown; that experience is going to stand me in good stead. My team-mates Tommy Price and George Wilks have also gone through this trying-to-keep-there hoop and their seasoned experience is going to prove mighty valuable.

Wembley are fortunate, too, in having second string riders who show no signs of nerves, no matter what the occasion. We already shown our strength on other tracks and ... we are lucky in having real team spirit at Wembley with Alec Jackson, the Lions manager, at hand with his stimulating and encouraging personality. Alec has been through almost everything connected with motor-cycle racing and his experience could not be bought for cash. He has the happy knack of making a lad feel at ease – his Yorkshire wit is always ready to take a youngster's mind off things until those tapes fly up.

And he can offer criticism which does not 'bite' but which makes a rider listen and act upon that advice. You see, matches are not entirely confined to the cinder circuit – if harmony is not present in the ranks no glittering prizes will come the way of the team. Wembley will lose more matches. We cannot hope to go through the rest of the season with a clean sheet: but we possess, I am sure, the right team spirit and talent to enable us to make a bold bid for the Championship crown.

Remember, you Wembley supporters, that we have very stiff opposition wherever we ride. Team riding this season is more marked than ever before – the pooling of strength has levelled individual clubs to such an extent that an away win is something of which to be proud. Another important factor in the race for the league crown is the support accorded a team. It bucks us up no end when we hear the Wembley cry on 'foreign' cinders, for, as I said before, league leaders, no matter who they are, have to treat each heat, never mind a match, as if it is the most vital race of the evening.

Critics are ready to exclaim 'I told you they were false favourites' when a reverse comes along. True, it is a nice feeling to know you head the league ladder, but never forget – as sportsmen of all ranks, be it cricket, soccer, tennis , boxing, etc. will confirm – it's a darned sight harder to remain there than it is to climb there!"

New Lions in 1946: Top left: Alf Bottoms; top right: Bill Gilbert; bottom left: Bill Kitchen (JSC); bottom right: Bob Wells.

Two riders who had ridden for Wembley before the War.
Top left: Tommy Price; top right: George Wilks.

Wembley Lions 1946 at Belle Vue: George Wilks, Tommy Barnett (Trainer),
Bob Wells, Tommy Price, Alf Bottoms, Alec Jackson (Manager), Charlie May, Bronco Wilson,
Roy Craighead. (JSC – Wright Wood)

A 71,000 crowd saw Odsal give the Lions a fright on 6 June. The visitors drew nine heats and were not beaten until heat 13. The report in the *News* said it was easily the best racing seen so far at Wembley, and that Wells and the second strings had been decisive in the Lions' victory. The *Gazette* said that Alf Bottoms had shown "considerable improvement". Both Gilbert and Wilson were nursing injuries. Charlie May and Phil Lewry had featured at reserve to cover for their injured colleagues.

In the middle of the month came the news that Lions chief Arthur Elvin had been knighted in the King's honours list. This was for his 'public services', and AM Low speculates that this was particularly for his work with youth in sport, which was also a cause important to King George VI. Probably his role in facilitating the 1948 Olympics to be held at Wembley also played a role in him receiving this accolade.

After running up 80 points against Birmingham in the National Trophy, the Lions faced a far more serious challenge from Belle Vue. The record crowd for a league match was broken again when 76,000 experienced 'an evening of excitement' according to the *Gazette*. But it finished in an anti-climax. Belle Vue had taken a one point lead with a 5–1 in heat 13, after the Lions had led by nine points at the end of heat eight. But in the final heat, both their riders fell, so Roy Craighead and Alf Bottoms took a 5–0 win and secured the league points.

Sir Arthur and Lady Elvin on the way to the investiture for his knighthood. (MKC & JCA)

The *News* said that the crowd had gone "haywire with excitement" during the meeting.

Despite facing a 53 point deficit from the first leg, a record crowd turned out at Birmingham to see the second leg of the National Trophy tie. The Lions won by 46 points this time, and provided 17 of the 18 heat winners.

An additional attraction for fans who watched Birmingham being massacred was the Match Race Championship first leg between Bill Kitchen and his former Belle Vue team-mate Jack Parker. Parker won 2–1, but Kitchen reversed that result two days later at Belle Vue. On 25 June a run-off was held at West Ham. Parker won 2–0, but Kitchen asked for his engine to be examined to make sure it was not oversize. This was done, but it was found to be within the proscribed limits.

Despite their success in the league, the ACU Cup was not so productive for the Lions. Team racing won the meeting for the home side at West Ham. Custom House was packed with 61,000 fans who saw West Ham veterans Watson and Harrison take a last heat 3-3 to confirm their four point win. In the return at Wembley two days later, the home side were flattered by a nine point win, although on this occasion it was the Lions' team riding that was notable. Bill Kitchen once again unselfishly nursed home the Wembley second strings.

It was not only the riders who were under pressure. The *News* reported that Alec Jackson never caught up with his post. He was receiving 150 letters a day, many with autograph books seeking signatures. He reckoned that 80 per cent were from new fans, and appealed for them to stop writing in for autographs.

At the beginning of July, Wembley were top of the league with 20 points from 11 matches. Odsal were second with 12 points from nine matches. In the ACU Cup, Wembley's team strength showed again with a 20 point home win against New Cross. The Lions second-strings were far superior to those of the visitors. Tommy Price had a particularly good meeting, and beat New Cross star Ron Johnson decisively.

Wembley were clearly dominant in the National League. But also at stake were the sport's two knock-out competitions: The National Trophy and the London Cup. The Lions had won the inaugural London Cup in 1930, and then won it again for three seasons running from 1932 to 1934. But after that they had not even reached the final. Could they turn their league form to winning this much sought after trophy?

Things did not look good after the first leg in Custom House. The Lions went down by 16 points, 62–46, in front of a record-breaking 62,000 crowd. The meeting was also broadcast on the radio. The *Gazette* said that West Ham won on their merits, and superb captaincy and team riding by Eric Chitty "completely confounded the powerful Lions." Wembley had fought hard against the inspired Hammers. Bill Gilbert was missing for the Lions, but replacement Charlie May at reserve scored four points. Bill Kitchen scored 14 from his six rides, and Tommy Price 10 from his, falling in one race. George Wilks scored nine, but it was clearly going to a hard task for the Lions in the return leg two days later at Wembley.

The return match is one of the greatest ever Lions meetings at Wembley. The crowd of 85,000 was then the biggest ever for any speedway meeting. Tom Morgan's report in the *Gazette* was on the magazine's front page, headed *Wembley – West Ham classic*: "The clash between the Lions and West Ham last Thursday gets the gold medal as the classic of classics. Rarely, if ever, has there been such a thrill-packed, sensational all-on-the-last heat 18 races as this London Cup tie which Wembley won to qualify for the final.

A record, perspiring crowd of 85,000 screamed themselves hoarse at the end of it, and it was several minutes before the announcer could make himself heard. With one heat to go it was anyone's match – more so when Kitchen and Price both reared at the gate leaving Chitty and Craven out in front for West Ham.

But the Wembley pair staged a sensationally terrific ride, Tommy Price putting up the best performance of his career to pass first Craven and then Chitty, and Kitchen coming along to do exactly the same thing and completely turn the tables. That race, however, was a repetition of what had gone before, for almost every heat was brimful of incident – so much so that I think this must be the longest 18 heats match ever staged at Wembley. Falls were frequent and in most cases races were justifiably stopped and rerun. Benny King completed 12 laps in two successive races, one of which had to be run all over again after the riders had been flagged home.

Part of Wembley's narrow win came from a he-man effort [in heat six] by Roy Craighead who pushed his machine for half a lap, shedding bits of his kit on the way, to get a third place point. Tommy Price, winner of this particular race, finished on a flat tyre and Colin Watson's machine faded out on the last bend but he managed to coast over the line for second. The fourth rider, Buck Whitby, had retired early on.

The crucial point of the match came in heat 11 in which West Ham appeared to have a reasonable chance of ultimately scraping home, but Eric Chitty stalled at the gate and Wembley went away to gain their third successive maximum. In each of two races Wembley had one rider only, for in one of them Craighead was disqualified and barred from the rerun, while in the following heat Wembley only had one eligible reserve.

If only for that sensational last heat Wembley well deserved their win. When they found themselves pressed during the last couple of heats they pulled out that little something extra which gives speedway racing its curious appeal to the ever-growing multitude.

In fact one could almost say that this match, with its tense electric atmosphere and a crowd comparable with any major sporting event in the world, was one of the finest advertisements the sport has ever had."

Faced with making up a 16 point deficit, the Lions were 9–3 up after two heats, but three successive 4–2 heat wins for the visitors made the score on the night 15–15 after five heats. The Lions had re-established a six point lead after heat 8. But they had lost the services of George Bason, who had been signed as cover for the injured Bronco Wilson, but was taken to hospital with concussion. The three successive 5–1 heat wins in heats 9 to 11 saw the Lions 18 points ahead. A 5–1 to West Ham in heat 13, after Craighead was excluded was countered by Bill Kitchen and Bob Wells beating Watson and King two races later. The Lions needed a 3-3 in that dramatic last heat, and their 5–1 win made their win look more comfortable than it really was.

Sadly, this was the last meeting that former Wembley captain Colin Watson completed. He was seriously injured in a second half race at Odsal two days later. He fractured his skull and punctured a lung and was on the critical list for weeks. He recovered, but never rode again. A benefit meeting was held for him at West Ham later in the season.

The Lions' attention now switched to the National Trophy. Two days after reaching the London Cup Final, they travelled to Belle Vue for the semi-final first leg. The competition had been launched in 1931, and the Lions had been the first winners, beating Stamford Bridge in the Final. They retained the trophy in 1932, beating Belle Vue in the Final, but had not won it since. In 1939, the Final never took place because of the outbreak of the war, but Wembley would have faced the Aces to decide the destination of the trophy.

The highest crowd of the season so far at Belle Vue, 35,000 saw the home team build up a 12 point lead. The Lions brought in Stan Hodson at reserve, and were missing Bill Gilbert and Bronco Wilson. After seven heats the Lions were 10 points down, but according to the *Gazette* "refused to be shaken and grimly held Belle Vue to this margin until the final race." Hodson rode in a few meetings for the Lions this season. In 1947, he rode for Sheffield and Wombwell before joining Exeter. In 1949, he was advised not to ride due to health reasons, but continued riding. He died at the young age of 27 in a nursing home from a heart attack on 17 June 1949.

Twelve days later, 80,000 attended the second leg at Wembley, with at least 10,000 locked out. According to the *News*, the stadium management only expected a crowd of 60,000. They prepared 80,000 rain check tickets, and when these were gone, closed the gates. But thousands stayed outside and listened to the results. During the interval the gates at the back of the pits were opened to allow the Pyramid display team of motorcycles to leave. Around 2,000 of the locked out fans tried to get in, and Alec Jackson had to assist the steward in locking the gate. After the meeting, mounted police controlled the half-mile long queue to Wembley Park station.

Left: Roy Craighead; right: Charlie May (JSC).

Given that Wembley's attendances had regularly topped the 60,000 mark, it is strange that the stadium management only expected 60,000 fans. Also, the stadium could hold 100,000, but the speedway attendances seem to have been capped at 85,000. Maybe with many families present the stadium management wanted to allow supporters on the terraces more space, but there must have been many disappointed supporters when the gates were closed, with potentially more room inside.

The *Gazette* called it "one of the most electrifying matches in the history of speedway racing." Their report said that the Lions were well beaten. After six heats, Belle Vue were 16 points ahead on the night. The *Gazette* said that "The vast crowd was staggered as heat after heat before the interval the visiting riders sprang furiously from the gate and tore round the track in a manner that made the Wembley team look slow by comparison." One highlight for the home fans was heat 11, when Parker and Kitchen had a "wheel-to-wheel duel, as these two crack riders threw themselves into the last bend in a spectacular nerve-racking bid for mastery the crowd screamed, hats and programmes were thrown wildly into the air, and seasoned riders hung over the railing of the pits with mouths agape. Kitchen run the race with nothing to spare."

In the league, the Lions had consolidated their position at the top with home and away wins over Wimbledon. In a seven point victory at Plough Lane, the Lions' heat leaders, Kitchen Price and Wilks were all in excellent form and together contributed 33 of the Lions' 45 points. Lions' reserve George Bason, recovered from concussion, returned to action and broke his leg. He was out for the rest of the season.

The match at Wembley was a farce. A crowd of 60,000 endured driving rain, a track that looked like a miniature lake and bikes stalling. Some of the races for second or third places were at 10 to 15mph. The riders struggled through to complete the match, but the second half was cancelled. The Lions were top of the table with 24 points from 14 matches, having lost their second league match of the season at Belle Vue at the end of July. The Aces were second, having ridden one less meeting, but were 10 points behind the Lions.

Tommy Price clearly liked riding at Plough Lane. He won the British Riders Championship qualifying round there with 14 points, and with Bob Wells won the Laurels Best Pairs competition, which was shown on television. The *News* said that Price was the 'man of the moment' in London, with 65 out of a possible 69 points, bringing him £250 in prize money. He had ridden at Wimbledon in the Riders Championship meeting with a chill, which he had caught in the rain-racked meeting at Wembley. The doctor had given him penicillin, then a fairly new drug.

The Lions rode four meetings in the ACU Cup in August, beating Odsal comfortably at home and then drawing at Odsal, battling through mud at New Cross for a 16 point win, but then losing at home to Belle Vue by four points in front of 75,000 fans. Belle Vue eventually won the Cup with 19 points from their 10 matches. Wembley were runners up with 16.

The fans' attention was now on two events – the forthcoming London Cup Final against Wimbledon, and the British Riders Championship. This event in practice took the place of the World Championship, which did not return until 1949. Qualifying rounds were held at all the tracks, and the final was to be made up of the top 12 riders from the National League rounds, and top four from the Northern League. Wembley staged two qualifying rounds in August, and by the end of the month, Bill Kitchen and Tommy Price had qualified for the final with 67 and 59 points respectively. The other Wembley riders scores were George Wilks with 42 (13 below the lowest qualifier for the final), Bob Wells 20, Alf Bottoms 15 and Bronco Wilson 10.

But before the final at Wembley on 12 September, the Lions faced Wimbledon twice in the last week of August for the London Cup. The dramas of the semi-final against West Ham were not repeated. The first leg at Wimbledon had been made all ticket, with an area reserved for Wembley supporters. The Lions won the match by two points. The *Gazette* said that the "lead changed hands four times in four races, but Wembley always had that little [bit] to spare and were the better all-round team." The Lions' teamwork won them the match, with every rider expect Roy Craighead doing well. Tommy Price had fallen heavily at Belle Vue two days before, had a slight concussion and was advised not to ride. Alec Jackson was against him riding, but agreed that if Price felt alright after his first race he could continue for the rest of the meeting. He did so, and scored nine points.

Three days later, Wembley won comfortably to win the Cup. But the *Gazette* commented that there were "Spills and excitement galore for a crowd of 78,000 despite the run-away nature of Wembley's ... triumph." The report said that Wembley were "complete masters throughout" and noted that George Wilks had returned to form with a new frame fitted to his bike. Price and Kitchen led the way for Wembley, but Kitchen had a nasty crash in the final heat, when he collided with Lloyd Goffe and both riders were carried off on stretchers. Kitchen had broken a rib and had severe bruising.

In heat 13, Wimbledon's Dick Harris had been forced wide on the first bend, and crashed into the safety fence. He became wedged between the track and the fence board, and attendants and ambulance men rushed to his aid. However, the race had not been stopped, and Roy Craighead swerved on the same spot, and just managed to stop his bike running into the people assisting Harris. Four heats later, Bill Gilbert remounted to beat Charlie Dugard who had crashed earlier in the race. Gilbert was also back to good form.

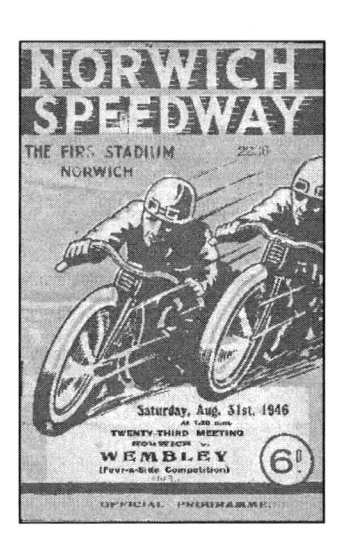

Programmes: Away to New Cross and Norwich (Challenge); at home to Wimbledon (London Cup Final)

The Lions fame spread throughout the speedway world. A four-a-side match at Norwich at the end of August attracted a capacity crowd. Ron Johnson rode in place of Bill Kitchen. After two wins against New Cross in the first week of September, the Lions needed just one point from their final four league matches to make sure of being League Champions. But before then, the British Riders Championship was to be decided.

A packed Wembley saw Tommy Price surprise many pundits by winning the British Riders Championship with a 15 point maximum. In his meeting preview, the *Gazette's* Basil Storey had not even mentioned Price. The *News* looked at each rider's chances and said that Price was like [West Ham's] Malcolm Craven, in his first big year. They said that he would have to "conquer that excitable trend which is noticeable on the big occasion. A tiger at Wembley, Tommy won't be far out if he can make a good start by winning his first race." Of Bill Kitchen, they said that a win for him would "lift the roof off the stands. He has an outstanding chance. But there is only one snag; he is a slow starter..."

The key race was heat six, when Jack Parker fell when challenging Price for the lead. The leather strap on Parker's steel shoe broke. The *Gazette* said that Price's victory "came right out of the blue." Bill Kitchen finished second with 13 points, having been beaten by Price and Jack Parker, who finished third. Tommy Price won £237/10 in prize money on the night, and £442/15 overall in the competition, which *Stenner's 1947 Annual* calculated was £10 a minute. There was talk of putting a waxwork of Price in the famous exhibition at Madame Tussaud's. The 1938 World Champion, Bluey Wilkinson, had been given this honour.

Price won despite suffering from concussion after a crash at Belle Vue in the qualifying round. He said after his win: "I had all the luck going. I owe a great deal to Cyril Spinks for super-tuning my motor and to Jack Parker for the advice he gave me when I was building a frame a couple of months back." (Quoted in article in *Classic Speedway* 30 by John Chaplin).

The Lions won the league comfortably, with wins at Odsal and West Ham and at home to the Hammers, when Tommy Price won nine races on the night. Two of his wins were against Jack Parker in the Match Race Championship. In October Parker got his revenge at Belle Vue, and won the run-off at Odsal to retain the title.

The final meeting of the season at Wembley was on 3 October, when Wimbledon were beaten by 20 points in the ACU Cup. There was a vast crowd, with 85,000 in the Stadium and 20,000 locked out, following the meeting on the loudspeaker system in torrential rain. There were 2,000 cars in the carpark, and some supporters in coaches stayed in their coaches to listen to the commentary. Extra police were needed to marshal the crowds.

Tommy Price scored 15 points with a maximum, well supported by Bill Kitchen and George Wilks. Bob Wells scored 10, as a last-minute replacement for Roy Craighead.

There was much interest in an experiment after the match with booster rockets being fitted to a bike which was ridden by Bill Kitchen. They only lasted for one lap, but Kitchen said that they gave the machine "a considerable push" and that he had "felt pretty scared before pushing the switch" as he did not know what was going to happen.

After winning at Wimbledon in the ACU Cup on 7 October, and returning two weeks later to win a Challenge match in front of over 30,000 people, the Lions finished the season with a tour. They drew at Newcastle, and then won at Glasgow, Middlesbrough and Birmingham.

In the *Gazette*, Basil Storey said that the Lions had been the 'team of the year'. He wrote "Their consistency under the able captaincy of Bill Kitchen earned them the National League championship and to crown this achievement and the winning of the London Cup, the Lions provided the season's star individual rider, Tommy Price, the British champion."

The magazine's editorial said that "Tommy Price [in the British Riders Championship] well deserved his success, is definitely the season's individual star, and many people are still wondering why they had not noticed his brilliance before that epic final at Wembley." They also commended Alec Jackson for the brilliant performance of his Lions.

When all the riders' points were totted up for the season in official team meetings, Jack Parker was top, Bill Kitchen second and Tommy Price third. George Wilks was eighth and Alf Bottoms 19th in the top 24 riders.

In December Wembley announced that the £7,800 receipts from the final meeting would be allocated to 14 charities, with the Speedway Riders Benevolent Fund receiving £3,000 and Wembley Hospital £1,000. A remarkable 1,211,355 people had attended speedway at Wembley in 1946, more than double the 1938 figure.

In his review of 1946 in the *1947 Stenner's Annual*, Tom Morgan said "There is no doubt that Alec Jackson under-estimated his Lions. At the start of the season the Wembley manager told me that he wasn't worrying much about winning championships and things. All he was doing was working to a three year plan so that he could build up a team of invincibles. Alec reckoned that he would be carrying too many novices in the side to be figuring in any prize giving. Well, Alec was proved wrong quite early. His novices Bottoms, Craighead, Gilbert and May proved receptive to the right kind of coaching and were able to pull their weight on more than one occasion." Curiously, he then went on to say that the Lions were not a great team, and that visiting teams always started with a disadvantage at Wembley. How Wembley was different from other tracks was not explained.

Overall, the season was a tremendous success. But one warning sign for the future was the number of easy home wins the Lions had. Five times the visitors had scored 30 points or less. But that was a problem for another day. The Lions had recruited riders who would serve them well in years to come, and attracted some of the highest attendances for any sporting event in England. With the prospect of speedway growing in 1947, particularly Harringay returning to the fold, and more young recruits from Rye House training school on the horizon, especially Freddie Williams and a young man just out of the Army, Split Waterman, things looked good for the Lions.

7. 1947: Champions again

On the track, the forthcoming season promised much for the Lions. In January, it was confirmed that Harringay's return to the sport would be in the National League's First Division, which would now have seven teams. While another London derby was undoubtedly welcome to the Lions, at the top level the sport still had a very narrow geographic focus, with only Belle Vue and Odsal outside the capital. Each team would race against the others four times, twice at home and twice away. The British Speedway Cup was also contested on a league basis; and the knock-out competitions were the National Trophy and London Cup.

However, overall, there was an expansion from the previous season's 12 teams. The Northern League in practice became the new eight-team Second Division, and a Third Division, also with eight teams, was also launched. In January, Alec Jackson announced that there would not be any changes to the Wembley team, and that the club would not transfer anyone if an eighth team was accepted into the First Division. He also said that he could not accept any applications for the nursery at Rye House, where there were 200 novices under review. In March he said that he had been able to concentrate on six riders, two of whom would be kept for the Lions in case of injury, and another four would be loaned to promoter Jimmy Baxter for his teams at Southampton and Plymouth.

The country was facing a major economic crisis at this time. A dreadful winter had meant a big demand for coal and cuts to production in industry. Shortages of paper and energy meant that all weekly publications had to be suspended for two weeks, and the *Speedway News* ceased publication for a couple of weeks in February.

Then, in March, came news that the Government was going to ban midweek sport. Their main concern was with association football. Their grounds had no floodlights at this time, and FA Cup replays on midweek afternoons were notorious for thousands taking an afternoon off to attend the matches. Midweek league matches were played as the evenings got lighter, with kick offs at 5.30pm or 6pm. The Government was also considering a two-shift pattern for industry, with people working either 6am to 2pm or 2pm to 10pm.

There was great concern that tracks would only be allowed to run on Saturdays, which could have meant racing at only four tracks, with others already committed to greyhound racing on that evening, which was also facing restrictions. Worried officials from the Speedway Control Board and the Auto Cycle Union (ACU) met Home Secretary Chuter Ede and agreed with him that the sport could go ahead, but with some restrictions on crowds. There was concern about whether the new Third Division would be able to go ahead, but in the end it did, with a delayed start to its season. Wembley temporarily suspended recruitment to its Supporters Club until the position became clear.

Although attendance figures for the Lions home meetings were not published this season, it seems that things went ahead much as normal. Off the track, the Lions had been busy. In January, the *News* reported that "Members of the world's largest family, the 50,000 registered members of the Wembley Speedway Supporters Club" each received a greetings card and brochure from the team. Many members were still in the Armed Forces, so this mailing was sent out worldwide. At the end of January, the Lions took over the Empire Pool for two dance events for the supporters. A special dance floor was laid over the ice, and 2,000 supporters danced, and another 8,000 could be accommodated as spectators. Over 10,000 attended; the Scooter Trophy was won by Tommy Price ahead of Bronco Wilson, and there was a Fancy Dress competition.

In March, as well as making final preparations for the new season, Tommy Price was being measured for his life-size waxwork model at Madame Tussaud's. Meanwhile, Wembley skipper Bill Kitchen had moved to Wembley from his Lancashire home. His brother Jack had taken responsibility for running their engineering business. Jack had ridden at Belle Vue before the War. It meant that Kitchen would not face the tiring commute from his Morecambe home.

On the track, Alf Bottoms was still convalescing from an operation that had included the removal of a kidney, and hoped to ride in three or four months' time. Wembley announced that their first home meeting would be on 8 May. The Lions were the only all-English team in the First Division, although Welshman Freddie Williams appeared, along with Split Waterman in a reserves match at Harringay as part of their opening evening on 4 April. Both riders would play an important part in the Lions' future. In the *Gazette* on 21 April, Basil Storey said that Wembley "are still the most powerful combination in the country. Alec Jackson's second strings have that touch of class which is do undeniably the Wembley hallmark. The Lions seem all set for another highly successful season."

The strength of the Lions' team-riding was shown in their first match, a comfortable win at Harringay against a Combined Harringay & West Ham team. Faced with the disadvantage of riding their first few meetings away from home, until the Empire Stadium was available, the Lions then lost three of their next four meetings, all in the First Division. A four point defeat, 43–39, at Wimbledon was decided in the last heat when Bill Gilbert and Bronco Wilson fell, so the two Wimbledon riders took five points unchallenged. The Lions three heat leaders, Price, Kitchen and Wilks, scored 32 points, but the other riders could only muster seven.

The Lions won at Belle Vue. The Manchester side were again to be their closest challengers for honours, but were missing Jack Parker and Eric Langton, and then lost Bill Pitcher, who was injured in the first race. The *Gazette* reported that "Bill Kitchen maintained his hundred per cent league record with another brilliant maximum, and, as usual, was well supported by Tommy Price and George Wilks. The latter is showing splendid form and threatens to upset the calculations of many of the stars this season." At West Ham, the Lions supporters were already celebrating a win when Bob Wells's engine failed three yards from the line when he was leading, and the resulting 3–3 gave the home team a one point win. The *Gazette* said that it was the "most exciting match seen in London this season."

The Lions' poor run continued at Odsal. The *News* said that they were "well and truly beaten". Bill Kitchen had asked for the track to be watered before the meeting, but then it rained. Most of the 22,000 crowd left and didn't see the Lions lose by 17 points.

On 8 May, the *News* reviewed Wembley's season so far. 'Red Lyon' asked if the Lions were slipping. He said that there were extenuating circumstances for the poor all-round form of the team. He felt that support from the second strings had been "feeble". At West Ham, all the Lions heat leaders were carrying injuries: Kitchen had a swollen left hand, Price had flu and could hardly ride, and Wilks had a boil under his arm. However, he did say that Wembley expected Split Waterman to be the "most outstanding find of the campaign" and that Bronco Wilson had a new frame and would now be appreciated by the Wembley fans. The editor noted that for many enthusiasts, Wembley's opening night marked the real start of the season. There were rumours that Jeff Lloyd would be signing for the Lions – in fact he ended up at New Cross. Alec Jackson said in the Wembley programme on 29 May that the Control Board considered the Lions to be strong enough, and had blocked any transfer of Lloyd to Wembley. He also said that Lloyd preferred to go to New Cross. George Bason, who had made a couple of appearances for the Lions in 1946, was now riding for Southampton.

The Lions could not turn round their fortunes on opening night. Wimbledon were eight points down with three races left, but sneaked home by a point. Their reserve, Archie Windmill, had one of his best nights ever with 11 points. In the final heat, Bob Wells fell at the first bend, Wimbledon's Dick Harris crossed the inside white line and was disqualified and so Cyril Brine and Bronco Wilson were left to fight for the win. Brine held off a 'herculean' last bend challenge by Wilson to take the chequered flag.

A comfortable win at New Cross on Wednesday 14 May, where the Lions rode hard 'to make every point count' was the start of an 18-match winning run, in the First Division and British Speedway Cup (BSC). Away from home, both Belle Vue on 31 May and New Cross, on 4 June, held the Lions to just a two point win. But at home, only Wimbledon, in a 47–35 win for the Lions, conceded less than 50 points.

Against New Cross on 15 May, the *News* reported that "Wembley's junior riders, Bronco Wilson, Bill Gilbert and Split Waterman rode in the best team spirit. Waterman is now beginning to show useful return for the many hours of practice put in on non-racing days. Wilson did not again make the mistake of riding too close to his opponent, obviously benefitting from the experience gained when opposed to Wimbledon last week." Against Harringay, the *News* said that the "Entire side rode with same spirit as last season. Reserves Charlie May and Split Waterman each performed with a brilliance that now has them ripe for a position in the team proper. In fact, it is to these junior Lions who are now finding their feet that Wembley owes so much for their recent success." Waterman also rode well in the return at Harringay, and early season predictions of his impact were being borne out.

Bill Kitchen was busy outside his team commitments for the Lions. In May, he rode with Ron Johnson in Prague, in front of at least 100,000 fans (some reports said 120,000). He also visited the Hoover factory in Perivale, where he gave the staff a pep talk and given a tour of the factory. He was also interested in sailing, and had a small yacht moored on the Thames at Putney.

Although the Lions were challenging for top place in the league table, after their poor start to the season, the home meetings were not always great entertainment. The *Gazette's* report of the Harringay match commented: "Pity that the Wembley track tends to make speedway racing appear so drab. When the teams are so unevenly matched ... the sport is practically deprived of all spectacle on the Empire Stadium circuit". The writer felt that this was speedway at its worst. The Lions won as they pleased. Wembley supporters seemed quite content, so maybe that is all that mattered. A week earlier, their reporter had said that the New Cross match was 'dreary' except for Tommy Price and Ron Johnson's riding. The Lions' win at home to West Ham, 60–24, was the widest margin in the First Division so far.

On the road the Lions were clearly a great draw and were involved in some thrilling encounters. At New Cross, on 4 June, the *Gazette* reported that the match was a "near classic, two teams almost at top of their form, packed with incident from start to finish and left the crowd in such a state of hysterical excitement that it did not quite know whether to barrack or cheer. The fans compromised by doing both with ecstasy."

In the last heat, New Cross were one point up and the crowd were in a frenzy, Lloyd crashed, Johnson came down on second lap, Bill Kitchen was disqualified for boring, and amid cheering and booing, Tommy Price finished alone, to give the Lions their win. The demonstration against Bill Kitchen continued to the end of the meeting. The reporter said it was a "wonderful match". In early July, Wimbledon were top of the First Division, with 25 points from 19 matches; Wembley were second with 20 points from 14 matches.

Split Waterman and George Wilks were attracting much praise at this time. In a wet meeting against Wimbledon at the Empire Stadium, Waterman was the "outstanding" performer, and the *News* said that he had the "force and grit that will carry him to the very top." After New Cross were hammered 60–36 on 3 July, the *Gazette* said that Wilks is Wembley's star at the moment, and the magazine also thought he could cause an upset in the British Riders Championship. He was nominated by the Lions to enter the competition, along with Bill Kitchen and holder Tommy Price.

According to the *Gazette*, Tommy Price spent some time at the seaside recuperating from Hay Fever during the team's unbeaten run. However, he was at his best against Harringay in July with a maximum. At West Ham, Wembley were six points down with seven heats left. Split Waterman, according to the *Gazette*, "beat Malcolm Craven, then Chitty and Lawson, then Craven and Lawson. Wembley won six of the last seven heats. The dauntless courage of Split Waterman saved Wembley." The Lions' first captain, Colin Watson, commented: "That boy is going places". Against Harringay at Wembley, Waterman had beaten Vic Duggan, one of the few thrilling races in a comfortable win.

The Lions' unbeaten run eventually came to an end at Belle Vue on 26 July, when they lost 49–35; according to the *News*, they were "outridden." In most sports, fans welcome a team being top of their league and winning regularly. That is also true in speedway, but with the sport's inbuilt advantage for home teams because of the different track shapes and surfaces, this can make a strong team's home meetings one-sided. In an editorial at the beginning of August, the *Gazette* reflected that the Lions were undoubtedly the strongest and best balanced team in post-war speedway. They had won the British Speedway Cup, the League Championship was within their grasp, the National Trophy and London Cup were more likely to find a home on the Empire Stadium sideboard than anywhere else, and Bill Kitchen, Wembley's popular captain, had been nominated for the Match Race Championship.

But, it went on "... merely the fact that Wembley are so much stronger than their rivals that tends to make racing at the Empire Stadium appear so dull and unspectacular. One would certainly expect something really special of Wembley in the nature of a track considering that Wembley are capable of providing everything else so much better than their contemporaries. .. The Wembley circuit is not in the true Wembley tradition ... It should be pointed out that the Wembley management works under a severe handicap as regards speedway racing. The track has to be rebuilt every season, due to the football matches staged there in the winter. To attain any degree of perfection a speedway track should be allowed to stay put throughout the winter. The weather does the rest. Under present conditions it is almost impossible for the Wembley circuit to be satisfactory.

Apparently it must remain a headache to the management and a pain in the neck to those people who visit other tracks in the course of the week's racing. It's a great pity, but there you are. Wembley has everything else."

In the same issue, Basil Storey highlighted George Wilks's good form in an article headed 'Wembley's man of the shadows': "George Wilks may yet prove to be outstanding British-born rider of 1947 season. A shy, quietly spoken little fellow; there isn't a rider in the game who treats riding more seriously than does Wilks. There are moments when I have thought that George takes it a trifle too seriously. A momentary lapse of form depresses him, and a slight error of judgement on his part can affect him for the remainder of a meeting... George Wilks is a far greater rider than many people are inclined to believe. George is not outstandingly popular anywhere else but his own Wembley track." Wilks rode at reserve for England against Australia at West Ham and won three races.

Vic Duggan leads Bill Kitchen at Wembley in the Match Race Championship that resulted in so much controversy. (JC)

There were two incidents involving Bill Kitchen in August, one serious and one not. The *Gazette* used to announce rider's birthdays, and fans would send cards to them. For some reason, they announced Kitchen's as 7 August, but it was not actually until December. Apparently hundreds of cards arrived for the popular Wembley skipper. It was not the first muddle involving him, in June the Wembley programme had to ask supporters not to phone a particular Wembley number anymore that belonged to a Mrs Kitchen. It was not, in fact, Bill's residence.

The second incident was much more serious. Bill won the first leg of the Match Race Championship at Harringay 2–1 against home favourite Vic Duggan. A few days later, the second leg was held at Wembley on the night that Harringay were the visitors. This time Duggan won 2–1. So both riders had won on their 'away' track. In its edition dated 14 August, the *News* announced that there was going to be an enquiry into the match race, probably based on the steward's report. A week later, the magazine announced that the two riders were not guilty of conduct prejudicial to the sport, but the inquiry panel issued a warning to all riders that if any race fixing was proved, drastic action would be taken.

This is very curious. These were two of the sport's top riders, who were both riding regularly. Their only gain from the match race going to a run-off was one extra booking. A run-off was not unusual, although both riders winning on the opponent's track was. As it was, the run-off was not held until 20 September, when Duggan won 2–0.

The inquiry also caused bad feeling. In a report headed "'Star Chamber' speedway justice?" Stenner's 1948 Annual commented: "The method of instituting the inquiry aroused much resentment. Neither Duggan nor Kitchen were informed that charges had been laid against them until they arrived at the inquiry. The nature of the allegations they had to gather from press reports appearing prior to the inquiry. In civil law, a man cannot be placed in the 'dock' without being charged, he must be told the exact nature of the offence and what law he is alleged to have broken. That basic legal principle should be adopted in speedway racing without delay."

In *Stenner's 1948 Annual*, Peter Wilson devotes around half a page of his article on the 1947 season to the Kitchen versus Duggan match race, but does not mention the enquiry. He does say that Kitchen beating Duggan on his own track was "one of the speedway sensations of the season". He went on: "I shall not soon forget the return race at Wembley. A gigantic crowd jammed Britain's finest stadium and I cannot remember a roar like the one which went up as the two men faced the tapes after each had won a heat. The thundering applause reached a crescendo as they began the final lap, for it looked as though Kitchen was going to upset all the odds by taking the championship in two legs. But when he was in the lead Kitchen drew out just too far and Duggan, seeing an opening, smashed his way through it..." The reason for the delay in holding the run-off was that Kitchen had bought a new yacht and entered for a race on 6 September. He offered to withdraw from the match-race, but the authorities accepted that he had accepted the race booking before he knew of the clash, and postponed the run-off.

After he had beaten Kitchen, Duggan announced that he would resign the title, so Jack and Norman Parker then competed for it. Duggan found the whole business upsetting, and never competed for the Match Race title again. Years later, he refused to discuss the matter with John Chaplin.

The second leg of the Kitchen versus Duggan match race was on the same night as their two teams met in the first round of the National Trophy. Wembley established a 16 point lead to take to Harringay eight days later. The Lions won the second leg by 11 points to comfortably go through to the semi-final, but the meeting was marred by tragedy.

Wembley's second string, Horatio Nelson 'Bronco' Wilson, crashed on the first bend in the first race. He was unconscious when the ambulance men got to him. He was taken to the Prince of Wales Hospital in Tottenham, but died early the next day, before his wife could reach the hospital. He had served in the Army in the War, and been spotted by Alec Jackson at Rye House. He had established himself in the Wembley team in 1946, and had moved up to partner Bill Kitchen. He had been ever-present for the Lions in 1947. The front page of the Wembley programme for 21 August carried a tribute to him which is reproduced elsewhere in this book.

He was the only rider who died while riding for the Lions post-war, and the first on any London track since Dusty Haigh at Hackney in 1936. This was an era when safety standards were not the same as today. That same weekend, Cyril Anderson also died in a Best Pairs event at Norwich. It was a very sad time for speedway.

With more Australians riding in the UK, a three match test series was held. The third was at Wembley on 14 August. England were already 2–0 up, and had won the series, but Australia won the match 57–49, with Vic Duggan top scoring with 17 points. Tommy Price and Bill Kitchen rode in all three tests, and for this one, George Wilks was promoted to the full team from a reserve spot in the second test at West Ham. He was partnered with Bill Kitchen, and scored nine points, as did Tommy Price. Kitchen scored seven.

Above: Split Waterman
Right: Freddie Williams

Wembley versus Wimbledon at the Empire Stadium in 1947. (MKC & JCA)

By the end of August, Wembley had virtually won the British Speedway Cup, with 11 wins from 11 meetings, had reached the London Cup Final and four days into September secured a place in the National Trophy Final, beating West Ham 68–40 after a surprise 55–51 defeat at Custom House in the semi-final first leg. In the First Division, Wimbledon were still top with 25 points from 19 meetings, but Wembley were third, with 20 points from 15 meetings.

Bill Kitchen, George Wilks and Tommy Price had all reached the British Riders Championship Final on 11 September. It was reported that Kitchen, Wilks and Split Waterman had been chosen to tour Australia in the winter, although none of them actually did tour with England.

In the British Riders Championship, Bill Kitchen ended up as runner-up again, after losing a run-off to Jack Parker. Both riders had finished on 14 points, and Kitchen led for the first two laps, but Parker passed him on the third to take the crown. George Wilks finished fifth with nine points, but Tommy Price finished 10th with just six points. After going through four qualifying rounds unbeaten, Vic Duggan could not reproduce this form at Wembley and finished seventh with eight points.

So could the Lions win all four trophies, as predicted in early August? In the league, a run of seven straight wins secured the title, with 38 points from 24 meetings, seven clear of runners-up Belle Vue. In the British Speedway Cup, a 64–32 win at Harringay gave the Lions a 100 per cent record. But in the other two trophies, the Lions fell at the last hurdle.

At the end of August, the Lions had won by six points at New Cross in the league. So it was no great surprise when they came away from south east London with a nine point lead in the first leg of the London Cup Final on 17 September. Bill Kitchen top scored for the Lions with 17 points from six rides; George Wilks and Split Waterman also reached double figures with 12 and 11 respectively. New Cross included former Wembley captain Lionel Van Praag, but he was now past his best, and only scored seven from five rides. The *News* said that Wembley had made the most of their good fortune to secure a nine point lead.

Earlier in the season, the Lions had beaten the Rangers by 16 points at the Empire Stadium, and two weeks after the second leg of the final won by a 30 point margin. But cup racing is different, and New Cross came away with the trophy after a shock 61–47 win. The *News* said that New Cross began with two 5–1s, virtually wiping out the Lions' lead in two races, and that after that Wembley were completely outridden. The *Gazette* said that "Wembley, the mighty Lions, were beaten at their own game. An inspired New Cross struck a team-riding formula, a complete confidence which shattered and finally almost demoralised their opponents. No one could have blamed the Wembley riders for considering that the issue was 'in the bag'. No one could blame them for under-estimating the opposition, which we are afraid they did and realised their mistake when it was too late to do anything about it." It was Wembley's first home defeat since 8 May and only their fourth post-war.

Having won the League, the Lions entertained Belle Vue in the first leg of the National Trophy Final on 9 October. In the League and British Speedway Cup, the Aces had been beaten decisively three times at the Empire Stadium in 1947.

On this occasion, the Lions could only take a two point lead to Manchester, and the *Gazette* said they were lucky to get that. Louis Lawson was excluded in heat 12, and the Lions then secured a 5–1. A couple of heats earlier, a disaster was narrowly averted: Split Waterman fell, then Lloyd fell and remounted, and had to dodge a track grader to finish third. The *Gazette* said that Wembley could not match Jack Parker and Eric Langton, despite inspired riding by Bill Kitchen and Tommy Price. Highlights from the match were shown by *Pathe News* in around 1,000 cinemas.

The Lions had already won twice in Manchester in 1947, but on this occasion, except for Split Waterman, the Lions' second strings made little impact, and the Aces held onto the National Trophy with a 63–45 win to triumph on aggregate by 16 points. The *News* said that the Lions were far from a well-balanced team and relied almost entirely on Bill Kitchen, Tommy Price and Split Waterman.

In the programme for the National Trophy Final, Alec Jackson wrote that it had been a "glorious season" for the Lions. To celebrate their achievements, he took the riders out to dinner in the West End and then to the Palladium to enjoy a show. The Lions were presented with the British Speedway Cup on the 16 October, and the National League trophy at their final home meeting on 23 October.

The previous week the *News* devoted an editorial to the Lions. The editor, R.M. Sammy Samuel, said that Wembley had been expected to take all the honours, but had fallen from grace, and lost the National Trophy and London Cup. With the Supporters Club membership at 50,000; he reckoned that five times that number were "devoted worshippers of the Lions." However, he believed that it was good for the sport that these reverses have come Wembley's way. He said "Only Wembley's attractive super-production saved some of the meetings from being monotonous. High spots were, of course, the test match and the [British Riders] Championship.

Now we know that Wembley are not an overwhelmingly powerful team after all. Wembley, both as a ground and a team, is so famous throughout the sporting world that an occasional set-back cannot dim the lustre of the name. But speedway racing as a sport has gained through the change of fortune which the Lions have so dramatically encountered. How greatly this turn of the wheel is going to stimulate next season's racing. Teams which threatened to become half-hearted will take on a new lease of life and Wembley should gain by meeting stronger opposition."

In *Stenner's 1948 Annual*, David Williams, The *Daily Herald's* speedway reporter, said that Wembley had "the greatest club spirit in the game. Times out of number when their stars faltered the lesser fry would come out of the blue with something extra, to shatter the hopes of the opposition. Tommy Price and captain Bill Kitchen were always expected to be to the fore and seldom did they fail, but their strength lay in the support of men like George Wilks and the find of the year, the ever wise-cracking Split Waterman."

Also writing in *Stenner's*, Peter Wilson from the *Sunday Pictorial* said that nearly a million and a quarter people "jammed the stands and terraces at Wembley". Figures were not published this season, but there is no reason to dispute his comment.

Clearly, Split Waterman had had an enormous impact in his first season, and was widely recognised as having star potential. In his final meeting of the campaign, at Birmingham, he won the Perry Barr Trophy with a maximum, ahead of Tommy Price and George Wilks.

As always, Wembley were planning ahead. Alf Bottoms had returned to action towards the end of the season, and it was felt that a move to lower grade racing may help him recover his form. Alec Jackson signed Gil Craven, younger brother of Malcolm Craven, for the Lions, and there was speculation that he would be loaned to a Second Division team. In fact, the signing was not approved by the Control Board and he never rode for the Lions. It was also reported that Stan Lanfear and Harold Sharpe, who had both been on loan to Plymouth, were now transferring to the south west club, but certainly Lanfear was regarded as a Wembley asset the following year.

Another rider who had come on the scene in 1947 was Freddie Williams. Alec Jackson had plans for another winter training school at Rye House, and the team's ability to find and develop new talent arguably put them ahead of any other team in the league.

But there was a cloud on the horizon for the 1948 season. For some time it had been known that the Olympic Games would disrupt the Lions 1948 season. In the Lions' programme for their final home meeting, Alec Jackson said that the Stadium would not be available for part of the season. He said that the Lions hoped to be able to open the season at Wembley, and then return on the third Thursday in August, but that what would happen would be confirmed in the next few weeks.

At the end of the year, it was confirmed that the Lions would ride some meetings at Wimbledon or Harringay, West Ham being considered too far away, despite its enormous capacity. In fact, 1948 would be fraught with problems.

8. 1948: A year in exile

The Lions had been very successful in the first two seasons after the War. But 1948 posed a set of new challenges for the team and their supporters. The 1944 Olympics had been awarded to London before the war, but after the War started in September 1939 all scheduled Olympic competitions were cancelled. Helsinki had been offered the 1940 games, but was in no position to stage them, so London was given the honour of staging the 1948 games. The Labour Government agreed to honour the commitment, despite the dire state of the economy. Wembley was the obvious stadium to stage the opening and closing ceremonies, the athletics and the football, although it is not clear whether White City, with a similar capacity and athletics track in place, was considered, and if not, why not?

Fred Hawthorn and Ronald Price, in their history of White City, *The Soulless Stadium*, say that before the War, in 1937 White City had approached the Football Association about staging the FA Cup Final when the FA's agreement with Wembley ran out. They offered to invest £250,000 in their facilities, and have a capacity of 150,000. Hawthorn and Price wonder whether Sir Arthur Elvin was determined to punish the Greyhound Racing Association (GRA) for their "impertinence" and thus "White City did not play any part in the 1948 Olympic Games." However, if there was a bad relationship between Sir Arthur Elvin and the GRA, this may also explain why the Lions moved to Wimbledon for their 'exile' period rather than the nearer and larger Green Lanes.

The Government could not put any funding into repairs at Wembley, so Sir Arthur Elvin persuaded his fellow directors that the Stadium would pay for the repairs, and hope to recover the money from ticket sales. Including the construction of Olympic Way from Wembley Park station to the Stadium, and repairs and improvements to the Stadium and the Pool, AM Low, in his rather laudatory book *Wonderful Wembley*, believes that the company spent £200,000. This was probably a factor in securing the games for Wembley – that no funding from outside was required. One tangible reward was establishing Wembley as a world-renown venue, and – of course – the improvements stayed in place.

However, for the speedway team and Wembley Stadium Limited, the consequences were very serious. The Lions had to ride elsewhere until 2 September; although the British Olympic Association did compensate Wembley for the loss of income from the speedway and 14 greyhound meetings which were cancelled so the athletics track could be prepared. However, there was still the cost of staging 'home' meetings for the Lions at Wimbledon.

The *News* was very concerned at the start of the year. Its editorial on 1 January outlined: "Let's be frank and admit right away that much of speedway's success hinges upon Wembley. We owe Sir Arthur and the go-ahead folk with whom he has surrounded himself far more than many realise. But if my news is correct we shall not see much speedway racing at Wembley in 1948. Can the sport stand this severe blow? I hope so. Of course, the Lions will race at other tracks. There are plenty invitations flying around. But there's a magnet in Wembley, and it has to be tested whether the 60,000 or so who flocked there regularly last year will visit other grounds quite so enthusiastically. Let's try to be optimistic about it." The *Gazette*, meanwhile, pointed out that the country was still in an "era of austerity", and that although the sport had problems, it also had ambitions and potential, one of which should be a bigger First Division.

The ban on midweek sport was still in place, which could cause problems for potential new tracks. The Home Office would only grant licences for new tracks in 'non-industrial' areas. By the end of February, it was agreed that the First Division would stay at seven teams, five of which were based in London. The Second Division grew to nine teams; Wigan closed, and Fleetwood and Edinburgh joined. The Third Division also grew, from eight teams in 1947 to 12 in 1948. Eastbourne moved down the south coast to Hastings, and the new recruits were Coventry, Hull, Poole and Yarmouth. Halifax had also been interested in joining, but could not secure the Halifax Town football ground for long enough to run a league season; Rayleigh and Leicester staged open meetings during the campaign with an eye on future league membership.

In March, it was announced that Wembley would stage 18 meetings at Wimbledon before returning to the Empire Stadium. The Lions season would open on 29 April, slightly earlier than usual, and after the Olympics finished on 14 August, it would take a couple of weeks to restore the speedway track. The *News* said that White City, which was owned by the Greyhound Racing Association (GRA) was not available for speedway because of contractual commitments with the Amateur Athletics Association (AAA). The *News* commented that this was probably a matter of regret for the GRA, who owned Harringay Stadium and had made good profits from the speedway there.

Wembley issued the following statement: "Due to preparations for the staging of the Olympic Games at the Empire Stadium, Wembley, the Wembley speedway team will race 18 of their home fixtures at Wimbledon Stadium. These will be held every Thursday evening from April 29 until August 26. Immediately on the conclusion of the Olympic Games on August 14, the Wembley speedway track will be prepared in readiness for a grand reopening on Thursday 2 September.

An important fixture at Wembley during Sept will be the [British] Riders Championship Final and, of course, it is possible Wembley may have reached the final of a Cup competition by that time. As the accommodation at Wimbledon is considerably smaller than that at Wembley only members of the Wembley Speedway Supporters Club, with the exception of a small number of the supporters of the visiting team, will be able to obtain admission to the track. No cash will be taken at the turnstiles and Wembley have devised a scheme for season and individual tickets to be available only to their supporters. A brochure, giving full details of the Wembley Speedway plans for this year, together with information on how to apply for these Lions matches at Wimbledon, will be sent to all members of the WSSC within the next fortnight or so."

The reaction to this announcement was not positive. On 11 March, the *News's* editorial was headed "Wembley's move to Wimbledon causes some criticism". The editor, Sammy Samuel, wrote: "Wembley's scheme for ticket only admission to Wimbledon during the Lions tenancy there seems to have aroused a rare hornet's nest. As I write I know of no more of the arrangement than appeared in Wembley's own announcement in last week's *Speedway News*, and the only reply I can make to hundreds who have written – many indignantly – for fuller particulars is to wait until all details have been worked out by the worried Wembley folk. All the complaints I have received appear to follow the same line: 'Why should I, a keen supporter of another team, have to join the Lions' club to get an additional evening's sport? I haven't had to do so in the past and I may say that I have been almost a regular attendant at Wembley merely because I can get a great kick out of speedway without my own team being concerned.' Thus writes Miss Phyllis Knowles of Herne Hill [in south London] and her comment can be taken as typical.

I am going to appeal for a little patience and reason, for I appreciate that Wembley are in more than a bit of a jam. The trouble all boils down to the comparatively small crowd capacity of Wimbledon considered in conjunction with the average attendance at Wembley last season. It is not policy to talk figures just now, but you must take it from me that, in its present blitzed state, Wimbledon cannot accommodate half the average crowd at Wembley last season. Remember, too, that the Lions Supporters Club has a membership of over 50,000.

The journey to Wimbledon from the districts north and north-west of Wembley, from which I believe the track draws most of its support, is not an easy one, and maybe only half of those who habitually attended Wembley last season will be prepared to travel so far this year. But even such a drastic reduction means an overcrowded Wimbledon, so where are we? Many will query why Wimbledon was selected as the Lions' 'home' when either Harringay or West Ham would have allowed for bigger crowds. I believe I'm right in saying that both were considered, but that there were good reasons why the choice fell on Wimbledon. My idea about Harringay is that it would have been foolish to have Wembley riding on Thursday nights with the local team following the next night. And West Ham is rather inaccessible for Wembley enthusiasts. Transport to the east London track is not easy.

Well, there it is for the moment. I believe we shall see some arrangement which will not work too harshly against those who want to watch speedway racing irrespective of what teams are concerned."

In response to the criticism, H.C. Hastings, the Stadium's chief press officer, wrote to the *News*:

"Dear Sammy,

I read with considerable interest your leading article in this week's issue of the *Speedway News*, and I afraid my recent bulletin concerning our 'transfer' to Wimbledon is responsible for the misunderstanding about tickets for members of the Wembley Speedway Supporters Club (WSSC). In the article you air the complaint of a neutral supporter who protests at joining the WSSC in order to gain admission to our Wimbledon meetings. I should like to emphasise that no new members can be admitted to our Supporters Club until we return to Wembley on September 2.

As you will appreciate with our membership of 56,000 we cannot accept new registrations with only a 22,000 accommodation at Plough Lane. Therefore, I should like to emphasise once again that only those who were members of the WSSC last season – and they have no need to re-register for the present season – will be allowed to obtain tickets for our meeting at Wimbledon. In other words, the 1947 membership cards are valid for the whole of this season, including the number of meetings we shall run at Wembley from September onwards.

I thought I would let you know this so as to clear up any misunderstanding which has arisen, as shown by the complaint of your reader."

The same issue had a letter from a D. Kew, arguing that Wimbledon was a very bad choice, and that Harringay or New Cross would have been more accessible.

On the Supporters Club, Mr Kew said that £1,400 a year was collected from members for privilege of being a supporter. He argued that there was no reduction in admission charges which are most expensive in London, and that Wembley get crowds two or three times larger than other teams, but their costs cannot be greater. He also said that Wembley made huge profits last year.

He said that the Wembley supporters should be given priority in the stadium, he couldn't leave work at 4pm, and often couldn't get into any part of ground except bends. He concluded that "All I have had from the Supporters Club were cards and calendars. Sixpence a year, I would pay five shillings, but why have a Supporters Club if nothing is gained?"

The editor replied, saying that there were difficult conditions at moment, with the Entertainment Tax and that Wembley's costs of staging a meeting were far higher than any other track. Samuel also said that the Wembley management assisted other venues and that Sir Arthur is continually assisting speedway racing as a whole.

The *Gazette* looked at the issue more from a racing point of view. At the end of February they commented: "Wembley are going to be put to a severe test during the 1948 campaign. To win the National League championship a team has to ride almost as well away as they do a home. Wembley has accomplished this feat two post-war racing years. If they can retain the Championship this year playing most of their matches away from home, and we believe they are quite capable of doing so, the Lions can claim to be Champions indeed.

The situation is rather unfortunate for Wembley's legion of supporters, but it certainly adds piquancy to the season; and what a magnificent test for Kitchen and his men."

So who was actually going to be riding for the Lions? Along with their statement about the move to Wimbledon, Wembley said their team would be Bill Kitchen (captain), Roy Craighead, Tommy Price, Bill Gilbert, George Wilks and Split Waterman. The reserves would be chosen from Freddie Williams, Peter Robinson, Bob Wells and Bill Kemp. Kemp had ridden with Split Waterman in Italy when serving in the Army. In the *Gazette*, Basil Storey said that Robinson's move to Wembley from Third Division Southampton was a surprise. He thought that Robinson, who had been the leading points scorer in the Third Division in 1947, might regret this "hastily sought promotion". Storey was proved to be correct, Robinson hardly rode for the Lions, and could not win a place at reserve.

Alf Bottoms had joined Southampton. Charlie May was also on the move, and looking for a team in the Second Division – he joined Birmingham for a fee of £400. Eric Williams was also loaned to the Brummies, but only to be used in the team in an emergency. But he then beat three of their riders and did ride for the team until he broke his thigh in a track crash.

Bill Kitchen had also been busy in the winter as vice-chairman of the Speedway Riders Association. With chairman Jack Parker riding in Australia, the *Gazette* said that Kitchen had "made quite a hit" with the Speedway Control Board as a 'level headed' man.

As usual, the Lions started the season with a run of away fixtures. Three riders rode in New Cross's opening meeting on 24 March; the next day the whole team comfortably beat Wimbledon 52–30 in a Challenge match at their new temporary home. But then they lost 49–35 at West Ham on Good Friday; although this was maybe a warning that the east Londoners were to be stronger in 1948 than in the previous campaign.

The Lions opened their defence of their National League crown at Harringay with a six point win. The Racers were missing the services of Vic Duggan, and the Lions were not impressive, according to the *Gazette*. However, four days later, Bill Kitchen fell in the opening heat at West Ham and was taken to hospital with a broken arm. The report in the *Gazette* said that this "seriously upset Wembley's chances of hanging onto the league championship. Tommy Price will be captain until his return. Kitchen, one of the safest riders in the game, rarely falls, and his spill was one of the simplest ever seen. Bob Harrison, close behind, did well to throw down his machine, but while he managed to avoid hitting Kitchen he could not miss Bill's machine. The bike smashed into Kitchen who, in great pain, was rushed to hospital. After treatment he went home." However, Kitchen had further problems with his arm and had to return to hospital for further treatment. It was expected that he would be out for three to four months.

New riders in 1948: Top left: Bruce Abernethy; Top right: Jim Gregory (JSC); Left: George Saunders
Bottom right: The cover of the Stenners' booklet on the Wembley Lions.

Peter Robinson asked to return to Third Division racing, and this was accepted by the Lions. Former Lion Wally Kilminster, who was living in Auckland, recommended Bruce Abernethy to the Lions, and Alec Jackson invited the young Kiwi to come over. Another new recruit before the Lions had even ridden a home meeting was George Saunders, who was signed from Wimbledon, and made his debut in a 29 point defeat at New Cross. He pushed home from the last bend for second place in one heat.

In April, the Government put forward proposals to restrict greyhound racing to one midweek evening. With so many teams sharing stadiums with the dogs, yet another potential obstacle faced the sport. The *News* outlined that the proposal that the greyhounds' night would be Thursdays would cause more problems for the Lions: "I am truly sorry for the Wembley management who have gone to no end of trouble to keep the sport this season, despite the upset caused by the Olympic Games. You will appreciate that speedway means quite a lot to Wembley in a normal season. Even after the considerable assistance which Sir Arthur is always ready to provide, the sport makes a substantial contribution to the Wembley balance sheet. This could scarcely be expected this year, and a less sporting management might reasonably have told the Board that they must get along without a Wembley side in the league. It would have been simple to loan the boys so that there would have been no hardship and, when the autumn came along some kind of 'snap' competition could have been arranged to bring the Lions back into the picture.

But that's not Wembley's way of doing things. It is well appreciated that First Division speedway racing would be very poor stuff without the League leaders. We should all be grateful to the Wembley chief that he has kept in the sport despite the prospect of huge difficulties and an overall loss instead of the usual handsome profit. This threatened further dislocation of plans is to be regretted all the more."

The next week it was proposed that the greyhounds would run on Wednesdays, which would cause problems for New Cross. In fact, they switched to Friday night home meetings without any great difficulties.

Meanwhile, the Lions were preparing for their first home meeting at Wimbledon. A special train service had been arranged, leaving Watford, Harrow, Wembley and Willesden, then changing at Clapham Junction to get an electric train to Earlsfield and then a bus to the stadium. The return left Clapham Junction at 10.38pm, and arrived at Watford at 11.30pm. With working hours far longer than today, one wonders how many supporters would undertake this journey and arrive home at approaching midnight.

The Lions comfortably beat Belle Vue 52–31 in their first 'home' match at Wimbledon. But, maybe put off by the restrictions on admission, there were no concerns about the Wembley thousands packing out the stadium. The *Gazette* commented: "The Lions supporters have not taken kindly to the change it seems, Plough Lane Stadium was half empty and the small amount of enthusiasm seemed forced. Bill Kitchen, with his arm in a sling, introduced his team and at the end had every reason to be proud of them, particularly Freddie Williams, who chose the occasion to record his first win in a league match. Split Waterman, his face decorated with strips of sticking plaster, gave a hectic display, his 10 points being topped with one more by Wilks. Tommy Price just failed to reach double figures when beaten into third place in the last heat. Bill Gilbert was satisfied with four second places."

Meanwhile, the *News* reflected on how Wembley established the presentation standards for other teams to aspire to: "Why has Wembley achieved the fine reputation it holds? Even when – as on occasions there last summer – racing there is very one-sided, folk still came away feeling they've enjoyed a great evening. And it is all due to the remarkable care which is taken in the presentation of racing – from the beautifully kept turf and the abundance of colour to the strict timing of the races. Many tracks are following the lead and are trying to introduce little touches of their own." The Lions had even bought their 'artillery' to their new home – their finishing gun was present at the first meeting, with a uniformed attendant.

In the meeting for the second home match at Plough Lane, against their hosts, Alec Jackson wrote: "It was nice to see you here at Wimbledon last Thursday. Granted you had plenty of space and there was room left for several thousand more. Naturally the position will be reviewed later if there is still unfilled accommodation."

However, it soon became clear that there was no need for restrictions on supporters wishing to attend the Lions' 'home' matches. The management quickly announced that one area would be reserved for Wembley supporters and that cash payments would be accepted at the turnstiles. Tickets could be booked for the following week's meeting at kiosks in the stadium and at Wembley during the week.

On the track, the Lions scrapped a draw at Belle Vue, where four home riders had machine problems. A narrow win over their landlords was followed by a brilliant display by George Wilks at home to Bradford, who beat Australian veteran Max Grosskreutz. Wembley offered Second Division Middlesbrough £1,800 for Frank Hodgson, but not for the first time, the rider preferred to stay on Teeside. After eight league matches, the Lions were third in the table, with 11 points. A comfortable win 'away' to Wimbledon followed, with the home team afflicted by falls and machine problems. But then, metaphorically speaking, the wheels fell off.

The Lions lost their next 'home' match to New Cross (programme above). Despite a maximum from George Wilks, Ron Johnson won the last heat to give his team a 5–1 and three point victory. Ten more matches were then lost, the worst run in the club's history. Three were League matches, and seven in the Anniversary Cup, which had replaced the British Speedway Cup. The competition was run on the same basis, but had been renamed to mark the sport's 20th anniversary.

There were some highlights for the Lions fans. Freddie Williams was improving every week, and moved up from reserve to partner Tommy Price in the Lions team. George Wilks, Tommy Price and Split Waterman all contributed to England's 61–45 win in the first test at Wimbledon. But then, three days after the test, George Wilks broke his thigh in the Lions' home match against Harringay. The *Gazette's* report said that the accident "completely demoralised Wembley who suffered the unusual indignity of losing their third successive league match."

It was now clear that the Lions needed strengthening urgently. In the *Gazette*, Basil Storey's column was headed "Wembley Woe". He wrote: "The boom team of post-war speedway, Wembley might have done well to withdraw from the 1948 scene, loan their riders to other tracks for one season and resumed activities in 1949 shorn of none of the famous Wembley glamour.

This statement will probably cost me numerous friendships out Middlesex way, but there you are Lions – from the word 'go' this was fated not to be a Wembley year. The rather pathetic ghost of a twice-crowned champ-winning combination rattles its chains each Thursday evening at Wimbledon. The mighty Lions roar (as good as a 10 point lead to everybody but the opposition) is missing; and the atmosphere at Plough Lane is so strained that I'll swear I haven't seen a Wembley 'home' match this season.

If, like me, you visited the Wimbledon track twice a week you would appreciate my meaning. Whereas Monday night has the electrifying atmosphere of a Wimbledon night, Thursday doesn't seem to be anyone's night. And an unkind fate continues to mock at the might that is really Wembley.

Homeless due to the Olympic Games until the end of the season, the League champs are fighting a losing battle. Miracles sometimes happen, but where's the comfort in waiting for a miracle? No Empire Stadium, no Bill Kitchen and now no George Wilks. Wembley are right up against it.

The injury to Wilks at a moment when he was riding at peak form was the hardest blow of all. It was bad enough having Kitchen nursing a broken arm following his West Ham crash at the beginning of the season. Only Tommy Price remains of Wembley's 'Big Three' and I fancy that the responsibility is weighing heavily on Tommy's shoulders. This is tragic for I was convinced that Price was booked for a good season.

Manager Alec Jackson is a man capable of handling problems. Alec justifies his title of 'Star Maker' but it is one thing developing stars in your own good time and quite another having to produce them over-night during a crisis. Alec has a number of promising young men in his Rye House school, but unfortunately none of them is quite ready for the Wembley League team, and less so in view of the fight facing the Lions for the remainder of the season,

For two years Wembley have been immune from the devastating set-backs of injuries to key men. Misfortune has caught up with the Lions all at once. West Ham, Belle Vue, Odsal and New Cross have all had their turn; Norwich had an alarmingly bad run of injuries last year in the Second Division, while Sheffield, Glasgow and Birmingham are well acquainted with similar tribulations. It is, however, doubtful whether any team has suffered as are Wembley at the moment. Vagabonds of the National League, the Lions have now almost completely lost their identity. At the moment the brunt of the work falls to deputy skipper Price, Waterman, Gilbert and Williams.

I little wonder that manager Jackson in desperation immediately thought of the Americans, Wilbur Lamoreaux, Jack and Cordy Milne. With tongue in cheek I suggest that this might be the signal for rival promoters to give three hearty cheers for the foreign riders ban."

With both Kitchen out for some time, although he was still working with the Lions off-track and coaching Plymouth, and Wilks out for the season, the SRA and the Control Board agreed that Wembley could sign pre-war Wimbledon star Wilbur Lamoreaux. However, this was only until either Kitchen or Wilks was back in the team and pulling their weight.

At the beginning of June, Roy Craighead was hit by West Ham's Australian star Cliff Watson in the Lions 'home' match, but managed to walk back to the pits. The *News* reported that Wembley were facing a big financial loss this year, and their gates had been "rather thin." The Lions then went down by a massive 66–30 at Odsal, winning only three heats. Split Waterman was the only Lion to trouble the home side. His development was shown by his triumph in the London Riders Championship at New Cross. The *Gazette* described his win as "Dynamic youth shook the Metropolis". It was his first major individual trophy and he was the first British winner of the title since the late Tom Farndon in 1935. He "completely shattered a field of stars" including Ron Johnson, Vic Duggan, Norman Parker, Eric Chitty, Tommy Price, Malcolm Craven, Aub Lawson and Jeff Lloyd.

Wilbur Lamoreaux arrived, saying it was "good to be home" and that he hated that it was at the expense of Bill Kitchen and George Wilks.

Wilbur Lamoreaux (left) and George Wilks (centre) with an admiring fan. (JSC)

Wembley Lions 1948 at Belle Vue (JSC – Wright Wood)

After a stormy journey from America, he arrived at Heathrow in the early hours of Thursday morning, and made his debut for the Lions against Belle Vue on June 10. The *Gazette* commented that he would give "new life to a Wembley team sorely in need of inspiration." He top scored for the Lions with 12 points in a narrow defeat at West Ham, and then fell twice two days later in the Lions' ninth successive defeat against Harringay at Plough Lane.

Writing in the programme for this meeting, Alec Jackson felt that part of the problem was with the team's second strings and reserves. He said that Bill Kemp and Jim Gregory needed to get more experience. He analysed the scores of the 'second string' riders in the last five matches, up to the previous weeks' home match with Belle Vue. George Saunders had a return of 20 points out of 51 for 39 per cent; then came Bob Wells with 33 per cent, Bill Gilbert on 28 per cent, Bill Kemp on 18 per cent and Roy Craighead on 15 per cent. To be fair to the riders involved, they were effectively riding every meeting away from home, even if they were becoming more familiar with the Plough Lane circuit. Jackson also recognised that Tommy Price had been starting badly which had contributed to his loss of form.

Split Waterman's 14 points, including a victory over Vic Duggan, was the only good thing for the Lions at Harringay. Then Bill Kemp broke his collarbone at New Cross, and was out for several weeks. Tommy Price broke his thumb in the same meeting, but managed to ride the next night when, at last, the Lions won a match. Split Waterman's second place in the last heat confirmed a two point win over New Cross.

Tommy Price was now using the frame with which he had won the 1946 British Riders Championship, and looked much improved. In July, the Lions rode every meeting until the penultimate day of the month at Plough Lane. A comfortable away win over their landlords was followed by four decisive victories before the Lions lost twice in two days to Harringay. During this run of six successive wins, Lamoreaux scored his first post-war 15 point maximum against Odsal. A week later, Tommy Price faced Belle Vue – and scored a maximum – despite burning his left hand in the workshops 24 hours before the meeting.

Lions second-string Bill Gilbert had qualified from the Second Division qualifying rounds of the British Riders Championship with 39 out of a possible 45 points. The meetings were on tracks which he only rarely rode. The *Gazette* said that he was the "most improved Lion" and that his partnership with Tommy Price had been an important factor in the Lions' revival. At Harringay, on a torrid night for the Lions when Waterman and Bruce Abernethy arrived late, Tommy Price was injured and missed the meeting, Lamoreaux retired injured after his forks snapped in heat seven; Gilbert won three races and was second in another.

Split Waterman rode for England in every test of the five match series against the Australians. At the end of July it was announced that he was going to challenge Jack Parker for the Match Race title.

Wembley's 'annus horribilis' continued when Tommy Price broke his collarbone in a qualifying round for the British Riders Championship. Basil Storey wrote that the Lions were now rivalling Odsal as the 'jinx' team of 1948. Lamoreaux now became the senior rider, with more responsibility on the shoulders of Split Waterman and Bill Gilbert, who had "improved beyond recognition". Even riders not currently riding for the Lions had bad luck. Eric Williams had been in hospital for three months with a broken thigh. It was improving when he had a nightmare, fell out of bed and broke it again.

The Lions did look to strengthen their team by offering Newcastle £1,000 for their 26-year-old New Zealander Jack Hunt. Alec Jackson planned to visit Newcastle to watch him ride against Lamoreaux and Waterman, but the rider stayed in the north east.

Bill Gilbert's good form saw him selected for England, and he scored 13 points in the fourth test, and seven in the fifth. England won the series 4–1. Along with Wilbur Lamoreaux, Gilbert qualified for the final of the British Riders Championship; a huge achievement for someone who had fought his way through the Second Division qualifying rounds. In Wembley's home round, at Plough Lane, Freddie Williams scored 10 points, riding in place of Tommy Price, showing the progress he had made.

It was clear that the Lions were not going to win the League or the Anniversary Cup, but the two main knock-out competitions, the National Trophy and the London Cup, were open to them. The Lions welcomed back Bill Kitchen for their away win at Wimbledon, and three days later, in their last 'home' match at Plough Lane, the Lions ran up a 22 point lead in the first leg of their National Trophy tie with Belle Vue. Lamoreaux led the way with 17 points from six rides and was unbeaten by an opponent. Heat 16 was controversial. Bill Kitchen rode inside Dent Oliver to pass him, but Oliver kept going and a lap later dived inside Kitchen, who fell. Belle Vue's Jack Chignall, in trying to avoid the fallen Kitchen, hit the fence with such force that he broke a water pipe. With water spraying onto the track, Split Waterman laid down his bike to avoid any further mishap and Oliver was the only rider left on his machine. A rerun was ordered with Oliver excluded, and many in the crowd felt that he was made the scapegoat for the whole incident. Chignall fell in the rerun, so Wembley won the heat 5–0.

But before the second leg against the Aces, the Lions had two clashes with West Ham in the semi-final of the London Cup. According to the *News*, West Ham deserved their 61–46 win in the first leg.

The second leg was the meeting that every Wembley supporter had been awaiting, the 'opening night' back at the Empire Stadium. In the *Gazette*, Basil Storey said that "The success of the 1948 Olympic Games is still fresh in the sporting memory, but Sir Arthur, who has done so much for speedway racing, will experience a feeling of personal satisfaction this week with his famous Lions back in their lair." Wilbur Lamoreaux was writing a regular column for the *Gazette,* and said that it would be a thrill "for those thousands of Lions fans who have been feeling all this season that somehow or other they have not been able to recapture so much of the old enthusiasm while their favourites have been staging home fixtures on the Wimbledon track." He admitted that riding for the Lions at Wimbledon suited him, because it had been his home track before the war. However, he did say that for the first time in nearly 10 years he would "ride from the historic Wembley pits to the starting gate" but this time as a Wembley Lion. He was waiting to hear the famous Lions roar, and concluded "Get cracking, you fans."

Including the first leg, the Lions had only beaten the Hammers once in five official meetings in 1948, although that had been a 24 point trouncing at Plough Lane, over 16 heats. This time, over 18 races, the Hammers were beaten by 27 points. It took the Lions seven heats to wipe out their deficit from the first leg, and the *Gazette* commented on the "apathy" of the West Ham team. The Hammers had no answer to Lamoreaux, Price, Williams and Gilbert, although Kitchen and Waterman did not enjoy a good evening.

Two days later, the Lions travelled to Manchester for the second leg of the National Trophy tie with Belle Vue. There was "tremendous excitement" according to the *News*, but the Lions went through by two points on aggregate. The tie went to the last heat, when Lamoreaux held off Jack Parker and Dent Oliver. He was only the Lions' fifth heat winner on the night, but it was enough to knock the holders out.

Twenty five Wembley followers were not doubt pleased at the Lions' win, but not so happy at having to spend the night in Stafford when their coach broke down on the way home. Not finding any cafes open on Sunday morning, they were given breakfast by nuns at a local convent. After parts and mechanics arrived, they set off for Wembley once again. The bus suffered a second breakdown, and they had to call out the AA who did the repairs to get them home at 7pm on Sunday. Mrs Jose Watkins, who reported all this to the Wembley programme, did say it was all worth it to be at Belle Vue and see the last race in particular.

Harringay came to Wembley for the first leg of the semi-final, and were taken apart 73–35. Lamoreaux contributed an 18 point maximum, and Bill Kitchen also showed some welcome good form with 11 points. The Lions also won the second leg at Green Lanes to go through to the final 133–87 on aggregate. In both the National Trophy and the London Cup, the Lions' opponents in the final would be New Cross, who were heading towards their first League title since 1938.

The British Riders Championship Final attracted a crowd of 90,000. Vic Duggan won the title; Bill Gilbert and Split Waterman finished joint fourth with 10 points apiece. Wilbur Lamoreaux must have been disappointed with his tally of six, although he damaged his best bike in a fall in his first race that involved the demolition of several yards of the safety fence.

Before the Cup Finals, the Lions returned to Manchester for a league match. There was little at stake for the visitors, but tragedy was narrowly avoided when after Wally Lloyd fell and was on the track, the riders came round again and Roy Craighead hit him. Craighead's bike flew into the crowd. The rider was ok after some treatment on the track, and two spectators received minor injuries. But it could have been much worse.

A 65–40 win in the first leg of the London Cup Final for the Lions put them in a strong position for the return at New Cross 24 hours later. The *Gazette* reported that "New Cross relinquished their hold on the London Cup when they failed to clear off more than eight of a 25 points first leg deficit against Wembley and were well beaten in the final by aggregate of 115–98. Wembley rode as a well-balanced team in both legs of the final, but Bill Gilbert is the man to whom they virtually owe the cup. New Cross were holding their own in the first leg at the Empire Stadium when Gilbert made his first appearance in heat 7... [He] forced two successive maximum wins and established a Wembley lead of 13 points.

All told, Gilbert figured in four maximum heat wins in six rides and this in spite of a torn leg muscle which prevented him riding in the second half of the programme. It was Gilbert again who rattled New Cross in the second leg 24 hours later on the Old Kent Road circuit. Defeating Ron Johnson in a thrilling final heat, the Wembley rider scored another 14 pts to bring his total for the final to 28 out of a possible 36."

Once again, the Lions were involved in controversy. Should Lamoreaux be able to stay with the team now that Bill Kitchen had returned? The *News* commented: "The Lions, having annexed the London Cup have a good chance for the National Trophy as well... [A] pleasing prospect for their supporters, but cannot say I feel very happy. Since Bill Kitchen returned, I have been inundated with letters – Wembley should give up Wilbur Lamoreaux. The Lions are recovering their old strength, but more due to 'come on' of Bill Gilbert rather than Bill Kitchen finding his old form. Tommy Price is good at Wembley, but not elsewhere. [The Lions are] also missing George Wilks, the real backbone of the team. The Lions should keep Wilbur Lamoreaux for the rest of the season."

The Lions won the National Trophy for the first time since 1932, beating New Cross in the Final. The *News* reported that the Lions "piled up a formidable number of points" in the first leg, and were the "all-over better team." Ron Johnson was excluded twice, but still scored 12 points. Only three times in 18 heats did a Lions rider fail to score, and one of those was an engine failure for Tommy Price.

The *Gazette's* report highlighted the contribution of Bill Gilbert: "Wembley's cup final specialist Bill Gilbert again proved the key man when the Lions defeated New Cross on aggregate 120–96 in the National Trophy final. In four legs of two finals Gilbert scored 56 out of a possible 72 and this crowned his greatest ever season. There is every reason to believe that this man of Kent has not yet reached the peak of his form and he is undoubtedly the most valuable rider on Wembley's books on 1948 performances.

Wembley built up a lead of 20 pts in the first leg. New Cross more than held their own in the opening heats and held a lead of two points when Gilbert made his first appearance in heat seven. After two successive rides, Bill had completely turned the tables on the Rangers, given Wembley a lead of six points and shaken the visitors' confidence. In six rides Gilbert scored 13 points, sharing the scoring honours with Tommy Price."

In the second leg, New Cross "...had pulled back eight points of Wembley's lead when Gilbert came out in heat seven to score the Lions' first heat win and eventually put his team right back into the picture. Only Ron Johnson, who won all his races to score 18 points, was capable of holding the match-winning Gilbert. The second leg went to Wembley by a four point margin."

New Cross returned to Wembley the following week for a league match – and won by two points, part of a late run that secured the title for them. After 12 races the scores were level, but the match was decided in the final heat, and once Ron Johnson got ahead, he could not be caught. A crowd of 70,000 saw the Lions last home match of a difficult season. New Cross secured the title with a comfortable home win against West Ham the next day.

The Lions finished fifth in the league, with 25 points from 24 meetings. New Cross headed the table with 34 points. The Lions had a better away record than home one, with 13 points on the road and 12 at home.

Bill Kitchen was involved in a controversial incident at New Cross in the Tom Farndon Trophy on 28 October. He allegedly collided with Ray Moore on the way back to the pits, and was disqualified for the rest of the meeting. In November, the SCB agreed that he should face no further penalty.

For the Lions, Bill Gilbert's progress was very welcome. He capped his successful season by winning the Borough of Wembley Trophy in the second half of the Lions last meeting. It was only for Wembley riders and had not been competed for since the War. Split Waterman had ridden regularly for England and won the London Riders Championship. The *Gazette* felt that compared to 1947, he was "slightly more subdued but nevertheless quite devastating". Another one for the future was Freddie Williams, who had developed during the season and held down a regular team place. Bruce Abernethy had benefitted from experience on loan at Rayleigh, and returned to New Zealand to ride in the winter. Stan Lanfear finally severed his ties with Wembley and was transferred to Plymouth.

The Entertainment Tax was still an issue. In December, the *News* said that at 48 per cent of gate income, it hit smaller tracks hard, and that speedway was a "working man's sport". Another issue in the early part of the season was midget car racing at various venues. Alec Jackson commented in the Wembley programme of 20 May that there had been a "fanfare of ballyhoo" about this import from America, and that he believed that "any form of car racing on our type of tracks is bound to be a flop." The cars did receive some coverage in the speedway press, but in the long term Jackson was wrong; stock car racing added to the sport's problems in a few years.

Left: Royalty made a rare visit to speedway when Prince Phillip presented the British Riders Championship trophy to Harringay's Vic Duggan. (MKC & JCA)

Below: Belle Vue star Jack Parker with Split Waterman.

9. 1949: Back home and another title

By 1949, life was slowly returning to 'normal', three and a half years after the end of the War. There were still many men in the Armed Forces. The 1948 National Service Act came into force on 1 January 1949. Men aged 17 to 21 were expected to serve for 18 months, which was extended to two years in 1950 with the onset of the Korean War.

There was still rationing on many consumer goods, although clothes rationing ended in May 1949. Television was growing slowly, but was not yet a real threat to attendances at live sport. The Entertainment Tax was still hitting speedway hard, at 45 percent compared to 15 percent for other mass spectator sports. In January, the SCB announced the appointment of Reginald Clifton, a 'senior member of a firm of Parliamentary agents' to campaign on the issue, and for speedway to receive the same classification as football and other mass spectator sports. By early March, it was reported that 183 MPS were supporting speedway's cause, but little progress was made. A Parliamentary delegation to William Glenvil Hall MP, the Financial Secretary to the Treasury, was led by the MP for Wembley South, Clarence Barton.

There was controversy around the thorny issue of promotion into the First Division. Birmingham were promoted to the National League Division One, despite having finished runners-up by five points to Bristol in the Second Division. Maybe the SCB considered Birmingham to have greater potential than their west-country rivals. However, the development of the sport's top tier outside London, Manchester and Bradford was to be welcomed. The Second Division grew from nine clubs in 1948 to 12. Middlesbrough had closed; a second team was formed in Glasgow, Cradley Heath and Southampton were both given places in the Second Division, leaving the 1948 champions Exeter in the Third for another year. Supporters must have wondered what the point of a league competition was if it did not lead to promotion for the Champions. The Third Division grew by one team, from 12 to 13, compared to 1948. From a London fans' point of view, the launch of a Second Division team at Walthamstow, in the famous greyhound stadium, offered an alternative to the five top flight teams in the capital. Overall, 33 teams started the season in 1949, compared to 28 in 1948.

For the Division One teams, the Anniversary Cup was abandoned, and the league programme involved meeting each team home and away three times for a total of 42 league matches. The issue of promoting a second, or even third meeting against opponents who had been beaten on their first visit by 30 points must have been a problem for all the top teams, not just Wembley. There would still be the National Trophy and London Cup for the Lions to compete for in knock-out competitions. A positive change for the sport was the re-introduction of the World Championship, another sign of a return of stability after the War.

Alec Jackson again recruited three novices from training at Rye House for the Lions, 'Bluey' Pay, Raymond 'Buster' Brown and Dennis 'Bing' Cosby. Cosby and Pay had not ridden a speedway machine before going to Rye House. Brown was described as a cycle speedway veteran for the Wembley Panthers. He had beaten Ronnie Genz twice, who was another cycle speedway star and went onto have a long speedway career. Wembley paid £100 to Rye House owner Dicky Case for four novices, including these three.

Eric Williams, Freddie's younger brother – another young hopeful – was loaned to Cradley Heath for the season; while Bill Kemp also moved to the midlands side, but for a £150 transfer fee. Veteran George Saunders decided to stay at Wembley to compete for a team place. Roy Craighead, who had ridden for the Lions since 1946, moved to Southampton in exchange for Alf Bottoms, who had enjoyed a successful season at the south coast club in 1948, following his injury problems. Craighead's form had declined in 1948, and he went on to find more success in the Second Division.

Basil Storey noted in the *Gazette* that young riders would be challenging the older stars in 1949. He highlighted Split Waterman, Bill Gilbert and Freddie Williams for Wembley, and also said that Williams was one of his 12 riders to follow in 1949.

West Ham star, Eric Chitty, broke his leg riding in Australia. There was speculation that Wembley would loan one of their top riders to the Hammers until Chitty recovered. After some speculation, George Wilks moved to the east end in return for a loan fee of £500.

In March, Alec Jackson proposed that a Junior League be run in the second halves of Division One meetings, with the two reserves and two other riders from each team riding in four heats. This caused controversy with the SRA threatening strike action, because more senior riders would have lost some second half rides. A compromise was reached with the Junior League being restricted to two heats, and the season began without any disruption.

One star who left the Lions was Wilbur Lamoreaux. Signed in 1948 to cover injuries to Bill Kitchen and George Wilks, the American veteran joined Birmingham for the new season.

Facing a massive league programme, the Lions did not ride any challenge matches at the start of the season, and went straight into league action with a comfortable win at Green Lanes over Harringay, for whom Vic Duggan seemed out of practice. But the next five matches on the road saw the Lions take just one point, from a 42–42 draw at Wimbledon. The Lions lost narrowly at West Ham, and managed to draw nine heats at Belle Vue in a six point defeat. Bob Wells was 'outstanding' for the Lions with nine points. The Lions were then 'trounced' – according to the *Gazette* – at newcomers Birmingham by 25 points. Freddie Williams was the only bright spot on the Wembley horizon at Perry Barr. Thousands had been locked out, and 35,000 fans saw Wembley collapse, lacking their usual 'fighting spirit' according to the *News*.

At Odsal a week later, the Lions only took a points advantage in three heats, and lost by 19 points. Split Waterman shocked the track doctor. He crashed and stood up, but then collapsed. He ignored medical advice to keep riding and scored five more points. A few days later, riding at Second Division Leicester, he showed his versatility by helping repair the start gate when it broke down.

After six matches, the Lions were bottom of the league with just three points. However, Six days before their first match at Wembley, they won at New Cross, and were "riding like champions" according to the *News*.

Normal service was resumed when the Lions returned home on 12 May. Bob Wells scored a maximum and Freddie Williams rode well in an easy win over New Cross, and then Kitchen and Waterman were "well to the fore" in a comfortable win against Odsal the following week. RM Samuel had been confident that the Lions would turn things round. Writing in the *News*, he said: "This week sees the re-opening of Wembley, which means to many enthusiasts the real start of the speedway season. All that has happened during April doesn't convey much to them – but those who have followed the fortunes of their local heroes must be a little shocked to find the Lions so far down in the league table.

For some obscure reason Bill Kitchen's side have made heavy weather of it so far, but that this loss of form is only temporary seemed indicated by their recent well-earned win over New Cross, highly placed in the table. For some weeks past, letters have been pouring in on me suggesting that Wembley are ill-advised to loan George Wilks to the Hammers, even though a substantial sum is being paid for him. I do not think this opinion will remain once the Lions begin riding at home again."

The Lions beat the league leaders, Odsal, comfortably at the Empire Stadium the next week. But the *Gazette* reported that the "state of the track marred the racing and deprived the home team of much glory... [It] would have been a keener match on a cleaner wicket. At times the racing was almost farcical and hundreds of fans made a bee-line for home at the interval." Too much dust was the problem.

The third meeting at Wembley in the Lions season was a test match against Australia. A 70,000 crowd saw the Australians win comfortably. Only Bill Gilbert had been chosen for the England team, Waterman and Freddie Williams were chosen as the reserves. Peter Foster, in his comprehensive history of the test matches with Australia, said that in a 'debacle' "only the reserves came out with any credit." Gilbert and Williams were joint top scorers with Jack Parker on nine points, Waterman contributed five. Four of the England team scored just nine points between them.

Two weeks later, after a defeat at New Cross that was covered on television, and a win at struggling Wimbledon, 'unfashionable' Harringay came to be the Lions' next victims. But a maximum from Vic Duggan inspired the rest of his team, who 'rode like champions' and won by four points.

After that, the Lions' form improved. The main drama when New Cross were the visitors was Bill Kitchen's journey to the Stadium. According to the *Gazette*, two hours before the meeting, he was at sea in his yacht at Cowes. He remembered his speedway booking, hailed a launch, was taken to mainland, chartered a plane, flew to Hendon, and arrived with 40 minutes to spare. The meeting itself was "just too easy for Wembley."

Alec Jackson reshuffled the team for the visit of West Ham, with Tommy Price partnering Bill Kitchen, and the Lions won by 32 points. At West Ham three weeks later, Price used an Erskine frame in his bike and scored his first maximum of the season, despite suffering his usual problems with Hay Fever.

Belle Vue held the Lions to 10 points at Wembley on the last day of June, and then beat the Lions by 20 two days later in Manchester. Bill Kitchen missed both matches against his former club. Bob Wells took his place in the team, and Kitchen followed medical advice to have a break from racing. The *Gazette* commented that he had never really been the same since his broken arm in 1948, and maybe he should have had a longer rest and not returned at the end of the 1948 season.

Tommy Price's World Championship campaign started earlier than the other Lions riders, and he won the qualifying third round meeting at Newcastle with a 15 point maximum. His form had not been considered good enough to be exempted until the Championship round.

Jackie Gates came into the team to cover for Bill Kitchen. The young Australian had come to England with Graham Warren, but had failed to find any form at Leicester. He sold his equipment and was going to work in a garage, but Aub Lawson arranged for him to have a trial with Wembley. Alex Jackson signed him up, and gave him a chance in the team. Gates never became a Wembley regular, but had more success at Glasgow Ashfield and St Austell.

July showed how dominant the Lions were, particularly at home. A 40 point win over Birmingham, who were missing Wilbur Lamoreaux and had Graham Warren injured in the meeting, at least saw Bill Kitchen return to form. A week later, the Lions ran up 58 points against Wimbledon, and a week later, Harringay only won one heat as the Lions won 65–19. In August, the Lions' programme said that it was their policy to have the finest possible racing in the second half of meetings, which was just as well because some of the matches were horribly one-sided.

The penultimate home meeting of July was a double-header, on a Tuesday night, to help the Lions catch up with their fixtures. This provided more competitive fare, possibly because the Lions had also ridden at Wimbledon the night before. Odsal were beaten by just six points, and Belle Vue by 12. The second home match against Birmingham saw Lamoreaux make a 'brilliant return' to the Birmingham team. Birmingham lost by 14 points, but the *Gazette* said that they were not disgraced.

From June 16 to 28 July, the Lions won 13 out of 14 league fixtures. But then they lost at home to West Ham by 10 points, and had another disastrous night at Belle Vue, going down 59–25. Split Waterman had been injured riding at Bristol, and was in Wembley Hospital with a spinal injury and broken ribs. Freddie Williams was also injured, and Tommy Price missed out on the Belle Vue match after being injured in the fourth test. Buster Brown and Den Cosby rode for the Lions, and the *News* commented that the visitors' display was "inept". They did not win a race. Wembley were now one point behind Belle Vue in the league, but with three meetings in hand.

The *News* said that: "Wembley is always an example of brainy team-building. Look at their progress this season against losses which would have crippled any other side. Kitchen has been a big disappointment though he still has time to reach his old form. Tommy Price, now coming on again, has been anything but the Tommy of previous years. George Wilks – a consistent points scorer in previous years – is a temporary Hammer and will finish the season there. But thanks to Wembley's many discoveries and the tremendous pride in which the boys take in upholding the good name of the Lions, the team hasn't felt these blows."

The Lions scraped home against Odsal by two points. A dispute arose in the meeting about Jackie Gates replacing Buster Brown. Medical evidence was required to allow this, and Alec Jackson confirmed in the Wembley programme that Brown had been ruled out of the rest of the meeting by the doctor after a spill. The meeting was at a crucial stage when the substitution happened, with Odsal only four points down before heat 12. Bill Kitchen's win over Jack Biggs in heat 11 was also vital, and he seemed to be coming back into form.

Tommy Price was not the only Lion to be affected by Hay Fever. Buster Brown was exempted from National Service because of it. He was healthy enough to ride speedway, but classified as 'C3' by the Army.

Good news for the sport was that attendances were up. From April to June, compared to 1948 all three leagues attracted larger crowds. The First Division had gone from 1,929,427 to 2,512893. The Second Division had risen by over 400,000 and the Third by over 100,000.

An anti-climax for the Lions' fans was a demonstration of jet rockets attached to bikes in the second half of the West Ham meeting. Afterwards, it was said that doubtful if they could contribute anything to speedway. On the same evening, Bill Kitchen and Aub Lawson had a three lap race on 'veteran' speedway bikes. Lawson leg-trailed, and Kitchen won with a time of 79 seconds for three laps, although it gave the "vast crowd a first rate pleasure thrill" according to the *Gazette*.

Twelve days later, the Lions faced the Hammers again, this time in the National Trophy over two legs. Wembley were missing Freddie Williams, Split Waterman and Bob Wells for the first leg at Custom House. They were six points up after five heats, but after the next four heats, West Ham had turned the meeting around to lead by six points, and eventually won 64–44. Two nights later, a Tommy Price maximum and heroics from Bill Kitchen, bought the Lions to within 10 points of West ham on aggregate. But as the *Gazette* commented "the remainder of the task was beyond Wembley's novices", although it was a "plucky" effort. Wembley won by four points on the night, but lost by 16 on aggregate.

New arrivals at Wembley in 1949:
Top left: Buster Brown (JSC)
Top right: Den Cosby
Bottom left: Jack Gates

75

Wembley Lions 1949

Tommy Price receives the World Championship Trophy from
Mrs Violet Attlee, the Prime Minister's wife. (MKC & JCA)

The Lions' colourful Kiwi, Bruce Abernethy, got some new support at this time – his parents came from New Zealand to watch him ride for the Lions. It was their first visit to England for 35 years. August concluded with another Tuesday double-header. The Lions beat Harringay comfortably, but then lost to a Birmingham team who the *Gazette* said were "fresh and in a fighting mood". Two days later, Wilbur Lamoreaux won the World Championship Qualifying round at his former home with a 15 point maximum.

By the beginning of September, the Lions were very close to reclaiming the league title. A win at New Cross was followed by a home win against Belle Vue. The *Gazette* said that Belle Vue's reserves were weak, and "Wembley's team of semi-invalids snatched the honours on their merits".

The Australians had won the test series, despite being heavily beaten at Odsal in the final test. Bill Gilbert made the most consistent contribution of the Lions riders who rode for England, and finished as third highest scorer for England in the series after Jack Parker and Dent Oliver. Curiously, he was dropped to reserve for the final test, despite scoring 12 – and being second highest scorer – in the fourth. Split Waterman, Freddie Williams and Tommy Price also rode for England in the series. Freddie Williams became the youngest rider ever to be selected for a tour down under.

With the league all but won, attention turned to two other competitions – the London Cup, and the first World Championship Final since 1938. In the London Cup, the Lions faced Harringay in the semi-final, with the first leg at home. The Racers had won at Wembley in June, but then been beaten heavily in two subsequent visits. On a rain-sodden track, Price, Wilks and Gilbert were the main scorers for the Lions as they built up a 22 point lead for the second leg. Price was only beaten once, by Vic Duggan. At Green Lanes the next night, the Lions won by six points to comfortably reach the final. There they faced West Ham.

The east London side had won at Wembley in the league in August, and knocked the Lions out of the National Trophy. The first leg was at Wembley, and things started badly for the Lions with Price excluded for boring. After five heats the score was 15–15, and the *News said* that few fans before the meeting thought that West Ham would hold the Lions to an eight point lead. Bill Kitchen top scored for the Lions, and Freddie Williams had a poor night, scoring only one point. On their own cinders, the Hammers would have a great chance to win the London Cup for the first time.

But at Custom House, in front of packed terraces, the Lions were unstoppable and West Ham were virtually beaten by the fifth heat, according to the *News*. Their report said that George Wilks produced form that the locals had not seen from him earlier in the season, Price and Kitchen rode at their top level, and Split Waterman showed some return to form. After the ninth heat, the Lions did not lost a race on points, and the Hammers provided only five race winners. The Lions romped home by 24 points to win by 32 on aggregate. It was their sixth success in the London Cup.

Between the semi-final and final, Wembley staged the first post-war World Championship Final. Basil Storey had tipped Tommy Price for the title, and he was right. Price became the first Englishman to become World Champion with a 15 point maximum in front of 93,000 fans. According to the *News*, he was a worthy title winner. His win over Jack Parker in heat 14 was decisive. For the Lions, Bill Kitchen scored nine points, and Bill Gilbert six.

It had been an uneven season for Price, who was not up to his usual high standard until mid-June. But then his form gradually recovered and at the end of July and into August he was back to his best. He had experienced some machine problems, and his annual battle with Hay Fever.

Basil Storey commented that during the last three months Price has been the most consistent rider... "He's a great rider and takes a well-deserved place among the speedway racing immortals." Price had prepared very thoroughly for the final, and spent three days in his workshop working on his bikes. He arrived at the Stadium with four spare wheels, each with a new tyre, for each race.

After his success, he missed the post-meeting dinner. Price's hobby was short-wave radio, and he had promised to tell a fellow radio ham about his victory. In his book, *Speedway Mixture*, Price recalls how his form had been poor early in the season, but had turned round and his confidence was restored by the night of the Final.

The *News* also recognised the standard of presentation at the final: "All thanks to Wembley for providing the most brilliant presentation of all time. Sir Arthur Elvin must have been a proud man as he watched the smoothness which distinguished the evening's show. Better racing has rarely been seen; the setting has never been more appealing. How lucky we are to have a Wembley."

The Lions received the National League trophy at their final home meeting, against West Ham, in front of a crowd of 66,000. It was a fitting end to the career of Alec Jackson as the Lions team manager. He had announced in September that he was retiring due to health problems, and would be replaced by Duncan King, the assistant manager.

The *Gazette* said that 50,000 Wembley fans would miss him, and that he "has played a mighty part in putting Wembley where they are today." Jackson himself said it had been a period of "discovery and development for the Lions. Split Waterman, Freddie Williams, Bill Gilbert, Bob Wells and Alf Bottoms stand out as particularly fortunate finds for me." Sir Arthur Elvin wrote the following tribute on the front page of the programme for the final meeting: "As all supporters are already aware, our speedway manager, Mr Alec Jackson, has intimated that he will resign from his post at the end of the current year. Mr Jackson, who has been in indifferent health for some years past, has decided to take this step on the advice of his medical advisers, and he proposes to take up a new life in the country, where he will be able to lead a less arduous existence than his duties at Wembley have permitted him in recent years. The departure from the sport of Mr Jackson, who has served us so faithfully and well since 1932, is not only a great blow to us all at Wembley, but is regretted by Control Board, promoters, riders, officials and supporters alike, and his going creates a gap in the world of speedway racing that it will be difficult, if not impossible, to fill.

All his colleagues at Wembley will miss Alec's cheery personality very much – not only is my company losing a loyal, efficient and valuable servant, and I, personally, will miss a very good friend.

I am sure I speak for many thousands of those who know Alec Jackson and appreciate his many sterling qualities when I say 'Good luck to you, Alec, in your new life. May you be blessed with better health and every success, and may you and your wife enjoy much happiness for many years to come. We all hope you will pay us a visit from time to time in the future and, when you do, I am sure the Wembley 'war-cry' will always be ready to welcome you.

'Au revoir and the best of good wishes from us all.'"

It was the end of an era. Jackson had been an accomplished motor-cyclist himself, and had ridden in the first speedway meeting at Audenshaw in Manchester in 1928. He had played a key role in the development of speedway at Wembley, particularly in the development of young riders after the War. His place was taken by Duncan King, who had been at Wembley for 20 years, since being Johnnie Hoskins's assistant in 1929.

The question of the Lions being too strong was – yet again – raised in Howard Jacobi's review of the First Division in the *News*. He said that the problem before 1950 is Wembley. No team deserves to prosper more than the Lions, and that with the exception of Bill Kitchen, every rider of their books has been discovered and nurtured by them, or else bought to his full stature by the Lions. But Wembley are too strong, six of the team could ride for England. Even in a season when they were dogged by injuries, they won two of the three major trophies. This was with Wilks and Eric Williams out on loan. Jacobi said that most team would be happy with Wilks, Waterman and Williams as heat leaders. He was not making an attack on the Lions, or suggesting that they give up part of their "hard earned wealth of talent". It was merely a statement of fact.

For the future, the Lions had signed Jimmy Gooch in September, when he was home on leave from the Army. He won the BAOR championship in Germany after his successful trial with the Lions. The *Gazette* also commented that Eric Williams was ready to move up to First Division racing.

The spread of talent in the Lions team was shown by the 'maximum' score records. Price had nine, followed by Gilbert with three and one each for Kitchen, Wells and Freddie Williams. Over the season the Lions used 13 riders; only Gilbert rode in every match.

The Lions had won the league by nine points from Belle Vue, with 28 wins and a draw in 42 meetings. While the fans no doubt enjoyed the success, in nine home meetings, the Lions scored 50 points or more; in only four meetings was the margin of victory six points or less, and two of those were defeats – one in the second half of a double header. However, the review by David Williams in *Stenner's 1950 Annual* made the point that the Lions lost or drew half of their opening matches, and that both Price and Kitchen were off form, and then as they improved, Waterman and Freddie Williams were injured. The dilemma between a winning team and one-sided matches was still there, although Wembley's attempts to develop the second-halves did offset this to some extent.

In September, it had been reported that attendances were up overall, but down in London. The general drop in London, which had only First Division teams, was 10 to 15 percent, although one track had a 40 per cent drop. The reasons given were shortage of money for spending on entertainment, and a natural tendency for attendances to reach a 'normal' level after three years of sport following the War.

One reason could have been the lack of variety in the First Division. In the *Stenner's 1950 Annual*, David Williams argued for a First Division of 14 teams in his review of the season. He welcomed the promotion of Bristol to the top tier for 1950, but said that the top six in the Second Division should have been moved up. He said that the 'good as over' long before the end of the season aspect of the top division must go. However, he was against re-pooling as had happened after the Second World War. While there may have been more variety of opposition, without some form of spreading the top riders, it is hard to see how his idea would have created more competition. Usually promoted teams struggled, especially away from home. A Division of 10 or 12 would have been a step forward, with some redistribution of the top riders, or more foreign riders in British speedway, something the SRA regularly opposed in most cases.

And finally, the team was honoured by London Zoo – a Lion cub there was 'christened' 'Wembley'. Its cage had a plate erected saying 'Wembley Speedway Supporters Club – Wembley Lion'. Bill Kitchen and six female supporters were photographed with the cub at the Zoo.

Above: Bill Kitchen and Wembley fans with the Wembley Lion cub at the London Zoo. (MKC & JCA)
Below: Belle Vue versus Wembley programme and the programme from the England versus Australia test at Wembley.

10. 1950: Arrival and departure

Going into the 1950 season, speedway could reflect on yet another huge rise in attendances in 1949, to 12,585,698 from 10,694,361 in 1948. While part of the reason for the increase may have been the Lions absence from their usual home for much of 1948, with a consequent effect on crowd figures, it was a still a very positive message.

But there were also warning signs on the horizon. Television ownership in March 1950 was 343,882, still less than one home in 20, but it had almost tripled from the figure a year earlier. And the punitive Entertainment Tax was still a burden to the sport, despite the campaigning work to reduce or remove it. Five years after the end of the war, a wide range of food remained rationed, although soap was removed from the ration, and in May 1950, petrol was no longer rationed. While this may have helped supporters who owned cars to get to speedway meetings, it also opened up a rival form of entertainment, with trips and outings by car being an alternative to a visit to speedway. However, private car ownership at this time was relatively low, although it did grow during the 1950s.

The number of teams grew by one, to 34. Bristol were promoted to the First Division, which now had nine teams, five in London and four elsewhere. It was agreed to run a Spring Cup in the early part of the season, but the Lions did not compete, due to the unavailability of the Empire Stadium as usual until mid-May. The Second Division had 15 teams and the third tier had 10. Former Wembley rider George Saunders was running the team at Aldershot, and his recruits for the new season included a young New Zealander called Trevor Redmond. Another young Kiwi new to British speedway joined Wimbledon – a 17-year-old Ronnie Moore.

Supporters from other teams had regularly argued in letters to the trade press and elsewhere that the Lions were too strong and should release a rider – or two. In a way, they got their wish when Split Waterman moved to Harringay in February, for a world record £3,000 transfer fee, beating the £2,000 that Wimbledon had paid for Alec Statham in 1948. The *News* said that Waterman's break with Wembley had been in offing for some time. A statement from the Lions outlined that: "Waterman asked for a change of track for personal reasons and, while regretting his departure, the club does not wish to stand in his way, particularly having regard to the desirability of helping Harringay to strengthen their weakened team." Waterman was 27 years old, and had the chance to be one of the top riders at Harringay, with Vic Duggan past his best.

Interviewed by John Chaplin in *Classic Speedway* (no.21), Waterman said that the top stars at Wembley, such as Bill Kitchen and Tommy Price, got very good deals from the management that were not open to him. Also, he said that they "monopolised the second half winnings", which could be very lucrative. Moving to Harringay, where he became their top rider, opened similar deals for him. But he did say, later in the interview, that he regretted leaving Wembley; and that there was a "magic about the name."

Freddie Williams and Bill Kitchen had been riding for the British Lions in Australia, but with little success – the Australians won the test series 6–1. Williams rode in five tests, scoring 19 points; Kitchen rode in two for 15 points. Kitchen did not ride after the second test, when he was injured. He broke his ribs and a foot, as well as being concussed. Bruce Abernethy had returned home to New Zealand for the winter, and won the New Zealand Championship in Taita with a maximum.

Alec Jackson was still involved at the Rye House training school. One prospect for the new season was Jimmy Gooch, who it was expected would ride in the junior league with Den

Cosby. Buster Brown was loaned to Third Division Oxford to gain experience. In April, young Australian Doug Ible, who had also been recruited from Rye House, was loaned to Aldershot for the same reason.

Cyril Spinks was promoted from chief mechanic for the Lions to assistant manager to Duncan King. He would continue to be in charge of the workshops and mechanics, and would also deal with transport and equipment.

Another issue for the riders before the season was the adoption of a new, narrower tyre, which had given trials in a Wembley second half towards the end of the 1949 season. Some riders favoured the new tyre, others did not.

The Lions' season opened with a Challenge match at New Cross, and the *News* reported that the Lions were "yards faster from the gate" than the home team. Tommy Price won five races from six rides for 15 points, George Wilks top scored with 16. The *Gazette* said that the Lions "look a strong combination".

Two days later, the Lions won at Bristol in front of 19,000 fans. Bill Kitchen set a new track record, and the *News* said that Bristol had been beaten by "one of the finest teams the sport has ever known." Further challenge matches at West Ham, in front of 58,000 fans, and Wimbledon were won. The rest of the top flight teams were then involved in the Spring Cup for three weeks, so the Lions went to Scotland for a match with the Second Division Edinburgh Monarchs. The home side fared better than the First Division teams the Lions had faced, going down by just eight points. They found the Lions team-riding hard to cope with. Tommy Price did not make the trip to Scotland, and the Lions team did include Jimmy Gooch, Jackie Gates and Den Cosby.

Bill Kitchen had built strong links with Plymouth when he was injured in 1948, coaching their team. He returned there for a match race, and was beaten by local favourite Pete Lansdale. It was reported as one of the best races seen at the stadium.

First Division action for the Lions started in May. They won by 18 points at West Ham, and immediately the *News* was saying that they had demonstrated their claims to the 'champions' label. But three days later, the Lions lost at Bristol. Bill Kitchen was injured in his first race, and a 15,000 crowd saw the Lions defeated by Bristol for the first time. The next night, normality was restored with a comfortable win at Birmingham, despite a slippery starting area and heavy track.

The Lions celebrated 21 years of speedway at Wembley with their first home meeting against New Cross. The visitors were missing Cyril Roger, who was injured, and a maximum from Tommy Price saw the Lions home by two points. In the *Gazette*, Clem Macarthy wrote that Duncan King had the strongest team in the league "with several good bodies to spare". He predicted that Wembley would sweep the board in 1950. He said that the Lions are a big attraction, with more than 50,000 supporters, who are among the most fanatical followers of the sport. Hundreds went to support them at the other London tracks.

The *News* reported that an editorial in the London *Evening Standard* had commented on the family atmosphere at Wembley, with many middle aged women there and families. This was very different from the crowds at football or cricket, which at this time would have been overwhelmingly male.

There was speculation about another established rider leaving the Lions. Bruce Abernethy was apparently going to Birmingham or Wimbledon; a rumour that Bill Gilbert was joining Bristol was denied by the club.

By the end of June, the Lions had ridden 12 league matches, and won 11 of them. In May, at home, Wimbledon provided some stern opposition; a 60,000 crowd saw the young Ronnie

Moore beat Bill Kitchen, George Wilks, Bill Gilbert and Freddie Williams in two heats. A week later, Belle Vue lost their unbeaten record to the Lions, going down by 12 points. The Lions won the last four heats 17–7 to go top of the league with 10 points from seven meetings. However, the weaker teams could not compete with the Lions at Wembley. When Bristol were beaten 58–26, the *News* said it was a "dull and uninteresting contest" with only Bill Hole able to compete with the Lions top riders. Only 35,000 saw the match, clearly fans were not attracted to a "slaughter of the innocents" as the *Gazette* put it.

Away from home, the Lions drew big crowds. At Odsal, the biggest attendance of the season so far, 22,600, saw the Williams brothers' 4–2 in the last heat win the match. George Wilks dislocated his shoulder in heat 11, and it was put back by the track doctor.

Tommy Price was chosen as the first challenger for the Match Race title. He flew to Manchester for the first leg – his machines went by road – but still lost 2–0. He was also chosen, with Freddie Williams, for the England team in the first test at West Ham.

Alf Bottoms rode in a car race in Dorset, and then won one. This was to become his main sport in 1951, with fatal consequences for him. Jack Gates showed his potential with nine points in an open meeting at St Austell. Some of the riders were experiencing problems with the switch back to the 'old' tyres, in particular George Wilks and Bob Wells. At home, the Lions wore masks to prevent cuts from flying red shale. Meanwhile, at London Zoo, the Wembley Lion cub had grown so much that he could no longer be petted.

In June, the speedway Lions beat Birmingham 60–24 and repeated the score-line the next week against West Ham. To be fair to the Brummies, Graham Warren had withdrawn from the meeting with concussion after a fall. Basil Storey reported on how Wembley "put on a super show" in the second half of the meeting, including the young Australian star Ken Le Breton. He saved the night, because the league match was a "string of processions". Le Breton won his heat, semi-final and final. Storey said that he "brought skill as well as colour to a drab meeting" and the crowd stayed on to cheer him.

As well as livening up the second half, the Lions management used these appearances to have a look at some of the up-and-coming riders from the second and third tiers, noting future prospects if the need should arise. At the same time, Bob Wells was offered to Birmingham on loan, because he could not get a place in the Wembley team.

In the West Ham match, the visitors were missing Howdy Byford and Aub Lawson was unwell. A young Reg Fearman won heat eight against Bill Gilbert and Bob Wells, which lifted the meeting from a "depressed state" according to the *Gazette*. There was certainly general concern in the sport at this time about falling attendances, partly due to bad weather, but also to uneven matches. Basil Storey felt that a majority of First Division matches were one-sided; and certainly for some teams, if their leading rider was missing or off form, they offered little else for the fans to enjoy.

On the road, the Lions had some great meetings. At Birmingham on 1 July, they won by six points. The *News* said that the home side put up a "magnificent fight against the might of Wembley" in a "first class meeting". Every heat was a "race in every sense of the word."

The Lions had already beaten New Cross twice before their next league meeting at Wembley. On a controversial night, the *News* reported that New Cross threatened to walk out of the second half. They did not agree with the exclusion of Bert Roger in the 10th heat. New Cross promoter Fred Mockford intervened and ordered them to complete the meeting. The meeting "provided more thrills, spills and extraordinary happenings than any seen at the Stadium this season. Bill Kitchen pulled out with a groin strain after his first ride. Only one rider finished heat 10. Bottoms was injured, Longley excluded, then Roger was excluded for unfair riding against George Wilks. The reporter said that the "decision was hard to understand, and in my opinion unwarranted." Bruce Abernethy fell twice in heat eight, In same place after remounting. With this victory, the Lions were in an almost impregnable position at the top of First Division.

But the next night, at Bristol, the Lions were missing Tommy Price, Bill Kitchen, Eric Williams and Alf Bottoms, all from injuries sustained the previous night. Wilks, Gilbert and Freddie Williams scored 32 out of the Lions' 35 points. It was a meeting full of spills, including a crash in heat eight after the race was over. The Lions only fielded seven riders with Jackie Gates the only reserve.

Then a weakened Wimbledon side "overthrew the mighty Lions" and became the first visitors to win at Wembley in 1950. Bill Kitchen was injured in heat eight, and again Ronnie Moore played a crucial role for the visitors. Seven Wembley riders had sustained injuries in the space of two weeks. Maybe not surprisingly, West Ham beat the Lions at Custom House, with a faultless maximum from Aub Lawson. Two days later, Belle Vue won by six points at Wembley. Price, Freddie Williams and Wilks were the mainstay of the Lions team. Eric Williams rode with an injured ankle, and Abernethy, Gooch, Gates and Cosby all contributed little, which the more senior Lions could not overcome.

Bill Gilbert was reported as having health problems at this time, and was soon told not to ride again this season by his doctor. There was some speculation initially that this was a 'diplomatic' illness. The Speedway Riders Association (SRA) was effectively a closed shop. Gilbert had refused to pay his subscription, having said that he was not satisfied with the organisation. At West Ham, the *Gazette* reported that the pits were "crowded with SRA reps", but then it was announced that Gilbert was indisposed and would not ride. In fact, he genuinely had nervous dyspepsia. He did eventually settle his dispute with the SRA.

The supporters annual day out saw over 2,000 head to Southend. Bill Kitchen and Tommy Price appeared on the light entertainment television programme *Kaleidoscope*. They gave a talk about speedway, and demonstrated their skills on midget bikes. The Lions match programme said that "Those Lions supporters lucky enough to possess television sets" would be able to watch.

The Lions beat Bristol comfortably at Wembley; the visitors were missing Billy Hole and Mike Beddoe. In the second half was Southampton's Bob Oakley, and the next day the Lions signed him for £1,500. He had been averaging over 10 points a meeting for the Second Division side. He had been a novice with New Cross in 1946 before moving to the south coast in 1947. He had captained the Great Britain team against an Overseas side in a Second Division international. However, the *Gazette* did speculate on who would drop out of the team when Gilbert and Bottoms were fit. The latter was developing his car racing, and headed the French Grand Prix 500cc class. He was also booked to drive at Brands Hatch.

Duncan King recalled in an interview with the *Gazette* in December that Oakley was leading in his second half ride at Wembley, but his machine had broken down. He was so disappointed that he had gone home. King had had to phone him the next day to tell him that the Lions wanted to sign him.

Bob Oakley made his debut at Odsal, and after eight heats the home team were 20 points up. Things settled down for the Lions, and that was their winning margin. Oakley and the Williams brothers had been the pick of the Wembley team. The *Gazette* said that Oakley was a "star in the making"

New Lions in 1950: Left: Bob Oakley (JSC); Right: Jimmy Gooch.

The 1950 Wembley Lions (JSC).

Eric Williams had made a big impact in his first season as a full-time Lion. But then he crashed at his former track, Cradley Heath, in a World Championship qualifying meeting, and fractured his skull. He was initially expected to be out for the rest of the season.

Oakley's home debut came in a 34-point win over West Ham. After the first two heats, the Lions "ran riot" according to the *News*. But then two days later, the Lions travelled to Birmingham, and experienced the biggest defeat in the club's history. The Lions had often achieved less success in the National Trophy than the league or the London Cup, but a 79–29 defeat was not acceptable. The *News* said that the Lions were "completely outridden", with only one heat winner. "A Wembley side can never have given a worse exhibition" was their verdict, with only Bob Oakley showing any semblance of form. The Lions won the second leg by two points, but lost Tommy Price with a dislocated collarbone. Graham Warren, McLachlan and Payne were in great form for the visitors; George Wilks and Den Cosby rode well for the Lions, the latter winning three races.

Eric Williams (JSC)

The *News* had an editorial on the Lions. It said that Duncan King believed that the only match where criticism was justified was at home to Wimbledon, where Ernie Roccio and Ronnie Moore excelled themselves for the Dons. His team had had a succession of injuries and in-and-out form. Bill Kitchen had pulled a muscle, George Wilks had a shoulder injury, Tommy Price's starting was poor, and Bill Gilbert could be out for the rest of the season. Eric Williams would be out for some weeks, but his injury was not as serious as first thought.

Alec Jackson visited London around this time, and seemed to be enjoying life in the Hebrides. He said he was planning to stay there for two years, and now slept at night, unlike when he was managing the Lions.

After their National Trophy disappointment, there were three issues to be decided for the Lions fans. The league was still there to be won; in the ever-competitive London Cup, the Lions would face Harringay, and the World Championship offered another chance for glory.

Split Waterman returned with the Racers to help hold the Lions to an eight-point lead in the first leg of the London Cup tie. The Lions were missing Tommy Price, and George Wilks was their best rider. The next night at Green Lanes, the *News* said that Bob Oakley effectively repaid his transfer fee for the Lions. Harringay had a slender lead, but in heat 13 he beat Vic Duggan, then won heat 17 and was second to Freddie Williams in the last race for a 5–1 that gave the Lions the tie. Interviewed in December by the *Gazette*, Duncan King recalled that his highlight of the season had been that race. Both Williams and Oakley had started poorly, but then Williams passed Dunton and Waterman on one bend, then Oakley passed Dunton and then Waterman on the last bend. The Racers won 56–51 on the night, but the Lions reached the final 109–106 on aggregate.

The last two weeks of August saw Wembley stage their World Championship Qualifying Round, and then the latest England versus Australia test match. The visitors won by two points; Tommy Price scored 15 for the home side, and Freddie Williams contributed 8 from six rides as reserve.

The London Cup Final against Wimbledon proved to be even tighter than the clash with Harringay. In the first leg at Wembley, the Lions won by five points. Alec Statham shattered the Lions hopes of a bigger lead in heat 16, when he beat Freddie Williams and Bill Gilbert to prevent a 5–1. Bill Kitchen had his worst night of the season, with only one point. On a positive note for the Lions, Eric Williams had returned from injury.

Bob Oakley provide his worth in the return the following Monday with 14 points from his first five rides. But he was last in a controversial final heat, when Tommy Price split the Wimbledon pair of Cyril Brine and Norman Parker to take second place. The *News* commented that the "manner in which the last heat was ridden displeased a large section of the crowd, and a demonstration is reported to have followed, which must have damaged considerably the good name which Wimbledon has always borne in the speedway world." The writer also reflected that it was a pity that Tommy Price was often given a hostile reception, because there was nothing of a bad sport about him. He could be forceful, but he had found out early on that there was no 'give and take' in speedway, only 'take'.

In the *Gazette*, Basil Storey attacked the Wimbledon fans who had booed Price. He said it was a "breath-taking match" which could only do speedway the power of good. In November, Price was 'severely reprimanded' by the Speedway Control Board for inciting the crowd at the end of the meeting. Wimbledon promoter Ronnie Greene was fined £10 for 'contravening the speedway regulations' in incidents in the meeting.

On 21 September, a packed Wembley saw a Lions rider win the World Championship. Tommy Price had been the first English winner, now Freddie Williams, who the *News* had tipped as the 'best outsider' before the meeting, became the first – and so far only – Welsh winner of the title. Williams broke the track record in his first race. The *Gazette* said his win was the "most surprising of all time", but he had ridden consistently during the season, been relatively injury free, and was riding on his home track. He dropped his only point to Jack Parker in heat 14, and finished a point clear of runner-up Wally Green and two of third placed Graham Warren. Tommy Price finished with eight points, after falling in his second ride. The *Gazette* commented that drama was packed into the first 10 heats, and that Williams made no mistakes. The *News* said that Williams gave credit to Cyril Spinks, his mechanic, but also said that his win was "surprising".

Williams did regret was spending his £500 winnings on a new car, a Jowett Javelin, which Alec Jackson encouraged him to buy. On reflection he said he should have bought a house, not a luxury car. He did not get a bonus from the Lions for his world title win, but did get more invitations to ride in open meetings, particularly on the continent.

The Lions returned to league action with a win at New Cross on 27 September. They were two points down after eight heats, but three consecutive maximums sealed their victory. Eric Williams, riding at reserve, scored 11 points, and was unbeaten by an opponent. The next night, Graham Warren managed the unusual feat of scoring a 12-point maximum for his team in a 59–25 defeat. Only once did a Lions rider fail to score. Bill Kitchen had a last place in the first heat, but followed this with three wins.

After a win at Belle Vue, the Lions were confirmed as league champions with a 20-point win over Odsal. They won seven of their last eight meetings to retain the title, and were presented with the trophy at the last meeting of the season against Harringay.

1950 World Final: Wally Green (runner-up), Freddie Williams and Graham Warren (third).

Basil Storey commented that the signing of Bob Oakley by Duncan King had been a 'masterstroke', and that without him, Wembley would not have won anything. He had been the Lions most consistent rider for the past 10 weeks.

The Lions finished the season with a tour of Sweden and Norway. They beat West Ham 45–39 in Stockholm. Bill Gilbert and Den Cosby were injured, and Cosby had to postpone his wedding because he was in plaster. Tommy Price was also injured near the end of the season at Wimbledon, and fractured his skull. He was in hospital with Gilbert and Cosby. By November, it was reported that he was recovering well and going out for walks. He had finished as the Lions second highest scorer in the National League, with 279 points from 29 matches, behind George Wilks. He had clearly felt the pressure of being World Champion. Interviewed by Clem Macarthy in the *Gazette*, he said of his year as World Champion: "Everybody, including the stewards, seemed to be down my throat for any slight infringement of the rules. It's a fact that I was disqualified more times than any other rider in the First Division last season! Whether I deserved such treatment is a matter of opinion of course. I read in the press that I am an aggressive type of rider. I have to be. I don't and won't give way on the track."

For the future, Jimmy Gooch had mainly featured for the Lions in the junior league matches. And in the Third Division, Aldershot's Trevor Redmond was the top scorer in the league with 342 points from 36 matches. Another issue for the future was the ongoing campaign against the Entertainment Tax. The Lions programme for the Odsal meeting on 5 October was only four pages due to strike action in the printing industry, but did contain a leaflet from the SCB protesting about the tax, and urging people to write to their MP. It was reprinted in the programme for the final home meeting against Harringay.

Alec Jackson and Duncan King. (JSC)

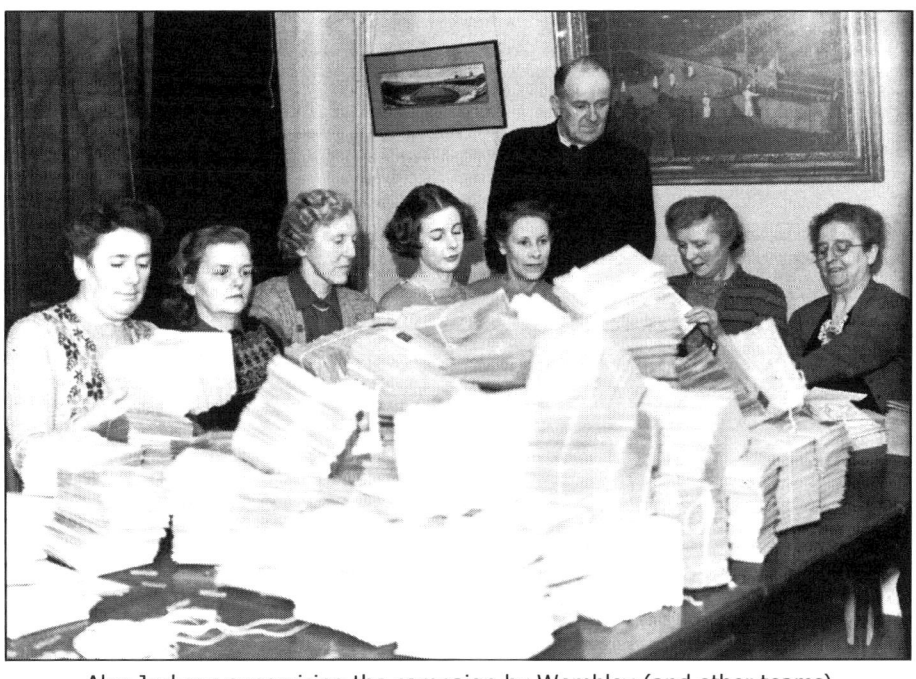

Alec Jackson supervising the campaign by Wembley (and other teams)
against the Entertainment Tax. (JSC)

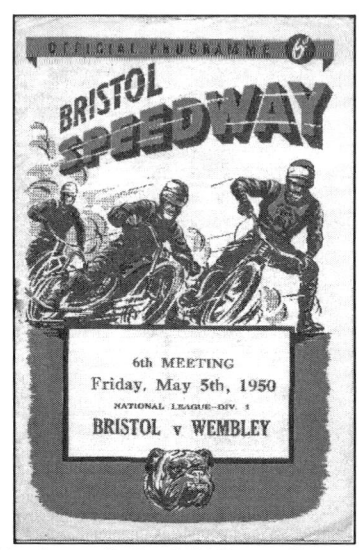

Lions programmes from 1950: At Harringay in the Middlesex Cup; at Bristol in the National League and against Harringay at Coventry in a Challenge match. Below left: The World Final.

One of the Wembley supporters' outings to the seaside. (JSC)

90

11. 1951: Another title and the London Cup

While the support for speedway in 1951 did not match the massive crowds of the immediate post-war period, the sport was still in a relatively strong and stable position. In 1950, total attendance was 10,349,397. This dropped by over a million to 9,013,013 in 1951. But speedway was not alone in this. Attendance at Football League matches had peaked in the 1948–49 season, and gradually declined in the 1950s, as did those at professional rugby league matches. After 1946, which was an all-time UK high of 1,635 million, post-war cinema attendances had fallen in 1947, maybe due to the bad winter, then peaked in 1948 at 1,514 million, and by 1951 had fallen to 1,365 million, a decline of just under 10 per cent in three years. They continued to fall throughout the 1950s.

The *News* claimed in January that in 1950 there had been a slight fall in attendances, but far smaller than other outdoor sports which were speedway's competitors, such as greyhound racing. Meanwhile, the ownership of television sets continued to rise. A change in leisure spending and activity was underway; combined with the developing post-war boom with full employment.

Another potential problem for speedway was the possibility of call-up of Z-class reservists for the Armed Forces. National Service was still in place at this time, but the demands of the Korean War presumably needed a further mobilisation. Former Wembley rider Peter Robinson was facing recall by the RAF, and mechanics and former Army technicians were also possibilities for call-up. Den Cosby also faced a possible call-up later in the season.

On the track, the make-up of the sport remained fairly stable. The First Division continued with the same nine teams as in 1950; leaving Second Division champions Norwich in the second tier. The Second Division grew from 15 teams to 16, while the Third Division stayed at 10. From 1950, Sheffield had dropped out of the Second Division, and Southampton pulled out in June, although the sport would return to both venues and Tamworth dropped out of the Third. Champions Oxford had been promoted from the Third Division to the Second, along with Liverpool who had finished eighth. Motherwell had entered the league, in the Second Division, presumably to provide local derbies with the other three Scottish teams.

Meanwhile, Plymouth were dropped to the Third Division, mainly to reduce travel costs. Wales was represented in speedway with a new Third Division team at Cardiff; Long Eaton and Wolverhampton were also new arrivals in that league. In reality, the Third Division was a midlands and south league, with eight teams from Scotland or the north of England in the Second Division. Confused? Imagine what supporters at the time made of all this. Winning a league did not guarantee promotion, meanwhile other teams could be arbitrarily dropped to a lower level. All this did not help the credibility of the sport's league structure.

From the Lions' point of view, there were still all the 'derby' matches with the other four First Division London teams, and Walthamstow continued to provide Second Division fare for London fans. The Lions started the season as league champions and London Cup holders, as well as fielding the World Champion for the second successive season, Freddie Williams now holding the crown.

Views on this Lions team varied. On 4 January 1951, an editorial in the *News* said that the Lions had the right to be considered the best side. They had wonderful talent, and no track could compete with their staging of meetings. But to the writer "the side always seemed to me to be a collection of individuals, each riding for himself. There are exceptions of course. Bill Kitchen, for example, is a born team rider." The writer also said that while Freddie Williams was World Champion, he was not the best performer of the season, and even in his own team, a couple of riders would beat him three times out of five.

These comments are curious, given the number of meeting reports which note the Lions' team riding. Two weeks later, the review of Wembley's 1950 season in the same magazine, probably by Len Went said "Some experts considered Wembley's 1950 combination a collection of individualists. I do not share that view. On the contrary, I should say that the Lions' successes in 1950 were largely due to the grand feeling between the riders. Some years ago Wembley were described as a slick, high geared racing machine with individualism at a discount. The same gracious tribute could be paid to Wembley's 1950 line-up."

Alf Bottoms had retired at the end of the 1950 season to concentrate on car racing. Eric Williams was one of the better performing riders in the England team in Australia in a 7–0 series defeat. Tommy Price went on a cruise to New Zealand and Australia for a rest. He acted as adviser to the England team in the third test, and then scalded his foot at Hot Springs in New Zealand, an injury that caused him problems in the forthcoming season and into 1952.

The Lions' line up showed little change from the previous year. Jack Gates was transferred to Glasgow Ashfield for £250 in February. Another young Australian, Doug Ible, was loaned to Aldershot and then Oxford, but made little impact at either track. Another new junior was Dennis Cross, who was briefly loaned to Wolverhampton midway through the season. He was discovered at Rye House by Alec Jackson, was aged 21 and worked as a fitter in the JAP works. Buster Brown had a more successful loan spell in the Third Division and was Swindon's top scorer.

There had been speculation at the end of the 1950 season that Bill Gilbert would retire. He did not ride in the team's early fixtures, and in mid-April said that he was retiring to concentrate on his business selling motor cars and helping in his father's grocery business.

The First Division clubs started the season with the Festival of Britain Trophy. As usual, the Empire Stadium was not available to the Lions until the middle of May, so they did not enter this competition. The early part of the Lions' season therefore included more challenge matches than usual. The league competition was based on two meetings at home and a further two away against each team, for a total of 32 league meetings, the same as 1950.

By the time opening night at the Empire Stadium arrived on 17 May, the Lions had ridden 12 meetings and a second half seven heat challenge match at Harringay. Despite the rain 'teeming down', 40,000 saw the Lions' opening fixture at West Ham. The Lions lost by four points, but 10 days later won by 18 at Wimbledon. Freddie Williams stole the show, and the *News* said that on this showing the Lions were in a class of their own. However, in the league, the Lions lost at Belle Vue despite the home side missing their best two second-strings. A rare trip to Scotland saw the Lions defeated by Second Division Edinburgh, but the next night they won comfortably at West Ham in the league. Bob Oakley won three races. But the same week the Lions lost at Bristol in the league; less than 10,000 fans watched "some of the finest racing they will see at the Bristol track this season" according to the *News*. Bob Oakley was again in good form in a challenge match win at New Cross and was unbeaten by an opponent.

Having been to Scotland, the Lions rode in Dublin on 2 May, and drew 42–42 with the local Chapelizod team. Five days later, they crossed north London to ride at Walthamstow, and, missing Tommy Price, lost by 14 points. The *News's* report said it was one of the most exciting encounters ever seen at the Chingford Road track. Again Bob Oakley was in form with a 12 point maximum. Two more league meetings followed before the first home fixture, a very comfortable win at Odsal, the home side's biggest defeat on their own track, and a 10 point loss at Wimbledon. Freddie Williams and Bill Kitchen refused to ride in heat nine. They said that the gate slots had not been swept. They were excluded under the two minutes rule and replaced by Jimmy Gooch and Bob Wells. They both rode later in the meeting.

After three league wins and two defeats on the road, 47,000 fans came to the Lions' opening match against Wimbledon. As the *News* said, for many fans the season was only really underway when Wembley opened, reuniting the thousands of enthusiasts whose interest was one team, the Lions. The Lions won by 14 points. Bruce Abernethy, who had come back from New Zealand towards the end of April, was on top form and Freddie Williams was unbeaten by an opponent. An injury to Ronnie Moore in heat nine, after which the Lions led 30–24, saw Wimbledon's challenge fall away.

There was sad news for the Lions' fans at this time. Alf Bottoms had retired from speedway at the end of the 1950 season to concentrate on car racing. But on 3 May he was killed in a crash in Luxembourg. He was driving a single seater miniature car that he had designed. He had joined the Lions in 1946, but after health problems saw him miss most of the 1947 season he joined Southampton. He had returned to Wembley in 1949, but had not had a regular team place, and in 1950 had started to do more car racing. He had a great reputation as a drive and designer in car racing, and was aged 32 when he died. The Lions programme for the Wimbledon meeting said that his wife and family thanked their friends and supporters for their kind thoughts at their recent bereavement.

Returning home usually gave the Lions a boost, and this season was no exception. The next 13 meetings were won. At home, only West Ham and Birmingham came close to the Lions, and of the eight home meetings in this 13 match run, the Lions scored over 50 points in half of them. At Birmingham at the end of May, the Lions scrapped home by two points, with a 12 point maximum from Bob Oakley. "Solid teamwork and superior starting" gave the Lions their win according to the *News*. At Odsal two weeks later, the ACU steward had to intervene in an argument followed by a 'scuffle' in the pits between Tommy Price and Oliver Hart over track tactics. Hart had fallen in heat 7 when Price won the race, but then beat Price and Bill Kitchen in the last heat. Hart was suspended from the second half racing and reported to the SCB. In the match, Odsal had been eight points up after five heats before three successive heat wins put Wembley ahead.

At Bristol six days later, just under 8,000 fans saw the Lions win at the Knowle Stadium for the first time in 13 years. According to the *Gazette* they rode "like champions" with lightening work at the starts. Freddie Williams was the first visiting rider to score a maximum there this season. Both Bob Oakley and Bruce Abernethy were receiving more recognition. Oakley was chosen for England for the first time, while Abernethy broke the Wembley track record in the first heat against Wimbledon. Tommy Price had worked on Abernethy's bike, but had then gone home sick with a kidney problem and missed the meeting. A week later, against West Ham he lowered it again, to 69.4 seconds. Jack Parker reduced it to 69 seconds before the end of the season. Abernethy was much in demand, and in one spell in June rode in 10 meetings in 11 days, including some second half appearances. However, he blew four motors, which cost him £200.

On 5 July, the Lions beat Birmingham by two points at the Empire Stadium. The *News*, in an editorial, said the riders had provided speedway as good as it ever was. However, the Lions had injury problems. Bob Oakley had been injured in the first test at Odsal. He had hit the fence to avoid hitting Freddie Williams and was expected to be out for several weeks with crushed vertebra. He also missed out on the Match Race Championship, where he had been chosen to challenge Jack Parker. Abernethy was also injured, having broken a bone in his hand at West Ham.

The Lions' unbeaten run ended at Belle Vue on 7 July. A solid two hour downpour on 12 July saw the Lions home meeting with Harringay abandoned after eight heats, a rare occurrence at the Empire Stadium. The next week, 54,000 fans came to see Australia take a 2–1 lead in the series. Freddie Williams was England's second highest scorer with 12 as the home team lost 58–49. George Wilks and Tommy Price were selected as reserves for England; Wilks scored seven points, Price just one. The next night, the Lions went down by 11 points to Harringay at Green Lanes, in "One of the most thrilling meetings seen [there] this season" according to the *News.*

In the London Cup, the Lions faced a tough test against Wimbledon in the first round. A crowd of 14,100 saw "real cup tie fare" at Plough Lane in the first leg according to the *News*. The meeting finished in 'blinding rain". Jimmy Gooch fell in heat 14 and cracked his collarbone, broke his nose and severed a vein in his right arm. He was expected to be out for a couple of weeks. Tommy Price and Freddie Williams both fell in the last heat to give Wimbledon a 5–0 and four point advantage to take to the Empire Stadium three days later. There, a 62,000 crowd, the largest for any British meeting so far in 1951, saw Wimbledon be competitive until the seventh heat, then the Lions pulled away to win 64–44 and take the tie 115–99 on aggregate.

Six days later, the Lions went to New Cross for the first leg of the semi-final. The home side were missing Cyril Roger, while Abernethy was missing for the Lions, but was replaced by Bob Oakley. Jimmy Gooch was back at reserve. The Lions had won by 24 points at New Cross in the league in July. This time, over 18 heats, the home side fared better, but still went down by 18 points. Freddie Williams was unbeaten by an opponent, Tommy Price was paid for 14 points, and Bob Oakley won his last two rides. The next night, the Lions reached the final with a comprehensive 70–38 win at the Empire Stadium, to win the tie on aggregate by 50 points.

The National Trophy had often eluded the all-conquering Lions. This season's campaign did not start well with a three point home defeat to Belle Vue. Jack Parker scored a 'magnificent' 18 point maximum for the visitors, who clinched the match with a 5–1 in the last heat. Bill Kitchen and Tommy Price were not fully fit, and scored five points between them.

The return leg was rained off on the 11th and 25th of August and was scheduled for the first week of September. The postponements cost Belle Vue £150 in travelling costs. Before then, the Lions rode two consecutive double-headers to catch up with their home fixtures.

The first match was against Harringay. The *News* reported that a "brilliant final heat ride by Bruce Abernethy", who had returned to the side after a lengthy absence through injury, "provided Wembley with one of their most narrow and thrilling victories this year." Jack Biggs won the race, and Abernethy's second place, keeping Split Waterman in third, won the league points for the Lions. The Racers had been eight points up after six heats, but the Lions then won four of the next six heats.

Freddie Williams withdrew from the evening's second match, a comfortable win over Bradford, and was fined £50 for this by the Speedway Control Board. The next week, the Lions beat Bristol and then New Cross, topping 50 points each time. But then two days later, the Lions lost by six points to Birmingham, their third successive away defeat. It was one of the best meetings seen at Perry Bar in 1951; Freddie Williams was the mainstay of the Lions according to the *News*.

Towards the end of August, Bill Kitchen dropped down to reserve. The Lions programme for the double header on 23 August commented: "Bill will be called upon during matches if, or when, any weak spots become apparent, and his wide knowledge of tactical moves, of which he is an undoubted master, will be utilised to the fullest extent in the Lions' bid for league and cup honours. With Bill ready to step into the breach, and with his vast tactical experience readily available in the pits, he may well prove to be the 'key' rider in the Lions' heavy and vital fixture list which lies ahead." Kitchen was approaching the age of 43, although he still had something to offer the Lions.

The Lions had overtaken Belle Vue at the top of the First Division after the second double-header. They travelled to Manchester for the National Trophy semi-final second leg. After eight heats the score was 24–24; after heat 16, the Lions had secured a place in the final with a 60–36 lead. In eight races they had won four 5–1 and four 4–2. Except for Bruce Abernethy, every member of the team made a contribution, led by Tommy Price with 14. Belle Vue won the last two heats 5–1 to make the final score slightly more respectable, but it was a remarkable win for the Lions over the team who would finish runners-up to them in the league.

The next night, the Lions lost at home to West Ham in the league. The club took the riders to Cromer for a few days break before the final crucial weeks of the season. All three team trophies could be won: the league, the National Trophy and the London Cup. And Freddie Williams would be defending his crown in the World Championship Final.

At Cromer, under the watchful eye of trainer Tommy Barnett, the riders enjoyed the sea breezes and some physical exercise, including long walks and golf. George Wilks could not make the trip because he was injured, and Bill Kitchen was riding in Copenhagen.

In the London Cup Final, the Lions faced Harringay, with the first leg at home. The Lions took a 10 point lead, 59–49 from a fascinating meeting, where their strength as a team was shown. For the Racers, Olle Nygren scored a paid maximum (17+1) from his six rides, and after a last place in his first ride, Jack Biggs won five heats. Their other six riders scored 17 between them. For the Lions, Eric Williams was the only rider in double figures, with 12 (+1); but they only had five last places, including a fall and an exclusion, and mustered 11 bonus points in 18 heats.

It was a similar story the next night at Harringay. Split Waterman returned for the Racers, and notched up 15 (+1), while Nygren again top-scored with 16 (+1). But again, as the *News* put it, there was "not a weak link to be seen" in the Lions, who only finished last five times in the 18 heats. Eric Williams again top-scored for the Lions, but their lowest scores were 4 for Wilks and Kitchen, who were paid for 3 and 2 bonus points respectively. The Lions had won the London Cup for the fourth consecutive time at the end of heat 15. A 5–1 by Freddie Williams and George Wilks was enough, and three consecutive heat wins in the last three races by Nygren were not enough. The *News* said that the Lions had "pulled out their very best" in the second leg.

Three days later, the league title was won with a 12 point win at Wimbledon. The *News* said that the Lions were a "credit to the sport". Bob Oakley was the only rider from either side in double figures. The Lions ended their league campaign with four more wins, including another double header, this one on a Tuesday night, against Belle Vue and Birmingham; who mustered 52 points between them, less than the Lions scored in both matches. Worryingly, on a wet night, only a "few thousand fans braved the elements. The league season finally finished on 18 October with a 30 point win against New Cross. Within 10 hours of the conclusion of that meeting, the speedway track was being torn up, and the football pitch restored for England to play the famous Austrian team in November.

In the National Trophy, a two point win at New Cross in the semi-final in reality decided the tie. The return was postponed for a week by rain, but after Bert Roger withdrew after his first race, the Lions won as they liked. Cyril Roger had scored an 18 point maximum in the first leg, and he top scored for the south London side in the second leg. Five Lions riders reached double figures, and a Wembley rider only finished last twice. The News said that it was a "one sided affair" and a "poor advert for the sport".

The first leg of the Final was the Lions fifth visit to Plough Lane in 1951, a track they were very familiar with. In official fixtures they had won once and lost twice. But at the Empire Stadium, the Lions had won all three matches, the most recent by 20 points. So it was no great surprise when Wimbledon built an eight point lead, 58–50, in the first leg, but most people believed it would not be enough to take the trophy. The *News* said that the Dons needed a 20 point lead. Over 20,000 fans has seen a "feast of thrills" in the first leg. Eric Williams top scored for the Lions with 11 points. *Stenner's 1952 Annual* said: "It looked as if nothing could stop the Lions ... from gaining the 'triple crown' for the first time since 1932."

But after Price gated badly and Abernethy had engine trouble in the first heat, to give Wimbledon an opening 5–1, they notched up four more in the next five races to build an unconquerable lead. The final result on the night saw the Lions defeated 67–41, their biggest home defeat for many years. The *News* commented: "So the virtually impossible happened. The highly geared Wembley machine was not only beaten but completely subdued before their own supporters at the Empire Stadium last Thursday ... Wimbledon proved that big names and big reputations are not impregnable."

The report also said that Wembley's machines seemed under-geared, but the Lions had no answer to opening onslaught. For the Dons, Dennis Gray scored an 18 point maximum. Ronnie Moore scored 14 (+3) and Cyril Brine 11 (+3). No Lions rider reached double figures.

The enduring pulling power of the Lions was shown in a challenge match at Exeter at the end of the season. The Lions stood in for Harringay at short notice. The SCB had put a limit of 14,000 on the crowd, but according to an article on the County Grounds in the *Speedway Star* (13 February 2016), the tickets sold out before the meeting started, and the real attendance was probably more than 16,000. The Exeter club had been inundated with requests for tickets from all over the west country. The Lions drew 42–42 on their first visit to the stadium. Bill Kitchen was missing from the Lions line-up, and was replaced by an interesting choice of guest rider, a young New Zealander who was riding for Aldershot in the Third Division: Trevor Redmond. He had ridden in second half races at Wembley before, and was clearly someone the Lions management were interested in for the future.

The Lions won the league by 11 competition points from Belle Vue. At home, in the league the Lions scored 825 points, averaging over 51 a meeting. Nine home league matches were won with more than 20 points to spare. From the end of June, only Belle Vue had offered any sort of challenge in the league. The season review in the *News* said that Bruce Abernethy had shown some "wonderful form" after his return from New Zealand, while Jimmy Gooch had "materialised into a first rate rider." Bill Kitchen had lost form mid-season and had finished the campaign at reserve. Bob Wells and Den Cosby were both valuable reserves, but Wells asked for a transfer towards the end of the season because of the limited opportunities for him. He was listed at £200.

The *Gazette* felt that Jimmy Gooch had a lot to do with the Lions' successes and was "probably the best reserve in the business." It also noted that the Lions had been relatively lucky with injuries compared to other teams. *Stenner's Annual* said that no rival team could match Wembley's all-round strength, but that Bill Kitchen's move to reserve covered a potential weakness insomuch that the club was weaker at reserve than before. However, Buster Brown, on loan from Wembley, had top-scored for Swindon in the Third Division.

The 1951 Lions with the National League Trophy at Harringay (JSC)

'Red' Lyon, writing in the *News* felt that Duncan King had managed the side with great credit. Throughout the season one rider or another had come to the front at the psychological moment when one of his team-mates was injured or had hit a bad patch.

One trophy that the Lions had failed to hold onto was the World Championship. Tommy Price had missed out on a final place due to health problems during the qualifying rounds, so it was defending champion Freddie Williams and his brother Eric who represented the Lions at Wembley, in front of 93,000 fans. In one of the most dramatic finals ever, neither made much impact. Freddie scored seven points and Eric, on his debut in the final, notched six. Jack Young won a three-man run off with Split Waterman and Jack Biggs. A single point for Biggs in heat 19 would have seen him take the title with 13 points, but he finished last, and then finished last in the run-off that decided the top three places.

The Supporters Club membership finished the season at over 50,000; maybe not quite as high as three or four years ago, but still a very substantial number who showed their support for the team. There was a target of 60,000 for 1952, and supporters were encouraged to renew their membership before the end of the season.

Left: Aub Lawson (West Ham) and Tommy Price.

Below: Split Waterman, Eric Williams, Tommy Price and Ron How ride through the water at Harringay.
(MKC & JCA)

98

12. 1952: A sixth title but no Cups

There had been speculation during the winter that West Ham would pull out of the league. But a new promoter, Alan Sanderson, took over the promotion at Custom House. He soon strengthened his team for 1952, and the club's prospects of survival, by signing the World Champion, Jack Young, from Edinburgh. So the number of London derbies for the Lions remained the same and the sport did not lose a well-established First Division team.

Walthamstow had been interested in taking over West Ham's slot in the First Division. Norwich had won the Second Division for the second consecutive season, and this time were given a place in the top flight, which was expanded to 10 teams.

The management at Walthamstow then said that speedway was only viable at their famous stadium if they could offer First Division action, so they withdrew from the league. Halifax, Fleetwood and Newcastle also all withdrew from league racing, and attempts to run open meetings at Fleetwood collapsed during the season, as they did at Wigan.

The Second Division fell from 16 clubs in 1951 to 12 in 1952. Poole, the Third Division champions, were promoted. The Third Division was renamed the Southern League, and started the season with 11 teams, Southampton having rejoined after a mid-season departure the previous year, and Ipswich joining after a season of open meetings in 1951. However, Long Eaton did not last the course and dropped out mid-season.

The budget in March saw a reduction in the rate of Entertainment Tax charged on admission to speedway meetings. The formula adopted was 1½d on a charge up to 1/1½d, then a 50% rate on everything above 1/1½d. So for an admission price of 3/4½d including tax (2/6 without tax), the tax rate overall would be around 25%, but was larger for the higher admission prices. The new rate was to be charged on sports which had previously paid the reduced rate from August 1952, which immediately saw a protest from the MCC on behalf of cricket. It was a step forward for speedway, but probably not what the sport really wanted, which was the tax abolished. For Wembley, with a higher proportion of seats that would attract higher prices, it was probably less beneficial than to other tracks with smaller seating areas in proportion to the size of their standing accommodation.

Jimmy Gooch had been selected for the England team to ride in Australia. They lost the test series 4–1, but the *Speedway Star* said in its first issue that the Wembley youngster had "shown brilliant spasms" and was probably the only man to gain good experience from the trip. Freddie Williams had been riding in New Zealand, where he had won the North Island championship and experienced an earthquake before a meeting. However, he aggravated an old injury and did not ride in the one test match that was completed between England and the Kiwis.

The Lions did not run any training sessions at Rye House, but did keep an eye on a couple of novices there. There was discussion about reducing team numbers, and Wembley were concerned that they could not offer rides to all their current riders. In fact, Division One matches were ridden again over 14 heats with teams of six riders and two reserves.

Tommy Price had built a new machine for the season. He trained with the Queens Park Rangers footballers to get fit for the campaign. However, he pulled a thigh muscle kicking a football, and the foot he had scalded in New Zealand had not completely healed.

The *News's* pre-season review said that the Lions had made no signings and did not anticipate any changes. They were expected to challenge for the Cups and Trophies, but expected stronger opposition in the league. Their columnist, Red Lyon, expected Wembley to "lead the pack" but then be faced with the urgent need for new blood.

Once again, the league made up the main part of the fixtures, with each team racing the others twice at home and twice away; 36 fixtures in total. There was also the National Trophy and London Cup to be fought for. Apart from West Ham's capture of Jack Young, Birmingham had signed Dan Forsberg, and looked very strong; Split Waterman was still the big star at Harringay, with Ron How and Maurice Dunn coming to the fore. South of the river, Wimbledon recruited well, with another young New Zealander, Barry Briggs, joining the Dons, along with Peter Moore and Cyril Maidment. However, the Dons were hit by the tragic death of Ernie Roccio at West Ham in July, and head injuries to Norman Parker and Dennis Gray.

Wembley's admission prices were 2/-, 4/- and 8/-, with reductions for children. Supporters Club members got in for 1/9, 3/6 and 6/-. The prices included a copy of the programme. Harringay's standard admission prices were slightly more expensive, but their top price was only 7/-. Belle Vue charged 1/6, 2/6 and 3/6. The average weekly wage for men in 1952 was £9, and for women £5.

The Lions' season started at Harringay. In front of a capacity crowd, they narrowly lost in the Middlesex Cup by two points. The next day they went down at Birmingham by 10 points in front of a 23,000 crowd. The meeting opened with a 'terrifying' crash. A bike jumped the fence into the crowd, although no riders or spectators were injured.

Freddie Williams was rested for these matches with knee ligament problems. The Lions were unsure if Bruce Abernathy would return to ride for them, so signed another Kiwi, Trevor Redmond, for £1,500 from Aldershot. It was said that when both Freddie Williams and Abernathy were available, Redmond would be loaned to Norwich, but this never transpired. However, the Lions did give the First Division newcomers permission to speak to Bill Gilbert. He had retired, but was still on the Lions' books. He proved to be a valuable signing for them.

There was, inevitably, some controversy about the Lions being allowed to sign Redmond. However, RM Samuel pointed out in the *News* that "It must not be overlooked that the fortunes of the Lions represent quite 50 percent of the advertisement value the sport gets in the newspapers."

The Lions' league campaign started in Manchester with a 10 point win over Belle Vue. The Aces were not the force they had been in recent years, with Jack Parker and Louis Lawson past their best. Parker missed the meeting, as did their South African star Henry Long. A Lions rider won five of the first six heats, and the *News* said that "Plucky little Belle Vue fought hard against what must be the sport's strongest club combination." The *Star* commented that it was a hard-fought match which "came close to speedway perfection and more than pleased a near capacity crowd." However, the home side only provided four heat winners, so the home fans can't have been that pleased.

Two days later, the Lions won by 25 points at Plough Lane against a Wimbledon team missing Ronnie Moore. After four heats the Lions were eight points up, and according to the *News* were already favourites for the league title. Bob Oakley showed a welcome return to form. But on the following Saturday, the Lions lost at Odsal, and were lucky not to lose by more according to the *Star*. Trevor Redmond was the Lions' top scorer with eight points.

The Lions opening night was on 8 May, five days after the FA Cup Final. Seventy men, two mechanical diggers, two bulldozers and six lorries had been used to lay the 700 tons of shale which formed the new Wembley surface. The track also had new mixed 400 watt mercury vapour and tungsten lights, which were 50 per cent brighter than the old ones. Wembley was the first track to use this system.

However, the opposition was newly promoted Norwich, who suffered a humiliating 62–21 defeat. Only Billy Bales and Bill Gilbert provided any opposition to the Lions, who won every heat. Maybe anticipating a one-sided match, the second half included World Champion Jack Young, former Lions favourite Split Waterman, Birmingham star Alan Hunt and Glasgow White City's Second Division star Tommy Miller. One surprise in the Lions' line-up was George Wilks riding at reserve, and the *News* speculated that he could be loaned to another track, as the writer felt that he was too good to ride at reserve.

Two days later, the teams met again, this time in East Anglia. The Lions won again, but this time did not have everything their own way, according to the *News*. It was a typical Wembley away win, with every rider contributing, and only on four occasions did a Lions rider finish in last place.

The Lions won their next two league matches by two points. The first, at New Cross, was very controversial. On a night of seven falls in 14 races, the Rangers were winning 39–32 after 12 heats. In heat 13, the *News* reported that Eric Williams threw off the challenge of Bob Roger; both riders went wide allowing George Wilks through for a Lions 5–1. New Cross team manager Alf Cole protested at Williams' riding, and the steward [referee] said it was borderline. In the last heat, with the score 40–37, New Cross needed at least second place to secure a win. Bert Roger led for two laps, then overslid. The Lions riders, Redmond and Kitchen, came through. However, Ronnie Genz then hit Roger's bike. Despite there being two bikes, two riders and four ambulance men on the track, the race was not stopped, and the Lions won it 5–0. According to the *News*, the crowd were "incensed". Stadium officials and the police had "great difficulty dealing with a highly infuriated crowd." Their reporter said that the crowd "had just cause" for their demonstration.

Eric Linden in the *Star* said that it was "downright bad stewarding". Amidst all this, the Lions showed their strength in depth. Freddie Williams had a bad night, but Tommy Price and Trevor Redmond made an effective pair. The Lions only had three last places and two falls. Their team riding is shown by six 'bonus points' in 14 heats.

The next night, the Lions scraped home in a "battle royal" according to the *News,* against Wimbledon at the Empire Stadium. Led by Ronnie Moore, with a four ride maximum, the Dons provided nine heat winners, and only a 5–1 from Bill Kitchen and Trevor Redmond in the last heat saw the Lions home. The *News* said that there was "pandemonium" in the crowd. Bill Kitchen said that he could hear the crowd during the race, for only the second time in his career. Apparently the race produced more cheers than Newcastle's goal against Arsenal in the FA Cup Final 12 days early. It was the first time the Lions had been ahead in the meeting. Kitchen won the race, and Redmond winning a "shoulder to shoulder" duel with Ernie Roccio saw the Lions take the two league points. The result left the Lions second in the Division One table, behind Harringay. Both teams had lost one meeting.

The attraction the Lions had throughout speedway was shown when between 18,000 and 19,500 fans crammed into Stoke's track for a challenge match. The Lions won, again by two points. The Lions lost Trevor Redmond after a crash in his second ride.

The Lions were pretty invincible at the Empire Stadium this season in the league. Only Harringay won at the Empire Stadium, and only the Dons, New Cross and Birmingham kept the home side to less than 50 points. The Lions topped 60 five times; no wonder the management put a lot of resources into the second halves of league meetings. This seemed to be the only way to ensure some close racing at times in the first half of the season.

However, away from Wembley, the Lions were less consistent. At West Ham, the Lions only provided three heat winners; and George Wilks was top scorer at reserve in a 15 point defeat. Jack Young and Wally Green both scored maximums for the Hammers. Together with Malcolm Craven, who scored 11 from his four rides, they outscored the Lions on their own. At Bristol, three days later, they lost by five points in what the *News* said was the "hardest fought and most exciting fixture at Bristol since the war." It was 36–36 after 12 heats, but Bristol won the 13th heat 3–2, and then a 5–1 clinched the match for the Bulldogs. A third defeat on the road followed on the last day of May; the Lions went down by over 20 points at Birmingham. Only Tommy Price, who was returning to form, and Bill Kitchen offered much opposition to the Brummies.

The *News* was publishing a record of how many maximums riders scored in the First Division. Towards the end of May, Jack Young led with seven, followed by Ronnie Moore with four. Wembley's riders had just one, by Bob Oakley.

In June, the Lions were told that Bruce Abernethy was staying in New Zealand, where he had a job selling cars. He had sent a bike to England, but in fact never returned to England to ride, despite numerous offers over the years. That bad news was offset by the announcement that Alec Jackson had sold his farm, and was returning to Wembley as Director of Racing.

The Lions' campaign in the London Cup started in June against Wimbledon, earlier than usual. They must have anticipated building a good lead to take to Plough Lane when they saw the visitors' line-up. It included four inexperienced youngsters in Maidment, Trott, Holmes and the 17-year-old Barry Briggs. But they pulled off the "greatest speedway shock of all time", according to RM Samuel in the *News*, with a 10 point win. The Lions were off form, only Redmond, Price and Oakley could stem the tide. It was 15–9 to Wembley after four heats, but then the Dons won six heats in a row to be 12 points up after heat 10. Four days later, the Lions went to Plough Lane. They fared better, but never really looked like riding consistently enough to pull back the deficit. A 5–1 in the last heat secured a win on the night for the Dons in front of a 22,000 crowd, bigger than for the England versus Australia test the previous week. It was the first time the Lions had missed out on the London Cup Final since the War. It was a warning of Wimbledon's forthcoming challenge to the Lions' supremacy in speedway.

Between the two London Cup matches, 16,000 fans endured heavy rain to see the Lions beaten at Norwich in the league. The second half of the meeting was abandoned. The night after a 20 point win over Bradford at home, with "many thrilling races" according to the *News*, the Lions drew 42–42 at Green Lanes. Split Waterman saved a league point for the Racers. Jack Biggs's bike failed in the last race, and Waterman first passed Bill Kitchen, then on the third lap Eric Williams to secure a 3–3. The teams were neck-and-neck in the title race, both had lost five meetings and drawn one.

In early July, the Lions made a rare trip to Scotland, and beat Edinburgh by 12 points in a challenge match. Tommy Price missed the trip with the worst Hay Fever he had suffered for 15 years. However, a new American drug was helping him.

Five days later, the Lions beat Harringay 61–23 at the Empire Stadium, although the *Star* said that the racing was "far keener and closer" than the score suggested. The Lions provided every heat winner and Freddie Williams was "streets faster" than any Harringay rider according to the report. Redmond was also unbeaten by an opponent.

The match against Harringay was the second of three consecutive home league meetings in July when the Lions topped 60 points. The *News* said that the West Ham match "involving two of the country's leading teams, was enough to discourage even the most rabid supporter." A rain-soaked track, when the Lions "battled through the mud" was not really an excuse for the Hammers, for whom Jack Young and Wally Green at least 'had a go'. Trevor Redmond scored his first 12 point maximum for the Lions.

Above: 1952 World Final: Freddie Williams (runner up), Jack Young (winner), Bob Oakley (third) (JSC)

Left: Trevor Redmond during his riding days. He went on to revive the Lions in 1970.

Wembley Lions 1952: Trevor Redmond, Eric Williams, Bob Oakley, Tommy Price, Duncan King (Manager), George Wilks, Den Cosby, Jimmy Gooch, Freddie Williams, Tommy Barnett (Trainer). (JCS – Alf Weedon)

The Bristol match was described as a "walk-over", with the Lions running rings round the opposition. By the end of the month the Lions were still battling with Harringay for the leadership of the First Division. The *News* said that a two-point win at New Cross had put them in a strong position to take the title. Bill Kitchen, riding at reserve, won heat 13 to secure the league points. Eric Williams's frame had snapped on a bend in the seventh heat, and he had a "miraculous escape" according to the *News*. The Lions consistent away form, apart from an awful night at Birmingham in early August, saw them take the league title comfortably.

Off the track, the Lions took a new initiative to involve some of their younger supporters. In partnership with the Middlesex County Army Cadet Force Committee, they started a Wembley Speedway Motorcycle Unit, affiliated to the Middlesex Army Cadet Force. It was to be the first such unit in the country, and was open to Wembley supporters aged between 16 and 18, who owned a motorcycle. Uniforms and other equipment would be provided by the Army authorities. The unit would provide training that would be useful during National Service. Alec Jackson, who had considerable experience of working with motorcyclists during the War, was involved in the project.

The Williams brothers were the men on form when the Lions built up a 25 point lead against Bradford in the first round, first leg, of the National Trophy. Freddie was unbeaten by an opponent, with five heat wins, while Eric scored 14 (+2). Bill Kitchen was also paid for a maximum at reserve over three rides, but Tommy Price, Trevor Redmond and Bob Oakley were all a long way from their best according to the *News*. The *Star* said that Bradford "put up a spirited fight", and it was their best effort on a London track this season.

Alan Hunt had been "outstanding" when Wembley got a "tousing" from Birmingham according to the *Star* on 2 August. The Lions avenged their 55–29 defeat with a similar win against the Brummies at home. In the National Trophy semi-final, two weeks after the Lions' defeat, the Brummies were 29–25 up after nine heats at Perry Barr. Then the Lions collapsed. The home team won every heat apart from heat 17 when Eric Williams and George Wilks managed a 4–2 for the Lions.

Birmingham 69 Wembley 39 did not augur well for the second leg. This was the most points the Lions had ever conceded, although West Ham 68 Wembley 16 – over 14 heats rather than 18 – on 27 April 1937 was arguably even worse. In the second leg, the Lions were 14 points up after 13 heats, but then two consecutive 5–1s saw Birmingham through to the final, where Harringay comfortably beat them.

Between the two National Trophy matches, the Lions won 63–21 at West Ham. Jack Young was injured in the first heat, and the Hammers only had one heat winner. Three Lions were unbeaten by an opponent, both Williams brothers and Tommy Price.

Two wins in a double-header at the Empire Stadium, against Norwich and New Cross, made the Lions clear favourites for the league title. A surprise defeat at home to Harringay the next week must have raised some doubts – a Split Waterman and Jack Biggs 5–1 in the last heat clinched the match for the Racers. But seven straight wins to finish the league campaign saw the Lions complete the campaign on 57 points, 11 clear of runners-up Birmingham.

In the World Championship, Bob Oakley was the highest scorer in the qualifying rounds with 28. He was joined in the Final by Freddie Williams. Trevor Redmond and Tommy Price narrowly missed out. In the final, on 18 September, it was Jack Young's night again. He won with 14 points. Freddie Williams was runner-up on 13. A defeat to Dan Forsberg in heat 14 cost him the chance of a run-off with Young. In third place was Bob Oakley on 12. However, he did beat Jack Young in heat 17, although the Australian knew that second place would give him the title.

The Lions finished their home season with a match against Second Division Stars, including Poole's young world-finalist Brian Crutcher. There was speculation that Crutcher would move to Wembley if Bruce Abernethy did not return.

The Lions concluded their season with a tour of Sweden, winning matches against five Swedish clubs. In December, the *Star* published a letter to Sir Arthur Elvin from two Swedish promoters, Arne Bergstrom and CC Ringblom: "We have been asked to convey the appreciation of the riders' performances and good behaviour both on and off the tracks. Everybody wishes the team heartily welcome back and we do sincerely hope that the conditions next year will still be such that a new invitation can be extended to visit Sweden."

In terms of organisation, the Lions were still ahead of the other teams. Tom Morgan commented in the *News* on 8 October: "Wembley win most of their matches before they go on the track. At West Ham at the end of August, there was slickness on the Wembley side of the pits – every Wembley mechanic knew their job and the riders did not have to worry about anything. Duncan King was quietly efficient, Alec Jackson was ever hovering in background." He said there was a "sense of workmanship so often missing from other teams." In the same edition, RM Samuel said that there was an "air of prestige" at Wembley lacking elsewhere.

The Lions had also again had relatively few riders missing with injuries – part of which must have been attributed to the facilities and training available to them. Tom Morgan pointed out that Den Cosby had ridden just five league meetings, and the Lions had virtually the same team all season. In their review of the season for the Lions, Rick Eldon said in the *Star* said that the strength of the team was obvious; any of them were quite capable of going out and beating every member of the opposition. At reserve, he said that Jimmy Gooch had disappointed, rarely showed form expected of him. Bill Kitchen, he thought, was the toughest reserve in the business. In any other team he would have been a heat leader.

He said that Tommy Price was back on top of the world, although he perhaps lacked a little of his former fire, his points potential was as high as ever. Eric Williams, Bob Oakley and George Wilks were among the best team men in country. However, he said that the Lions lacked novice talent, and thought that if any two of their riders had been injured at the same time they would have been scrambling round looking for another rider. He said that this is where they must improve to remain a force without constantly using their cheque book.

Stenner's 1953 Annual was more critical. Basil Storey said that the Lions "plodded through to the championship" with the "least spectacular team in the club's history." He said that Freddie Williams returned to the "fiery form that won him the 19050 world title" in the closing weeks of the season, and acknowledged that Bob Oakley rode well." He also said that Trevor Redmond would improve. He concluded that "Wembley need a shot in the arm. Youth, new faces and a healthy struggle for team places". But of the team, Gooch and Redmond were relatively young, while Oakley and Eric Williams were fairly new to the top flight. Even Freddie Williams had only ridden six seasons at the top level. Certainly Price, Kitchen and Wilks were past their best, but still rode consistently. Bruce Abernethy seemed to have lost interest in riding for the Lions, so they were scouting the Second Division for new talent, and inviting some riders to ride in second-halves at home meetings, as they had with Oakley and Redmond.

In July, the Lions had claimed 50,000 members in the Supporters Club, aged from three months to 70 years old, evenly split between men and women, and living throughout the Home Counties. They did not know how many branches there were. In August the annual outing to Southend attracted 1,500, lower than previous years, although this may have been due to greater travel and holiday opportunities for supporters then compared to in the 1940s. The Lions still had a large base of support in changing times for the sport.

Tommy Price in the Wembley workshops. (JSC)

Cyril Spinks (Wembley chief mechanic) and Freddie Williams (JSC).

13. 1953: Champions for the last time

1953 was a seminal year for both the country and speedway. It saw the Coronation of the young Queen Elizabeth, who had succeeded to the throne when her father, King George VI, had died the previous year. On the sporting front, 1953 is memorable for the 'Matthews Cup Final', when Sir Stanley Matthews finally won an FA Cup winners medal; Edmund Hillary and Sherpa Tensing climbing Everest, and Sir Gordon Richards won his only Derby, six days after being knighted.

The Coronation was on 2 June, and dominated the national consciousness for the first half of the year. In speedway, the early-season competition for First Division clubs was renamed the Coronation Cup. Thousands of people made plans to come to London for the event, or to celebrate the event locally. Significantly for speedway, and other forms of live sport and entertainment, combined with the FA Cup Final – which had been shown live on television – the Coronation saw a huge growth in the ownership of television sets. At the end of 1950, the figure was 578,000; by the end of 1953 it had grown to 2,957,000, an increase of 2,379,000. The cost of paying for the sets, and the entertainment provided for free and in people's living rooms hit speedway hard. The sport, relying on private ownership through promoters who aimed to make a living from their business in running the sport, was less stable than football, rugby league and cricket, which also suffered from falling attendances. Another reason that speedway was hit harder was that it primarily took place in the evening, in direct competition with television.

Even during the post-war boom years, teams had gone out of business. Since 1950, some had started to fall by the wayside mid-season, further undermining the sport's credibility. But 1953 saw the mid-season closure of New Cross. To lose an established First Division team, and a London team at that, was a major blow to the sport.

New Cross closed in mid-June, due to lack of support. Longstanding promoter Fred Mockford said that he could not afford to keep losing money. In an article in the *News*, he said that television was the sport's "number one menace". The other reasons for the closure were a general lack of spending money, taxation levels and the Entertainment Tax, which was at 33 per cent. Tom Morgan wrote that football clubs and cricket were losing crowds. He said that a First Division track needed a weekly 10,000 crowd to survive and New Cross had not been getting half of that. Pay reductions agreed with the SRA came too late to rescue the promotion. There was an issue about rising Swedish star, Olle Nygren, being refused a work permit extension, resulting in the team being weak, but it is difficult to see how Nygren could have drawn enough fans to New Cross to keep them alive.

A letter in the *News* at the time said that the slump in attendances was due to television. The writer said that people's holiday money went on a deposit for a set, and the weekly HP (hire purchase) payments could be up to £1. He added that the sport had healthy attendances in Scotland until television arrived there.

For the Lions, in the winter, Bill Kitchen, Eric Williams and Jimmy Gooch had been riding in New Zealand. Trevor Redmond had been part of a developing speedway scene in South Africa, and Tommy Price made a short trip to Sweden to coach some riders. Freddie Williams announced his engagement to Pat Devries, an Olympic skater.

There was speculation – yet again – about whether Bruce Abernethy would return to the Lions from New Zealand. The Lions said they would only pay a steamer fare, not an air fare.

In the event, Abernethy did not return. In March, the *News* predicted that Harringay would be the main threat to the Lions. Including Abernethy, the Lions had 11 riders registered for eight team places. The report said that the team was often wrongly described as a team of "old men". In fact, this really only applied to Bill Kitchen, Tommy Price and George Wilks. The report also said that the Lions were "a great team to watch and a very sporting combination." Buster Brown was loaned to Swindon, and the Lions signed a new novice, Bill Simpson.

The sport continued to have three leagues, as in 1952. Glasgow Ashfield pulled out, and Wolverhampton took Cradley Heath's place in the Second Division. There was talk of speedway returning to Sheffield, but this did not materialise. However, during the season Cardiff and Liverpool both pulled out of league racing.

The question of seven-man teams was raised by the promoters – presumably to save costs – but in fact the format stayed the same for league and cup matches as in 1952. Another area where there was little change was in the use of foreign riders. At the beginning of April, Sir Arthur Elvin commented that "I hope the Riders Association will let in the foreign riders – let them all come, there cannot be more than 20 good class foreigners. This might save many tracks from extinction."

However, the SRA stuck to their position that foreign riders could not join a team on permanent basis, but only for one month if team had injuries. This meant that some riders rode for more than one team on a short-term basis, which was not good for the credibility of the sport. Also, some of the foreign riders were an attraction to the fans, and could have boosted attendances.

In March, it was reported that the Lions had agreed to hold five of their Coronation Cup meetings at Wimbledon, because the Empire Stadium would not, as usual, be available until mid-May. This was despite their disastrous experience there – certainly in terms of attendances – in 1948. Why meetings at Green Lanes were not tried is not clear – maybe the stadium was not available, or the Harringay management did not want the traditionally more high profile Lions riding on their track – but a few more Wembley fans might have gone. In fact, only three 'home' meetings were held at Plough Lane.

The Lions' first meeting was at Green Lanes, the traditional season-opener for the Middlesex Cup. The Lions went down by 21 points, but it was a weak Lions team, with Den Cosby in the team, and novices Bill Simpson and Mike Meacher at reserve. The Williams brothers and Tommy Price scored 25 of the Lions' points between them.

Six days later, the Lions won at Birmingham in a challenge match. Trevor Redmond returned to action, and Bob Oakley found the form he had been lacking at Harringay. The league programme had been reduced to 16 meetings for each team, and the Coronation Cup fixtures were run in the first half of the season, on the same basis as the league. The Lions first 'home' meeting was against Norwich at Plough Lane on 9 April, in the Coronation Cup. The Lions won by 12 points on what was really a neutral track, but victory was not assured until heat 13. Trevor Redmond was unbeaten by an opponent, and the Lions team had a more familiar look to it, although Bill Kitchen was missing.

However, the next week the Lions lost to Bradford at Plough Lane. The Yorkshire side rarely did well in London and this was their first win in the capital since 9 June 1950. Dent Oliver led the way for the Tudors with a four win maximum. The *News* said that "established Wembley stars" were victims of his "tearaway tactics". Freddie Williams couldn't settle, Oakley was "hopelessly out of touch" while Wilkes and Kitchen tried hard but got nowhere. The *News* also commented on the "poor attendance" for an entertaining match.

The Lions recovered to win at Birmingham. Alan Hunt got a maximum for the Brummies, but the home side fell apart after Graham Warren fell in heat six. Tommy Price had one of his occasional outings in road racing at Silverstone in the afternoon before the meeting. He finished 10th out of 52 riders, and then scored 8 (+1) at Perry Barr. Not bad for a 40 year old.

RM Samuel commented in the *News* that Wembley were waiting for news about Bruce Abernethy. He felt that the Lions needed younger riders, although Alec Jackson and Duncan King had looked for new talent in the winter.

The Lions return to the Empire Stadium was set for 7 May. Before then, a "faultless" Price maximum could not stop Belle Vue winning at Plough Lane. But the Lions also lost at New Cross and then got "mauled" at Odsal in the return match with Bradford, 55–29. The Lions only had one heat winner – Eric Williams – and won only one heat.

The Lions final scheduled meeting at Plough Lane, against Bristol, was rained off and rearranged for later in the season. Before the Empire Stadium opening night against Harringay, Bob Oakley announced his retirement to concentrate on his business interests in Southampton. So the Lions moved to sign Poole's young rising star, 19-year-old Brian Crutcher. The transfer fee was £2,500 and Buster Brown moved to join Poole as part of the deal. Arguably, this was one of the most important signings for the Lions in the post-1950 period. Crutcher had already ridden in a World Final, and part of the reason he joined Wembley (according to an interview with him in the *Star* in January 1955) was that the Lions had invited him to ride in a second-half before the big night so he would be more familiar with the track. Advice and support from Freddie Williams also impressed the youngster, and a final clinching factor in the deal was that the Lions did not require him to move to London.

Apparently the Lions also looked at Exeter's Goog Hoskin and Yarmouth's Fred Brand. Wolverhampton's Harry Bastable had turned down the Lions – he did not feel he was ready for the First Division. He later joined Birmingham.

However, opening night turned out to be a disaster for the Lions. Not only did the team lose by eight points to Harringay, with Brian Crutcher falling in his first three races, but the track was clearly under-prepared. The stadium management had put down the track in four days after the FA Cup Final. Clearly they would have been wiser to have waited a week to welcome the Lions home. The *Star* said that it was the worst track surface seen at Wembley for years, and that the Harringay riders had ridden under protest. Their report said that it would have been no surprise if the steward had stopped the meetings due to the track conditions.

For the *News*, editor Len Went wrote: "At Wembley, the brooms stand to attention. If ever the trumpeter misses a note there is consternation. The Empire Stadium on speedway night is an acme of perfection. To see it as a shambles is unthinkable. But a shambles it was on opening night. Spills in each of the four races had the crowd spellbound and the ambulance men dizzy. In all they had to cope with three stretcher cases while a fourth rider had to be assisted off. Rarely in post-war racing have men been called upon to ride on such a bad track."

He said that the track was bumpy in parts but improved as the match progressed. For the second half it had bedded down considerably. Bill Kitchen said that it was the "roughest I have seen our track". Harringay manager Wal Phillips commented: "It's positively dangerous". The steward sent word for rakers to do their stuff, but covering pot holes on a hastily prepared track was hardly sufficient.

Ron How looped in heat one, but there was no blame on track for that. In the second race George Wilks hit same bump as Brian Crutcher in the third heat, and broke a rib. In heat four, Racers' reserve Stan Clark hit a bad patch by the pits, went to ground, was hit by a machine and went to hospital. In heat seven, Crutcher fell again. He was taken off on a stretcher but came out again in heat 11, when he fell again, and heat 14.

Went concluded: "All the riders deserve special congratulations for putting up such a grand show on a very treacherous track. Knowing Wembley, this matter will be put right – and very quickly too." Trevor Redmond commented in his column in the *News* that rarely has any first class speedway track had so many bumps and potholes.

After advice from Freddie Williams and Tommy Price, Crutcher settled down. But after the defeat against Harringay, the Lions were bottom of the Coronation Cup table with just two wins from eight meetings. George Wilks was clearly going to be out of action for a few weeks, the *News* reported that he had pneumonia, so as a temporary replacement, the Lions signed their first Swedish rider, Rune Sormander.

Normal service was resumed the following week, with the Empire Stadium track back in its usual condition, and the Lions comfortably dispatching Wimbledon by 18 points. Crutcher won his first heat for the Lions, and Jimmy Gooch had a good night, scoring 8 and three bonus points. Sormander made his debut the following week. He had bought a set of handlebars and a saddle with him from Sweden, and scored four points in a comfortable win over Birmingham. Sormander went onto have a distinguished career, including six World Final appearances, but made little impact with Wembley. Riding at reserve, he rode four meetings, with his best performance 5(+1) from two rides against Belle Vue in the first league match on 4 June. Then George Wilks returned to take his place in the team.

Apart from a 10 point defeat at Wimbledon on 8 June, the Lions won the rest of their Coronation Cup matches to finish second in the table with 18 points from 16 meetings. Harringay were at the top of the table with 24 points, and were clearly going to be the main challenge to the Lions for the league title in the second half of the season.

The Lions had last won the London Cup in 1951. Their campaign started – and finished – much earlier than usual this season, in the last week of May. The Lions went to Plough Lane on Monday 25 May, and lost 61–46. Australian Peter Moore reeled off four wins for the Dons after a last place in his first ride. At heat eight, the scores were level, but then the home side only lost one more heat. The Lions suffered three engine failures, which made their task in the home leg even harder. Freddie Williams was the Lions' top scorer, with 14 from six rides including an engine failure.

But three days later, the Dons took ample revenge for their earlier defeat in the Coronation Cup. They won the second leg 56–52 to go through by 19 points on aggregate. The *News* said that with the exception of Freddie Williams and Brian Crutcher the Lions had "little or no fight in them". Harringay retained the cup they had won in 1952, beating West Ham in the final.

RM Samuel commented in the *News* at the end of May about the Lions' campaign so far. He suggested that "Wembley's poor show at start of season may be the best thing that could happen to them. The team has been on top of the world so long that their own supporters began to get a little bored. Persistent success can be satiating. It can also sap endeavour in a side. Everyone gets a little lethargic. Now that just won't do in speedway. Everyone likes to see the team they follow beat the other fellows, but isn't it refreshing when the under-dog suddenly comes to the top and either scares you stiff, up to the last heat – or even perhaps, gets home by a couple of points? That's the kind of racing that makes the turnstiles click, and that's why I welcome Wembley's stiffer passage."

He went to say that he thought that there was over-confidence in two or three of the Lions riders. He was in favour of a prominent Wembley, but not powerful. He concluded that he would rather see a sporting team than always a winning one at the Empire Stadium. The team should be good enough to keep the reputation of a world-famous organisation. The money spent on the purchase of young Crutcher, he though, would prove to be common sense.

The closure of New Cross saw their riders signed by other tracks. In *Stenner's 1954 Annual*, Basil Storey argued that "The Control Board lost a great opportunity of easing the strain on struggling teams by placing the riders of the disbanded New Cross in the open market. Allocation of the stranded riders to those teams really in need of strengthening was, in all probability, such an obvious move that the Board missed it." The Lions signed England international Eric French from the disbanded Rangers. However, he never hit the form he had shown at New Cross, although the difference in home tracks between Wembley and the smaller track at New Cross could explain that. However, although Norwich signed Cyril Roger, Basil Storey does have a fair point, although whether French would have wanted to ride for Bristol or Belle Vue, with the additional travelling involved, is not known. French cost the Lions a £1,600 transfer fee.

Sadly, New Cross was not the only track to close during the season. Cardiff and then Liverpool both withdrew from the Second Division. Cardiff's attendances had dropped to 3,000, and they faced high running costs. However, there was more encouraging news for the sport in August. The *News* reported that attendances had jumped by 25 percent in the last month. The First Division was averaging 118,000 a week, the Second Division 68,000 and the Southern league 49,000. The report said that attendances usually fell in the holiday season, and put the increase down to all-out endeavour by the riders, sunshine and close matches. The fact that the Coronation had taken place may have had something to do with it as well.

The league campaign started at the beginning of July, although the Lions had already raced one match, a home win against Belle Vue on 4 June. With only 16 matches, the whole issue was settled by the two clashes with Harringay in the first week of September. At home, the Lions were consistent winners, notching 50 points or more in their eight home matches. In the other two, they scored 49 against Bristol in the second half of a double header, and, incredibly, lost at home to West Ham in July by five points. The *News* said that Jack Young was the match winner for West Ham. However, for the Lions both Tommy Price, with an uncharacteristic three last places, and Brian Crutcher had poor evenings. The report in the *News* said that this was a strong West Ham team capable of winning anywhere; in fact this was their only away win in the league in 1953.

Away from home, the Lions lost twice in the first three days of August, at Norwich by five points and Wimbledon by just one. The *News* said that this was the 'match of the season'. Brian Crutcher fell in the last race, and Don Perry, who also fell, started to push for home for the crucial point to win the match. His bike sprang into life and he made it by 18 seconds. Earlier in the meeting, Tommy Price was booed after fallen to avoid Don Perry who had fallen. Price was excluded, and acknowledged the jeers with a "cheerful wave" according to the *News*. Price was never popular with the Dons fans. The Lions' only other defeat in the league was in the last match of the season at Birmingham, when they had already won the league title. They won by 18 points at West Ham in September, which showed what a shock the earlier result at the Empire Stadium had been.

In *Stenner's 1954 Annual*, Basil Storey said that Harringay were "by far the best balanced team we have seen in post-war senior racing" – although Wembley fans would probably have disputed that. He said that they "failed to clinch the league championship as the result of injuries, particularly the indisposition of Split Waterman in the closing weeks of their league schedule."

New Lions in 1953: Top left: Brian Crutcher; top right: Eric French; bottom left: Dennis Newton (JSC); bottom right: Rune Sormander.

Wembley Lions 1953 (JSC).

Programmes from 1953: Left: The Lions' National Trophy Semi-final at Birmingham;
Right: The World Championship Final.

When the two teams met on 3 September, they were level at the top of the league with West Ham. All three had won seven matches and lost three, although the Lions' points difference was easily better than the other two. The match was really decided by a pile-up in the first race. Bill Kitchen fell, and Split Waterman went into the fence to avoid him. Ron How touched Kitchen's back wheel and also fell. Waterman was carried off from the dog track on a stretcher. The Lions won the rerun 5–1 and never looked back. Waterman did not ride again, having sustained a bruised shoulder, and also missed the return at Green Lanes two nights later. The visitors fought hard, according to the *News*, but with the Williams brothers and Tommy Price all scoring double figures, the Lions won comfortably. Trevor Redmond returned to action at reserve.

At Green Lanes, the Lions took the lead in heat five with a 5–1 from Eric Williams and Crutcher, and never looked back. Only Jack Biggs got into double figures for the home side, and Wembley rode consistently, only finishing last twice. The Lions won by 18 points. In the league table in mid-September, the Racers were top with 20 points, but with only one match left. The Lions were second on 19 points, but had three matches to ride.

To conclude their campaign, the Lions drew the largest crowd of the season to Belle Vue. They witnessed the Aces securing a draw with a 5–1 in the last heat. After winning at West Ham, the Lions clinched the league at Bristol the day after the World Final. As the Lions season had finished with the World Final, because Wembley had to be prepared for two England football matches in October and November, the Lions actually received the trophy at their first home meeting in 1954.

While the Lions had dominated the National League since the War, the National Trophy was another story. Their only success had been in 1948, when they were out of contention for the league due to riding most of the season at Plough Lane. In 1953, their first tie was against Harringay, with the first leg at the Empire Stadium. It has been argued that the Racers were really the best team in 1953, and that they should have won the league. But over two legs, the Lions blew the Trophy holders away. In the first leg, before rain came after heat eight, the *News* said that the meeting "appeared to be developing into a real sizzler." After nine heats, only four points separated the sides, but 5–1s in heats 10 and 11 saw the Lions finish the tie 12 points up. Two days later, at Green Lanes, racing was delayed by half-an-hour by a thunderstorm. There were several inches of water on the bends, and riders and officials helped to clear it. The *News* said that the Racers were "outclassed" on their own track. Tommy Price top scored for the Lions with 16 points; five straight wins from Brian Crutcher, before he fell in his last race, helped clinch a 68–40 win, and a 40 point win on aggregate. The *Star* said that Wembley gated better, which was a considerable advantage in the conditions. Overall, between the two teams, the Lions won four times and the Racers twice in official fixtures.

In 1952, the Lions had been embarrassed by a 30 point defeat at Perry Barr in the National Trophy. This time, Birmingham had to ride the first leg at the Empire Stadium. The Lions' revenge was sweet, with a 78–29 win, although the *Star* said that their win was "too easy to be interesting". The *News* said that in the second leg, Birmingham had "no difficulty in a convincing win, but could not overcome the calamity of the first leg." The *Star* said that there was "grand racing" with the home riders "fighting their way through from the back". But the Lions had secured their place in the final by heat 12.

There, they faced Wimbledon, who had easily dispatched Bristol in the semi-final. The Dons had knocked the Lions out of the London Cup in May, but had been beaten by 32 points in the league at the Empire Stadium at the end of August.

Ronnie Moore had missed the league match, but returned for the Cup Final, and a six ride paid maximum contributed to a 68–40 win for the Dons at Plough Lane in the first leg. The *News* said that the "highly geared Wembley team failed to click" and Freddie Williams had his worst match of the season. He was pulled out of heat 12, and could have been withdrawn earlier. Brian Crutcher was also a disappointment. Eric Williams was the best rider for the visitors, with five second places in an 11 (+1) return. But the Lions only won two heats on a track they were very familiar with. The *Star* said there was "good racing and plenty of thrills."

It was a different story three days later at the Empire Stadium. A 40,000 crowd experienced "excitement without parallel at Wembley this season" according to the *Star*. The Lions notched up three 5–1s in the first five heats. The *News* said that the "gap slowly but surely closed as the match progressed." However, the report noted that the Wimbledon second-strings never let up, and Wembley needed two 5–1s in the last two races. However, in the 17th heat, Norman Parker Gated ahead of Trevor Redmond, and would not leave the white line, winning the Trophy for his side. However, the *News* questioned Wembley's tactics in that race. Redmond replaced Eric French, but Bill Kitchen was left in the race, despite a poor third in his previous race.

The *News* said that apart from Freddie Williams, who was unbeaten by an opponent in six rides, Tommy Price and Trevor Redmond, the Lions did not rise to the occasion: "several 5–1s went by the board because of lack of fire of the second strings." Eric French, Brian Crutcher and Bill Kitchen "must bear the brunt of the criticism" according to the magazine's reporter. However, Crutcher had a "wonderful win" over Ronnie Moore in heat six. The final result was 66–42 to the Lions, but the Dons won the Trophy 110–106 on aggregate. It was Wimbledon's third win in four seasons.

An interesting part of the tournament had been the lower-level teams entering the early rounds, with the First Division teams joining in round four, which is how the FA Cup is run. Glasgow White City gave a good account of themselves against Birmingham, but Stoke, who scored just 19 at Wimbledon in 18 heats, and Motherwell, with 23 at Harringay, showed the problems of the idea, with one-sided fare for the fans.

In the World Championship, Tommy Price was involved in some controversy. Wembley could only nominate two riders into the Championship round, and chose Freddie and Eric Williams, who were the top two scorers at the time. Other First Division riders joined in the International round, including Bill Kitchen, Trevor Redmond and Brian Crutcher. Price withdrew from the Championship and asked for a transfer. He missed the Lions' win at Belle Vue, and the home win over Bristol, although this was apparently due to tonsillitis. Although a transfer to Birmingham had been agreed, fortunately for the Lions Price backed down and withdrew the request. Whether this was because of strawberries and cream being delivered to his house by supporters when he was ill is not known. According to the *News* he said that he had "acted childishly" although he thought the World Championship system was wrong.

Freddie and Eric Williams both qualified for the Final, along with Brian Crutcher and Rune Sormander, although the latter's links with the Lions had finished. The *News* thought that former World Champion Freddie could outshine his brother on this occasion. The event was to be shown live on television, and Brian Crutcher was the youngest finalist.

A 90,000 crowd saw Freddie Williams win his second World title. He earned £587/10 for just under six minutes racing time according to the News. There had been problems with the starting gate, and five heats were started on the green light. The only point Williams dropped was to Jeff Lloyd in heat 13. The decisive race was heat 17. An unbeaten Split Waterman faced Freddie Williams. Second place would have secured a run-off for the title for the former Lion, but he could not get past Olle Nygren and finished as runner-up on 13 points. Brian Crutcher finished on six points, one ahead of Sormander, and two ahead of Eric Williams. Former champion Jack Young finished on 10 points, after failing in his last race. RM Samuel said that Williams had won the World title "fairly and squarely" and he "rode cleverly in each of his five races."

Looking towards the future, Bill Kitchen had ridden at reserve for the Lions at times, and was clearly in the twilight of his career. George Wilks had also reached the veteran stage, and only rode in four league meetings. Trevor Redmond, in his column in the *News*, said that he expected Wilks to leave Wembley because of the lack of rides he had got this season. Of the Lions up-and-coming riders, Dennis Newton had ridden at St Austell. Bill Simpson, Mickie Meacher and a young New Zealander, Hec Mayhead, had all taken part in second half and London Junior League matches. In December, the Lions announced their list of 12 retained riders. This included Bruce Abernethy and Bob Oakley, but not Den Cosby. He had stopped riding due to a back injury, but did maintain a connection to the sport by in December asking Tommy Price to be godfather to his new baby.

On the international scene, Freddie and Eric Williams, Brian Crutcher and Tommy Price had all ridden for England against Australia in the three match series. New Zealand also faced England in a three-match series. Freddie Williams rode in all three tests, Eric Williams in two and Price once, while Trevor Redmond appeared three times for the Kiwis.

The *Star's* review of the Lions season said that Brian Crutcher was a "fine signing" by Duncan King, and the youngster had done well after an uncertain start. Bill Kitchen was still useful to the team, but the writer felt that Jimmy Gooch had not progressed to establish a team place. He felt that the Williams brothers, supported by Tommy Price, were responsible for Wembley winning the league again.

However, there were concerns as well. RM Samuel noted that "In Coronation year, every theatrical venture and outdoor entertainment, except cricket and Wimbledon tennis, experienced bad business." There had been a 12 percent drop in attendances compared to 1952, although this is partly explained through track closures if Samuel was comparing the aggregate figures. More worryingly for the Lions, it was reported in the *Star* on 14 April 1954, in an article on the Entertainment Tax, that at 22 speedway meetings at the Empire Stadium in 1953 not a single penny profit was made. But the Chancellor of the Exchequer benefitted to the tune of almost £12,000.

After the end of the season there was debate in the trade press about the way forward for the sport. Wembley favoured nine heat league matches, and presumably a more developed second half, possibly involving other forms of motor sport. In December, it was reported that there would be an attempt to launch stock car racing in Great Britain in 1954. More problems for speedway were on the horizon.

14. 1954: Two Cups

The New Year opened with a potential split in the sport. The *News* reported that there were plans to set up a breakaway London–Provincial League of 18 teams, including Wimbledon, West Ham and Bristol. There was talk by the smaller promotions of dictatorship by Wembley and Harringay. The editor, Len Went, said that these allegations can be taken with a pinch of salt. He commented that "Wembley chief, Sir Arthur Elvin is one of the greatest showmen in the country. Naturally he holds strong views on speedway – he's been associated with the sport for a very long time – but that must not necessarily be interpreted as dictatorship." He said that had been deadlock in the promoters meetings. However, the new league also faced many problems. These included the question of evening up the teams and pay rates, especially for the top riders, such as Ronnie Moore and Jack Young. For Wimbledon, there would also be the loss of matches against Wembley.

The teams for the new league were to be: Wimbledon, West Ham, Bristol, Coventry, Leicester, Poole, Yarmouth, Wolverhampton, Glasgow White City, Edinburgh, Motherwell, Raleigh, Exeter, Swindon, Ipswich, Oxford, Southampton and Plymouth.

This clearly posed major problems for the six teams left in the First Division, four of which rode their home meetings on Saturdays. However, two weeks later, the idea had collapsed, following a meeting of the Speedway Control Board. It "went out like a damp squib" according to the *News*. The Board did agree that Bristol could return to the Second Division, which their promoters believed would be more viable for them. It was also agreed that the Second Division and Southern League would amalgamate and run under the title of the Second Division.

The issue that was not resolved was that of promotion and relegation. Howard Jacobi, the *News's* Midlands correspondent said that there was support for two divisions of 12 teams with promotion and relegation. But there were "two flies in the ointment": "We have two promotions in London – Wembley and Harringay – whose attitude towards speedway, by virtue of the enormity of their financial commitments, is different from that of any other track in the country – with the one possible exception of Belle Vue. Wembley and Harringay have to fill the Empire Stadium and Harringay Stadium. And if speedway doesn't bring its anticipated quota of customers, then it becomes necessary – from their viewpoint – to alter things." He argued that the sport should expand the First Division, not cut it down, and that one team relegated and one promoted, would have speedway on a "firm and sane basis".

For the new season, the First Division had eight teams, and would again run league meetings over 14 heats. Each team would meet the others twice at home and twice away. The RAC Cup would be the early season competition, but the Lions decided to ride all their matches away from home. The experiment tried in 1953 of staging meetings at Wimbledon had seen "extremely thin attendances".

The Second Division originally consisted of 15 teams, but Glasgow White City and Wolverhampton withdrew without racing a league match. The Scottish club lost money on their first two meetings and closed down, while Wolverhampton shut up shop in June. The possibility of the team moving to Stoke was turned down by the SCB.

Edinburgh and Plymouth also pulled out mid-season, so 11 teams finished the campaign. With only Motherwell flying the flag for the sport in Scotland, and facing substantial travel costs in a league based largely in the southern half of England, their long-term future looked in doubt. Yarmouth were refused admission to the Second Division, because they only wanted to run a four month season. With the decline in the number of tracks, this seems a surprising decision by the SCB. The Second Division also hit problems at the start of the season when a short pay dispute postponed the opening of some tracks.

A new initiative was a 'training league' based in the south. This became the Southern Area League and gave opportunities for new riders to participate in the sport. It started with six teams, but Aldershot dropped out in mid-season.

The SCB also said that there should be no stock car racing on speedway tracks, although how they could enforce this was another matter. In January, the *Star* had an interview with John Pugh, who was organising the stock car meetings, and he said they were "negotiating for several provincial tracks where speedway has failed." The sport planned to launch with a meeting at New Cross on Good Friday.

One positive piece of news for the sport was that evening fares in London were to be reduced, which could help boost attendances. However, the Budget in April provided little help to the sport. A halfpenny reduction in the hated Entertainment Tax meant from an attendance of 5,000 the promoter would gain £10.

Prospects for the Lions looked good. Four of the riders, Trevor Redmond, Brian Crutcher, Freddie Williams and Bill Kitchen had been riding in South Africa. Redmond had been in great form, far better than his performances for the Lions in 1953. In February, he reported that the Lions were favourites to sign Fred Lang, one of the local stars of the sport in South Africa. In March it was confirmed that Lang would be joining the team on a two year contract. However, not so good news was that Freddie Williams broke his collar bone in a match race with Brian Crutcher. He was expected to be fit for the new season at home, and when he arrived in London was given special exercises by Wembley trainer Tommy Barnett.

The pundits expected the Lions to do well in 1954. In the *Star*, both Angus Kix and Frederick Philpott expected them to retain the First Division title. In the *News*, RM Samuel said that Trevor Redmond and Eric French needed to improve to be of Lions standard. He said that Harringay were a better side than the Lions in 1953.

Something that did not worry the Lions was the prospect of their young star, Brian Crutcher, being called up for National Service. The *Star* published a profile of him in March, and revealed that he was exempt due to a perforated eardrum.

Another change for the Lions was that cinders would replace shale as the track surface at the Empire Stadium, reverting to the 1949 surface. The cost of this was £1,000 and Sir Arthur Elvin believed that it would "bring back thrills and spectacle." In fact, the change only lasted until early August, when the shale track was restored.

In April, Bill Kitchen announced that he would only ride if the Lions suffered injuries, although he continued as non-riding captain. Bob Oakley came out of retirement, but after a couple of early season meetings for the Lions was loaned to Norwich. Dennis Newton was loaned to Oxford for the season.

The Lions campaign began with a four team tournament at Wimbledon. They finished last behind their London rivals, Wimbledon winning the meeting. Four days later, the Lions won the Middlesex Cup at Harringay with a 5–1 in the last heat. The RAC Cup was organised in two pools, and the Lions faced West Ham, Birmingham and Norwich. A Jack Young maximum saw the Lions go down by 12 points at West Ham on Good Friday. Tommy Price's mood was probably not improved when on the way home, his car was hit by a trolley bus. Both his bikes and the trailer sustained extensive damage.

On Easter Monday, the Lions lost by eight points in a challenge match at Wimbledon, although the crowd enjoyed a "feast of good racing" according to the *News*. The Lions first win of the season was at Norwich. They provided all but three of the heat winners, and a Brian Crutcher maximum saw them home by nine points. As well as Bob Oakley, former Lion Roy Craighead was riding for the home team.

The Lions lost at Birmingham in the RAC Cup, which effectively ended their interest in the competition. The top team in each pool met later in the season to decide the trophy, and Wimbledon beat West Ham comfortably over two legs. The Hammers won their pool with 11 points from six meetings, Birmingham were runners-up with five, then came Wembley and Norwich with four each. The Lions' only other win was at Birmingham on 22 May.

In the league, the Lions faced a tough encounter in their first match with a trip to Green Lanes to face Harringay, the night before their home opening meeting with the same opponents. However, falls and engine failures "cost the Racers dearly" according to the *News*. However, the report also said that the better team won, and "by a margin that did not flatter them unduly." Eric Williams and Brian Crutcher were both unbeaten by an opponent.

The Racers fared better the next night, and went down by six points. Riding was difficult on a wet cinders surface. Once again, the Lions were almost invincible at home. They racked up 50 points in six meetings, and 60 three times. At the end of May, Birmingham went down 65–19. The *News* said it was a "humiliating slaughter of the pride of the Midlands." Worryingly, the report said that, apart from Ron Mountford and Eric Boothroyd, some members of their team rode "as if they couldn't care less." In June, the *News* said that Belle Vue were "putrid and ineffective" in only scoring 17 points.

After the Harringay match on opening night, only Norwich, who held the Lions to 44–40 on 1 July, and West Ham, who lost 49–35 in August, conceded less than 50 points. However, the Lions lost two home matches, both to Wimbledon, which effectively decided the outcome of the First Division. On 10 May, the Lions lost at Plough Lane by just three points. In an "intense atmosphere", according to the *News*, Freddie Williams was excluded for unfair riding in heat nine, which was unusual for him. The Lions were 11 points down with three races left. Freddie Williams and Trevor Redmond produced a 5–1. Jimmy Gooch replaced Tommy Price in the next heat and followed Eric French home to make the score 40–37. In the final heat, Ronnie Moore's bike shed a chain, but Cyril Brine won the race, and the match for the Dons, despite being pressured by Brian Crutcher.

The Lions then lost at West Ham the next day in the RAC Cup, and went down by 18 points at home to the Dons on the Thursday night. The Williams brothers, with eight points apiece, were the top scorers for the Lions. Brian Crutcher had a poor night, and Tommy Price got two third places in four rides. The Lions only won five heats.

The Lions' second home league encounter with the Dons came on the last Thursday of July. The *News* reported that the new shale surface was "rough and bumpy." The teams were level after five heats, but from then the south Londoners never looked back. Freddie Williams beat Olle Nygren in heat eight, and in heat 13, Price and Crutcher were ahead, but the latter developed engine trouble, and Nygren won the race on the line. Nygren was on a short-term deal with the Dons, covering for the injured Ronnie Moore.

Four days later, on August Bank Holiday Monday, a large crowd saw the Lions lose by two points at Plough Lane. Eric French top scored for the Lions with 10, but Geoff Mardon's final heat win clinched the match, and effectively the league title, for the Dons. In the final table, Wimbledon had 44 points from 28 matches, Wembley had 40, with a marginally better points difference. One win over the Dons would have won the league for the Lions. Odsal finished in third place in the league, 10 points behind the Lions.

One of the few times the three Williams brothers rode together in an official meeting: Fred, Ian and Eric at Wembley in 1954. Ian rode for the Swindon Robins. (JSC).

Jimmy Gooch, Ken Walsh, Fred Lang and Frank Lawrence at the start: Wembley versus Harringay 1954. (JSC).

Wembley Lions 1954 at Norwich with the National Trophy (JSC).

Left: Wembley's South African recruit, Fred Lang.

121

In June, the *News* had reported that there was a slump in speedway attendances in London. Len Went said that some people blamed the weather, television, the cinema and stock car racing. However, he added that the standard of racing had been very low, with some "shocking" performances by provincial teams, resulting in one-sided massacres. Attendances were holding up at the provincial clubs, where the London teams were attractive visitors.

Certainly television ownership was growing, but cinema attendance was in a gradual decline, so it is hard to see how that would affect speedway. It is true that it was a poor summer, with above average rainfall, which is also apparent from the speedway match reports.

One step Wembley took to improve their meetings was to introduce handicap racing in the second halves of meetings. This was well received, and there were letters both in the *News* and the Wembley programme saying how exciting it was and that it should bring the crowds back to speedway. There were five riders in a race, and in July the Wembley management said that novices would not ride in these races. Wembley's programme for the match against Birmingham on 15 July said that those who had been spreading gloomy stories on the future of speedway had been routed by news of the test match series and the development of handicap racing.

A further sign of speedway's problems came in early July. Harringay announced that their season would finish early, and they would run double-headers to complete their home league programme by 18 August. In the same week it was announced that Plymouth and Edinburgh would close after staging their World Championship qualifying round meetings. Harringay's attendances had been low all season, not helped by their management being slow to deny rumours in early May that the team was going to move to New Cross so that stock car racing could be run at Green Lanes.

Stock car racing had started at New Cross on Good Friday. There was a huge attendance, with 10,000 locked out according to reports. In June, they moved to Harringay, which was advertised on the front page of the *News*. At the end of May, the *News* had reported an attendance of 28,000 (or 40,000 according to a different article in the same edition!) at Odsal for stock cars. That compares with 11,000 watching Odsal beat the Lions on 5 June. While part of these attendances can be explained by people wanting to see something new and different, they must have been demoralising for long-term speedway fans who were seeing their sport in decline. Towards the end of the season, various other cities and current or former speedway venues staged stock car racing, including West Ham. In October, a crowd of 45,000 was reported for a meeting in Sheffield. For the speedway promoters and stadium managements, concerned at declining speedway attendances, this must have seemed a great opportunity to bring in revenue. Some current and former speedway riders took part as well.

In all the Lions' success since the War, the National Trophy had usually eluded them. As in 1953, the Second Division teams fought out the early rounds, with Coventry and Poole winning through to face First Division opposition in Odsal and Belle Vue. Both lost both legs to their higher grade opponents. As before, the meetings were run over 18 heats.

The Lions faced West Ham in July with the first leg was at Custom House. The *News* said that the shortened starting area "added to first bend thrills". Only Jack Young and Wally Green could mount a serious challenge to the Lions, and they scored 29 of West Ham's points between them. For the Lions, who won by eight points, Brian Crutcher was paid for 17 points, and Trevor Redmond for 12; it was a typically solid Wembley team performance. Two nights later, the Lions won the return leg comfortably to take the tie 128–87 on aggregate. The Lions were superior from the gate, and "won as they pleased" according to the *News*. There was a nasty incident in heat 17 when Jimmy Gooch lost control and Howdy Byford ran into him. Byford went to hospital with a head injury, and Gooch sustained cuts.

Two weeks later, Odsal came to Wembley for the semi-final first leg. The visitors provided eight heat winners in the first 12 races, but then four Wembley 5-1s in five heats turned the tables. However, Odsal manager Bruce Booth said that "This result gives us a fighting chance of reaching the final." Arthur Forrest and Eddie Rigg scored 29 of the visitors' 44 points; while for the Lions, who won 63-44, Tommy Price was paid for 15 points, and Eric Williams for 14, although that included four bonus points.

The return leg was three weeks later. The *News* said that it was "one of the finest meetings ever seen at the Bradford track." The Lions riders had protested at the state of the track, but according to the *Star,* extra grading made everyone happy. The *News* said that the steward took no notice of the Lions' concerns.

Arthur Forrest scored a six ride maximum for Odsal, and Eddie Rigg was unbeaten by a home rider. After nine heats, the home side were eight points up on the night, but a 5–1 from the Williams brothers "slumped Odsal spirits" according to the News. In heat 16, Freddie Williams's second place meant that Odsal needed two 5–1s to win the tie in the last two races. Eric Williams's second place in heat 17 meant that the Lions just needed a point from the last heat, which they duly secured. Eric Williams was carried back to the pits shoulder high by his team mates. The Lions had reached the final 108–107 on aggregate.

There they met Norwich, who had comfortably beaten Wimbledon in the other semi-final, winning by six points at Plough Lane, and 20 at The Firs. The first leg of the Final was the Lions' last home match of the season. The *Star* said that Norwich "staged a wonderful battle", in particular due to their reserves, Bob Oakley and Fred Brand. Oakley was unbeaten in three rides, scoring 7(+2), and Brand scored 10 from five rides, including three heat wins. The *News* said that better use of their reserves could have seen Norwich going into the second leg with more points in hand. For the Lions, Brian Crutcher was paid for 17 points, and Fred Lang had one of his better meetings, scoring 7(+1). The Lions won 61–46 to take a 15 point lead into the return match.

However, the second leg was an anti-climax. A heavy storm an hour before the scheduled start left the track heavy and waterlogged, and the meeting only began after a 30 minute delay. The *Star* commented that "Wembley mastered the conditions early on" and that the "processions got monotonous". Two 5–1s and two 4–2s stretched their lead to 27 overall. Racing was stopped after the fourth heat, and the track was inspected. The *News* said that times were six seconds slower than usual, and once it was decided to continue after the delay, it was clear that the Trophy would go to Wembley. Norwich's first heat winner came in heat 11, and the Lions had the Trophy won by heat 12. The *News* said that the weather ruined the match as a spectacle, but that Wembley were worthy winners on the night. Their reporter did wonder what would have happened under normal racing conditions. Crutcher again led the way for the Lions with 14(+1), Trevor Redmond scored 12 and Freddie Williams 10(+2). Except for Jimmy Gooch, who had a poor night, every member of the team contributed to the Lions 123–92 aggregate win. The last time the Lions had won the Trophy was in 1948, when they also failed to win the league, and it was the fourth time they had won the Trophy overall.

The closure of New Cross meant that there were just four teams in the London Cup. In early June, the Lions comfortably knocked out Harringay in the semi-final. A 5–0 in the first heat at Green Lanes, when Waterman stalled and Lawrence broke a chain, was the start of a 19 point win for the Lions. Freddie Williams was unbeaten until his last race, when Waterman beat him.

The return leg the next night was closer. It was 21-21 after seven heats, but then two consecutive 5–1s made it a comfortable win for the Lions. Freddie Williams's win in heat 13 confirmed their place in the final; 123–92 on aggregate at the end.

There they faced Wimbledon. The final had been put back to August after Wimbledon's Ronnie Moore cracked a bone in his leg riding in Denmark. According to the *Star*, the Lions were "yards faster than their opponents" in their 69–38 win. The *News* said that the Dons had ridden poorly, although their reporter said that they should have used their reserves earlier; Barry Briggs and Cyril Maidment had seven scoreless outings between them before they were replaced. The Lions gave a solid team display in wet conditions. Ronnie Moore and Peter Moore (no relation) won the first heat 5–1, but the Lions were ahead after heat five and never looked back. Freddie Williams was "magnificent" with 17 points, and Price, Crutcher and Eric Williams all scored double figures. The Dons only provided four heat winners. Ronnie Greene subsequently complained about the track surface at Wembley, saying it was bone hard and the first man out of the gate won every time. Len Went commented that he believed that the Lions had won on merit.

The second leg at Plough Lane 11 days later was a fairly hopeless task for the Dons. But, according to Cyril Hart's report in the *News*, they "fought like tigers throughout the intense 18 heats battle". Brian Crutcher scored an 18 point maximum, and was "effortless, immaculate and supremely confident" according to Hart. He said, however, that Wembley "rode solidly as a match-winning combination". Eric Williams was paid for 16 points, and both Wembley reserves, Eric French with 8 (+1) from four rides and Gooch with 5 (+3) from his four rides, enjoyed some success. In reality, the Lions had the trophy won when they reached 29 points in heat eight. Wembley won 61–47 on the night, and 130–85 overall.

This was the final London Cup competition in Wembley's first period in post-war speedway. It was revived in 1964, when Wimbledon beat West Ham, and then became part of the new speedway set-up that started in 1965. This was the Lions' sixth post-war win in the competition, and ninth overall.

The Lions riders World Championship campaign started earlier than usual. Bill Kitchen qualified for the European Final with third place in a meeting in Oberhausen in West Germany. He and Fred Lang rode in the European Final in Linkopping in Sweden. However, neither qualified for the next round; Kitchen scored eight points and Lang four.

Freddie and Eric Williams, Tommy Price and Brian Crutcher were all seeded to the final series of qualifying rounds. Trevor Redmond also battled his way through to join them. However, World Champion Freddie Williams had a bad night at the qualifying round at Belle Vue. He only scored seven points after crashing in his first race. He needed a 15 point maximum from the round at Wembley to qualify. However, he ended up with 14 points, having been beaten by his brother Eric in his second race. Eric had been last in his first heat, and did not qualify for the final. The meeting was one of the few occasions when all three Williams brothers rode together in an official meeting. Eric finished the night on 10 points, Ian, who rode for Swindon, got seven.

Brian Crutcher and Tommy Price made it to the final through the qualifying rounds. They were joined by Trevor Redmond, who was second in a three-man run-off to decide the final two places. Olle Nygren won the race, and Alan Hunt was third, becoming first reserve. Freddie Williams was second reserve, and did not get a ride.

More than 80,000 fans saw Ronnie Moore win the title with a five ride maximum. Brian Crutcher won a run-off with Olle Nygren to take second place on 13 points. Price and Redmond scored five points apiece. This was Brian Crutcher's best performance in a World Final, for Price, Redmond and Freddie Williams, it was their last appearance at Wembley's biggest night of the year.

Over the years, the Lions made little impact on the Match Race Championship. However, in July Eric Williams and Bradford's Arthur Forrest were nominated for the vacant title. They both won their respective home legs, then Forrest won the run-off 2–0 at Birmingham.

In September, the *Star* reported how Eric and Helen Williams's three-year-old daughter enjoyed watching her father race. If he won, she yelled "Good old Eric", but if he fell, was heard to say "He felled off". Her dad's comments on the latter were not recorded!

In October, the Lions and Wimbledon toured Sweden. The Lions beat a Stockholm Combination 58–32, Folkare 49–34 and the Swedish champions Vargana 54–35. A London side lost to a Swedish Combination 59–49.

Wembley had been well-represented on the international stage during the season. England had beaten Australasia 3–0. Brian Crutcher was the Lions' top scorer in the first and third tests, and finished the series with 42 points. Eric Williams rode for England in all three tests, scoring 21 in total, and his brother Freddie rode in the first test, scoring five. For Australasia, Trevor Redmond rode in all three matches, scoring 18 points.

In his review of Wembley's season, published in the *News* in January 1955, Len Went commented on the individual performances of the riders: "Individual honours in the Lions were shared by Crutcher and Eric Williams. These boys rode hard and true all the season. Many were surprised to see Eric displace his brother Freddie in the scoring honours. Yet the ex-World Champion had a fairly good season and had a league average of well over 9 a match [His Calculated Match Average – CMA –was 8.89].

Tubby Trevor Redmond surprised a few, too. He came back to something like the Redmond of old, full of fight and throttle. Maybe he solved some of his weight difficulties. We've yet to see the best of Freddie Lang. The slick Wembley circuit was not his cup of tea, but he was improving all the time.

Tommy Price is still very much a valuable team member. Price is the man for an emergency and there will be room for him in the 1955 Wembley side. Jimmy Gooch still remains something of an enigma. At one time last season it seemed that he was on the threshold of stardom. But he never quite made it, and had to be content with a reserve berth for most of the season. We mustn't forget Eric French either. He is getting on in years, but can still show the young 'uns a thing or two. Should the Lions find it difficult to fit him in in the new season, certain other clubs are bound to make an offer for his services."

So at the end of a difficult season for the sport, the Lions had won two trophies. But with Harringay's future in the sport clearly uncertain, the presence of stock car racing and the prospect of a commercial television channel on the horizon after the passing of the 1954 Television Act, speedway still faced an uncertain future.

Freddie Williams fixing his bike, ably assisted by his wife Pat. (JC)

15. 1955: No trophies!

1955 was a problematic year, both for speedway and the Lions. It became clear that Harringay were not going to return to the sport, so the First Division would have only seven teams. Poole had applied for promotion from the Second Division, but were turned down. There were only three London tracks, so the London Cup was not run. The competition did not return to the sport until 1964, when Wimbledon and West Ham, as the only two National League teams in London, rode for it. Why a three team tournament could not have been organised is curious; the Cup was an attraction, and there were enough dates for it.

There was pre-season speculation that World Champion Ronnie Moore would switch to car racing. In fact, he did return to the UK, and continued to ride for the powerful Wimbledon team. In the Second Division, Motherwell closed, so there was to be no league speedway in Scotland. The *News* reported that they had paid out £2,000 in Entertainment Tax, but lost £500 on the season.

However, the sport's morale were raised when Weymouth joined the Second Division. This was the first new track for a couple of years. Sadly, the promoters pulled the plug after just six homes meetings, before the holiday season had started, which surely would have produced better attendances. Bristol also did not complete the season – they withdrew from the league after only 2,027 came to a match against Rayleigh – so the final Second Division table had only nine teams. The Southern Area League also lost a track, when Ringwood closed two thirds of the way through their season. However, this league remained important for the sport; it was one of the few opportunities for new riders to develop their skills.

In the First Division, it was agreed that league matches would be over 16 heats, with seven-man teams, one of whom would be a reserve. Guest riders would be allowed to cover for injuries, and would be selected from a pool of Second Division riders. Also, a tactical substitute rule was introduced, and could be used if a team was six points in arrears after heat four. Both these initiatives, it was hoped, would make league matches closer and more exciting. However, in the case of some teams, the damage had already been done, and their reputations as weak opponents saw the Wembley management make a remarkable move that effectively gave away the league title before the season had started.

It was already clear that the Lions would be pushed to challenge Wimbledon for the title. The league was based on each team facing the others twice at home and twice away. Wembley said that they would only ride against each other team at home once, and would ride away to them three times. The six home dates not used by league matches would be filled by individual open meetings.

RM Samuel commented in the *News* on 4 May that Wembley wanted to introduce more novelty or variety into speedway. He said that Sir Arthur Elvin would prefer shorter league meetings with brighter programmes. Wembley were prepared to try any variety of motor cycle racing or design to help kill monotony. "Big or small twins, stripped road machines, compulsory trailing, anything for variety, that is the policy at Wembley", he wrote.

Three weeks later, he examined the thinking behind Wembley's decision over their programme of meetings: "Sir Arthur, I imagine, is fully alive to the fact that league racing has so deteriorated that only one or two clubs draw really paying crowds to the Empire Stadium. I don't want to individualise, but can you think of a team, other than Wimbledon, that would attract a 15,000 crowd... Belle Vue or Birmingham ... they have poor performances last season to live down ... West Ham is only a shadow of its former strength. Odsal are yet to convince.

From Wembley's point of view both the demise of Harringay and New Cross – both clubs which used to give the Lions plenty to think about – must dictate policy. Whether the combination of a restricted season coupled with a limited number of home league engagements is the right line remains to be seen. At least it is worth trying."

Whatever the pros and cons of this for Wembley, it did not help the image of the sport. How could the league championship be taken seriously if this is how the sport's most famous team treated it?

The Lions' riders and supporters were used to their home season starting in the first or second week of May, once the football and rugby league cup finals were over. But this season, it was put back to 26 May, because the Stadium was being used for two weeks by the American Christian evangelist Billy Graham. The *News* reported that some of the Wembley and Wimbledon riders had attended one Dr Graham's meetings. Trevor Redmond said that "A revivalist such as Dr Graham is badly needed in speedway."

In the *Star*, Eric Linden said that the late start would not encourage the Lions' regular supporters. He said that in ice hockey, it causes problems for the fans when ice shows take preference over the Lions fixtures. It also meant that for the first two months of the season, only West Ham and Wimbledon would be running in London. He did say that it would not be possible to have speedway in a "House of God" which is what Wembley would temporarily become. He did point out that Wembley had always championed speedway, and that the sport should not lose that support.

In terms of the Lions team, their South African recruit, Freddie Lang, did not return. Dave Nelson outlined in the *Star* that he came with a great reputation, but never settled on the trickier English tracks. On his second visit to Harringay, he scored nine points, then the Lions dropped him. He was put back in the team for his second visit to Birmingham, and scored seven, but after that scrambled for odd point. It would have been better for the modest, likeable youngster had he signed for a Second Division side to accustom himself to English tracks - as he had expected to in the first place.

It may have been better for the Lions to have loaned Lang out for a season to a Second Division team. The basis of the team was the same as in 1954. However, in May, Eric Williams, asked for a transfer because of the late opening and changes to the league fixtures. The Wembley management set the fee at £2,850 – more than they had paid for Brian Crutcher in 1953. Eric Williams stayed at Wembley, but the *Star* said that he was "not the only person left completely cold by the exceedingly late Wembley opening this year."

George Wilks had retired, and while Bill Kitchen was still racing on the continent, it was extremely unlikely that he would return to league racing. So the Lions really only had seven riders, although there was always the possibility of using Second Division guests. Their lack of depth became clear in early June, when Jimmy Gooch asked for a transfer. He wanted a team place, and more rides than he was getting at reserve. Gooch got his move, on loan to Second Division Swindon. His form improved with more rides, albeit in the sport's second tier. The *News* commented that "At one time Gooch promised great things in the senior grade. He tried hard all the time, but, somehow, never really turned the corner." He could still ride for the Lions in National Trophy matches, which used eight man teams.

He was replaced by Ken Adams, who joined the Lions when Weymouth closed. Adams was 30 years old, and had ridden for most of his career at Stoke, before having a season at Southampton in 1954 before signing for Weymouth. He was a pragmatic signing for the Lions, and was riding in the sport's top tier for the first time. Later in the season, the Lions did give some of the Southern Area League riders second-half rides, which did pay dividends for 1956, when Mike Broadbank was signed. Towards the end of the season, former New Cross Australian veteran Bill Longley signed for the Lions. He rode once, at Norwich, before retiring from British speedway.

In April, Angus Kix in the *Star* was pessimistic about Wembley's chances, given their fixtures: "...To regain the title, they are expecting Brian Crutcher, the Williams boys, Tommy Price, Eric French, Jimmy Gooch and Trevor Redmond to ride like supermen for the entire season. Those boys are good, but they aren't that good. League champions? Not Wembley – not this year – not likely ... This year they are going to be fighting lambs led to the slaughter. This year they are going to finish further down the league table than they can remember doing before."

Wembley started their season with a short tour to Austria. With Trevor Redmond away in South Africa, they used West Ham's Gerry Hussey as a guest. He was top scorer in the first two matches. The Lions beat a Continental team 59–31 in Vienna, 49–41 in Linz and 60–30 in Bruck. The crowds were very enthusiastic, with 40,000 watching the meeting in Vienna.

Back in the UK, the Lions had three challenge matches, at West Ham, Belle Vue and Wimbledon before their league campaign started. A 17,000 crowd saw them win by 10 points in Custom House, although West Ham were missing Jack Young. At Wimbledon on Easter Monday, there was a fight in the crowd after Ron How had fallen with Brian Crutcher close to him. The Lions' first league match was also at Plough Lane. The Dons won by three points, after Tommy Price was excluded in the last race after having bike problems at the start. In heat 10 his motor was blown out of the frame, and he salvaged some of the parts before getting off the track. Brian Crutcher led the way for the Lions, with 12 points from his 5 rides.

Twelve days later, the Lions rode at Belle Vue. The Aces were much improved on 1954, and won by 18 points. The *Star* reported that the Lions have never been so obviously rattled in a post-war meeting at Belle Vue and that Wembley failed to match the fierce enthusiasm and team spirit of Ken Sharples' youngsters. Only veteran Tommy Price appeared to grasp what was needed against such an onslaught. Eric Williams and Price were the Lions' only heat winners. "Of the rest of the Wembley team, it could not be said they faded out. They just didn't get started!"

The Lions did manage two wins on the road before their home season began. At West Ham, they faced former Lion Split Waterman. He had originally been allocated to Belle Vue, but had insisted on staying in London and joined West Ham. A 15 point maximum from Jack Young could not stop the Lions winning by four points. The home team needed a 5–1 in the last heat to force a draw, but Eric Williams and Tommy Price kept Bert Roger in last place for a 3–3. At Odsal five days later, the Lions won by the same score. The *Star* said that they took greater risks on a wet track, and were sharper out of the gate. Brian Crutcher dominated with a five ride maximum, but it was Tommy Price's win in the last heat clinched the match for the Lions. In their final away meeting before opening night at Wembley, the Lions lost to Birmingham by five points. So after five away meetings, they had four league points out of 10. It was going to be a tough campaign.

The first meeting at the Empire Stadium saw Wimbledon facing the Lions for the third time this season. The *News* said it was a "feast of racing thrills." Tommy Price had broken two fingers, so Rayleigh's Gerry Jackson stood in as a guest. A 5–1 from Crutcher and Eric Williams settled the match in the Lions favour. The *News* said it was a "rousing start to the season at Wembley and a great fillip for the Lions." The second half included sidecar and handicap races. Later in the season, another novelty the Lions tried in the second halves was having non speedway motorcycle races. There were eight riders in each heat, with the top four in each heat going through to the final.

The Lions' results for their other five home league meetings seem to bear out the Wembley management's doubts about the ability of the other First Division teams to provide decent opposition. Only West Ham, who lost 50–46 at the end of July, conceded less than 60 points. Ironically, the Hammers finished bottom of the league. It was a strange match. West Ham only had four heat winners, and Jack Young had to be content with five second places. Brian Crutcher, as so often in this season, saved Wembley's night with a 15 point maximum. The *News* said that West Ham were value for money, and that, apart from Tommy Price, the Wembley riders seemed overanxious after their defeat at West Ham two nights earlier.

Of the others, Bradford lost 61–35, Norwich and Belle Vue 66–30, and Birmingham 68–28. In July, there was a letter in the *News* about Wembley and their strength. The writer said that it will take a long time to live down the reputation of early 1950s. Rarely was there a match worth seeing entirely due to the way in which the Lions overshadowed all and sundry; "Gradually the crowds fell away, simply because they tired of the inevitable 5–1 heat after heat. They'll take some winning back." Part of the Wembley versus Belle Vue match in June was shown on television. The *News* said that it was a poor advert for the sport; the racing was poor and the commentary worse. The writer said that "Commercial television may turn out to be a very happy event for the two-wheeled sport." Certainly, many years later, ITV did give the sport some excellent coverage, as *Sky* do now, but in the short-term, commercial television was yet another counter-attraction for speedway fans.

A letter in the programme for the All Star Trophy meeting on 7 July showed some of the problems the Lions were having in maintain their crowds. It was from a supporter who had organised coach trips from Thame in Oxfordshire to home meetings. Lack of support meant that the trips may have to stop. If that happened, maybe up to 50 supporters were lost in one go. Travelling from Thame to Wembley today would be manageable, but in the 1950s, when car ownership was far lower, most supporters would not be able to continue without their coach journeys. The Lions programme, a bit defensively, said that the Empire Stadium still drew one of the largest speedways crowds in the country.

In *Sport for the Million*, published in 1958, Tom Stenner wrote: "...when television became a craze speedway followers, almost all in the lower income group, bought sets and put up aerials invariably on the hire purchase system. The ever-increasing cost of living meant cutting down, and the stream of motor-coaches that poured from the Home Counties and outlaying districts to London speedways became within a year little more than a trickle."

Away from home, the Lions were involved in some exciting meetings. A 48–48 draw at West Ham in June was "nail-bitingly exciting" according to the *Star*, with a "larger than usual crowd." The *News* said it was a "wonderful night's racing." At Wimbledon on 1 August, the Lions lost by three pints, having been nine ahead after seven heats.

It is interesting to look at the results of the six 'home' meetings that the Lions rode on opponents' tracks. They won at Bradford and Norwich, and lost the other four meetings, three by 10 points or less. In the final league table, Wimbledon finished top with 34 points, Belle Vue were second on 32, and Wembley third on 23. However, had the Lions ridden those six matches at the Empire Stadium, and won them all, the final table would have seen Wimbledon top with 32, Wembley second with 31 and Belle Vue third with 30. But, maybe at the end of the day the Lions weren't quite good enough. RM Samuel said at the end of the season that Wembley "lacked the spirit of previous years", which was hard on Duncan King and their captain Tommy Price. He said that they were still a talented side, as shown by their clashes with Wimbledon, when they had to ride hard. As it was, this was the Lions' worst league campaign since 1948, when they had also only ridden away from the Empire Stadium for much of the season.

For only the second time since the War, the Lions started the season as holders of the National Trophy. The seven First Division teams were joined in the first round by Poole, who had won the Second Division competition. The Lions were drawn against Belle Vue. In the first leg at Wembley, according to the *News*, some "odd decisions" from the steward helped Wembley to their 67–41 win. In the return at Belle Vue two days later, the Lions reached heat 8 on level terms. Belle Vue would have needed to win every heat after heat 12 to win the tie, but only won two. The Lions went through to the semi-final comfortably enough by 12 points on aggregate.

The other semi-finalists were Wimbledon, Norwich – the 1954 beaten finalists – and Poole, who had knocked out Birmingham. The Lions were drawn against the Dons, with the first leg at Wembley. In the other semi-final, Norwich overwhelmed Poole 82–26 at The Firs in the first leg. Poole won the second, but it was the East Anglian side who faced Wembley in the final.

The Lions got there by building up an 18 point lead in the first leg at the Empire Stadium. The Dons were missing Ronnie Moore. Brian Crutcher was only beaten by Barry Briggs to score 17, and Freddie Williams had a good night, with 13 (+2).

The *News* said that the second leg was a "thrill-a-second" match. The key factors in Wembley's win were 12 points from Eric French, who was one of the Lions' reserves, and Eric Williams' win over Barry Briggs in heat 15. That left the Dons eight points behind on aggregate with three races left. A win Eric French in the next race, and a second for Eric Williams in heat 17 saw the Lions through to the final by four points, 110–106. It was just as well for the Lions that French rode so well, because Tommy Price had a poor evening with just two points, and Freddie Williams had three last places before being replaced.

The Trophy Final first leg was the Lions' last home meeting of the season. Earlier in the season, the Lions had beaten Norwich by 36 points, but since then the East Anglian side had signed one of the Swedish up-and-coming stars who would later lead a Wembley revival – Ove Fundin. He made his debut at the end of June against Belle Vue, and only rode six league matches for Norwich that season. One of his other appearances for the Stars was the first leg of the final.

Fundin was the Stars' top scorer with 16. Tommy Price beat him in the first heat, and then did not score another point. Brian Crutcher beat him in heat 12, and won four other races before falling in heat 18. Fundin's win in that heat over Eric Williams – Cyril Roger had also fallen – secured a 64–43 win for the visitors. For the Lions, apart from Crutcher, only Eric Williams, with 9 (+1) made any impression. Freddie Williams could only muster six points from five rides, and the Lions only provided eight heat winners.

Nine days later, the Lions travelled to The Firs for the second leg. This was a very different match. The Stars were missing both Ove Fundin and Aub Lawson, who had broken his collarbone. Then Billy Bales, after winning his first race, went into the safety fence at the start of heat seven. Eric Williams was excluded and Bales was taken to hospital with concussion. After 12 heats, the scores on the night were level at 36–36. The Lions won the last six heats 27–9, but it was not quite enough, and a second place by Fred Brand in heat 17 saw Norwich home. Phil Clarke, with 15, including winning his first four races, had been the saviour for the home side. For the Lions, Tommy Price top-scored with 13. Brian Crutcher only managed 11 (+1) from his six rides, but the meeting was two days after the World Championship Final, where he had scored 10 points to finish fifth. Trevor Redmond got 11 for the Lions, but Eric

Williams, who had finished fourth in the World Final, just scored three – a heat win – from his five rides. It was Norwich's first National Trophy win, and a night, according to the *News*, that the 13,500 crowd would remember for a long time. The *Star* said that Norwich had had to fight for the Trophy, and that their win at the Empire Stadium in the first leg was the "greatest performance of the year."

In the World Championship, for the first time four European riders qualified direct for the final, leaving just 12 places for the riders who competed in the British rounds. Freddie Williams and Tommy Price did not qualify. Brian Crutcher had won the Wembley qualifying round with 14 points, but faced a run-off with Eric Williams and Billy Bales for the last two places. The two Wembley riders qualified, but they were joined by Bales on the night, who replaced his Norwich colleague Aub Lawson, who was injured.

Brian Crutcher scored 10 points from the four rides he completed. But his chance of a rostrum place went in heat 13, when he fell and was excluded, although many fans felt the decision was harsh. Eric Williams won three heats, but third place in heat eight, behind eventual winner Peter Craven, and Arthur Forrest meant that he finished on 12 points, along with Ronnie Moore and Barry Briggs. The three of them went into a run-off for second and third places. Moore won the race comfortably, but the battle between Briggs and Williams ended in both riders falling on the last bend. Briggs remounted and rode home. Williams pushed home, hoping that Briggs would be excluded, but it was not to be.

This was the last World Final to be staged on a Thursday night. The crowd was 60,000 – good in the circumstances, but from 1956 the Final was moved to a Saturday.

The short home season the Lions ran meant that they only held four of the individual meetings they planned. The Wembley Open was in June, and won by Barry Briggs. The editorial in the *News* before the meeting anticipated a "feast of excellent racing". However, its report said that the first 20 heats were not particularly exciting, despite the star-studded field. The second semi-final was the best race; although Brain Crutcher's engine failure cost him a place in the final and £24 prize money.

In July, the All Star Trophy was won by Jack Young. The *News* said it was a "good night's racing with surprise galore." Two weeks later, Ove Fundin was the big attraction for the Empire Trophy in July. He pushed home 150 yards after a crash with Ian Williams, when both machines were on the precious Wembley turf. However, they were both disqualified for 'outside assistance'. Ron Johnston scored a 12 point maximum in the heats, but the Trophy was won by Ronnie Moore, who also won his semi-final.

The final individual trophy was a Handicap meeting in August. The riders were re-handicapped after heat eight, which the report in the Star thought didn't work. Rayleigh's Gerald Jackson won on the night with 13 points.

The figures below do show that some of the Lions riders did do worse in these meetings – and therefore earn less – than if they had ridden in the same number of league meetings. Certainly, Eric Williams, Eric French and Trevor Redmond did not do as well. We do not know what the pay rates were for these meetings in comparison with a league meeting.

Wembley individual open meetings Lions riders' results

Rider		Meetings	Rides	Points	CMA
Ken	Adams	1	5	11	8.80
Brian	Crutcher	4	23	47	8.17
Eric	French	4	19	22	4.63
Jimmy	Gooch	1	5	11	8.80
Tommy	Price	4	21	42	8.00
Trevor	Redmond	4	19	22	4.63
Eric	Williams	4	19	22	4.63
Freddie	Williams	4	22	39	7.09

NB: Jimmy Gooch and Ken Adams only rode in one of the meetings, the handicap one, so their averages are probably artificially high.

Towards the end of the season, the Lions staged a couple of challenge matches with Wimbledon. They won 67–40 at home, but then crashed 77–31 at Plough Lane. "Very tame Lions" said the headline in the *News*. Only Tommy Price won a race for the Lions, and the report said that Freddie Williams and Trevor Redmond were "shocking", and Eric Williams wasn't much better.

The *Star's* editor, John Anthony, said after this rout that the Wembley legend was rapidly evaporating: "The second strings have been scoring spasmodically throughout the season, and many of the Lions defeats can be traced to their failure to consistently outride their opposite numbers. Wembley are ... the back-bone of speedway. It is essential that they resume as soon as possible their previous invincibility."

Clearly this was not a happy Lions team. The Wembley management had reported Trevor Redmond to the SCB when he failed to turn up at Rayleigh for a Lions challenge match. He was fined £5 by the SCB. In October, the *Star's* Eric Linden presented his 'end of season awards'. The 'worst decline' was "Definitely Wembley at the end of the season, a year in which they won nothing. All the pep and fire seemed to go out of their riding. It had been a tough year for them, with all those away fixtures, and they gave the impression that they were darned glad to see the end of it. Only one rider escapes criticism, skipper Tommy Price. For an 'old un' he was terrific. (He'd have been terrific for a young one too)."

Linden's review of the Lions' season was equally damning: "Wembley third in a league of seven. Thus are the mighty fallen ... And that they were darned lucky to finish third. If they had run into anything like the number of injuries as Bradford they would have been in a sorry plight. Beg pardon, an even sorrier plight than they were... Only two of the team kept sparkling, in my eyes, for the whole of the season. He wasn't top scorer by a long way, but I'll hand the No.1 position to ... skipper Tommy Price.

After him I'll hand a smaller sized medal to Brian Crutcher, for his scoring power... You don't need me to tell you what Crutcher meant to Wembley. Just take a look at the scoring chart. He darn near racked up 300 league points. Nobody was within 100 of him among the other Lions. He was the only man to top the 200 mark in the side, and that's unusual in a team like Wembley's.

He practically doubled the total number of points scored by another rider in the Trophy. Lucky, lucky Wembley that Brian did not suffer the same decline as the Williams brothers, Trevor Redmond and Jimmy Gooch. ... Wembley were lucky regarding injuries. They had to use guest riders on only two occasions. Of the teams below them, Birmingham had nine, Bradford seven, Norwich four and West Ham seven.

And three of those teams, being Saturday sides when the guest rider scheme was liable to flop on its face, had to make up sides with novices on occasions. Something else that Wembley did not have to do. All in all, I reckon that in a way it was again a case of 'Lucky old Wembley' last year. They could rise to the heights though. If you saw the way they smacked it out, heat after heat, with deadly rivals Wimbledon, you'll know that without my spotlighting it.

But 'trouble' was the 1955 watchword for Wembley. Brian Crutcher made himself unpopular and finally landed himself up before the Control Board, with a habit of missing unofficial matches at Wimbledon. The crowd didn't like it, his team-mates were not particularly impressed by it either… Yet, through all [their] troubles, Wembley were still the biggest draw in the league. There was still a magic about the name which drew fans who might ordinarily have passed up a meeting.

And considering the great handicap of riding six home matches – all of which they won – and 18 away fixtures, they did do remarkably well. By virtue of riding more away league matches than any other side, they also won more. In all, they scored 11 out of a possible 36 away points. Now compare this: A percentage of very nearly 30, with Belle Vue's 27 per cent, Birmingham's 4 per cent, Bradford's 9 per cent, Norwich's 19 per cent, West Ham's 19 per cent or Wimbledon's 45 per cent … only one side topped them – the league champions.

Then, again, they did get through to the final of the National Trophy. And, but for the sorriest display they can have given in an uncountable number of years on their own track, they would have taken the Trophy.

There will undoubtedly be changes next season. An influx of new youngsters are needed, while a skipper like Tommy Price is still around to school them in the Wembley tradition. A tradition of victory and glory which should be jealously guarded. It has not been easy to make. It could be easy to break."

The *News* was also concerned about what was happening with the Lions. In November, it wondered what sort of season Sir Arthur is planning for Wembley in 1956? In 1955, the "riders were discontented and a proportion of the patrons were grumpy too. Will the Lions run a full league schedule, or just a dozen meetings?" RM Samuel wondered that if the two divisions amalgamated, would Wembley compete? He said that anything at the Stadium must be top grade. Could it be challenge matches, championships and the World Final? Wembley must make a profit for shareholders, anything staged there is costly and speedway was scarcely encouraging financially. However, he did believe that Sir Arthur would support speedway as far as he could.

Basil Storey joined in the debate a couple of weeks later in the *News*. He asked "What do Wembley have in mind? A strong, well supported Wembley is vital for speedway. Recent seasons have wrought a change at the Empire Stadium. The old Wembley dynamite has been missing. The streamlined line-up, for so long the most colourful in the game, has somehow lost character. Last season saw a sort of rebel policy – six league meetings with open meetings. In my view this certainly didn't help the sport."

He also said that it was alarming how Wembley's home crowds dwindled, and that it was more noticeable at the Empire Stadium. He said that an apathetic Wembley can have a disastrous effect overall.

Ken Adams was the only new recruit for the Lions in 1955.

He hoped that some of that old, concentrated Wembley dynamite of behind-the-scenes direction could spark off a speedway revival: "Wembley has terrific pulling power and Sir Arthur has a genius for inspired drive. And maybe the fact that he will be practically starting from scratch will fire his endeavour. The lost thousands, too, may be brought back, and the Lions team to be rebuilt." There was still a nucleus in Tommy Price, Brian Crutcher and Freddie Williams, although Crutcher was the only long term asset. He pointed out that some colourful characters had left – Split Waterman, Bill Kitchen, Bill Gilbert, Bruce Abernethy and George Wilks. Eric Williams was also leaving. Eric Williams emigrated to New Zealand, and did not return to England to ride again until 1960, when he joined New Cross.

He concluded that the glamour has gone to Wimbledon, but a strong Wimbledon can never be the same as Wembley. Another Wembley season like 1955 would be as good as nothing at all. In fact, the sport couldn't stand it.

In December, it was confirmed that there would – at last – be promotion and relegation between the two divisions. Wembley said that their home programme would start as usual, but Harringay confirmed that speedway would not be returning to Green Lanes. And soon another blow would hit speedway in London.

Bill Kitchen, Tommy Price and George Wilks,
three stalwarts of the Wembley Lions in the post war period. (MKC & JCA)

16. 1956: The last season

The year started – yet again – with a debate over amalgamation into one league. Coventry promoter Charles Ochiltree, a supporter of one league, commented that First Division fans had only seen 42 opposition riders in the 1955 season. Promotion and relegation was accepted, so at last the Second Division champions were guaranteed a place in the top flight. The 1955 Second Division champions, Poole, had been accepted into the First Division anyway. But the disappointment that Harringay would not be coming back into speedway was added to when it was confirmed in March that West Ham would not run. The Hammers had struggled on and off the track in 1955, and there had been regular reports that their promoter, Alan Sanderson, was trying to reach an agreement with the stadium owners for the team to continue. In March it was confirmed that this had not proved to be possible. Jack Young not returning to the UK and a fall in support were given as the main reasons for the Hammers' demise. Speedway would return to West Ham in 1964.

Club speedway never returned to Harringay. Another longstanding team who went under were Exeter, but speedway would be seen again at the County Ground.

Basil Storey said in the *News* in January that speedway now had two divisions of eight teams. The sport should aim for two divisions of 12 teams. He pointed out that 30 tracks had closed since the 'boom'. In fact, speedway ran in 1956 with two divisions of seven teams. Another change was a return to 14 heat meetings with teams of six riders and two reserves in the First Division. The guest rider scheme was abandoned.

Also in the *News*, Len Went said that it cost £450 a week to run a Second Division track. A gate of 4,500 would produce £400 after tax. The promoter would have to sell programmes, car parking and refreshments to make up the difference, let alone be in profit. Sir Arthur Elvin said in a speech that the Entertainment Tax was still a problem for sport, which was being "taxed to the point of extinction."

However, one positive point about 1956 was that – for the first time since 1950 – no teams pulled out of speedway during the season. Apart from the two professional divisions, the Southern Area League (SAL) continued to offer opportunities for new riders. However, the Lord's Day Observance Society caused problems for some of the tracks, who had to either change their race day, or charge for admission through programme sales or run a membership scheme. In those days it was illegal to charge for admission to a sports event on a Sunday. Membership schemes or admission by programme was a way of side-stepping the law!

In January, the *News* reported that things were quiet at Wembley. There was no talk of new signings or any major announcements. It said that the Lions fans should sit tight, something would be on the way. Alec Jackson would have something up his sleeve. However, Len Went also said that "Man for man, the present team represents the weakest bunch of Lions in post war years, if not for all time." Eric Williams had gone, and there was speculation about Trevor Redmond's future.

Eric Williams was a loss for the Lions. Although often outshone by his brother, RM Samuel wrote that he was a great trier, and in 1955 had shone, although he could be inconsistent. He also said that maybe his plans to emigrate had something to do with his indifference.

He had put in a transfer request, and the price put on him by the Wembley management meant that he stayed with the team for the rest of the season. Trevor Redmond had said that the programme Wembley had run in 1955 had made it difficult for a 'medium class' rider to make the sport pay.

Wembley did confirm that they would be running a full home programme of league matches. They also expected to open at their usual time, after the FA Cup and Rugby League Challenge Cup Finals were completed. In March, Wembley announced a long list of retained riders, but the reality was that five of them had either retired, emigrated, or – as with Bruce Abernethy and Freddie Lang – there was no realistic prospect of them returning to England. The seven other riders included Jimmy Gooch, who had mainly been riding for Swindon, and Dennis Newton, who had minimal top flight experience.

Split Waterman had been without a track since West Ham closed. He was running a garage in New Malden, so was keen to stay in London. Wembley welcomed him back. Two other recruits came from the SAL, Mike Broadbank and Merv Hannam. Broadbank was signed from Rye House for £150. He went on to have a very successful speedway career. Hannam was Brian Crutcher's uncle, although he was only four years older than his nephew. In 1955 he had ridden for Ringwood, and then Eastbourne after that track closed.

The Lions were also linked with a young Australian, Bill Bryden. He did not join the team, but another young Aussie, Ray Cresp, signed for the Lions in June. Recruiting Cresp meant the departure of Ken Adams, who returned to the Second Division by joining Ipswich. Apparently the fee for a one season loan was £30.

As the season was starting, there was also a change in the speedway trade press. The *Speedway News* had ceased publication in the middle of February. On 14 April, it merged with the *Speedway Star*. (It is referred to from now on as the '*Star*'.) The number of publications had gradually declined from the sport's 'boom' period.

The Lions started their season with a series of away meetings before opening at the Empire Stadium on 17 May. The Lions were the only team not to participate in the Inter-Divisional tournament. This was an early-season competition, organised somewhat haphazardly, and not an 'official' competition. The Second Division sides hosted up to three First Division teams. Eric Linden wrote that the Lions riders were upset at lost meetings, and there was no statement from Wembley about why they were not involved. Some thought that the Lions were being snobbish, although they had regularly ridden in challenge matches at Second Division tracks over the years.

The Lions lost their first two challenge matches, narrowly at Belle Vue and by 15 points at Wimbledon. Only Brian Crutcher, Eric French and Ken Adams showed any form at Plough Lane, and Adams was not given any extra rides from reserve. New team manager John Evans was very critical, saying that the whole team was unfit.

However, the Lions did make a promising start to their league campaign. A 'disappointing' crowd of just under 7,000 saw a thrilling 42–42 draw at Norwich, where there were never more than four points between the teams. Brian Crutcher scored a 12 point maximum, and Split Waterman only dropped one point to an opponent. Two weeks later, a similar size crowd saw the Lions win by 20 points over a weak Bradford side. Brian Crutcher again led the way with a maximum, Split Waterman was unbeaten by an opponent, and only a young Nigel Boocock challenged the Lions. A week later, the Lions won by 17 points at Birmingham. The Brummies couldn't match the Lions' all round strength. Ron Mountford stopped Crutcher recording a third maximum; Trevor Redmond was paid for 12 points, although his tally included three second places.

Three days before the Lions' opening night at home, they travelled to Poole for their first league encounter with the Pirates. The Pirates had beaten Birmingham (over two legs) and Norwich (at Wimborne Road) in the National Trophy in 1955. However, no one predicted their "almost unbelievable" 55–29 win. Price, Waterman, Williams and Redmond contributed just four points between them. Brian Crutcher won three heats before an engine failure in his last race, and was still clearly "master of the Poole track" according to the *Star*. The report added that Mike Broadbank put more into his riding – for six points – then the rest of the Wembley team, except for Crutcher and Eric French. He was clearly a star in the making.

After that, the last team that the Lions wanted to face twice in five days was the old enemy from Plough Lane. The lead changed hands four times at the Empire Stadium before Wimbledon pulled away to win 46–38 on a 'bumpy' track, as reported in the *Star*. A 5–1 in heat 12 by Peter Moore and Cyril Maidment clinched their win. More worryingly for Wembley supporters, the Lions only provided six heat winners. The *Star's* reporter said that Broadbank looked a winner, and Waterman and French looked set for good seasons. The rest needed a dose of the Dons' team spirit. To be fair to Brian Crutcher, he won three heats, and was clearly Wembley's top star. He was only 21 years old, and apart from his speedway commitments was running a garage. He had grown up fast since joining the Lions in 1953.

Crutcher did restore some pride for the Lions when he became the first rider to beat Ronnie Moore at Plough Lane in 1956, winning the first heat the following Monday. But Tommy Price was Wembley's only other heat winner in a 12 point defeat.

Things returned to normal in the Lions' subsequent home league matches. Birmingham, Belle Vue and Bradford were all comfortably beaten. The *Star* said that Belle Vue's riders, apart from Bob Duckworth, "were almost too shocking for words." Bradford were described as looking like a "mediocre Second Division team." After this match, Wimbledon were top of the First Division with 19 points from 14 matches; the Lions were fifth with 11 points from 10 matches.

Both Poole and Norwich made more of a fight of it at the Empire Stadium. Poole lost by six points on 14 June in the "best match at Wembley this season". This was partly due to good use of tactical reserves by Poole's manager John Rapson. An engine failure for Cyril Roger in heat 13 saw Waterman and French get a 5–1 to secure the match for the Lions. Norwich went down 48–35, although Ove Fundin contributed almost half their points with a 15 point maximum. The second halves for these meetings included either speed car or sidecar races – anything for some variety.

June also saw two major team changes for the Lions. Jimmy Gooch was loaned to Bradford for the rest of the season. The Odsal side were struggling; but Gooch found less success at Odsal than he had at the Empire Stadium. However, he went on to have a long and successful speedway career, including a World Final appearance.

Freddie Williams had opened a motorcycle business in Wembley in 1955. Bizarrely, this involved him having to take a test to have a licence to allow him to ride motorbikes on the road. His form had dropped in 1955 – his CMA had fallen from 8.89 in 1954 to 6.75. Danny Carter had written in the *Star* in May that Williams and Gooch's places in the team were in danger. Gooch had left, then, after a poor show by the Lions at Belle Vue, when they did not win a race or have a heat winner, Williams announced his retirement.

Interviewed by Tony McDonald (*Classic Speedway* 19), Williams said that he was "no longer riding as hard as I should have been". He had only scored a couple of points and said to Duncan King "That's it, I'm finished." King said that he would put in a reserve, but Williams said that he was "finished with speedway". The *Star* reported that close associates of the Welshman were not surprised, and there was not much likelihood of a comeback. Basil Storey said that Williams's retirement was a blow to Wembley, in spite of his indifferent form this season. Williams was only 30 years old. The Lions management were worried about the team, and Alec Jackson tried to talk him into a change of heart. Storey also said that "Attendances at the Empire Stadium this season have been shockingly low ... and although Williams has never been a particularly big crowd puller at other circuits, he has retained a good following at Wembley." The Wembley management regarded Williams's retirement decision as a calamity. Tommy Price was to retire at the end of the season, and Wembley's experienced riders were slipping out the back door as fast as promising new talent entered at the front.

While the Lions were fairly consistent at home, it was on the road that the team's weaknesses showed. They only won four times, and two of those were at Odsal, where the home team were struggling and finished bottom of the league. At Perry Barr, in a 50–32 defeat in June, the Lions only had two heat winners; Crutcher and Waterman did not win a heat between them. In early August, they conceded 50 points again at Poole, and then lost by 20 points at Norwich in their last away match of the season. Their only other away win, apart from their early season triumph at Birmingham, was at Belle Vue, when a Tommy Price maximum inspired a 10 point victory. The Lions did finish as runners-up in the league, with 29 points from their 24 matches, six points behind Wimbledon.

The National Trophy offered the Lions another chance for glory. They were drawn against Birmingham. The Lions lost the first leg by 14 points. The *Star* said that Brian Crutcher was "terrific" and was only beaten once, by Ron Mountford. Ray Cresp provided good support with nine from six rides. The match at Wembley had been scheduled to be on 19 July, but was rained off, so it became the second leg a week later.

The Lions missed out on winning the tie by one point. The *Star* reported that the Brummies went into the last heat needing a 5–1. Alan Hunt shot out of gate to beat Crutcher for the second time. Behind him, the Wembley pair battled it out with Doug Davies. Waterman pulled a big lock and Crutcher bounced off him to avoid his team mate; Davies shot around the outside and bounced off Crutcher. All three stayed on machines, Davies went after Hunt, and stayed there, fighting off Crutcher's every effort, resulting in the maximum that Birmingham needed. Ron Mountford had pulled out after one race, and the Brummies kept the Lions just in reach.

Crutcher was slightly off form, with 13 from six rides. Eric French was bang on form, with four heat wins; Cresp and Waterman both rode well. Tommy Price was excluded in heat 12 and his engine stalled in his next ride when he and Cresp were miles ahead. But for the Lions it was not to be. The Wembley programme the following week said that the Brummies had "two amazing slices of good luck – when Price's engine 'packed' when our skipper looked all over a winner, and when Crutcher and Waterman slid into each other in that final heat." However, they did give Birmingham credit for their "never-say-die spirit."

The Lions did better on the individual front; well Brian Crutcher did on their behalf. He won the World Championship qualifying round at the Empire Stadium with a maximum, and was the only Lion to qualify for the Final. Split Waterman missed out by a point. Tommy Price had to miss the qualifying rounds due to concussion.

The Final was the last meeting at the Empire Stadium in 1956. Staged on a Saturday night for the first time, a 65,000 crowd saw Ove Fundin win with 13 points. Crutcher finished eighth with nine points. He had been excluded after a fall in heat 16; second place in that heat, which was won by Fundin, would have put him in a run-off for third place.

Two weeks earlier, Crutcher became only the second Lion since the War to win the London Riders Championship. It was staged at Wembley for the first time since the War, and the field was just Wembley and Wimbledon riders. Crutcher beat Ronnie Moore in a run-off to win the competition.

New Lions in 1956: Left: Mike Broadbank; right: Ray Cresp.

Future Wembley star Ove Fundin leads Wembley's Brian Crutcher in the 1956 England versus Sweden test at Wembley. (MKC & JCA)

141

Over the years, Wembley had enjoyed little success in the Match Race Championship. In May and June Crutcher beat Ronnie Moore, then Barry Briggs and finally Alan Hunt. Peter Craven finally beat him in a run-off at Norwich in October. Crutcher said before the second leg against Hunt that "Golden Helmet racing has put the finishing touches to my racing experience: it has sharpened my gating technique".

On the international front, England had raced a three match series against Sweden, including one test at the Empire Stadium. Crutcher, Waterman and Price all appeared for England. Crutcher and Waterman also rode against Australasia; Ray Cresp made one appearance for the Australasia side. Waterman rode for England on an end-of season tour of Sweden, but Crutcher declined to ride, citing business responsibilities. He was criticised for this in the *Star*. Trevor Redmond made his usual trip to South Africa at the end of the season, accompanied by Ray Cresp.

Between the London Riders Championship and the World Final, the Lions met Wimbledon in a challenge match at the Empire Stadium. They included end-of season loan signing Gerald Jackson. They won 44–40, with a Crutcher maximum and 11 points from Tommy Price. It was a nice ending for Price to beat the old enemy from Plough Lane. And it was the final Wembley Lions home meeting for 13 years, although no one knew it at the time.

Angus Kix's season review of the Lions in the *Star* in November was headed "Wembley achieved ... Not a thing". This was a bit unfair – they had finished up as runners-up in the First Division, an improvement on the previous season when they had ridden so many away matches. He did praise Mike Broadbank, who he said would merit a full team place in 1957. He said that Ray Cresp had the potential to be one of the Lions' top three in 1957. He thought that Split Waterman was a far better rider than when he first rode for the Lions, albeit less spectacular. Eric French also was praised, and was still the 'backbone' of the team. The Lions would miss Tommy Price, who had finished as the Lions' second top scorer. But only Brian Crutcher had enhanced his reputation in 1956.

The Lions programme had said there had been a series of wet Thursdays. Maybe one indicator of falling support was that the Supporters Club now did a draw for free tickets, using membership numbers rather than members' birthdays. Of the winners' membership numbers, none were over 10,000; one indicator of the reduced numbers following the Lions.

The thorny question of amalgamation into one league was again discussed in the autumn in the *Star*. Their midlands correspondent, Howard Jacobi, often no friend of the Lions, asked whether it would be "Wembley versus The Rest" on this question. He felt that the Second Division had no future. He was borne out, but sadly because of the sport's decline, not strength. Danny Carter wrote in November that supporters of amalgamation would be prepared to go ahead without Wembley if needs be.

In December the Lions announced a list of 17 retained riders for 1957. But only seven were realistic starters for the new season, eight if Jimmy Gooch was included. Others were permanently overseas, or retired.

The sport's ongoing problems were shown when Odsal withdrew from speedway in December. The team had struggled in 1956; the stadium could hold 100,000 people and must have lacked atmosphere with crowds of less than 10,000. The stadium lacked cover for the terraces as well, which hit attendances at both speedway and rugby league, which was starting to decline. The sport did return to Bradford in 1957 for part of the season.

One issue that seems to have receded was competition from stock car racing. Maybe the novelty had worn off, but there was little mention of it in the speedway press.

17. Mister Wembley

Wembley is a London suburb similar to many other areas in the suburban belt around central London. But one feature has made the name world famous. Wembley Stadium is an iconic international sporting venues. In British sport, it has staged the FA Cup Final since 1923, most of the important England international matches and many other domestic football matches. In rugby league, older players talk about how many 'Wembleys' they played in – meaning appearances in the Rugby League Challenge Cup Final. Internationally, in football it staged the 1966 World Cup Final and 1996 European Championship Final; the Olympic Games in 1948 and football in the 2012 Games. And away from sport, concerts such as Live Aid in 1985 which was broadcast world-wide from Wembley. The Empire Pool, today known as the Wembley Arena, was used during the 1948 Olympics, was the home of the Wembley Ice Hockey teams for many years, as well as staging concerts and many other forms of entertainment and sport.

Speedway is often overlooked in the numerous histories of Wembley Stadium. But without the regular income from speedway and greyhound racing, it is hard to see how the Stadium could have survived on a handful of football matches each year.

Sir Arthur Elvin was the driving force behind Wembley from when he purchased the Stadium in 1927. He had ran tobacco kiosks during the Great Exhibition on the site from 1924; and then agreed to purchase the Stadium from Jimmy White in 1927. White then committed suicide, and Sir Arthur managed to raise enough money in two weeks to take control of the Stadium. At the age of 28 he was managing director of the Wembley Stadium and Greyhound Racecourse Company, which became Wembley Stadium Ltd. He ran it for the rest of his life. Had he not taken it over, according to Simon Inglis in *Played in London*, "… with only one football match guaranteed (the FA Cup Final) and one international every two years (v. Scotland), the stadium would have been demolished."

Greyhound racing was established in 1927, and then the new sport of speedway in 1929. He realised that anything connected with Wembley had to be of a high quality, and – despite obstruction and opposition from other promoters – developed a strong team. He also developed the idea of a Supporters Club as part of the speedway business.

As outlined earlier, the first few speedway meetings had only attracted a handful of fans. He employed Johnnie Hoskins to develop the team and find new riders. AM Low, in his book *Wonderful Wembley*, comments on the Supporters Club: "In essence, like most good ideas, this one was very simple. By offering various small concessions, advertising by word of mouth, and offering the attraction of new riders, the Supporters' Club came into being and grew rapidly. There were soon 10,000 enrolled – four times the total average attendance of the first meetings." The speedway team turned the corner, and was soon attracting 25,000 a week. By the second season, 1930, the Supporters Club had 25,000 members. By 1931, they were the top team in the country. Sir Arthur also developed the idea of interval attractions. Some of the early ones involved Alec Jackson, who later became the Lions manager. However, one – involving two cars which were being driven while on fire – nearly ended in disaster, and Wembley took more care in future, according to Low.

AM Low describes the immaculate organisation of Wembley speedway meetings: "The Wembley organisation was drilled to perfection by Arthur Elvin's passion for getting every detail exactly right." He outlines how every member of the track staff knew exactly what they had to do and when to do it.

Also, the facilities made available to the Wembley riders, both in terms of physical fitness and workshops and mechanics for their bikes, were better than any other team. The quality of second halves at Wembley meetings were also among the nest in the sport.

There was, particularly once the post-war boom years in the sport were over, debate in the speedway press about the amount of influence that Wembley – and Sir Arthur – had on the sport. Another question about the post-war Lions is whether they were 'too successful', which is considered in more detail in the next chapter. Clearly, he did believe that a smaller, elite top division was best for the sport – and Wembley. However, what is not in dispute is that he was a great fan – and supporter – of speedway. He realised the importance of the Lions for speedway's credibility as a national sport. His unexpected death on 4 February 1957 while on a cruise was a great blow to the sport.

The *Star* on 23 February 1957 included a tribute by Basil Storey to the man he called "the sport's greatest champion". He said that "speedway racing has lost its greatest and most powerful friend. Powerful … because of his dynamic drive and personality he virtually ruled the sport. Friend … because he loved his speedway and wielded his power to further the sport and nurse it, even in the current dark days of the 1950s."

Storey said that "drivel" had been written about the "alleged harmful influence of Wembley's power in speedway." He argued that Wembley was a "beacon of hope" as track after track closed. His involvement made it possible to secure more press coverage in an often hostile Fleet Street environment.

Storey talked about the "mere handful of spectators at Wembley's vast stadium on Lions' Night." He continued "Yet, the man who should have been the most despondent of all, Sir Arthur Elvin, remained doggedly at his speedway post. In spite of his legion of other money-spinning interest, he stayed loyal to speedway." Storey said that he was 'Mister Speedway' and that "we shall never again see his like". He concluded that the sport was "greatly indebted to him".

Interviewed in Phillip Dalling's *The Golden Age of Speedway*, Freddie Williams points out that Wembley meant more to the sport than just status: "What was not generally realised was that Elvin and Wembley were indirectly financially subsidising the other surviving Division One tracks, particularly in London." Apparently the Lions received 10 per cent of the gate from away meetings, and the reverse applied when the Lions were at home. Because the Lions' gates were larger than the other teams, this gave the other teams some financial support.

Sir Arthur had been made MBE in 1945, and a Freeman of the Borough of Wembley. He was knighted in 1946. When he died he was on a cruise to South Africa to try to improve his ailing health. He was buried at sea, off the coast of Madeira.

He was mourned by people in a wide variety of sports and the wider community. A friend and fellow Wembley resident, Lord Walter Citrine, the former General Secretary of the TUC, wrote in *The Times* "The passing of Arthur Elvin will be mourned by a wide circle of friends such as few men are privileged to possess. He gathered together at the many functions, entertainments, and sports events at Wembley men and women distinguished in almost every phase of public, economic and social life." Citrine also said that he "prided himself on maintain a standard of clean and enjoyable entertainment… He was supreme as an organiser and inwardly fumed when any infringement of his high standards occurred."

The new Wembley Stadium has a bust of Sir Arthur in its entrance hall. The old stadium had the bust above the gates to the Royal Tunnel, facing Olympic Way. It looked down onto the crowds flocking to the stadium along the road which he had built for the 1948 Olympics.

Sir Arthur Elvin

A question that cannot be answered is whether even Sir Arthur would have been able to continue running the speedway team, in the face of ongoing losses and the opposition of his fellow directors. As Freddie Williams said "We should never forget that despite his love for speedway, Elvin was first and foremost a businessman ... Whether [his] head would eventually have overruled his heart is again something we can only guess at."

In the same edition of the *Star* as Basil Storey's tribute, Danny Carter wondered "whether there will be any Lions" for the 1957 season. Sadly, within three weeks that question would be answered.

Left: The programme from the 1956 World Championship Final.

Right: The programme from the last Wembley Lions home meeting in 1956.

18. The Lions leave speedway

The sad death of Sir Arthur Elvin also saw speedway lose his team. On 14 March, the remaining Wembley Stadium board members announced that the Lions would be withdrawing from league speedway and that all the Lions riders were available for transfer.

In 1949, the four directors of Wembley Stadium were Sir Arthur Elvin, WH McGrath, Lieutenant Colonel Hon Arthur C Murray, and Captain AE Brice. In March 1951, Arthur Murray became the third Viscount Elibank. His background was in politics and the Army, and he does not seem to have had any particular sporting interests. Captain Brice was director of greyhound racing at Wembley. WH McGrath was a barrister and Queen's Counsel.

In July 1955, Sir Bracewell Smith joined the board. He was a business man and politician as well as chairman of Arsenal FC. The last board meeting Sir Arthur Elvin attended was on 24 January 1957. There was a meeting on 13 February with only four directors present, and Sir Bracewell Smith in the chair. Their next meeting was on 14 March, and it was these four directors who took the decision to close down the speedway team.

On 30 March, the *Star* published a letter from KW Innes saying that he had written to the Wembley Stadium directors protesting at the decision. He also wondered whether the Supporters Club had been consulted about the closure. The *Star* said that they had received "dozens of letters from Wembley fans expressing indignation at the closing of their track."

However, the *Star* also said that Wembley Stadium was a 'commercial venture' and that the Wembley directors clearly did not think that league speedway was a viable financial proposition at the moment. It said that the terraces had been "sparsely lined" at Wembley on most occasions in 1956. The heavy costs in running a huge arena such as Wembley meant substantial losses on each meeting. The article said that West Ham faced the same issue, and maybe smaller venues such as New Cross, Hackney Wick and Walthamstow would be more viable at the moment. In fact, New Cross and Hackney did stage speedway again when the Provincial League started.

In the same edition of the *Star*, Danny Carter wondered how much damage Wembley pulling out would do. Ronnie Greene, the chairman of the Promoters Association, commented: "It's no use thinking that their loss is not a blow. But to suggest that it is the end of speedway is an awful lot of rubbish."

Carter said that "people who allocate publicity space in national newspapers aren't going to think that way, unless they see signs of speedway staging a comeback, even to a small extent, this year. It's up to the promoters now."

The World Final would still be staged at Wembley, and the Stadium continued to stage one big meeting a year until 1981. In 1964, the first test match against the Soviet Union was held at Wembley, and attracted a crowd of 26,000. But for now, the Lions were no more.

Of the 1956 Lions, Freddie Williams had already retired, and Tommy Price had said that 1956 was going to be his last season. Brian Crutcher returned to the south coast with Southampton, before he retired at the start of the 1960 season, aged just 25.

Split Waterman rode for Wimbledon in 1957, then Southampton before switching to the Provincial League with New Cross. In his final season, 1962, he rode for Ipswich and then Belle Vue. Eric French, already in the veteran stage of his career, rode for Rayleigh in 1957 before retiring.

Jimmy Gooch rode for a number of clubs in a successful career which finished at Hackney in 1970. He and Mike Broadbank were the only riders whose careers covered both post-war Wembley eras. Broadbank rode until 1977, at his peak in the 1960s featured in five world finals, and regularly rode for England. Ray Cresp rode consistently until he retired in 1966 at the age of 38. Merv Hannam did not ride in senior speedway after 1956 apart from a brief spell at Southampton in 1960.

Trevor Redmond continued to ride until 1964, and then developed his promoting ambitions full-time, leading to his return to Wembley in 1970 as joint promoter

As the sport declined in the second half of the 1950s, it became more difficult for riders to find teams. In 1957, there were 11 teams in the National League; 10 in 1958 and just nine in 1959, although there was also a second team competition run by the National League sides. The SAL also continued to run, but never with more than five teams.

The sport turned the corner in 1960, with the launch of the Provincial League. This led to the merger in 1965 that created the British League, which in 1970 saw the return of the Lions to league speedway.

But before looking at that period, it is important to look at the reasons both for the withdrawal of the Lions from the National League and the decline in speedway in the first half of the 1950s. The decline of support for the Lions has to be seen in the context of the sport's overall decline, from 34 teams in the late 1940s to just 11 in 1957. But arguably there were issues specific to Wembley.

The Lions under Sir Arthur Elvin had to win and had to be successful. But one of the dilemmas for speedway as a sport is that a dominant team can produce one-sided home matches. The Lions were always a great attraction on the road, but at home, some of the provincial teams had a bad reputation for providing weak opposition. A letter in the *Speedway Star* in 1956 said that the writer "had even been to the Bradford match" at Wembley to show his dedication to the sport.

When teams came twice or even three times to the Empire Stadium because of the relatively small size of the First Division, it is not surprising that fans at times voted with their feet. Wembley tried to counter this in 1955 by one staging one home meeting against each team in the league, and running individual meetings instead. This may have temporarily helped the Lions on the business side (the lack of information on attendances makes it hard to assess), but it clearly damaged morale among the riders and undermined both the credibility of the First Division as a competition and their chances of winning it.

Of the teams who conceded 60 points, Birmingham 'led the way' with six matches, Belle Vue and Odsal were on four, West Ham and Norwich three, Harringay two and Bristol and Wimbledon one each. Obviously the number of times the teams had ridden at Wembley from 1946 to 1956 varied, but it does show the problem of some teams as an attraction. A 50 point score meant at least a 16 point win for the Lions in 14 heat matches; so in 11 seasons, just under two-thirds of home meetings were won by this margin by the Lions. And just under 18 per cent of home matches saw the Lions score 60 points, at least a 36 point winning margin in 14 heat matches.

One sided meetings was not solely a problem for the Lions. But they were, from 1946 to 1956, the most consistently strong team. Wimbledon were the top side from 1954 onwards, but they had not always been one of the top sides in post-war speedway.

The lack of close home meetings is shown by the table below.

Wembley home league matches at the Empire Stadium

Season	Number of matches	Lions Score 50+	Percentage	Lions Score 60+	Percentage
1946	10	5	50%	0	0%
1947	12	9	75%	2	16.5%
1948	2	1	50%	1	50%
1949	21	8	38%	2	9.53%
1950	16	10	63%	2	12.5%
1951	16	10	63%	2	12.5%
1952	18	14	78%	6	33.3%
1953	8	7	88%	0	0%
1954	14	9	64%	3	21.4%
1955	6	4	67%	3	50%
1956	12	7	58%	3	25%
Totals	**135**	**84**	**62%**	**24**	**17.8%**
1955	55 points + (16 heats)			1955: 65	
1948	Excludes league matches at Wimbledon				

Another issue that faced the Lions in their declining years was having a small crowd in a massive stadium. Even if the Lions were still attracting 20,000 to home meetings in 1956, in a stadium that held 100,000 – and many of the fans would have remembered the huge crowds of the 1940s – there must have been a lack of atmosphere. The same issue faced the other London tracks who closed in this period – West Ham with their 80,000 capacity; Harringay who were drawing 6,000 in 1954 to a 40,000 capacity arena; and New Cross with 5,000 in a stadium that held around 30,000.

The Lions were often criticised by some of the regular speedway columnists for failing to recruit young riders. But, the Lions signed and developed a young Jimmy Gooch, and then, in 1953, the 18-year-old Brian Crutcher. Mike Broadbank and Ray Cresp were new recruits in 1956. The team did evolve in the 1950s, although whether the Lions needed Eric French in 1953, when he could have played a more prominent role with a more struggling team, is debateable. It is interesting to note that French had his best season with Wembley in 1956, when the Williams brothers had gone, and more responsibility fell onto his shoulders. The Lions also gave Fred Lang his chance, although a year's experience in the Second Division could have helped him more than riding for the Lions.

Similarly, could foreign European riders have made a difference? Certainly, there was interest in some of the Swedish riders that started to appear in Britain in the early 1950s, but this was a wider question for speedway overall, not just Wembley. Rune Sormander made little impact in his short spell with the Lions. International stars were a draw, and may have slowed the fall in crowds, but the other problems and changes the sport faced were too large for them to have made a major difference. The Lions did not lack for stars and glamour. However, for most of this period, the SRA only allowed foreign riders to have short spells at clubs, such as Wilbur Lamoreaux's with Wembley in 1948. Once they were allowed to become regular team members, they could have more impact, such as Ove Fundin at Norwich. The

SRA, from a trade union standpoint, were protecting their members' jobs; but this did not help the sport overall.

Wembley were hit by the loss of the other London tracks from 1953 to 1956. The 'derby' matches against Harringay, West Ham and New Cross were often closer than meetings with some of the provincial teams, and presumably they also brought in more away supporters. The London Cup was a big draw and the two-leg finals semi-finals could be a very big attraction. In some ways, this was a vicious circle. The mid-season closure of New Cross hit the sport hard. Harringay, whose stadium was also owned by the GRA, were next to go. Stock cars appearing on the scene at both stadiums added to speedway's frustration. West Ham struggled on the track in 1955, and the loss of Jack Young, combined with falling gates saw their departure at the end of 1955.

The departure of the Lions has to be seen in the context of the decline of speedway nationally in the 1950s. It is easy to look back and criticise the way the sport was run; but there were decisions that could have been made that could have made a difference.

Two issues stand out: the size of the First Division, and the lack of any consistent policy to try to keep teams at the same level. Clearly, when teams were promoted from the Second Division, they often struggled. The lack of a consistent promotion – and relegation – policy also undermined the league structure. In other sports, particularly football, winning the Second Division meant something; this was not the case in speedway.

When teams were promoted, there was little support for them. For teams such as Norwich and Bristol, their stars could cope with the First Division, but often their second strings couldn't, especially away from home. For Norwich, a rider such as Bill Gilbert became a leading rider for them, but couldn't have got a team place at Wembley when he came out of retirement to join the Stars. In reality, the control on transfers was not enforced by the SCB. They could have used the New Cross riders better to even up team strengths, although this was made more complicated because some wanted to stay in London. Eric French could have been a heat leader at most of the provincial teams, rather than making Wembley even stronger.

International riders could have been allowed more, and the restrictive practices of the SRA in the early 1950s, while understandable in terms of protecting their members' jobs, did not help the development of the sport overall. People wanted to watch the top star riders. One reason that Norwich survived for so long was the presence of Ove Fundin. While Olle Nygren would probably not have saved New Cross in 1953, he may have kept some supporters watching the team.

To be fair to the people running speedway at this time, the sport had only run for 11 seasons after its launch in 1928 prior to 1946 (i.e. taking 1929 as the first season of team meetings.) It takes time for a new sport to establish a structure. For example, rugby league until the First World War and in the 1920s and 1930s had teams that closed for lack of support or even failed to finish a season. Football, although well-established locally, developed a league structure gradually. Both these sports had clubs which were long established, which was something speedway lacked.

Speedway was run on commercial basis and couldn't sustain losses for most promoters, unlike football, cricket or rugby league. Also, usually the teams did not own their stadiums, although this was not an issue for the Wembley Lions. However, in 1948 the Lions had to move to Wimbledon for six months because of the Olympics, always started later than other teams because of the stadium's football and rugby league commitments and in 1954 did not start home meetings until the end of May because the stadium was let to Dr Billy Graham for his evangelical Christian meetings.

The issue of stadium ownership did contribute to instability as the sport declined. The stadium owners could restrict how often stadiums could be used, and on which evenings. Even where the stadium also ran the speedway, such as Harringay, alternatives such as stock cars could take over if they offered more income in the short-tem.

And there was a rent to be paid to the owners by the speedway promoters. The stadiums speedway used were commercial ventures – and could stage any sport. For example, Mitcham Stadium in south London was considered for speedway in the 1940s. It had staged rugby league before the war, but the owner, Sydney Parkes, really wanted a licence to run greyhound meetings. When this was refused in the summer of 1936, the rugby league team only lasted for another eight months and the stadium was a white elephant until it was demolished in the mid-1950s.

Other sports' attendances dropped after the post-war boom, but it was very rare for teams to go out of business; mainly because they were better established in the community. County cricket and some rugby league teams were members' clubs; in football there were strict limits on the dividends that directors could receive at this time. Often they were local businessmen; running their club was often seen as a service to the community and often carried considerable local prestige.

There were also factors that were out of control of speedway. One of the key ones was the Entertainment Tax. Ironically, it finished in 1957; too late to save many tracks which had become unviable partly because of it. It was seen as unfair for two reasons – for much of the post-war period the rate charged on speedway was higher than other spectator sports. Secondly, it was a tax on revenue, rather than profits. A promotion could be making a loss, but still have to pay a substantial amount of their gate receipts in tax.

A second factor in speedway's decline at this time was the growth in television. This affected other forms of live entertainment and sport; and the growth of television ownership and availability has been outlined in the chapters above. In an age today where we use screens all the time for entertainment, information and work; it is hard to imagine the enormous change that the arrival of television was. The impact of being able to watch live pictures in people's own living rooms – for free apart from the cost of the set and the licence fee – must have been enormous.

There were other social changes in the 1950s. Food came off ration, resulting in a change in household expenditure, with more spent on food which was now more widely available. There was a growth in ownership of household appliances such as refrigerators and washing machines. Frozen food sales grew enormously. Motoring, to some extent, also grew once petrol was no longer rationed, although arguably mass car ownership did not arrive until the 1960s. There was a more stable society, with close to full employment. The post-war baby boom also saw the people who had come home from the war settle down and have families. All this reduced the amount ordinary people had to spend on live sport and time to watch it.

The sport survived – just. And 13 long years after the closure of the original Wembley Lions, a new team was born. Their story is told in the next part of this book.

Programme from the Great Britain versus USSR test at Wembley in 1964.

Part Three: 1970 and 1971

19. The Lions reborn

"One man's loss is another man's gain" is an old saying; and very true of speedway at this time. With an arguably better managed structure than in the past, there were a limited number of places in the British League. For a new team to join the league, another team closed – or sometimes later on accepted demotion to the Second Division. While Wembley's return to league speedway was welcome news in north west London, and generally in speedway as a whole, it did mean the closure of Coatbridge.

In 1948, the redevelopment of Wembley to stage the Olympic Games caused huge problems for the Lions that season. It was another athletics event, the 1970 Commonwealth Games, which led to the demise of the Edinburgh Monarchs, and the subsequent place for the Lions in the British League's First Division in 1970.

In the 1968 *British Speedway Handbook*, Ian Hoskins, Edinburgh's promoter from 1960 to 1967, wrote that "With the closure of Old Meadowbank due to redevelopment for the 1970 Commonwealth Games project, Scottish speedway lost its finest venue, and Edinburgh will be without the sport for the first time since 1960. A tragedy, as the Monarchs finished 1967 with their greatest team and their most successful season to date."

The Monarchs had finished fourth in the league. Reidar Eide and Bert Harkins had been regular performers for the Monarchs, and Brian Collins appeared in six meetings.

Ian Hoskins recalled in his book, the *History of the speedway Hoskins*, that he was approached by Allied Promotions to switch his licence to Reading, but he wanted to keep the team in Scotland for the loyal Edinburgh supporters. This was, he said on reflection, "a costly mistake". He had approached the Powderhall Greyhound Stadium in Edinburgh, to move the Monarchs there, but had been turned down. The owners admitted later that they had made a mistake in rejecting his offer, and the sport was subsequently staged there.

Instead, he moved the team to Coatbridge, and they took that name. They rode at Albion Rovers FC, five miles from Glasgow and 30 from Edinburgh. It was too far for the Edinburgh fans, and not enough locals came. So when Trevor Redmond and Bernard Cottrell contacted him to say that they had agreed with Wembley Stadium that they could run speedway there, he cut his losses and "soon signed away my Scottish speedway inheritance." In 1967, Trevor Redmond had sold the Glasgow Tigers to Danny Taylor, who subsequently sold the team to Les Whaley. This was Redmond's last speedway promotion before Wembley returned.

The *Star* reported on 9 January 1970 that the story that league speedway would return to Wembley was 'gathering momentum'. A proposal for a season of 12 meetings had been turned down, but now 20 dates were available, making a British League season viable. The report said that one of the current First Division teams could move into Wembley. A week later, Eric Linden reported that it was Trevor Redmond who was "fighting to establish a right to open speedway at Wembley". The key decision would be taken by the British League Promoters Association conference. The report also mentioned that Japanese rider Jimmy Ogisu had been in contact with Redmond. This rider featured regularly in the *Star* at this time, but never rode for the Lions. Although it was not covered in the press, Bernard Cottrell was behind the bid, and was working with Trevor Redmond. Cottrell provided the financial backing, Trevor Redmond had the speedway contacts.

As well as being a former Wembley rider, Redmond had considerable experience in promoting the sport. He had regularly ridden and promoted in South Africa in the 1950s, then promoted an open season at St Austell in 1958, Provincial League seasons at Neath in 1962 and St Austell in 1963, and then Glasgow from 1964 to the start of 1967. He had also promoted stock cars and super-rods at Newton Abbott and St Austell.

Two weeks later, James Oldfield confirmed that Wembley had bid to take over the Coatbridge licence. He said this was "appealing for southern speedway followers and appalling for the Scottish speed devotees." The Empire Stadium was available for 21 meetings, including the World Team Cup. He said that the Division One promoters would spend a lot of time deciding about whether Wembley should join the league. The "return of regular speedway to the Empire Stadium will be a tremendous boost for speedway, but ... if the promotion is not a success – a regular gate of 10,000 is an estimated break even figure – then Wembley's withdrawal after one season would be a bitter blow." Saturday had been identified as the Lions regular race night. This avoided any clashes with the other London tracks, but six other First Division teams staged their home meetings on Saturday nights.

On 30 January, it was confirmed that the British League Promoters Association had accepted Wembley's application. The Lions were back! There were to be 16 Saturday dates, three Wednesdays and a Monday (which was never actually used) and the World Team Cup. The first home meeting would be on 30 May, reflecting the growth in the length of the football season since the 1950s.

It was unlikely that all the Coatbridge riders would switch to Wembley. Reidar Eide was seen as a probable starter, and there would be a work permit for another foreign rider. In the Star, Dave Stevens commented: "Everyone wishes the Lions well. Their return to regular speedway will do the sport a power of good and one would hope for the immediate benefit of greater press coverage for the sport. Wembley has, and always will have, a magic name that should get the scribes running around for a speedway story.... Great revival of our sport which culminated last week in Wembley's return to league racing."

In February, Peter Oakes wrote in the *Star* that some fans were – unsurprisingly – very bitter about the move. However, the week before, one of their Scottish correspondents, Jock Anderson, had said that it would have been financial suicide to keep Coatbridge running.

The 1969 Monarchs had been strong at home, but weak away. They finished 11th out of 19 in the league table. Four of their top five riders moved to Wembley: Reidar Eide, Bert Harkins, Wayne Briggs and Brian Collins. Third heat leader George Hunter moved to Newcastle. Doug Templeton was a veteran of Scottish speedway and did not move to Wembley; nor did Alex Hughson and Alistair Brady.

The third heat leader slot was filled when Swedish veteran Ove Fundin signed for the Lions. While still one of the biggest names in the sport – he had won the world title for the fifth time in 1967 – he had business and speedway commitments in Sweden. Apparently he told Trevor Redmond that he wanted to come, but only if his wife Mona agreed. When she did, he signed up for the Lions. There had been speculation in the *Star* about him signing for a 'northern' track before Wembley came on the scene.

At the beginning of March, the *Star* carried a major interview by Harold Hastings with Bernard Cottrell. The Wembley-based businessman's office overlooked the stadium. He had risen from being a newspaper boy as a youngster, and had once sold a paper to Sir Arthur Elvin! He was a Wembley fan in the 'old days' and now made his living from garages, showrooms and restaurants.

He wanted to have more than racing at the meetings, with "well-known disc jockeys" and "stars from the entertainment world" involved, as well as cheerleaders. He said that already supporters from the 1950s were contacting him about the dates of meetings. He was hoping for 25,000 to 30,000 fans to attend the opening night. He said that the top price for tickets would be 16 shillings, and the lowest six shillings, with half price for children.

The Supporters Club was to be relaunched, and he was proud of having the 'number 1' membership card. He hoped that Bill Kitchen would become the team manager. Hastings concluded that "His enthusiasm and courage deserve success."

While the heat leader positions were sorted out, and Brian Collins and Wayne Briggs were First Division standard 'second strings', the Lions were not strong at reserve. Des Lukehurst was recruited from Second Division Romford. Another possibility was Stan Stevens, who had been released by West Ham, but he was not keen to ride for a Saturday track because he had a lucrative job on a newspaper that night. Graeme Smith and Brian Davies were other names mentioned in connection with the Lions. Trevor Redmond told the *Star* that overall he was happy with the team, but was hoping to sign one more former international rider. He said "I'm hoping for big things from the Scots boys in the squad. Harkins is a great character as well as a very good rider, and this boy Collins is going to shake a few people."

New Zealander Graeme Smith, who had ridden for Hackney and Rayleigh in 1969, but had fallen out with promoter Len Silver, was allocated to the Lions. Interviewed by Tony McDonald in *Backtrack* (issue 47), Smith recalled that he had been allocated to the Lions in 1970 and "With hindsight it's my biggest regret in speedway that I didn't join them. I think I would have learned a lot more by riding in the First Division and made my mark." He said that he was offered a good financial deal by Trevor Redmond, who was annoyed to be turned down, but Smith had given his word to veteran promoter Johnnie Hoskins that he would join Canterbury, and did not want to renege on that commitment. He could have added to the Lions' strength in the lower half of the team in the first half of the season.

Off the track, Bernard Cottrell and Trevor Redmond set up a new company, Wembley Speedway Limited, in February. The new company's objects were quite broad:
"1. To promote, manage, conduct and participate in Motor Cycle Speedway Racing, Stock Car Racing, Motor Cycle Racing, Motor Car Racing, Motor Car Rallying and Motor Cycle Rallying.
2. To acquire and manage Motor Cycle and Motor Car Racing Tracks, Public Arenas, Sports Stadiums, any place of entertainment or any place for the conduct of any sport.
3. To promote, manage, conduct and participate in any public entertainment, sport, pastime or game. 4. To carry on business as Restaurant Proprietors, Licenced Victuallers, Tobacconists, Publishers, Club Promoters and Managers and to make, buy or sell or otherwise deal in sports requisites, motor cars, motor cycles and motor car and motor cycle accessories."

Cottrell and Redmond were the first directors, along with Redmond's wife. Cottrell's wife was also a shareholder, although Cottrell and Redmond held 49 shares each, and their wives one each. The company was set up as a private limited company on 9 March 1970.

There is no indication that the company ever planned to run anything except speedway. This formulation was probably used by Trevor Redmond at other tracks where he was the promoter, and did allow the company flexibility to promote different events. He did later run stock cars at Wembley (see chapter 23) but under a different company.

The track being relaid in 1970. The stadium is very different from the 1950s – the roof was extended to cover the terracing in the 1960s. (JSC)

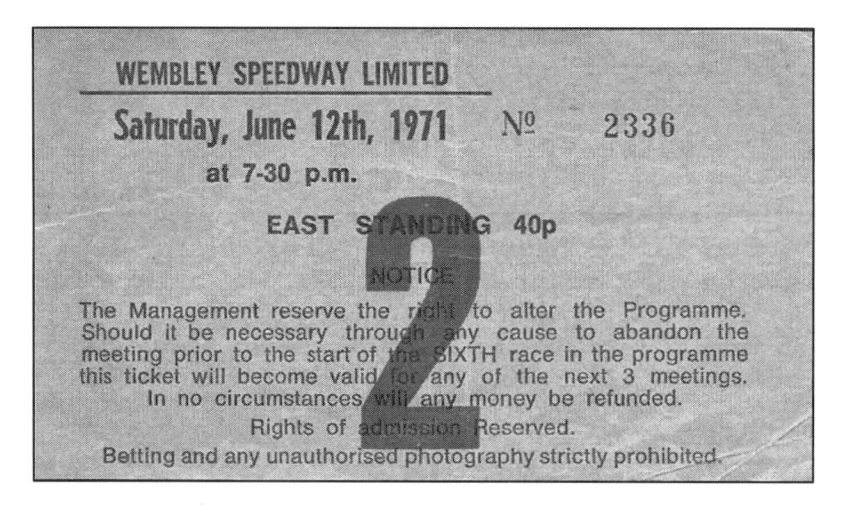

WEMBLEY SPEEDWAY LIMITED
Saturday, June 12th, 1971   Nº   2336
at 7-30 p.m.

EAST STANDING 40p

NOTICE

The Management reserve the right to alter the Programme. Should it be necessary through any cause to abandon the meeting prior to the start of the SIXTH race in the programme this ticket will become valid for any of the next 3 meetings. In no circumstances will any money be refunded.
Rights of admission Reserved.
Betting and any unauthorised photography strictly prohibited.

An admission ticket for 1971.

20. 1970: Back on track

The significance of the return of the historically biggest name in the sport to team racing was not really acknowledged in the fixtures. While, as with their predecessors, the Lions had to ride a series of away meetings before opening at the Empire Stadium, surely a more glamorous fixture could have been found that a Friday night challenge match at Newport! A match at Wimbledon – renewing the great rivalry of the 1950s – would have been better, although there was always the risk that the Lions might be heavily beaten by a strong Wimbledon team, undermining the whole project.

Wembley had a programme of 11 scheduled away meetings before 30 May. The challenge match at Newport on Good Friday resulted in a two point defeat. Bob Radford's report in the *Star* gave the team a very positive write up, saying that the Lions should add 'plenty of glamour' to the league. Ove Fundin missed the meeting, and guest Dave Gifford scored just one point in his place. Wayne Briggs top scored with a 12 point maximum, and the Lions would have got a draw, but for an uncharacteristic last place for Reidar Eide in the rerun heat 13.

Five days later, the Lions went to Poole, the 1969 Champions, and won 41–37 at Wimborne Road. Barry Briggs was seen helping Ove Fundin in the pits. The Pirates had been unbeaten at home in the league in 1969, but with Eide, Fundin and Bert Harkins scoring 30 points between them, a 4–2 in the last race confirmed the Lions' first league win. Their main weakness was at reserve, where Stan Stevens and George Barclay contributed one point between them.

The Lions could not repeat this form over the next eight weeks. They won at Cradley Heath 40–37 on 9 May, but lost five more league matches and two challenge matches. Their worst results were 49–29 at King's Lynn and 48–29 at Swindon. Ove Fundin had scored nine from five rides at Swindon and repeated the score at Coventry. However, his absence from the match at King's Lynn, resulted in "several thousand extremely long faces" according to Martin Rogers in the *Star*. His plane had been delayed because of fog in Copenhagen. Many of the Kings Lynn supporters would have remembered Fundin from his days with Norwich. The Lions used rider-replacement, and went down by 20 points. As identified early on by the Lions management, the team's main weakness was at reserve. Reidar Eide was an established number one, Fundin and Harkins were clearly heat leader class, and Brian Collins and Wayne Briggs were both adequate second strings, although Collins improved more as the season went on. But Des Lukehurst and Tim Bungay, who were the most common pairing at this time, rarely won a race; although to be fair they were riding away from home all the time.

To be fair, their 4–2 win in heat two at Cradley did make a difference in the Lions' three point win. The Lions were never behind after heat one, and a 5–1 from Fundin and Harkins in heat 12 put them seven points up with only one heat left. Curiously, those two away wins were the only ones the Lions achieved in 1970.

It was certainly correct not to try to ride any 'home' matches at Wimbledon or Hackney, but to focus on the big opening night on 30 May, when Hackney would be the opposition. Gradually, things were taking shape. Disc-jockey Ed Stewart was to be the announcer, along with Bob Danvers Walker. David Hamilton also became involved in this role later in the season.

Interviewed in *Backtrack* (issue 30), Stewart showed "genuine enthusiasm about his role with the Lions and enjoyment at being involved with speedway." He particularly recalls having a race after the last meeting with Hamilton and two pop singers, Leapy Lee and Troy Dante. That was when they realised that speedway bikes did not have brakes!

Bill Kitchen was appointed as speedway's national track inspector in May, so could not be the Wembley team manager. Trevor Redmond managed to get his former team mate – and double world champion – Freddie Williams to fulfil the role. Wembley's centre green would not its usual immaculate self for the start of the speedway season because a new pitch was being laid. Bert Harkins would probably be the Lions' most colourful rider – he had ordered a set of yellow and blue leathers when still with Coatbridge. Later, the Lions wore smart red leathers.

Saturday 30 May saw the Lions return to the Empire Stadium. The *Speedway Star* published a colour picture of Ove Fundin, Bert Harkins – in his blue and yellow leathers and with a tartan scarf – and Reidar Eide. The magazine, which had had a colour cover since the beginning of April, said that the Lions had "a side which will do justice to the traditions of Wembley" and that traditionally the Lions "have always been blessed with 'villains' and 'clowns' who have always made them an attractive team."

Interviewed by Martin Rogers in the *Star*, Trevor Redmond said that for years he had "wanted to bring speedway back to Wembley" and explained how he had had talks with the Stadium management every couple of years, but "this year everything seemed to be right to bring it back." Rogers pointed out that the Lions had quit the sport when it was "in a state of depression" and were returning "when it was booming again." He said that a 30,000 crowd was anticipated for the opening night, and regular crowds of 20,000 would please Redmond, Bernard Cottrell and the Stadium management.

Rogers also said that he now understood Redmond's sudden appearance at the Sweden versus Great Britain test match in Malmo the previous September. It was to contact Ove Fundin, who was a friend of Redmond's. There was clearly great enthusiasm for the return of the Lions, and Rogers hoped that "the country's most famous sporting arena will again be alive and buzzing with excitement." Freddie Williams was taking over as team manager for the Hackney match, and Redmond was "pretty satisfied" with the Lions team. He also made it clear that Wembley and the promoters were committed to the project for the long term.

In the match programme, Redmond said that it was a "red letter day" for the sport, and how it has been 13 long years since the Lions "slipped away from the speedway scene". All the riders had been "pretty choked" when the team had folded, and that he had always had a burning desire to "get the Lions rolling again."

The Wembley team for this historic night was Reidar Eide, Des Lukehurst, Ove Fundin, Wayne Briggs, Bert Harkins, Brian Collins and Tim Bungay. Hackney fielded two riders with a Wembley connection. Veteran Jimmy Gooch had started his long speedway career with the Lions almost 20 years before. And at reserve for the Hawks was Australian veteran Jack Biggs, who had ridden at the Empire Stadium against the Lions many times, and will always be remembered for being so close to becoming World Champion at Wembley in 1951.

A crowd of 21,000 saw the Lions win by four points. Reidar Eide was excluded in the first race after a fall, so the Lion lost their first heat at home 5–1. But with everyone contributing, led by Ove Fundin with three wins and a tapes exclusion, the Lions got home 41–37. Fundin's win in the last heat secured the win.

In the *Star*, Danny Carter commented that many of the old supporters headed back to their favourite spots as if they hadn't been away. Many of the old-time riders turned up. Peter Oakes said that the crowd was near 30,000, including various television stars. Ed Stewart was involved with the presentation, and David Hamilton "obviously enjoyed his night out". The crowd included a couple of hundred Coatbridge fans, and reputedly some from King's Lynn, who came to watch Ove Fundin. Another Lions tradition reborn was having a dance after the meeting. Whatever the actual attendance was, the norm for First Division crowds at this time was between 2,000 and 5,000; with more for derby matches. So a 20,000 crowd for a league match was exceptional.

Apart from Ove Fundin, the Lions riders had very little experience of riding their new home track. This was reflected in their home results. One of the issues with the team of the 1940s and 1950s had been their domination of home meetings. This was clearly not the case for the 1970 team. My memory of that time, as a supporter new to speedway, was that any Lions win bigger than 41–37 was a 'big win'. This was not quite the case.

For supporters who last watched speedway in 1956, there were changes both to the format for league matches and to the Stadium. In the 1960s Wembley Stadium had undergone an improvement programme that saw both ends fully covered. On the track, league meetings now consisted of 13 heats, there were tactical substitutes and guest riders. As in the 1950s, second-half races at Wembley were better presented than at most tracks.

The Lions hopes of being unbeaten at home only lasted until Sheffield were the visitors a week after the opening night, and won by a point. An 11 point return from Ove Fundin was not enough for the Lions, who needed all their heat leaders to be on form. Eide scored 8(+1), but Bert Harkins had an off night with just three points (+1) from three rides. The track record was lowered four times, ending up with Sheffield's Arnie Haley at 69.6 seconds. There had been minor changes to the shape of the track since the 1950s, so the records from that time were not used.

The Lions' biggest home win came the next week, when West Ham were vanquished 47–31. The meeting was memorable for a 15 point maximum from Christer Lofqvist, who scored nearly half his team's points. After that, the Lions won by 12 points twice, six three times four three times and two three times. There were two draws, against Belle Vue and Wolverhampton, and defeats against the 'other' Lions from Leicester and King's Lynn. Thrilling finishes were the order of the day, but this was not the sort of form that was going to bring home a league title.

Away from home, the Lions held their own. They did not secure another win on the road, but their worst result for the rest of the season was a 52–26 loss at Hackney on 12 June, when Ove Fundin could only manage three points (+1). After that, the Lions never conceded more than 50 points again.

There were two other reasons that may have contributed to the Lions' inconsistency. One was the amount of travelling they were doing. Ove Fundin was commuting to and from Sweden. For the first part of the season, Bert Harkins was based in Scotland, although he moved south later on. In June, he rode at Wimbledon for Wembley on Thursday, for Scotland at Hampden Park on the Friday and then was back in London on the Saturday again for the Lions against Swindon. Wayne Briggs still lived in Scotland, although he also had a base in Southampton with his brother Barry. The second reason was changes in the team. Looking to solve their weakness at reserve, the Lions signed Dave Jessup from Eastbourne.

Wembley 1970: Dave Jessup, Bert Harkins, Tim Bungay, Freddie Williams (Manager), Wayne Briggs, Reidar Eide, Brian Collins, Ove Fundin (on bike).

Reidar Eide.

New Lions: Left: Brian Collins; Right: Brian Leonard.

Left: Dave Jessup; Right: Ove Fundin

New Lions: Left: Bert Harkins; (JSC) Right: Wayne Briggs, with Reidar Eide in the background. (JSC)

Bert Harkins and Steve Bast alongside John Boulger. (JSC)

It was the highest cash transfer for a Second Division rider to the First Division at the time. He was initially signed as Wembley's 'number 8', but rode regularly for the Lions and the Eagles throughout the rest of the season. Looking back, there are similarities between the recruitment of Jessup and the signing of Brian Crutcher from Poole in 1953. Both riders quickly rose to the challenge of being part of the Wembley set-up, and challenged for the sport's highest levels without every winning the World Championship.

As Jessup signed, and made his debut against West Ham on 13 June, Des Lukehurst temporarily retired from the sport. He came back later in the season, returning to the Second Division at his former Romford base. Trevor Redmond was looking for new recruits, with the Lions again having a bare seven riders, and signed former West Ham second string or reserve Brian Leonard, who had just left Newport. Leonard had previously ridden for Swindon and Poole before joining West Ham in 1965. He was part of their great side that won the inaugural British League, Knock out Cup and London Cup that year. He was 24 years old when he joined the Lions, and went on to serve the team well. Interviewed in *Backtrack* (issue 64) by Rob Peasley, Leonard commented: "Who could turn down the chance to ride for Wembley? It was an incredible feeling riding round there every week." He believes that Mike Erskine, one of the top engine tuners who did Leonard's bikes for him, contacted Trevor Redmond to suggest Redmond approach Leonard to join the Lions.

In early July, Philip Rising reported in the *Star* that Redmond was delighted at the progress of Brian Collins and Dave Jessup. The promoter felt that Collins had "made great strides this year", making up for some of the other disappointments in the Wembley team. Rising said that it was important for speedway as a whole for Wembley to succeed but at present their side is not as strong as it might be. Reidar Eide and Bert Harkins had not been consistently in the heat leader class – although Eide's form improved in the second half of the season, while Ove Fundin had missed too many matches for the Lions to maintain a championship challenge.

The issue of Fundin's availability was raised again on 17 July in the *Star*. Peter Morrish asked whether Fundin had a future in British speedway. He wondered whether Fundin would be missing for more than just the two weeks that have been threatened. Due to "urgent domestic matters", Fundin had been unable to ride for the Lions on 11 July and was not be available for the home match with Belle Vue because of the European Final in Leningrad.

Morrish said that "Fundin has heavy business commitments in his homeland and with his virtual knock-out from the World Championship [he was reserve for the European final, but did not attend the meeting] he will not have that extra bit of incentive which he often seems to need. [The] Lions are not panicking, however, and while they keep a weather eye on the Fundin situation, Bert Harkins has been made captain for the two meetings Ove misses and Dave Jessup and Brian Leonard get more chances to prove themselves in the team."

He also said that the Lions' clash with Wimbledon had been "one of the best meetings seen anywhere this season with Reidar Eide's form the most pleasing feature for the Lions."

Things came to a head with Fundin at the end of July, and Wembley released the former World Champion. Bernard Cottrell and Trevor Redmond commented in the Lions programme on 8 August: "... A word about Ove Fundin, whom, it seems, feels that his riding days are over insofar as this country is concerned anyway. Ove has heavy business commitments back home in Sweden, and obviously is of the opinion that it would be too much strain to combine the two. ... Fundin isn't getting any younger and your management is not content to have Ove here in the role of a 'part-timer. We salute Ove for his great deeds on the track but now we must seek a replacement." There had also been issues around Fundin's work permit.

In Ove's time with the Lions, there had been 19 league matches. He had ridden in 14 of them. Of the five he missed, the home meeting against Belle Vue went ahead with the Aces missing Ivan Mauger, who was also involved in the European Final that weekend. The Lions had ridden three challenge matches in Ove's time with the team and he had ridden in one. For many supporters, his absence did a leave a bad taste in the mouth, and he was booed at the World Team Cup Final at Wembley later in the season. He was invited back to ride for the European Stars against the Lions in their final home match of the season, and won his first three races before being excluded for breaking the tapes.

It is fair to point out as well that the issue of Swedish riders commuting to ride in the British League was a contentious one at this time. The commuting was not on the scale of today's top riders, but it did cause problems with disappointment for fans missing out unexpectedly on seeing a top rider who did not turn up, as had happened with Fundin at King's Lynn early in the season.

In John Chaplin's comprehensive biography of Fundin, he says that Trevor Redmond had said to Fundin "You will love Wembley. Come and do a few meetings." Ove says in the book that Redmond was a good friend, and that Ove "took it seriously when I was there, but I forgot about it as soon as I left." He also recalls how Bernard Cottrell would pick him up at Heathrow in his Rolls-Royce. In a feature on Ove and Ole Olsen in *Backtrack* (issue 45), Richard Bott says that Fundin told him "It has been said that I let Wembley down. But these people do not know the whole truth. When I agreed to ride for Wembley ... I made it clear that I would not be able to ride in every meeting because of my commitments in Sweden. Then I had to go home, suddenly – for domestic reasons. And I could see no point in returning. My machinery was not properly maintained in England and I did not even have a good bike for the Nordic-British Final..."

Ove ended the season with an average of 7.93, only behind Reidar Eide. Whatever the rights and wrongs of his departure from the Lions, what is clear is that he was never adequately replaced.

Interviewed by Mike Hunter in *Backtrack* (Issue 1, 2004) Brian Collins remembers riding with Fundin, who he thought "... was a weird character, didn't really mix with anyone, and he either liked you or he didn't. Luckily for me he did like me. He used to say 'You get off the start and go as hard as you can. I'll keep them back.' But come the last lap, he always wanted to be first – I thought I was doing well until he went past me at 100 miles an hour."

The first replacement for Fundin was a young American. Steve Bast had won the American national title in 1969, and had worked with Jack Milne at the Costa Mesa track. But Bast found the British tracks very different to what he was used to in America. Having to ride immediately in the First Division, in a heat leader slot, did not help his progress. He made his debut for the Lions at home to Poole on 15 August, rode in the abandoned match at West Ham three days later, and at home to Leicester the following Saturday. In Dave Lanning's Diary in the *Star* dated 4 September, he said that he found the bends difficult at Wembley, because they were bigger than what he was used to in America. But on the next page of the magazine, it was reported that he had flown home. It said that he had far fewer meetings than he expected. Also, apparently he was homesick – Trevor Redmond had a large bill for international phone calls by Bast, and he clearly missed his girlfriend. His younger brother Mike went on to have considerable success in the USA.

Bast won the American title again in 1974, and rode in Australia and South Africa. He died at the young age of 55 in 2007. In the obituary in *Backtrack* (issue 23), Bert Harkins recalled that "A mixture of strange tracks, motorway food, grey skies, cold, wet weather and having to travel from Glasgow with me, made Steve very homesick for the Californian sunshine and burgers, so he flew home to Los Angeles without realising his full potential." Harkins felt that he had the potential to do as well as Bruce Penhall had he persevered with riding in Britain.

The Lions' final attempt to fill the heat leader slot was equally unsuccessful. Bengt Andersson was released by Exeter, and made his debut for the Lions at home to Coventry on 5 September. But in nine matches he scored just 14 points (plus three bonus points) from 28 rides. He was not retained for the 1971 season, and joined Cradley Heath, where his average in 18 matches was marginally worse than his one for the Lions.

The Lions finished the season with 15 wins in the league, two draws and 19 defeats for 32 league points. They finished 14th, well clear of Newport who took the wooden spoon. Four teams finished on 32 points, converting the two home draws into wins would have put the Lions almost at halfway. In the Knock-out Cup they had lost at Newcastle in the second round, having had a bye in the first. Due to their lack of home dates they did not enter the London Cup. The suggestions of riding the matches at home in the second halves or riding just away for double points were rejected by the other teams. This was a pity, the Lions had a rich history in this competition, and it could have given the Lions growing support more chances to visit the other London tracks to watch their heroes. As it was, they rode for a North London Cup against Hackney. The Lions lost at Waterden Road by 10 points and failed to make this up in a five heat second-half contest. Hackney promoter Len Silver then complained because the Cup was not presented to his team.

With the World Championship Final being staged in Poland, Wembley hosted the World Team Cup on 19 September. Sweden won comfortably, with Great Britain as runners-up. Ove Fundin scored 11 points for the Swedes, was booed and refused to ride in the second half of the meeting.

In the end of season British League Riders Championship, which brought together the top riders from each team, Reidar Eide finished ninth with seven points. Dave Jessup won the Second Division version on behalf of Eastbourne.

International honours did not come to the Lions very often in this period. Bert Harkins and Brian Collins rode for Scotland, and Harkins – along with Jim McMillan – reached the final of the first official World Best Pairs competition. In the semi-final at Belle Vue they were runners-up to New Zealand, but did beat England! The 'Sassanachs' got their revenge in the final in Malmo. New Zealand won the meeting, hosts Sweden were second and England came third by a single point ahead of the Scots. McMillan scored 10 and Bert Harkins eight.

Trevor Redmond said at the end of the season that the Lions were looking to develop more riders of their own. He confirmed that their home season would not start until 5 June 1971 because of football matches at the Empire Stadium. He was sure that the Lions would run in 1971, and had already got 16 Saturday dates agreed, and would use Wednesdays if necessary. He said that there were usually five figure crowds on a Saturday, but only half that for midweek meetings. Towards the end of the year it was reported that Redmond had visited White City to see if that could be used for some early season meetings, but an agreement had already been made for stock cars to run there.

Bert Harkins set off to ride in America and then Australia in the winter, but confirmed that he would return to ride for the Lions in 1971. It was clear that the Lions would make changes to the team for 1971; beyond the urgent need for a recognised third heat leader.

In the *Star* on 6 November, Danny Carter wrote that: "Apart from establishing themselves back in the sport, Wembley did not make a big impact on speedway this year. Mind you, if all their three heat leaders had ridden up to known form it would have been very different. As it was, Bert Harkins was up and down, Ove Fundin was in and out; and Reidar Eide was way down for a fair while. In the end only Eide completely recovered." However, Carter misses the point. What other team at this time regularly attracted five figure crowds? If the Lions had flopped, and been forced to close for financial reasons at the end of the season, it would have been a blow to the sport. As it was, league speedway was established back at the national stadium, and thousands of new fans had come to watch, including the author of this book.

Angus Kix, in his review of the season in the *Star*, was critical of the team's inconsistent performances. But he said "...they did one good thing, they re-established speedway at Wembley and re-established it as a success. Crowds were good. Racing was generally excellent from the start and got better every week."

Reidar Eide had found his form in the second half of the season, particularly at home, although his average fell by almost a point. Fundin had generally scored consistently in what was really a cameo to a magnificent career. Bert Harkins's average dropped by half a point compared to 1969, but that could be explained by moving to a new home track. Wayne Briggs's average also fell, and it looked likely that he would seek a move back to Scotland. Brian Collins had improved; Dave Jessup was clearly one for the future, and Brian Leonard had strengthened the reserve slots after he joined the Lions. Tim Bungay had averaged less than a point a ride, and retired after a handful of meetings in 1971.

Interviewed in the *Star* at the end of the year by Martin Rogers, Trevor Redmond said that the rebirth of the Lions had been a success: "We had considerable commitments but we were pretty satisfied nevertheless. The big complaint was that it seemed to be so difficult to get hold of a team worthy of the name. And I believe that is essential for Wembley's image and reputation to be maintained." Despite the shorter home season, there were riders interested in joining the Lions, and he was looking at touring America to provide some extra meetings. That never happened, but there was optimism for the future of the Lions, especially in the context of a sport that was growing and successful.

The company accounts for the period covering the 1970 season do not provide a great deal of information. The only fixed asset listed is the 'team and licence' valued at £3,000. Payments to four directors amounted to £4,700, of which the largest was £1,300.

21. 1971: The Lions rampant

The Lions were now re-established back in British speedway. The issue facing Trevor Redmond and Bernard Cottrell was to improve the team to start challenging for honours. Another problem was the lack of dates available at the Empire Stadium, with the opening meeting not due to happen until the first Saturday in June, due to the Stadium staging the football European Cup Final on 2 June.

The make-up of British speedway was remarkably stable at this time. As in 1970, there were 19 teams in the First Division and 17 in the Second Division. There was one change in the top flight – Newcastle closed and were replaced by Reading. In the second tier, Crayford and Doncaster both closed, and were replaced by Birmingham and Sunderland. The return of the sport to Birmingham, who had pulled out of the National League in mid-season in 1957, then ran an 'open' season in 1960, was particularly welcome. The formation of Sunderland meant that the sport kept a presence in the north-east. Speedway would return to Newcastle in the future.

In the winter, Dave Jessup had joined a group of British riders riding in Rhodesia. He had needed special permission because of his young age; letters home to his parents and girlfriend said that he was having a good time. Bert Harkins broke an ankle in America, and then broke a scaphoid. It seemed possible that he would miss much of the 1971 season; in fact that injury healed more quickly than expected; although he did have other injury problems.

Bernard Cottrell and Trevor Redmond had been trying to find a temporary home for the Lions before June. London's White City was a possible option, but had been leased out to stock car racing. Hendon Stadium, which was soon to be demolished to make space for the M1 extension and the Brent Cross Shopping centre, was also not an option.

In idle moments, the author has speculated whether the Lions could have been saved by a move to White City. In 1976 Oxford moved there, but although the team was successful on the track, struggled to be viable, with crowds under 2,000. Wembley would have bought a much higher hard core of support had the Lions moved there, but the magic of going to Wembley Stadium would have been lost. Ultimately the stadium was demolished anyway; we'll never know.

Rider control operated at this time, with the aim of evening up teams to make for a better competition. But riders often would not go to a track which they had been allocated to, although the system did have some success in avoiding the one-sided meetings that had been an issue in the National League in the early 1950s.

Early rumours were that Reidar Eide wanted a move; that Wayne Briggs wanted to return to Scotland and that Reg Luckhurst could move to Wembley from Wimbledon. A possible move for Reidar Eide was a return to Scotland with Glasgow; but the *Star* said that they probably couldn't afford his wages, and that he might price himself out of the sport. Eide did have a reputation for driving a hard bargain wherever he rode. In fact, he ended up at Poole, who were to be Wembley's first opponents at the Empire Stadium. Wayne Briggs was not wanted by Glasgow, and ended up at Exeter, even further from his Scottish base.

Interviewed in the *Star*, Briggs said that he had found Wembley to be a gater's track. He had stayed in Southampton for the first month of the 1970 campaign, but then had moved back to Scotland and commuted to London. He also expressed concerns about Wembley's late start for the forthcoming season and the lack of match practice this caused.

Reg Luckhurst was allocated to Wembley, along with West Ham's Tony Clarke. Clarke had fallen out with the Hammers and was looking for a new start with a move across London. He had watched his first speedway at Wembley with his father in the 1940s. But with Sverre Harrfeldt's future at West Ham unclear, Luckhurst ended up in east London. The Lions were offered Hasse Holmqvist instead – after Ken McKinlay had turned down a move to Wembley – but he never materialised. His wife had health problems and then gave birth to twins, who were also unwell. Although he hoped to ride for the Lions at various stages of the season, he never actually did.

It was reported that Trevor Redmond had found a new rider for the Lions in South Africa or Rhodesia. Later in the season Peter Prinsloo did join the Lions, but was clearly not ready for the First Division and was loaned to Ipswich, where he made some progress. He made his debut for the Lions in a 48–30 defeat at Sheffield in the Knock-out Cup, and rode in 11 meetings for the Lions. He was not the first Rhodesian in British speedway, Tom and Dick Sayer had ridden for Norwich in the 1950s.

One link with the Lions' past ended in April, when Jimmy Gooch announced his retirement from the sport. This left Mike Broadbank as the only rider still active in the sport from the Lions set-up in the 1950s.

Towards the end of April came news that there were changes in the promotion at Wembley. Trevor Redmond was to go it alone, after a split with Bernard Cottrell. There had been rumours that the Lions would not run, but Redmond dismissed this, confirming to Eric Linden that the lease had been signed and that he had promoted on his own before and would do it again. The following week, in the *Star*, the position was clarified in an article by James Oldfield. Cottrell explained that he still had a 50 per cent stake in the company, and had resigned in protest at the SCB's decision over the allocation of Reg Luckhurst. He had retained his promoter's licence and his wife was still a director of Wembley Speedway Limited. Cottrell was still involved in the sport; he was involved in trying to set up speedway in Majorca, and was working with Ian Hoskins to stage motorbike racing on a third of a mile track in Welwyn Garden City later in the year.

He accepted that there had been differences of opinion between Redmond and himself, but said that was not why he had resigned. According to Ove Fundin in John Chaplin's biography of him, Redmond and Cottrell "ended up as deadly enemies", but Ove does not say why. Given that Trevor Redmond died almost 20 years ago, and Bernard Cottrell has also passed away; it is not possible to develop this area further and verify Ove's comments.

Still hoping that Hasse Holmqvist would join them later in the season, the Lions signed Tommy Jansson on a short term basis, but released him after three meetings. In his review of the season in the *Star* (11 March 1972), Danny Carter points out that Jansson reached the World Championship Final, and maybe the Lions were too quick to release him. Maybe. But at that stage of the season they did not know that Holmqvist would never materialise; and the Lions would not have been able to sign Gote Nordin had Jansson stayed.

As in 1970, the Lions started the season 'on the road.' However, this time there were no challenge matches arranged; the team went straight into league action. The other London teams and Reading competed in the early season Metropolitan Gold Cup, and it could have given the Wembley riders more early-season meetings if the Lions had entered this competition, maybe riding for double points on opponents tracks. As it was, a respectable 12 point defeat at Wolverhampton was followed by a 40 point massacre at Belle Vue, the worst defeat in the Lions' modern day history and it was only the second time they conceded over 50 points.

New Lions in 1971:
Top: Tony Clarke
Bottom left: Sverre Harrfeldt (JSC)
Bottom right: Gote Nordin (JSC)

The Lions used rider-replacement for Brian Collins, which it later transpired they were not entitled to do. So a 58–20 defeat on the night became 59–19 after the scores were recalculated excluding the rides taken in Collins's place. Only Dave Jessup won a heat for the Lions, all the Aces heat leaders were unbeaten by an opponent and the Aces won the last six heats 5–1.

The Lions put on a better display in the "home" match on 16 April, which was staged at Newport. Later in the season, Danny Carter wrote in the *Star* he had never understood why the meeting had been ridden at Newport. Belle Vue, including World Champion Ivan Mauger, were one of the most attractive teams in the league. Mauger had missed the 1970 match at Wembley because of a fixture clash with the European Final. The Aces were also a 'Saturday' track, but surely a midweek date could have been found at Wembley later in the season. If the match had to be ridden away from Wembley, why not use one of the London tracks, or even Reading. Some Wembley supporters, including the author of this book who remembers getting a slow 'milk train' through the night back to Paddington, did get to Somerton Park. The Lions lost 47–31 on the night, which was changed to 48–30 because Tim Bungay had not completed two rides. Ipswich star John Louis rode as a guest for the Lions. Dave Jessup top scored for the Lions with nine (+1) and Tony Clarke won a couple of heats.

Things did improve for the Lions. On 15 May, Sverre Harrfeldt made his debut for Wembley at Swindon. Harrfeldt had been runner-up in the 1966 World Final, with 14 points. He had made his debut in British speedway for Wimbledon in 1963 before moving to West Ham. But in 1968 he suffered horrific injuries in the European Final in Wroclaw. He returned to West Ham in 1970, but broke his arm early in the season. This meant he missed the dreadful Lokeren accident, and deputised as team manager following the death of Phil Bishop at Lokeren. He did not agree terms with West Ham for 1971, so Wembley snapped him up. He started slowly with the Lions, but became one of the most exciting riders to represent the Lions in the modern era.

His arrival meant there were four riders in the team with West Ham connections. Clarke, Leonard and Harrfeldt had all been first team regulars with the Hammers; Dave Jessup had some of his first rides on a speedway bike at Custom House before joining Eastbourne.

The Lions picked up their first league point of the season at Cradley the following Saturday, albeit re-enforced by Charlie Monk and Bob Paulson as guests. Six days later, they went one better – and won at Hackney. In 1970 the Lions had one of their worst nights of the season at Waterden Road. With Bob Andrews and Graham Plant as guests, because Tony Clarke was still on international duty in Poland with Great Britain 'B' and Holmqvist unavailable, the Lions were six points up after 12 heats, and a 5–1 to Hackney in the last race made no difference. Harrfeldt moved to reserve and scored six points from four rides.

With Holmqvist still unavailable, Trevor Redmond acted decisively to sign Swedish legend Gote Nordin on a short-term contract until the end of July. In the *Star*, Martin Rogers said that he was "the one world class rider not regularly employed in British League racing" he was an obvious choice for Wembley. He had finished third in the 1961 World Championship Final, and won the Internationale in 1966 and 1967. He had previous British experience with Newport, Poole and Coventry, and was aged 35. He was studying a course in Sweden for his business, and it was clear that he would only be available for a couple of months for the Lions. In his two months with the Lions, he only missed two meetings – both at Sheffield – and scored double figures five times. As Sverre Harrfeldt gradually built up his scores, and Bert Harkins was injured, he was exactly what the Lions needed. Had he been available for the rest of the season, the Lions could have challenged for a place in the top four in the league. As it was, when he left, young Christer Sjosten was never an adequate replacement.

Wembley Lions 1971: Dave Jessup, Tony Clarke, Brian Leonard, Gote Nordin, Sverre Harrfeldt, Brian Collins, Peter Prinsloo; on bike: Bert Harkins (captain), Freddie Williams (manager)

The Lions team that faced Poole: Bert Harkins, Brian Collins, Gote Nordin, Tony Clarke, Dave Jessup, Sverre Harrfeldt and Brian Leonard; not necessarily riding in those positions, was arguably the best Lions line-up in 1970 and 1971. There were no weaknesses in the team; Tony Clarke spent a few weeks at reserve because of the side's strength. Nordin was the star, with an average of just nine, but this was a real team, with Bert Harkins 8.19 average only 2.4 more than Brian Leonard's 5.79 at reserve. Harrfeldt averaged just under 8, while Dave Jessup averaged an impressive 7.41 in his second season in the First Division.

After losing to Poole by four points, with Nordin winning two races and falling twice, the Lions won their next eight home meetings comfortably. It was almost like the 1950s, with a 52–26 win over Halifax, 51–27 against Cradley Health and 54–24 against Exeter. The Lions also won 46–32 at West Ham, their largest away win in the modern era.

Nordin could have continued to ride on Saturdays for the Lions, but they felt that a 'part-time' arrangement would not have been acceptable, and parted on good terms with the Swedish legend. His replacement, Christer Sjosten, only rode in six meetings; maybe the Lions would have done better keeping Nordin. After he left, they lost at home to Coventry and drew with Leicester, having drawn at Blackbird Road two weeks earlier. At the beginning of September they won at Oxford; and finished their home league programme with a 20 point win over Wimbledon.

Generally, the Lions' crowds were up compared to 1970. Trevor Redmond wrote in the last programme, for a Pairs event, that the "spirit of the Lions had triumphed over all adversity." The *Star* reported that Redmond told the 14,000 crowd: "We have been delighted by the performances of the team in recent months. In spite of a lot of problems we have finished well up the First Division table and next year we're going to have a go at winning the league."

In his season review in the *Star*, Danny Carter said that the team was not the "almighty Lions" of yesteryear, but added that "as far as the faithful thousands who flocked to support them in their second comeback year were concerned, that didn't matter one little bit. After all, they had all they could cope with in the cheering field." He pointed out that Bert Harkins improved on 1970 and "could always be relied upon to shake the opposition when they least expected it". He also scored four maximums – one full and three paid, and reached the Nordic British Final in the World Championship, where he only scored three points due to riding with a collarbone injury. Gote Nordin "seemed to dominate every match." Sverre Harrfeldt "became one of the idols of the crowd with his fast starts and wide, full throttle sweeps." Dave Jessup "tackled his Division 1 first full season with a deal of enthusiasm and verve" before an injury curtailed his campaign. Tony Clarke's scoring fell compared to 1970, but he got "better and faster and more daring and greater with every match that went on". He was another entertainer. Brian Collins was hit by early season injury, but was consistent in the second half of the campaign; with Brian Leonard, he gave the team great strength in reserve, something the Lions often lacked in 1970, particularly in the first half of the season.

The Lions finished ninth in the league, with 37 points from 36 matches. If they had beaten Coventry, Poole and Leicester at Wembley, the extra five points would have put them into fifth place. But it was still a considerable improvement on 14th place the previous season. With some quality young riders in Jessup, Collins and Leonard, combined with the experience of Harkins, Clarke and Harrfeldt, this was certainly a team that could have gone on to achieve more, and even challenge for titles.

22. Memories of the Wembley Lions
By Mark Lewisohn

I'm always mindful of the significant dates in my life and every year on August 8th I note the anniversary of my first speedway meeting, which was in 1970. I went to Wembley with my friend Jeremy Moore and his family. I'd watched a bit of motor-cycle scrambling on *Grandstand* on Saturday afternoons but had never been to a live motorsport event. The meeting was the Southern Riders Championship qualifying round, and we sat on the second bend in the great stadium.

My abiding memory is that I'd never heard anything so incredibly *loud*. I saw almost nothing of the first few heats because I was covering my ears and turning away from the action – no speedway meeting was ever louder in my experience. I quickly got used to it, though, had an unforgettable night and learned how to fill in a programme, which shows that Reidar Eide won with a 15 point maximum. He quickly became my favourite; as a twelve-year-old I was amused that a rider was called Reidar.

Another memory from that first meeting is that during the interval all the riders dispersed around the stadium to collect money for the Lokeren disaster fund – it was just four weeks after several of the West Ham team had been killed in a road crash in Belgium. As they walked through the crowd, the riders stretched blankets between them and everyone threw coins in. We'd just been watching these guys roar around the track and suddenly they were among us in their filthy leathers and steel shoes, giving me an amazing close-up.

Quickly hooked, I went to three or four other meetings that season, including the World Team Cup Final. Wembley Stadium was packed, *really* packed, and I stood on the terrace on the third and fourth bend. Ove Fundin was booed throughout. I knew he'd been the Wembley Lions' captain at the start of the season and then walked out midway through, but I didn't understand why he was being jeered to such a degree until the people around me explained he had 'let the Lions down'. Still, he returned for our final home meeting of 1970, a challenge match against the European Stars, riding for the opposition

By the time of that final home meeting I was a seriously dedicated fan, fully in love with the Lions and a sport I'd not heard of two months earlier. I ordered *Speedway Star & News* (as it then was) and the monthly *Speedway Post* from my local newsagent, I joined Wembley Lions Supporters Club, started buying badges and the like, and already *could not wait* for the next season to start. From the moment in February when the *Star* printed the 1971 fixtures I knew precisely how many days to count until our first home meeting on Saturday June 5th – another date I still nod to once a year. I was truly, madly, deeply envious of other teams' supporters whose home seasons began in March.

It took f-o-r-e-v-e-r, but June 5th did finally arrive. We lived in Pinner, only five stops from Wembley Park on the Metropolitan Line, and I went very early to that and every other meeting, before five o'clock, to take photos of the riders as they arrived and get their autographs. I certainly went to all the Saturday-night meetings in 1971, but missed some of the Wednesday ones because my mum wouldn't always allow me to go and I had school the next morning.

Reidar Eide had moved to Poole in the close season and actually rode against us in the opening match, which was strange. We'd signed the Swedish rider Gote Nordin as his replacement. He was always friendly with the fans, but one time – hoping for an autograph – I was leaning over the pits wall, shouting his name over his revved engine, and he never once looked up to see who was calling him. Years later I asked a Swedish friend how to pronounce

'Gote' and realised I'd been saying it completely wrong, so probably he didn't even realise I was calling for him! We loved Gote even though he lost us the match that first night, falling on the first bend in his third and fourth rides. It happened right in front of me because I sat in the same first-bend seat throughout the '71 season. That opening night defeat really hurt because I was always desperate to see the Lions win, but at least Bert Harkins, our captain, our new number 1, raced to a 12 point maximum. I thought he was brilliant.

I liked *all* the Lions team and was very passionate about cheering them on in the war cries and all that. Dave Jessup and Sverre Harrfeldt stand out in my memory. Sverre was a former top-line rider who'd suffered a career-threatening injury and was a bit of a crock, but week by week I watched him regain his strength, fitness and confidence, returning to heat-leader status. His gating was sensational, the best I ever saw. He'd shoot out of gate four and often be clear by the first bend. I was ecstatic the night he scored a 12 point maximum, apt reward for his courage.

Dave Jessup was instantly great in my view, a young and exciting champion to be. If memory serves, he had a 7.41 average with us in 1971, his first full top-flight season. I was proud that Wembley was continuing a long tradition of giving youth a chance.

The 1971 Lions were a real team – we didn't have an Ivan or an Ole or a Briggo but we had three or four riders often scoring 8 or 9 points a meeting, and with good second strings and reserves picking up plenty of points, we won many matches. We became quite formidable at home, hitting 50 points a few times.

Wembley also staged very watchable second-half races after the league match, up to eight heats in competition for a trophy of some kind, and different ideas like one-lap flying starts. Star riders were invited along just for the second-halves, including Ole Olsen on one occasion. He always won – it was rare for Ole to be beaten at Wembley. It was here that I first saw the rider who later became my all-time favourite, Gordon Kennett, when he was an Eastbourne youngster riding in a Wembley second-half junior race.

At that time most speedway riders wore black leathers, but in 1971 the Lions had matching red and white team leathers. It was special, like everything at Wembley was special. Even speedway can have a 'glamour team' and I knew Wembley was it and took pride in the Lions, just as the programme notes and announcements encouraged us. I knew I was supporting our sport's Manchester United, the headline-makers and, in the past at least, regular winners.

The last meeting of 1971 was a fairly uninspiring best pairs event won by our Scottish duo Bert Harkins and Brian Collins, and that was that: I knew I was in for another painfully long eight-month wait until the Lions roared back in June 1972. I was counting the days (really) when, in February 1972, newspapers reported a Wembley Stadium policy announcement, which was that the Lions were withdrawing from the league because they couldn't run a full season at the stadium. I was devastated – a consuming part of my world fell away in an instant. All speedway fans know that tracks close but I never thought it would happen to the Lions because we got such great crowds. I went to an emergency 'Save Our Speedway' meeting of the supporters club, held in a place called the Norfolk Arms, near North Wembley station. I was thirteen and it was a dark, cold wintry midweek night, quite a venture on my own – and I hadn't realised that the Norfolk Arms was a pub. The landlord took one look at me and said I couldn't come in, but I said I was there for the speedway supporters club meeting and he just *had* to let me stay. As the meeting was being held in a side room, he waved me through.

Mark with his hero – Bert Harkins – in 1971.
(Photo: Courtesy Mark Lewisohn)

I thought the place would be packed but there were only about 25 of us in there, everyone in their red and white scarf. It was like that sad scene in *Ripping Yarns* when Michael Palin goes to a supporters club meeting of his beloved football club and hears their ground has been sold to a developer. It was quite hopeless for us – how could we few change the mind of Wembley Stadium management? I do distinctly recall Lions supporters being told the hiatus was strictly for one season, that the team would return in 1973, because all through 1972 I phoned the stadium to ask for confirmation and for the date of the Lions' first 1973 meeting. It never happened, and once we missed 1973 as well that was definitely that. It hurt, badly.

I have the programme, but did I get to a four-team tournament at Hackney in 1972 which had a Wembley team in it? I certainly wanted to, but it was a long and dangerously edgy solo journey across London for a lad of 14. I was definitely at Wimbledon in 1973 when they raced an end of season challenge match against Ex-Wembley. Bert Harkins rode for us against his own side; he had to – he was the Lions' great captain.

I never missed another speedway meeting at Wembley, going to all the one-a-year European and World events up to and including the last in 1981, Bruce Penhall's big night. I revelled in the chance to sit again on the first bend and watch great racing ... but it was the Lions I really wanted and nothing else came close. I went to Wimbledon quite often in 1974–75 because Bert was there, but I could never bring myself to support the Dons and never warmed to the stadium or the racing at Plough Lane.

White City was a new beginning – I was a strong supporter from the first announcement, deeply back into it like I'd been at Wembley, and now I was seventeen and had a car. The Rebels opened in 1976 – in March, thankfully – but the crowds were always hopelessly small and there was zero atmosphere in the big stadium, whereas Wembley had always been electric. Our great year was 1977, when we won the British League – it was my best ever season in speedway because I went to most of the away matches as well. White City's eventual closure was inevitable, though, and after just three seasons the licence was transferred to Eastbourne. I followed the Eagles just as much, driving down to Sussex every Sunday afternoon for five seasons and going to plenty of away matches, cheering heroes like Gordon Kennett, Kelly Moran and Paul Woods. By 1984, though, my life had changed. I was twenty-five, I'd become a full-time writer and was in a steady relationship, so after 14 seasons of speedway – mostly enjoyable though sometimes frustrating – the sport fell away for me. I'm delighted to say I got back into it about eight years ago, watching the Grand Prix on television, but this is presently on hold until it returns to Sky or Eurosport because, on principle, I refuse to subscribe expensively to yet another channel on top of those I already have.

I've never parted with my speedway paraphernalia – it's all here along with the rest of my life's gatherings, so I still have my complete set of Lions programmes home and away for 1970–71. Amazingly, I've also made a real friendship with Bert Harkins. He lives just down the road from me in Berkhamsted, and he and his wife and me and mine get along very well, going for dinner and nice days out. The first time I went to Bert's house he hung his Wembley Lions race jacket – Number 1 – on the door outside, so I would know which house was his.

I've always been sure that Wembley Lions' 1970 revival was a great fillip for British speedway, and its sudden closure lost the sport not only a big chunk of its magic but also a large body of fans for whom speedway became something they 'used to go to'. Imagine the effect on British speedway today if there was a team riding in the national stadium. Nothing is impossible but, let's face it ...

It did happen all those years ago, however, and I'm still cherishing the memories of a wonderful and happy chapter in my life.

Bert and Mark at a social occasion more recently.
(Photo: Courtesy Mark Lewisohn)

Mark Lewisohn is a best-selling author and the only professional Beatles historian. He has also written on other subjects, including a biography of the comedian Benny Hill. For more information visit www.marklewisohn.net

23. The end

The problems the Lions had in 1971 securing enough dates at the Stadium put the 1972 season under question, particularly given the problems of trying to obtain an alternative venue to use for part of the season. Whether this would have worked, given the experience of the Lions at Wimbledon in 1948, we shall never know.

In November, in the *Star*, Eric Linden flagged up that the ever increasing use of Wembley for football could cause even more problems for the Lions. He also said that some riders were not happy with the short home season, and that this was one reason that Ken McKinlay had refused to join the Lions in 1971. Later in the month, the *Star* reported that Trevor Redmond already had an alternative venue available, and that more Wednesday night dates could be used by the Lions. It is hard to see how this would have worked – the occasional Wednesday night meetings were already not as well attended as the Saturday night meetings, and would the fans – let alone the riders – have been happy with a Wembley season crammed into three or four months. There was an England fixture planned for September, in fact it was not played until the second week of October.

In December, it was announced that West Ham were withdrawing from the First Division, and that the Greyhound Racing Association (GRA) were selling the stadium for redevelopment. While the Hammers had not had a great season in 1971, either on the track or at the gate, the vulnerability of speedway to losing teams because they did not own their own stadiums was shown yet again. The Romford Bombers moved in for a couple of months, having lost their track after a court case about noise nuisance; but by June they were also gone, with their licence transferred to Barrow. Ipswich took over the Hammers' First Division spot.

Meanwhile, Bert Harkins was riding in Australia for the British Lions. Dave Jessup, Brian Collins and Peter Prinsloo were riding in Rhodesia. In December, the *Star* reported that Trevor Redmond was "confident" about the Lions riding in 1972, and that he was looking for a title bid by the Lions.

Honours from the government and the monarchy are very rare in speedway. The *Star* made up for this by having its own 'honours' for the sport. Sverre Harrfeldt certainly deserved the 'Mister Courage' award for his return to track action and how he had worked his way up from reserve to 'star'. A couple of weeks later, Trevor Redmond confirmed that Harrfeldt would be invited back to ride for the Lions in 1972.

In February, Dave Jessup asked for a transfer. He said that he had enjoyed his time at Wembley, but needed to ride more meetings. Then came the announcement that every Lions fan had been dreading – "Wembley Out!" was the huge headline in the *Star*. A Wembley spokesman said: "We cannot guarantee regular speedway because of a possible extension of the football season and other events that may be held at the Stadium." Trevor Redmond said that it was a "bombshell". Redmond was going to look for an alternative venue, and it seemed that the stadium may be available in 1973. The World Final was still going to be staged on 16 September. In 1972, England played at Wembley on 23 May, and then Yugoslavia on 11 October. Unless there were other events on Saturdays, using midweek dates a Wembley speedway season could have been fitted in. The track was going to be laid anyway, for the World Final.

Redmond had been told in January that the Stadium would be available, and had arranged four extra dates at Wimbledon. He had paid an increased rent in 1971 of almost £1,000 per meeting, but despite that did better business than in 1970. The Lions had been the best supported track in the country. Martin Rogers said that the return of the Lions to British speedway had been beneficial for the sport. Redmond commented that it was a financial blow, he had tried several other venues in London, and even considered St Austell, where he ran stock car racing. Harringay, White City and Walthamstow all had tarmac tracks for stock car racing, which ruled speedway out. White City did stage speedway from 1976 to 1978, but the attendances were poor, and despite winning the league, the team was moved to Eastbourne.

West Ham and New Cross were both to be redeveloped. He said that he would make arrangements to loan the riders out for 1972, and hoped to bring them back to Wembley in 1973. A week later, he announced plans for the Lions to ride some challenge matches in 1972, to keep the name alive. But apart from a four team tournament towards the end of the season, these never materialised.

Dave Jessup remained a Lion, but with Leicester. Brian Collins moved to Poole, where he lived. Bert Harkins moved to Sheffield; Tony Clarke and Brian Leonard were allocated to Newport, but Leonard did not want to return to the track he had left in 1970, so joined Swindon. Sverre Harrfeldt was allocated to Oxford, but retired from British speedway.

On 27 October, Bert Harkins, Brian Leonard, Dave Jessup and Tony Clarke rode as 'Ex Wembley' in a four team tournament at Hackney. The hosts won with 40 points, Ipswich were runners-up on 26, and the Lions took third place with 14, two ahead of Wimbledon. Harkins top-scored with seven, Leonard and Jessup got four each, while Tony Clarke scored one point.

Early in January 1973, it was announced that the Lions had been unable to secure a return to Wembley Stadium, or secure an alternative venue in London. A transfer of their licence to Ellesmere Port was being muted, but that never happened. For the Wembley Lions, and their thousands of supporters, the dream was no more.

The Lions last appearance was an end of season challenge match at Wimbledon. Riding as 'Ex-Wembley', the Lions lost a 'lively' match 43–35. Brian Leonard top scored for the Lions with 11, Dave Jessup got eight, Brian Collins seven, Tony Clarke five and Bert Harkins, who wore his Wembley leathers but had bike trouble all night, one. Rogers Johns with two points and Ian Fletcher, who scored one, rode at reserve for the Lions. Dave Jessup was their last heat winner, and Brian Collins won a second half trophy for the Lions.

Most of the Lions riders continued to ride for a variety of teams, and their careers are covered in Part Four of this book.

Wembley Stadium continued to stage a big speedway meeting each year until 1981. The last meeting was the memorable 1981 World Final, won by Bruce Penhall. I made a last minute decision to go, so I saw the last meeting; and had also been to the Lions' last match at Wimbledon in 1973.

John McNeil and Peter York – when he was BSPA manager – at different times tried to get more speedway staged at Wembley, but the financial guarantees involved made it unviable. Indoor racing was staged at the Arena from 1979 to 1983.

The document setting up Wembley Speedway Ltd mentioned stock car racing. Trevor Redmond did run two stock car meetings at Wembley in 1974, but under the banner of his Auto Speed Circuits company. It was the first time that stock car racing had been held at Wembley, and it was not run again at the stadium.

All of the other London venues from both the Lions eras have not staged speedway for many years, and most are now demolished or about to be. Redevelopment and the price of land in London makes it very unlikely that we will see speedway again within the M25. Arena

Essex, Rye House and Kent are the only venues now reasonably accessible for London speedway followers.

It is extremely unlikely that Wembley will ever stage speedway again. Barry Briggs did organise an 'End of an Era' dinner in 2000 before the old stadium was demolished. It was attended by 600 people, double that which had attended a similar football event.

The Grand Prix is well-established in Cardiff. But with the new Olympic Stadium in Stratford having the flexibility to stage different events, us old-time London fans can dream that one day we will see and hear speedway bikes in action in the capital again, if the Grand Prix ever decides to come to the capital.

The invitation to the last speedway event at Wembley. It is based on the design of the Wembley Lions programme from 1950 to 1956. (Courtesy Mark Lewisohn)

The last time: An 'Ex-Wembley' team rode at Wimbledon in a challenge match on 18 October 1973.

Part Four: The riders

24. The Lions' riders 1946 to 1956

Bruce Mackenzie Abernethy (1948 to 1951)
Kenneth Peter (Ken) Adams (1955 to 1956)
George Bason (1946)
Alfred John Herbert (Alf) Bottoms (1949)
Michael John (Mike) Broadbank (1956)
Raymond Arthur Alfred (Buster) Brown (1949)
Dennis G. (Den) Cosby (1949 to 1952)
Roy Allan Craighead (1946 to 1948)
Raymond (Ray) Cresp (1956)
Robert Thomas (Bobby) Croombs (1956)
Brian Thomas Crutcher (1953 to 1956)
Eric French (1953 to 1956)
Jack W. Gates (1949 to 1950)
William Charles (Bill) Gilbert (1946 to 1950)
James Everard (Jimmy) Gooch (1950 to 1956)
James William (Jim) Gregory (1948)
Austin Mervyn Roy (Merv) Hannam (1956)
Stanley (Stan) Hodson (1946)
Gerald Richard Jackson (1956)
William (Bill) Kemp (1948)
William (Bill) Kitchen (1946 to 1954)
Wilbur Leonard Lamoreaux (1948)
Fred Lang (1954)
Phil Lewry (1946)
William (Bill) Longley (1955)
Charles Edward (Charlie) May (1946 to 1947)
Dennis Ronald Newton (1953)
Robert Lawford (Bob) Oakley (1950 to 1952)
Thomas (Tommy) Price (1946 to 1956)
Trevor John Redmond (1952 to 1956)
George Henry Saunders (1948 to 1949)
Rune Bertil Leopold Sörmander (1953)
Squire Francis (Split) Waterman (1947 to 1949, 1956)
Robert (Bob) Wells (1946 to 1951)
George Wilks (1946 to 1954)
William Eric Williams (1951 to 1955)
Frederick Owen (Freddie) Williams (1947 to 1956)
Horatio Nelson (Bronco) Wilson (1946 to 1947)

This chapter is based on research by Matt Jackson, who also provided the statistics for the National League and National Trophy matches and the Lions appearances for other clubs. These are usually only included where the rider still had a connection with Wembley. Riders who appeared in any National League, National Trophy, London Cup or other cup match are included. The early season Middlesex Cup matches with Harringay and other Challenge matches are not included. The statistics for the riders are for meetings for Wembley unless otherwise indicated; their achievements cover their whole career.

Bruce Mackenzie Abernethy
Born: 14 May 1928, Wellington, New Zealand.
Died: May 1999.

One of the most colourful and entertaining riders the sport has ever seen, Bruce was a Kiwi who spent four seasons with the Lions, having being recommended to the club by the former New Zealand international Wally Kilminster after some impressive showings on the Taita track in his home town of Wellington. He spent most of the 1948 season on loan at non-league Rayleigh and showed impressive form as the Rockets took on Third Division sides in challenge matches. These performances earned him a call up to the Lions side in 1949 and, despite being a second string rider in the main, his extravagant personality made him one of the most popular riders of his time.

He played an important role in the Lions championship winning sides of 1949, 1950 and 1951 and his last season in Britain proved to be his best. He was paid for double figures on 11 occasions during the league and cup campaign and looked certain to reach the World Final until blowing his chance in his last qualifying round at Harringay when he suffered three falls. Despite not returning to Wembley after the 1951 season, 'Abner' rode intermittently in New Zealand for many years and resisted numerous approaches to return – including a bid by West Ham as late as 1964. For at least two years after 1951, there was hopeful speculation by the Lions fans that he would return, but it never happened. Once he even sent a bike to Britain, but then changed his mind and did not follow it. Twice the New Zealand Champion, Bruce died in May 1999.

Year	Club	Division	M	R	P	BP	TP	CMA	FM	PM
1948	Wembley	NL1	1	2	2	0	2	4.00	-	-
1949	Wembley	NL1 & NT	35	100	99	25	124	4.96	-	-
		London Cup	2	4	2	0	2	2.00		
1950	Wembley	NL1 & NT	31	86	99	25	124	5.77	-	-
		London Cup	4	18	20	4	24	5.33		
1951	Wembley	NL1 & NT	31	124	202	31	233	7.52	-	3
		London Cup	4	21	26	5	31	5.90		
	Totals		108	355	450	90	540			

Individual Honours: New Zealand Champion 1950, 1951.
Team Honours: National League Division One Championship winner 1949, 1950, 1951. London Cup winner 1950, 1951.

Kenneth Peter (Ken) Adams
Born: 28 August 1924, Kensal Green, London, England.
Died: 1 May 1998.

Ken was a tremendous club man who had a career spanning nearly 20 years at a host of different venues, but his name will remain synonymous with the Stoke 'Potters', with whom he spent almost 10 seasons in two separate spells.

He joined the Army in 1943 and served in the Royal Tank Corps. He was a despatch rider instructor, and on leaving the Army in 1947, attended Tiger Stevenson's speedway training.

A Londoner who was born near Wembley, he joined Stoke in 1948 and made progress quickly through the ranks at Sun Street, scoring over 500 points in helping the club win the Third Division title in his second season. He made the transition into Division Two in 1950, taking over the captaincy of the Potters from Dave Anderson, and progressed to be a solid heat leader in the Second Division. This was despite having to overcome rupturing a liver in Sweden in the winter of 1950–51 while ice racing.

He was transfer listed at his own request in 1952 but stayed with the Potters and only left Sun Street when the club closed its doors to the sport at the end of 1953. A season with Southampton followed, and he then joined the new team at Weymouth for the 1954 campaign. After they prematurely withdrew from the league, he was a surprise signing by Wembley, given that his whole career had been spent in the Second or Third Divisions. He served the Lions well at reserve or second string, but lost his place in 1956 and moved back to the Second Division with Ipswich. After spells with Rayleigh, Poole and Oxford, Ken returned to Stoke during the 1960 Provincial League campaign and reasserted himself as a heat leader at the Potteries circuit, regularly averaging over eight points per match.

He moved on when the sport ended in Stoke at the end of the 1963 season, having scored well over 2,000 points for the five towns outfit in league and cup matches alone. He rode for Long Eaton and King's Lynn in the twilight of his career. He retired in 1966, but stayed involved for a while as team manager at Crewe in the late 1960s.

Year	Club	Division	M	R	P	BP	TP	CMA	FM	PM
1955	Wembley	NL1 & NT	22	46	42	16	58	5.04	-	-
1956	Wembley	NL1 & NT	1	2	2	2	4	8.00	-	-
	Totals		23	48	44	18	62			

Team Honours: National League Division Three Championship winner 1949.

George Bason
Born: 1 October 1913, Farnham, Surrey, England.
Died: 2004.

George started his speedway career in 1937. He rode one London Cup match for Wembley in 1946, having signed from West Ham as cover for Bronco Wilson. He broke his leg and did not ride for the Lions again. In 1947 he signed for Southampton. He moved to Liverpool Chads in 1949. He rode a full season that year, but only three meetings in 1950. In 1952 he rode briefly for Swindon, and in 1954 for California in the Southern Area League before retiring.

Year	Club	Division	M	R	P	BP	TP	CMA	FM	PM
1946	Wembley	London Cup	1	2	0	0	0	0.00	-	-

Alfred John Herbert (Alf) Bottoms
Born: 20 June 1918, Kensington, London, England.
Died: 3 May 1951.

The management at Wembley in the years immediately following the war had a fine knack of plucking riders from obscurity and thrusting them into the limelight of riding against world class stars in front of tens of thousands of spectators, often with superb results. A prime example of this was the progress of Alf Bottoms, who came to the Empire Stadium via their training scheme at Rye House.

He was an ever present in the Lions side in 1946 and won a championship medal in his first season, proving to be one of the discoveries of the year. After missing almost the whole of 1947 following an operation in which he had a kidney removed, Alf was allowed to join Third Division Southampton, despite comments that he was too good to ride at that level.

Those views were well founded as Alf dominated the league, scoring 35 maximums and a massive 625 points. For a rider to beat Alf that year was a feat and it was no surprise when he returned to Wembley in 1949. He settled into a reserve berth back in Division One and played a part in two more championship winning sides before retiring in mid-1950. Away from speedway, Alf had a passion for cars and was a successful performer on four wheels, but was sadly killed in a car crash in Luxembourg in 1951 at the age of 32.

Year	Club	Division	M	R	P	BP	TP	CMA	FM	PM
1946	Wembley	NL & NT	24	101	125.5	26.5	152	6.02	-	-
		ACU Cup	10	50	59.5	13.5	73	5.84		
		London Cup	4	20	24	5	29	5.80		
1947	Wembley	NL1 & NT	2	4	2	1	3	3.00	-	-
1948	Southampton	NL3	52	224	625	7	632	11.29	28	7
1949	Wembley	NL1 & NT	40	111	135	25	160	5.77	-	-
		London Cup	4	14	21	5	26	7.43		
1950	Wembley	NL1 & NT	11	23	19	6	25	4.35	-	-
		London Cup	2	4	1	0	1	1.00		
	Wembley	**Totals**	97	327	387	82	469			

Team Honours: National League Championship winner 1946, National League Division One Championship winner 1949, 1950. London Cup winner: 1946, 1949.

Michael John (Mike) Broadbank
Born: 25 September 1934, Hoddesdon, Hertfordshire, England.

Despite the fact that Ivan Mauger rode in the Southern Area League early in his career, the finest true product of the league was Mike Broadbank, who developed his talents at his local Rye House track. He had ridden at the circuit in his late teens before completing National Service and returned to take his place in the side for the 1955 season. Mike scored a full maximum on his league debut at Brafield and went on to have a fantastic first season in the sport, culminating in winning the Southern Area League Riders Championship.

These performances attracted the attention of the bigger clubs and Mike signed for the biggest of them all, joining Wembley for a season of racing in the First Division. He spent just one season at the Empire Stadium, and showed what a good prospect he was with an average of over six. When the Lions called a halt to league racing, he was signed by Swindon after at least one club turned him down. Mike's transfer proved to be a master stroke for the Robins. He developed into a world class rider, spending 16 fantastic seasons with the club to become one of the most popular riders ever at Blunsdon. Mike was an instantly recognisable figure in speedway for more than 20 years, but his best days were with Swindon. He reached the first of his five World Finals in 1958 and the following year took over as number one at Swindon, establishing him as one of England's leading riders.

His average dipped slightly in the early 1960s as he struggled with ill health but, when the British League was formed in 1965, he recorded a career best average of 10.53 points per match which put him fourth in the league averages. This was the peak of Mike's career as his average fell annually until 1972 when he finally left the Abbey Stadium, having made 418 appearances for the club and scoring well over 3,000 points.

Fast approaching the age of 40, Mike could have retired, but decided to continue and joined Division Two newcomers Stoke to lead the side for the 1973 season. He put his experience to full use with a new lease of life at Loomer Road, topping the Potters' averages with a figure of over nine points per match and repeated this form in 1974 in a second season with the club. He returned to the top flight in 1975 for a season at Hackney before ending a glorious career in 1977 after spells at Crayford and Newport.

In his five World Finals Mike never really did himself justice and his best performance was ninth place in 1964, but he was essentially a team man rather that an individual and will be remembered with legendary status, particularly by supporters of the Swindon Robins. Mike rode throughout his career with the surname of Broadbanks, the extra 's' being added at the start of his riding days and never corrected. He was one of two riders from the 1950s Wembley Lions to still be riding when the Lions returned in 1970.

Year	Club	Division	M	R	P	BP	TP	CMA	FM	PM
1956	Wembley	NL1 & NT	25	60	83	9	92	6.13	-	-

Individual Honours: World finalist 1958 (12th), 1961 (16th), 1962 (15th), 1964 (9th), 1966 (13th), Southern Area League Riders Champion 1955.
International Honours: England international – 28 caps, 167 points, Great Britain international – 8 caps, 30 points.
Team Honours: Southern Area League Championship winner 1955, National League Championship winner 1957, British League Championship winner 1967.

Raymond Arthur Alfred (Buster) Brown
Born: 21 April 1931, Greenford, London, England.

Born Raymond Brown, but known as 'Buster' from his schooldays, he was a leading cycle speedway rider before turning to the shale at the Rye House Training School under the tutelage of Dick Case, and had his first rides on Christmas Eve 1948. Interviewed by Phillip Dalling in *The Golden Age of Speedway*, he recalled that he was invited back a week later and "Alec Jackson offered me a contract, at £28 a week, which was a lot of money for an apprentice draughtsman. Alec also had to pay the firm for which I worked to get them to allow me time off for practice." His dad bought him a new road bike to try to dissuade him from signing for the Lions, but he took up speedway anyway.

He made nine appearances for the Lions. He was loaned to Oxford in 1950 to gain experience and won a Third Division championship with them. However, he never returned to Wembley, moving on loan to Swindon in 1951 where he had his best spell in the sport and later to Poole; he was part of the deal which took Brian Crutcher from Wimborne Road to Wembley. He rode for England 'C' in 1951 against New Zealand, the USA and Sweden.

Buster surprisingly quit the sport at the age of just 22. The 1952 edition of *Coming Speedway Stars* said that "…all he now needs is more and more racing experience and then he will be ready to hold his place in the senior division." But his premature retirement meant that never happened. In his interview with Phillip Dalling, he said that he "did not really settle at Poole and retired to start a driving school." He returned to the sport in 1962. He captained non-league Weymouth and had four outings for Swindon.

Year	Club	Division	M	R	P	BP	TP	CMA	FM	PM
1949	Wembley	NL1	9	18	7	4	11	2.44	-	-
1950	Oxford	NL3	40	131	179	23	202	6.17	-	1
1951	Swindon	NL3	41	168	284.5	29	313.5	7.46	3	2
1952	Swindon	SL	37	137	204.5	24	228.5	6.67	-	2
1953	Wembley	Coronation Cup	1	1	0	0	0	0.00		
	Wembley	Totals	10	19	7	4	11			

Team Honours: National League Division One Championship winner 1949, National League Division Three Championship winner 1950.

Dennis G. (Den) Cosby
Born: 1927, Uxbridge, Middlesex, England.
Died: 2009

Den served in the Army as a despatch rider and came into the sport via grass track racing. He joined Wembley, the strongest team in the world and in each of his four seasons at the Empire Stadium the Lions won the league. However, due to the strength of the side, he played only a minor role in this and only made 25 appearances in four years. He preferred to stay with the Lions rather than join a lower league club where he would have gained more experience and points. His best performance came in a National Trophy match against Birmingham in 1950, scoring nine points. He suffered with a back injury towards the end of his career which clearly affected his progress, and eventually saw him retire from speedway.

Year	Club	Division	M	R	P	BP	TP	CMA	FM	PM
1949	Wembley	NL1	8	27	18	2	20	2.96	-	-
1950	Wembley	NL1	9	24	20	2	22	3.67	-	-
		London Cup	2	10	3	1	4	1.60		
1951	Wembley	NL1	3	6	3	1	4	2.67	-	-
		London Cup	1	2	4	2	6	12.00		
1952	Wembley	NL1	5	10	4	0	4	1.60	-	-
1953	Wembley	Coronation Cup	4	7	1	0	1	0.57		
		Totals	32	86	53	8	61			

Team Honours: National League Division One Championship winner 1949, 1950.

Roy Allan Craighead

Born: 11 September 1916, Ilford, Essex, England.
Died: 17 March 2007

Although Roy was one of the lesser publicised riders, success seemed to follow him around the tracks throughout his career. He had ridden on the grass track circuits of southern England prior to the war and was spotted by Wembley in 1946 after some impressive practice sessions at Rye House.

He was a consistent middle order scorer for the Lions and played an essential part in the back-to-back title winning sides of 1946 and 1947 – adding vital points to those scored by the more illustrious members of the side such as Kitchen, Price and Wilks. After a poor season in 1948, during which he suffered from illness, Roy moved into the Second Division with Southampton and spent most of the rest of his career in the lower leagues.

He had his best season with Southampton at Bannister Court in 1950 before moving along the south coast and helping Poole to the Third Division championship in 1951, followed by the Second Division title the very next year. The strength of the Pirates team in 1952 was shown by the fact that Roy finished ninth in the Pirates averages that year with an end of season figure of 6.69 which would have made him third heat leader at Oxford.

After this success with the Pirates Roy rode only occasionally over the next nine years, but still the league championships followed him and he was able to play a minor role in Rayleigh's success in the Provincial League in 1960.

Year	Club	Division	M	R	P	BP	TP	CMA	FM	PM
1946	Wembley	NL & NT	24	85	100.5	27.5	128	6.02	-	-
		ACU Cup	9	43	38	14	52	4.84		
		London Cup	4	20	15	5	20	4.00		
1947	Wembley	NL1 & NT	27	79	107	15	122	6.18	-	-
		British Speedway Cup	9	28	47	7	54	7.71		1 (3)
		London Cup	4	14	12	1	13	3.71		
1948	Wembley	NL1 & NT	24	76	53	13	66	3.47	-	-
		Anniversary Cup	11	35	28	7	35	4.00		
		Totals	112	380	400.5	89.5	490			

Team Honours: National League Championship winner 1946, National League Division One Championship winner 1947, National League Division Two Championship winner 1952, National League Division Three Championship winner 1951, National Trophy winner 1948. London Cup: Winner 1946, runner-up 1947.

Raymond (Ray) Cresp

Born: 25 August 1928, Melbourne, Victoria, Australia.

Ray was a protégé of the Australian international and fellow Melbourne resident, Jack Biggs, and come to prominence in the 1955–56 Australian season. After only a short time in the sport, Ray took the plunge and travelled to England for the 1956 season, accepting an offer to ride in the Southern Area League with the Eastbourne Eagles. He made his league debut at California on 22 April and scored 34 points in just three matches for the club. This not only demonstrated that he was too good for that standard of speedway, but set the big clubs clamouring for his signature.

Wembley won the race and Ray completed a remarkable first couple of months in British speedway by turning out for the Lions at the Empire Stadium against Birmingham on May 24. His first three matches in a Lions race jacket saw him score paid eight and two hauls of paid 10 in a sensational spell which had him tipped as a future champion. Highlights of the season were his first paid maximum and a defeat of the reigning World Champion Peter Craven as he raced to a six point plus average.

Wembley pulled out of league racing in March 1957 and Ray was forced to seek pastures new, joining Oxford for 1957, and from then on he rarely settled with any one club throughout his 11 year spell in Britain. This lack of continuity possibly contributed to the fact that Ray never reached the world class rating his early performances had suggested, but he was a consistent and respected top flight performer. In 1961 Ray averaged a career best 8.34 points per match for Ipswich and reached his one and only World Final. This was the historic Malmö staged event, the first ever not held at Wembley. Ray finished 14th with three points. He represented both Australia and Great Britain at international level and ended his British career in 1966 after a two season spell at Long Eaton, at the age of 38.

Year	Club	Division	M	R	P	BP	TP	CMA	FM	PM
1956	Wembley	NL1	20	79	106	16	122	6.18	-	1

Individual Honours: World Finalist 1961 (14th).
International Honours: Australian international – 4 caps, 14 points, Great Britain international – 6 caps, 3 points.

Robert Thomas (Bobby) Croombs
Born: 21 April 1931, Kingston-upon-Thames, Surrey, England.

The son of former World Finalist and England international Tommy Croombs, Bobby emigrated to Australia with his family in the late 1940s after his father had finished his racing career. He began riding in Sydney and returned to England in 1952. He completed his National Service and was due to join Harringay, but the track closed. He linked up with Rye House in the Southern Area League in 1956 and was one of the top riders in the championship winning side, missing just two matches that season and scoring double figures on four separate occasions. He rode one match for the Wembley Lions near the end of the 1956 season.

Despite another fine season with Rye House in 1957, senior outings were hard to come by and it was not until New Cross reopened in 1960 in the National League that he got his big chance in the top tier. He showed occasional glimpses of form in south east London, but his best season came in 1962 when he contributed some vital points to Poole's Provincial League championship winning side. Bobby started the 1963 season with the Pirates, but retired due to increasing work commitments.

Year	Club	Division	M	R	P	BP	TP	CMA	FM	PM
1956	Rye House	SAL	12	51	92	11	103	8.08	-	1
1956	Wembley	NL1	1	2	0	0	0	0.00	-	-

Team Honours: Southern Area League Championship winner 1956, Provincial League Championship winner 1962, Southern Area League Knock-Out Cup winner 1956.

Brian Thomas Crutcher
Born: 23 August 1934, Parkstone, Dorset, England.

The son of former Exeter rider Tom Crutcher, Brian was one of England's finest ever products and can be counted as one of the best riders never to win the World Championship. At the age of 16, Brian signed for his local Poole Pirates side and burst onto the speedway scene like a whirlwind, sending all the top clubs in the country scurrying for his signature. He made his official debut for the Pirates in the Division Three fixture at home to St. Austell in May 1951 and showed signs of what was to come by riding unbeaten in his two outings from reserve.

He got better and better as the season progressed and, once out of the reserve position, began to chalk up some sensational scores to end the season with an average of 9.41 points per match – second only to Ken Middleditch – as Poole won the Third Division championship. The 1952 edition of *Coming Speedway Stars* said that he would develop into the greatest post-war discovery of speedway. "Watch this boy for future honours!" Fans of Peter Craven would probably dispute that accolade, but he went on to enjoy more success.

Brian's second season proved to be truly remarkable as he qualified for his first World Final at the age of 18 and made his debut for England. He also repeated the 9.41 average of the previous year, with the Pirates now taking the Second Division by storm. Brian playing a huge role as they won back-to-back championships. It was clear that Poole were going to struggle to hold on to him, with the only question being which lucky club would win the race and be able to afford the substantial transfer fee.

The answer was Wembley who shelled out a reported £2,500 to sign 'Nipper' in time for their opening home league match in 1953 as he departed Wimborne Road in May, having scored a fitting maximum in his last appearance. He had been invited to ride in second half races at the Empire Stadium in 1952, partly to help him prepare for the World Final, and also so the Lions could see how he performed.

He was undoubtedly one of the most important signings Wembley made. Bill Kitchen had retired, Bob Oakley had also gone, George Wilks was well past his best, Freddie Williams gradually declined after 1953, and Tommy Price was still effective, but was well into the veteran stage of his career. Crutcher was the young rising star that the critics had been saying the Lions needed for years.

He quickly settled into the rigours of top flight racing, helping Wembley to their final league championship and completing a remarkable personal feat by winning league titles at all three levels of the sport in his first three seasons. Brian took over as Wembley's number one and, for a time was England's top rider, finishing second in the World Final in 1954 and becoming England's youngest ever captain when he led the national side in the second test against Australasia at Wembley in 1955 at just 21 years of age.

Brian stayed at the top of the Wembley averages until the end of the 1956 season. When the club pulled out of the sport he moved back to the south coast to race for Southampton. In his three full seasons at Bannister Court he was still one of the leading riders in the world with some superbly consistent riding at club level. However, he had invested wisely in his business dealings and speedway began to become secondary in his life. He turned down all open meeting bookings and did not partake in overseas tours for England as he could not afford time away from work. When he missed part of the 1959 season suffering from a reported nervous exhaustion, it became clear that Brian's days in speedway were numbered. He announced his retirement at the start of the 1960 season aged just 25. In Tom Wareham's biography, he says that "When Wembley closed, well, for me that was it really. Where do you go after that? And when I went off on doctor's orders, well all of that was because I was fed up with the game. My car business was doing well and I could see that speedway was dropping off..."

During his time in the sport Brian won many individual and team honours, but the world title always eluded him. His decision not to ride for his country on occasions limited him to just 23 caps. This should not detract from the undoubted fact that Brian remains one of the finest English riders ever to have ridden in the sport of speedway, and one of the best in the 1946 to 1956 Lions set up.

Year	Club	Division	M	R	P	BP	TP	CMA	FM	PM
1953	Wembley	NL1 & NT	22	92	164	22.5	186.5	8.11	1	1
		Coronation Cup	10	40	58	10	68	6.80		
		London Cup	2	11	16	4	20	7.27		
1954	Wembley	NL1 & NT	32	135	322.5	18.5	341	10.10	9	3
		RAC Cup	6	24	48	2	50	8.33	1	
		London Cup	4	21	45	5	50	9.52	1	
1955	Wembley	NL1 & NT	30	163	369	11	380	9.33	3	2
1956	Wembley	NL1 & NT	26	112	279	5	284	10.14	7	-
		Totals	132	598	1301.5	78	1379.5			

Individual Honours: World finalist 1952 (11th), 1953 (10th), 1954 (2nd), 1955 (5th), 1956 (8th), 1959 (6th), British Match Race Champion May 1956 to August 1956, July 1958 to September 1958.
International Honours: England international – 23 caps, 257 points.
Team Honours: National League Division Three Championship winner 1951, National League Division Two Championship winner 1952, National League Division One Championship winner 1953, National Trophy winner 1954. London Cup: Winner 1954.

Eric French
Born: 4 August 1913, Cork, Republic of Ireland.
Died: February 1974.

By far the best speedway rider to hail from the Republic of Ireland, Eric was brought to England by his parents as a child and took up grass track racing in 1935. He had ridden for Wimbledon as a reserve prior to the war but, after working in an aircraft factory during the hostilities, he was still relatively unknown when he was chosen by New Cross in 1946.

He developed steadily into a consistent scorer and played a critical role in the Rangers title winning side of 1948 which interrupted Wembley's stranglehold on the league championship. He made his test debut for his adopted country at his home track in the 1949 series against Australia, but ended his second test at Harringay in hospital with shoulder injuries after scoring a creditable seven points.

Although he never appeared in a World Final, Eric graduated to full heat leader class in 1950 and his form was so good that in June he made an unsuccessful challenge for Jack Parker's Golden Helmet Match Race title. By the time New Cross closed early in the 1953 season Eric held the post-war appearance and point scoring records for the Rangers and fittingly ended the club's last full season in that period as their number one. When the unemployed Rangers were allocated to other tracks, Eric joined Wembley at the age of 39, and although he did not show the same form as a Lion he was a member of their league winning side in his first year at the Empire Stadium and claimed a National Trophy winner's medal in 1954. His best season came in 1956, when due to the retirement of Eric Williams and the premature departure of Freddie Williams, he finally could claim a heat leader slot.

Eric remained in the top flight throughout his career and ended his racing days with a season at Rayleigh in 1957. In retrospect, he may have done better to move to one of the First Division's weaker teams rather than the Lions, where he often struggled for recognition amidst the stars.

Year	Club	Division	M	R	P	BP	TP	CMA	FM	PM
1953	Wembley	NL1 & NT	21	80	99	20	119	5.95	-	-
		Coronation Cup	3	12	16	5	21	7.00		
1954	Wembley	NL1 & NT	30	95	133	22	155	6.53	-	1
		RAC Cup	6	21	27	3	30	5.71		
		London Cup	4	7	5	2	7	4.00		
1955	Wembley	NL1 & NT	30	141	166	41	207	5.87	-	-
1956	Wembley	NL1	26	102	163	23	186	7.29	-	2
		Totals	120	458	609	116	725			

International Honours: England international – 8 caps, 43 points.
Team Honours: National League Division One Championship winner 1948, 1953, National Trophy winner 1954. London Cup Winner: 1954.

Jack W. Gates
Born: 3 December 1926, Sydney, New South Wales, Australia.
Died: 14 May 2012

A former New South Wales triple jump champion, Jack made his first voyage to the UK in 1949 and was given opportunities by Leicester in the Third Division. He was dropped by the Hunters before he had chance to settle and was surprisingly taken on by Wembley later in the season. After a period in the second half at the Empire Stadium, short term injuries to Bill Kitchen and Freddie Williams gave Jack a chance in the reserve berth and he was able to play a minor role in the Lions' league title triumph that year.

After another season with limited chances in 1950 he moved to Ashfield where he averaged over six points a match for the Giants. Returning home that winter, he showed his best form on his native tracks and twice scored double figures for Australia against England in the unofficial test series. He missed out on the 1952 British season before returning for spells in the south west at St Austell and Plymouth to end his British career.

He returned to Australia, and died after a stroke in May 2012 at the age of 85. He had been living on the Gold Coast in Queensland.

Year	Club	Division	M	R	P	BP	TP	CMA	FM	PM
1949	Wembley	NL1	10	22	19	3	22	4.00	-	-
1950	Wembley	NL1	4	11	3	0	3	1.09	-	-
		Totals	14	33	22	3	25			

Team Honours: National League Division One Championship winner 1949.

William Charles (Bill) Gilbert
Born: 7 December 1916, Eltham, London, England.
Died: April 1992.

Wembley were often criticised for being too strong and regular calls were made for them to give up some of their talented riders to lesser clubs. In truth, many of the Lions riders were spotted by the unerring eye of manager Alec Jackson and were plucked from obscurity to be groomed to become stars of the sport. A fine example of the club's far sighted policy was the development of Bill Gilbert, who, after riding at Dagenham as a novice just before the war on a bike which once belonged to the Danish star Morian Hansen, was signed by the Lions after spending the war years serving in the RAF.

He was still a relative unknown and was plunged into the main body of the side from the start of the 1946 season. He responded with some consistent scoring and claimed the first of four league championship medals in his first year. A year of consolidation followed, when Leonard Sandys wrote that he had "recovered admirably" from the crash that wrecked his season in 1946, and said that he was "one of the finest second strings in the country."

Bill made rapid progress during the 1948 campaign with an impressive showing in the British Riders Championship and secured his first international cap in the fourth test against Australia at Harringay. Thirteen points on his debut for England underlined his development and 1949 was his finest year, putting another point on his average to finish as second heat leader behind Tommy Price and reaching his only World Final.

With the competition being held on his home track he may have been disappointed to finish in 11th place, but the fact that he was there showed the remarkable progress he had made. This proved to be the pinnacle of Bill's career as he reached his mid-30s, and after a troubled 1950 season during which he was in dispute with the Speedway Riders Association as well as fracturing a vertebrae, he announced his retirement from the sport. After taking a year out to work in the family grocery business, Bill was tempted back into the saddle to ride for Norwich and provided some useful scores in a difficult first season in the top flight for the Stars before hanging up his leathers for good at the end of 1952.

Year	Club	Division	M	R	P	BP	TP	CMA	FM	PM
1946	Wembley	NL	16	58	64	17	81	5.59	-	-
		ACU Cup	6	29	22.5	3	25.5	3.52		
		London Cup	2	10	17	3	20	8.00		
1947	Wembley	NL1	30	126	133.5	38.5	172	5.46	-	-
		British Speedway Cup	12	49	68	19	87	7.10		1
		London Cup	4	20	16	5	21	4.20		
1948	Wembley	NL1	30	129	225	32	257	7.97	1	1
		Anniversary Cup	12	49	63	19	82	6.69		1
		London Cup	4	23	46	5	51	8.87		
1949	Wembley	NL1	44	179	369	31	400	8.94	3	4
		London Cup	4	21	29	6	35	6.67		
1950	Wembley	NL1	27	107	171	26	197	7.36	1	2
		London Cup	2	10	13	3	16	6.40		
		Totals	**193**	**810**	**1237**	**207.5**	**1444.5**			

Individual Honours: World finalist 1949 (11th). British Riders Championship: Finalist 1948 (5th)

International Honours: England International – 6 caps, 60 points.
Team Honours: National League Championship winner 1946, National League Division One Championship winner 1947, 1949, 1950, National Trophy winner 1948. London Cup: Winner 1946, 1948, 1949, 1950, runner-up 1947.

James Everard (Jimmy) Gooch
Born: 16 November 1928, Dagenham, Essex, England.
Died: 18 June 2011.

Some riders reach world class status in a short space of time and some take a little longer, but there can be few riders in the history of speedway who took 15 years to break into the top echelons of the sport. That was the case with Jimmy Gooch, who began his career on the Army tracks in post-war Germany and won the 1949 Combined Services Trophy. He had joined the Army as a regular soldier in 1946, and served in the Royal Army Service Corps. He was initially in Palestine, but when he was posted to Germany, started riding regularly in the Hanomag meetings. He met Bill Kitchen who was on a brief visit to Germany. 18 months later he was riding with him for the Lions.

His success and a trail with the Lions when on leave won him a contract with Wembley. His brother paid the fee to 'buy him out' of the Army and Jimmy managed to win a reserve spot in the 1950 season. He was renowned for his wholehearted efforts and was a popular figure at the North West London venue, but struggled to lift himself into the main body of the team year upon year. He never quite made the progress that was predicted for him during his time with the Lions.

Eventually, tiring of the struggle of Division One speedway, he went on loan to Swindon in the Second Division in 1955 and moved to Bradford the following year in an attempt to step up to the next level. When Wembley closed early in 1957, Jimmy moved to Ipswich, but endured a torrid time at Foxhall Heath and quit the sport, sitting out the whole of the 1959 season. He was tempted back by New Cross in 1960, but continued to be a little publicised rider of no better than second string standard until a move to Oxford in 1964 suddenly brought Jimmy to the forefront of the sport.

Now aged 35, he should have been in the twilight of his career but the move brought more of an Indian summer as he added over two points to his average to record a figure in excess of eight points per match for the first time in his life as the Cheetahs won the National League title. If 1964 was a success, then 1965 was a sensational year for the popular veteran. The first season of the British League brought Jimmy an average of just under 10 points per match, a World Final appearance and place in the Great Britain World Team Cup Final side. His World Final appearance at Wembley was indeed the peak of his career and it was impossible for him to retain his fantastic form as he approached 40. Nevertheless, Jimmy remained a force to be reckoned with in later spells at Newport and Hackney and proved a shining example to other riders as to what could be achieved with hard work and perseverance.

Jimmy Gooch and Mike Broadbank were the only riders from the post-war Lions era to also be riding in 1970, and Gooch rode for Hackney on Wembley's opening night in 1970.

Year	Club	Division	M	R	P	BP	TP	CMA	FM	PM
1950	Wembley	NL1 & NT	12	30	22	4	26	3.47	-	-
		London Cup	2	4	5	0	5	5.00		
1951	Wembley	NL1 & NT	38	96	128	22	150	6.25	-	-

		London Cup	5	11	23	0	23	8.36		
1952	Wembley	NL1 & NT	40	87	83	25	108	4.97	-	-
		London Cup	2	4	10	2	12	12.00		
1953	Wembley	NL1 & NT	21	55	58	22	80	5.82	-	-
		Coronation Cup	16	49	59	18	77	6.29		
		London Cup	2	10	10	5	15	6.00		
1954	Wembley	NL1 & NT	34	114	144	24	168	5.89	1	-
		RAC Cup	6	15	14	4	18	4.80		
		London Cup	4	6	13	2	15	10.00		
1955	Wembley	NL1 & NT	14	43	50	7	57	5.30	-	-
1955	Swindon	NL2	23	116	175	28	203	7.00	1	2
1956	Wembley	NL1 & NT	6	14	18	6	24	6.86	-	-
1956	Bradford	NL1	13	47	55	8	63	5.36	-	-
	Wembley	Totals	202	538	637	141	778			

Individual Honours: World finalist 1965 (14th).
International Honours: World Team Cup finalist 1965, England international – 10 caps, 35 points, Great Britain international – 3 caps, 16 points.
Team Honours: National League Division One Championship winner 1950, 1951, 1952, 1953, National League Championship winner 1964, National Trophy winner 1954, 1963, 1964. London Cup: Winner 1951, 1954.

James William (Jim) Gregory
Born: 29 May 1927, Willesden, London, England.

Jim Gregory was another rider whose speedway career started in the Army. He was a despatch rider in Cairo in the Royal Corps of Signals and rode in the 1948 Egyptian Championship, scoring 11 points.

A former Wembley junior, Jim made his only official appearance for the Lions at Harringay in July 1948 before figuring in a £50 move to Third Division Rayleigh the following year, after an initial loan spell at the Essex track. In only his third match for the Rockets, Jim scored double figures and he proved to be one of the success stories of the season at The Weir, putting together a fine run of scores and recording his first ever maximum at home to Liverpool at the beginning of September to finish the campaign as third heat leader.

His form attracted the attention of Wimbledon and in 1950 he was back in the top flight, helping the 'Dons' to third place in the league for two successive years with some useful points at the lower end of the team. He rode in the first leg of the successful National Trophy Final against Bradford in his first season at Plough Lane, but his best performances were in the lower leagues. He was a fine addition to the Oxford side when he joined them early in 1952, topping the Cheetahs averages in a difficult year for the club. He remained with Oxford until a loss of form prompted his retirement during the 1954 season, but he stayed interested in the sport and was still riding display races on vintage speedway machines into his 80th year.

Year	Club	Division	M	R	P	BP	TP	CMA	FM	PM
1948	Wembley	NL1	1	3	0	0	0	0.00	-	-

Team Honours: National Trophy winner 1950.

Austin Mervyn Roy (Merv) Hannam
Born: 3 September 1931, Poole, Dorset, England.

The uncle of Brian Crutcher, Merv began his career in the Southern Area League with his local Ringwood track in 1954. He was one of the stars of the new division and provided excellent back up to the heat leader duo of Ernie Lessiter and Alby Golden at Matchams Park. He took over as number one in 1955 after the departure of the previous season's top scorers, but the club closed during the season and Merv finished the year at Eastbourne before winning a dream move to Wembley. Joining his nephew at the Empire Stadium, Merv took over the place vacated by the retired Freddie Williams in mid-season and spent the rest of the year in the reserve berth, recording a top score of four, paid five, at Birmingham. After the closure of Wembley, Merv reverted to second half rides at various southern venues before making a final league appearance for Southampton in 1960.

Year	Club	Division	M	R	P	BP	TP	CMA	FM	PM
1956	Wembley	NL1	15	31	17	5	22	2.84	-	-

Stanley (Stan) Hodson
Born: 4 March 1922, Nottingham, Nottinghamshire, England.
Died: 17 June 1949.

Stan appeared occasionally for Sheffield and Wembley in 1946 before the advent of the Third Division the following year gave him the opportunity for a more regular speedway career. Finally establishing himself in the sport with Exeter, he played a vital role in the Falcons' Division Three title win in 1948 and was a popular performer with the Devon fans. His performances around his home County Ground circuit were particularly impressive, recording five of his six paid maximums in that championship winning season at the Devon track but, such was the strength of the Falcons that year, a 7.48 final average could put him only sixth in the team's end of season figures. During 1949 concerns developed about his health and he was advised to retire during the season. However, he continued to ride, contrary to medical opinion, and tragically died of a heart attack in June in a nursing home in Paignton in Devon at the age of 27.

Year	Club	Division	M	R	P	BP	TP	CMA	FM	PM
1946	Sheffield	NrL	9	19	12	6	18	3.79	-	-
1946	Wembley	NL	2	4	2	0	2	2.00	-	-

Team Honours: National League Division Three Championship winner 1948.

Gerald Richard Jackson
Born: 14 October 1925, Teddington, London, England.
Died: July 1997.

One of the sport's most under-rated riders, Gerald was the son of pre-war Wembley rider Jack Jackson and was initially on West Ham's books as a junior. However, he made his name in the lower leagues as a mainstay of the Rayleigh Rockets and spent seven years at The Weir, establishing the club point scoring record. By 1952 he had reached a nine point figure as he formed a superb spearhead with Jack Unstead and Peter Clark which enabled the club to win the Southern League. He became the Rockets' number one the following year. By the time he had left the club at the end of 1956 he had clocked up almost 2,000 points in league and cup matches alone and had appeared for the Rockets on 234 occasions. Towards the end of the 1956 season he rode one official match for Wembley.

In 1957 he joined Wimbledon and was something of an unsung hero in a team that included Barry Briggs, Ronnie Moore and Ron How. Nevertheless, he was recognised by the international selectors and while he was never a regular choice for England, did score a paid maximum on his debut for his country against Poland. Eight seasons at Plough Lane brought four league championship winner's medals before he was allocated to Hackney when the British League was formed in 1965. Gerald emerged as the Hawks' number one in his first season, averaging over eight points per match at Waterden Road and finishing the year in the top 30 riders in the new league. He finally retired in 1967, approaching the age of 42.

Year	Club	Division	M	R	P	BP	TP	CMA	FM	PM
1956	Rayleigh	NL2	28	142	258	36	294	8.28	1	3
1956	Wembley	NL1	1	4	3	0	3	3.00	-	-

Individual Honours: Southern League Match Race Champion August 1952, July 1953 to September 1953.
International Honours: England international – 9 caps, 54 points.
Team Honours: Southern League Championship winner 1952, 1953, National League Championship winner 1958, 1959, 1960, 1961, National Trophy winner 1960, 1962.

William (Bill) Kemp

Born: 20 December 1921, Rainham, Essex, England.

A milkman prior to taking up the sport, Bill first rode speedway in 1945 in Italy while serving in the Army. He was outstanding and was almost unbeatable. He overcame a broken leg which took him out of the sport for some time, and joined Wembley on leaving the services. Failing to establish himself in the Lions side, he was loaned to Cradley Heath where he made an immediate impression, averaging over seven points per match at Dudley Wood and helping the Midlands side into the runners-up spot in the 1948 Third Division.

A move into Division Two with the Heathens came too soon for a rider of Bill's limited experience and he joined Oxford in the middle of 1949, spending the rest of his career with the Cowley based side. A fine middle order rider in the lower leagues, Bill was a popular figure with the fans at Oxford and played a major role in the Cheetahs Third Division championship triumph of 1950. He made over 150 appearances for the club before retiring at the end of the 1953 season.

Year	Club	Division	M	R	P	BP	TP	CMA	FM	PM
1948	Wembley	NL1	4	8	5	0	5	2.50	-	-
		Anniversary Cup	3	7	5	1	6	3.43		
1948	Cradley Heath	NL3	15	58	82	27	109	7.52	-	-
	Wembley	Totals	7	15	10	1	11			

Team Honours: National League Division Three Championship winner 1950.

William (Bill) Kitchen
Born: 7 December 1908, Galgate, Lancashire, England.
Died: May 1994.

Bill Kitchen was a legend in two eras with two of the greatest clubs the sport has ever known. A former trials, sand racing and Isle of Man TT exponent, Bill joined Belle Vue in 1933 with little experience and became a star almost immediately, gaining international honours for England within weeks of starting his career with the Aces.

He reached two pre-war World Finals and was a member of the Belle Vue side which dominated the sport in Britain, winning four championship medals in his first five years with the Aces. He would have most likely gained another championship success in 1939 but for the league being abandoned following the outbreak of the War. He was an automatic choice for his country in the annual tests against Australia and top scored in both the 1938 and 1939 series, making 31 appearances for England in those pre-war years, and 39 overall.

He rode at Belle Vue during the War, and in 1945 and 1946 was part of a group of riders who rode overseas to entertain the troops.

When racing was reorganised in 1946, the clubs drew lots for the right to choose riders and Belle Vue were expected to pick Bill to be their number one. However, when the Aces plumped for Jack Parker, Bill was snapped up by Wembley and helped to mould the Lions into the principal force of the early post-war years. That year saw Bill captain Wembley to the league title and, on an individual basis, he finished second in the British Riders Championship to his team mate Tommy Price, as well as being the inaugural holder of the British Match Race Championship in May. He was to lose the title to his great rival Parker, who also pipped him to top spot in the league averages.

Bill remained living in Lancashire for his first season with Wembley, getting a late night train home after meetings at the Empire Stadium. He ran an engineering business with his brother, and moved to London for the 1947 season.

In 1947 Bill recorded another 10 point plus average as well as leading the Lions to a second successive league title, and again finished runner-up in both the British Riders Championship and the league averages.

He missed a large proportion of the 1948 season after breaking his arm in a crash at West Ham and this was to prove a turning point in his career because he struggled to maintain his pre-injury scoring. He proved that he could still live with the best when finishing sixth in his third and last World Final appearance at the Empire Stadium in 1949, but was unable to lift his average above the eight points per match figure following his injury. Widely recognised as one of the finest team riders and captains the sport has ever seen, Bill continued to ride for the Lions until 1954, at the age of 45, and played a large part in seven league championships in eight fantastic years.

In a feature on Bill Kitchen by John Chaplin in *Classic Speedway* (Issue 5), Eric Williams recalls visiting Wembley to watch his brother ride. They walked with Bill Kitchen from the changing rooms to the pits. He was amazed at the huge reception that Kitchen got.

In *Broadside to Fame*, published in 1948, Leonard Sandys commented on Kitchen's team riding: "Right from the gate Bill lets his novice take the lead, while he weaves, slides and blocks the way of any eager rival. Sometimes things go wrong and the rival gets through. Then Bill opens his throttle and gives the offender a run for his money, often as not beating him to it. Whenever Bill turns out we see team racing as it should be – brought to a fine art by a master, full of clever tactics, where brain triumphs over speed. His skilful and unselfish riding gives he second-strings unbounded confidence and gave Wembley the most cohesive and successful team in the country."

Although he declined in 1953, and even rode at reserve on occasions, until then his average would have made him a heat leader in almost any team. He rode in Australia for England, and in South Africa, as well as in various European countries after he had retired from riding for the Lions. Interviewed by John Chaplin, he said that he thought his last ride was for the South African version of the Wembley Lions. Apart from speedway, Bill enjoyed yachting, and kept a boat on the Thames. He was also involved in the 'rocket bike' experiments in a couple of second halves at Wembley, which attracted great publicity.

Even after retiring as a rider, he continued as non-riding captain with the Lions, and still rode abroad even when not riding regularly with Wembley. In 1970, Trevor Redmond had hoped to make him the new Lions team manager, but he was offered a role by the SCB instead, as national track and machine inspector, which precluded him from taking a post with Wembley.

Year	Club	Division	M	R	P	BP	TP	CMA	FM	PM
1946	Wembley	NL	24	102	254	16	270	10.59	4	3
		ACU Cup	10	50	117	15	132	10.56	1	2
		London Cup	2	23	56	6	62	10.78		
1947	Wembley	NL1	30	128	305.5	28.5	334	10.44	5	4
		British Speedway Cup	12	58	135	10	145	10.00	2	1
		London Cup	4	22	45	2	47	8.55		
1948	Wembley	NL1	14	59	90	17	107	7.25	-	-
		London Cup	4	21	28	2	30	5.71		
1949	Wembley	NL1	42	170	281	41	322	7.58	1	3
		London Cup	4	23	48	7	55	9.57		
1950	Wembley	NL1	29	108	180	25	205	7.59	1	2
		London Cup	4	16	22	1	23	5.75		
1951	Wembley	NL1	38	124	190	36	226	7.29	-	1
		London Cup	6	23	40	6	46	8.00		
1952	Wembley	NL1	40	122	179	38	217	7.11	-	-
		London Cup	2	4	4	2	6	6.00		
1953	Wembley	NL1	21	78	85	27	112	5.74	-	-
		Coronation Cup	15	50	66	17	83	6.64		
		London Cup	2	4	3	0	3	3.00		
1954	Wembley	NL1	1	3	1	1	2	2.67	-	-
		Totals	**304**	**1188**	**2129.5**	**297.5**	**2427**			

Individual Honours: World Finalist 1937 (8th), 1938 (5th), 1949 (6th). British Riders Championship: Runner-up: 1946, 1947 (after run-off with Jack Parker for first place), British Match Race Champion May 1946.

International Honours: England international – 41 caps, 372.5 points.

Team Honours: National League Championship winner 1933, 1934, 1935, 1936, 1946, National League Division One Championship winner 1947, 1949, 1950, 1951, 1952, 1953, National Trophy winner 1933, 1934, 1935, 1936, 1937, 1948. London Cup: Winner: 1946, 1948, 1949, 1950, 1951, runner-up 1947.

Wilbur Leonard Lamoreaux
Born: 26 February 1907, Roseville, Illinois, USA.
Died: June 1963.

Illinois born Wilbur moved to Pasadena, California at an early age and worked with the famous Milne brothers, Jack and Cordy, as a motorcycle messenger. He began riding on the Californian circuits in 1932 and became one of the top riders in the States, along with the Milnes.

Joining Wimbledon in 1937, Wilbur made his World Final debut that same season and finished second in an all American 1-2-3, amazingly flanked by Jack and Cordy with whom he had spent so many of the previous years. A second World Final followed in 1938 and another rostrum place was the result, thereby cementing his status as one of the world's leading riders of the pre-war era. In 1946, after the war had ended, Wilbur won the American Championship at Lincoln Park, Los Angeles but was not able return to the UK due to a ban on overseas riders which affected the Americans and Europeans rather than riders from the Empire.

When Wembley hit massive injury problems in 1948, with Bill Kitchen and George Wilks suffering a broken arm and a broken thigh respectively, the Lions applied to the SCB for special dispensation to bring in Wilbur as cover. The request was granted and he proved to have lost none of his pre-war skill and speed as he recorded a succession of high scores including full maximums in his first two league matches. He was an important recruit for a Lions team who were having to race home meetings at Wimbledon and had been hit by an injury crisis.

His arrival in Britain was like a breath of fresh air to the First Division and he capped a superb return by assisting Wembley to National Trophy and London Cup success in what otherwise was a relatively bleak season for the club. With Kitchen returning from injury, there was little chance of the Lions being able to keep Wilbur for 1949, and so it proved with Birmingham being the beneficiaries.

The Brummies had been granted promotion to the top flight and Wilbur formed a spearhead with Graham Warren that was among the best in the league. His season was interrupted by injury, but he was hugely popular everywhere and managed to reach the World Final which had been reintroduced that year. Starting the meeting among the favourites, he again figured prominently, finishing 5th on the night at Wembley, some 12 years after his debut in the competition. This was his last season in Britain as, at the age of 42 and with a devalued pound, he declined to return. While overshadowed somewhat in the pre-war years by the Milne brothers, he left a legacy of being the USA.'s leading rider of the immediate post-war era and was highly regarded by the all fans in the UK who were lucky enough to see him in action.

Year	Club	Division	M	R	P	BP	TP	CMA	FM	PM
1948	Wembley	NL1	17	76	175	10	185	9.74	5	1
		Anniversary Cup	10	47	105	2	107	9.11	1	
		London Cup	4	23	54	1	55	9.57	2	
		Totals	31	146	334	13	347			

Individual Honours: World finalist 1937 (2nd), 1938 (3rd), 1949 (5th), U.S.A Champion 1946. British Riders Championship: Finalist 1948 (6th)
International Honours: U.S.A international – 3 caps, 13 points.
Team Honours: National Trophy winner 1938, 1948. London Cup: Winner 1948.

Fred Lang
Born: c. 1931, South Africa.
Died: 2004

Fred was a diminutive and spectacular performer who shot to the awareness of the British promoters when racing in South Africa against an English touring side in 1953–54. An almost frenzied bidding war developed for the untested youngster with Edinburgh, Ipswich and Wembley all involved in the process. In the end, he opted to join the famous Lions and was given a team berth at reserve for the 1954 season.

He was racing alongside riders like Trevor Redmond and Freddie Williams who had been close compatriots the previous winter and the Empire Stadium seemed the ideal place to hone his skills and settle into British racing. However, despite occasional flashes of form, which included an unbeaten two ride display from the reserve berth at home to Birmingham and a second place to Billy Bales in the Bilner Cup individual event at Norwich, he generally failed to live up to the publicity he had received. He found the smaller tracks particularly difficult and returned home at the end of the season. Fred was unable to agree terms to return in 1955 and retired altogether in December of that year.

He may have done better to have started his British career in the second tier, where he would have been under less pressure to produce results. On occasions, Wembley dropped him after he had ridden well, which cannot have helped his confidence. He is, however, the only South African to have ridden for the Lions.

Year	Club	Division	M	R	P	BP	TP	CMA	FM	PM
1954	Wembley	NL1	32	75	64	16	80	4.27	-	-
		RAC Cup	6	16	24	1	25	6.25		
		London Cup	4	11	6	1	7	2.55		
		Totals	42	102	94	18	112			

International Honours: South African international – 8 caps, 48 points.

Team Honours: National Trophy winner 1954. London Cup: Winner 1954.

Phil Lewry
Born: England.

A little known junior at Wembley in 1946, Phil made one league appearance for the Lions against Bradford at the Empire Stadium on June 6 that year, scoring a creditable two, paid three, from the number eight berth.

Year	Club	Division	M	R	P	BP	TP	CMA	FM	PM
1946	Wembley	NL	1	2	2	1	3	6.00	-	-

William (Bill) Longley

Born: 11 November 1911, Dandenong, Victoria, Australia.
Died: 29 April 2005.

A diminutive and hugely popular Australian, particularly at New Cross, Bill had a long career and will be best remembered for his association with the Rangers. He rode for the Old Kent Road club from 1937 up until the outbreak of the War, and was as a favourite with the south east London crowd, and served with the RAF as a fitness instructor during the conflict.

Bill returned to the saddle in 1946 and was chosen by Bradford in the allocation of riders but, despite achieving his best post-war average – a figure of 9.21 – he did not settle with the Yorkshire club and hankered after a return to New Cross. His wish was granted following a three-way deal which saw Oliver Hart move to Bradford from Wimbledon and Les Wotton to Wimbledon from New Cross. Although his average dropped by more than a point per match, Bill regained his status as a crowd favourite and helped the Rangers to the First Division title in 1948. He was a regular in the Australian side in the test match battles against England, and reached the first World Final to be held after the war in 1949.

Bill stayed with New Cross until promoter Fred Mockford closed the doors during the 1953 season, but by this time Bill had lost his heat leader ranking and had endured some stick from his home fans who were clearly frustrated by his dip in points. On the wrong side of 40, Bill was unlikely to improve after leaving the Rangers and a brief return to Bradford was followed by spells at Wimbledon and Rayleigh before he made his final league appearance in the colours of Wembley in a match at Norwich in August 1955.

Year	Club	Division	M	R	P	BP	TP	CMA	FM	PM
1955	Rayleigh	NL2	10	31	25	4	29	3.74	-	-
1955	Wembley	NL1	1	5	3	1	4	3.20	-	-

Individual Honours: World finalist 1949 (9th). British Riders Championship: Finalist 1946 (12th).
International Honours: Australian international – 39 caps, 250 points.
Team Honours: National League Division One Championship winner 1938, 1948, 1954.

Charles Edward (Charlie) May

Born: 18 October 1917, Southampton, Hampshire, England.
Died: May 1997

Charlie started and finished his 20 year speedway career with his home town club, Southampton, after having begun as a junior at Bannister Court in 1937.

He did not achieve a great deal of success before the war but, after practising at Rye House, he was signed by Wembley for the 1946 season. He added useful points from reserve at the Empire Stadium as he claimed two consecutive league winner's medals with the club, but moved down a division to join Birmingham in 1948 for a £400 fee.

In the lower leagues Charlie was a fine performer, particularly in his first season with Walthamstow when he was a heat leader in Division Two, and later at Cardiff where he was the mainstay of the Welsh side's line-up. When the Penarth Road track closed down during 1953, Charlie had half a season with Exeter before re-joining Southampton in 1954. This was his third spell with the club and he remained with the Saints until he retired in 1956.

His son Richard (Dickie) May also became a professional rider, and rode one match for the Lions as a Second Division guest in July 1970. His father Charlie proudly came to watch his son riding for his old team.

Year	Club	Division	M	R	P	BP	TP	CMA	FM	PM
1946	Wembley	NL	18	41	45	13	58	5.66	-	-
		ACU Cup	9	10	7.5	3	10.5	4.20		
		London Cup	4	8	10	0	10	5.00		
1947	Wembley	NL1	16	32	25	6	31	3.88	-	-
		British Speedway Cup	4	12	11	2	13	4.33		
		London Cup	3	6	5	2	7	4.67		
		Totals	54	109	103.5	26	129.5			

Team Honours: National League Championship winner 1946, National League Division One Championship winner 1947. London Cup: Winner 1946, runner-up 1947.

Dennis Ronald Newton

Born: 2 March 1929, Stepney, London, England.

Dennis was a charismatic rider who often appeared to be on the verge of a breakthrough into the big time, but always seemed to suffer injury at the most crucial point. He had started his career at High Beech in 1950 and was on Cradley Heath's books that season, without making his debut for the Dudley Wood club. After a spell racing in Spain, Dennis joined Swindon in 1951 and was averaging over nine points per match in the early part of the season when he broke his leg in a crash at his home track. He never really got a chance to establish himself at Wembley, and rode his one league match for the Lions in 1953.

It took quite some time for Dennis to get his promising career back on track and, despite a successful winter tour to Australia in 1953–54, it was not until 1955 that he returned to form in Britain. There were some indifferent performances but several double figure scores for Oxford combined with a shock fifth place in the Midland Riders Championship Final at Leicester showed that he had plenty yet to offer. In 1957 Dennis looked like he had finally fulfilled his promise as, racing in the top flight on a regular basis for the first time, he lifted his average to over six points per match and beat the World Champion Ove Fundin twice in a week. However, every time he ran into some decent form he picked up an injury which set him back. He fell out of favour at Cowley in 1958 and joined Norwich in mid-season. Dennis had spent quite some time in South Africa in the close seasons of the previous years and settled there in 1959. He came back for further spells at Norwich and Long Eaton in the 1960s, but his main racing activities were confined to South Africa, riding in representative matches for his adopted country. Dennis retired after winning the South African Championship in 1973, aged 44.

Year	Club	Division	M	R	P	BP	TP	CMA	FM	PM
1953	Southampton	SL	3	8	3	0	3	1.50	-	-
1953	Wembley	NL1	1	2	0	0	0	0.00	-	-
		Coronation Cup	1	2	1	1	2	4.00		
	Wembley	Totals	2	4	1	1	2			

Individual Honours: South African Champion 1973.

Robert Lawford (Bob) Oakley
Born: 31 December 1921, Southampton, Hampshire, England.
Died: November 1999.

Bob started his speedway career during the war while serving with the Army as a despatch rider and rode in grass track and scrambles events in 1946. He also had a handful of second half races at New Cross, but opted to join his home town club, Southampton, on their entry into the Third Division in 1947. This sparked a dispute between the two clubs over Bob's contract. The matter had to be settled by the SCB who ruled in favour of the Saints, who had to pay a £25 fee for his signature. The evidence of why both clubs were so keen to secure his services was soon clear as Bob took the Third Division by storm, scoring nine maximums, averaging over nine points per match and almost helping the club to claim the Third Division title. After two seasons in the lower league Southampton moved up into Division Two and Bob, after considering retirement during the winter, made the move with them. He was a huge success at the higher level and his performances attracted attention from First Division clubs.

His big move finally came in July 1950 and it was Wembley who came up with the cash, splashing out £1,500 for the 28-year-old. He was an important signing for the Lions, and played his part in winning the league in 1950. He showed some excellent form and had recorded two maximums by the end of the season which concluded with the first of his three championship medals in three seasons with the Lions. The following season saw further progress with a nomination to challenge Jack Parker for the Golden Helmet Match Race Championship and, while this bid proved unsuccessful, he was in no way disgraced. He was also picked for the England side to face Australia at Bradford, although this meeting ended in disaster as he fell in his first ride and broke his ribs. Amazingly, Bob was not selected again for his country and he failed to complete a ride in official test matches.

In 1952 he qualified for his only World Final and was ranked among the outsiders for the event as he had shown only mediocre league form during the season. However, he shocked the field with a third place podium finish behind Jack Young and Freddie Williams in front of a huge Empire Stadium crowd. If that performance was a surprise, however, it paled into insignificance with the incredible announcement that he was quitting the sport weeks into the 1953 season – just a matter of months after coming within a couple of points of the World title. Bob wanted to concentrate on his business interests in Southampton, but was seen in second half events later in the season. He decided on a full time return to the sport in 1954 and started the season back with the Lions. However, he was loaned to Norwich, as Wembley had a surplus of riders. He quit again after a poor season which saw him average only 6.65 points per match. Seven years later Bob was tempted out of retirement to join Wolverhampton in the 1961 Provincial League. He looked useful in his short spell at the end of the season but rode in just six matches for the Monmore Green outfit.

Year	Club	Division	M	R	P	BP	TP	CMA	FM	PM
1950	Southampton	NL2	12	55	117	9	126	9.16	2	1
1950	Wembley	NL1	12	49	82	7	89	7.27	2	-
		London Cup	4	22	42	4	46	8.36		
1951	Wembley	NL1	34	141	256	24	280	7.94	2	-
		London Cup	4	20	29	5	34	6.80		
1952	Wembley	NL1	39	146	245	21	266	7.29	1	1
		London Cup	2	11	19	0	19	6.91		

1953	Wembley	Coronation Cup	3	10	11	0	11	4.40		
1954	Norwich	NL1	31	113	165	23	188	6.65	-	1
	Wembley	**Totals**	**98**	**399**	**684**	**61**	**745**			

Individual Honours: World finalist 1952 (3rd).
International Honours: England international – 1 cap, 0 points.
Team Honours: National League Division One Championship winner 1950, 1951, 1952. London Cup: Winner 1950, 1951.

Thomas Hubert (Tommy) Price

Born: 2 December 1911, Cambridge, Cambridgeshire, England.
Died: January 1998.

England's first ever World Champion, Tommy Price was a superb rider who graced the sport in both the pre- and post-war eras, despite suffering from Hay Fever for many years. He was also Wembley's longest serving rider. He was born in Cambridge in 1911, and first rode a motorbike when he was eight years old. In his book, *Speedway Mixture*, published in 1950, he recalled that his father, who had considerable engineering skills, built it for him. His family moved to London in 1927, and he became an engineering apprentice with AEC, who built London buses. He saved up to buy a motorbike, which he soon traded in for a 1926 AJS, with the aim of doing grass track racing.

He realised his bike was not suitable for grass track racing, so traded it in. The friend who did the trade was later killed practicing for the Isle of Man TT races. At his first grass track meeting, a competitor died from his injuries.

A road accident on his way home from the meeting, which resulted in a broken leg, did not deter him. He rode at Barnet, which was run by the North London Motor Club. In Wembley's early days he had a trial, but Johnnie Hoskins told him that he would never become a speedway rider.

He was a fine grass track rider in the early 1930s and had trials with Harringay in 1934, but was rejected by the north London club. He fell in the junior race, which was won by George Wilks. He was signed by the Racers and Tommy was let go.

In 1935, he was with his friend, the Australian rider George Hannaford, who had just returned from the TT races. They realised that George was unwell, and found out that he had a fractured skull! He was due to be riding for Wembley Juniors at Luton, so Tommy rang Alec Jackson and the Wembley manager offered Tommy the chance to take George's place. He was the top scorer for his team, was invited to take part in the Novices' race at Wembley and won it for six successive weeks.

Tommy spent almost the whole of his career with the famous Lions, although he was loaned out to Cardiff to get more experience in his younger days. Just four years after that unsuccessful trial at Green Lanes, Tommy reached his first World Final in 1938. He scored four points on the night, and with four bonus points finished with eight to take 12th place. He made his England debut in 1939 when he was selected for two tests against Australia in the final pre-war series.

In 1937, he rode 24 league matches for the Lions, with an average of 5.48; in 1938 he increased this to 6.07 and in 1939 increased it again to 7.57.

He rode at Belle Vue regularly during the War. He resumed his association with the Lions in 1946e war and was a superbly consistent heat leader during the next decade as Wembley almost completely dominated the league year after year.

The World Championship was resumed in 1949 after a 10 year absence and Tommy hit form at exactly the right time of the season, taking the crown with a 15 point maximum ahead of the Belle Vue pair of Jack Parker and Louis Lawson. He was 37 years old at the time of his success and took the crown three years after winning the British Rider's Championship, the closest competition to the World title at that time. He had not ridden well in the first half of the 1949 season, and Wembley had not nominated him to the Championship Round. So he had to ride in the third round at Second Division Newcastle, where he won the meeting with a 15 point maximum. In the Championship Round he was the top qualifier for the Wembley Final along with Graham Warren. Both had 38 points from three meetings. He had spent three days in his private workshop at Wembley preparing his bikes for the World Final. In his next ride after the Final, the engine blew! One honour was given was to be portrayed in wax in Madam Tussaud's.

In *Speedway Favourites*, Basil Storey recalled that Price was a surprise winner of the British Riders Championship in 1946. He had "been 10 years [including the War] a Wembley rider without firing anyone's imagination, yet overnight he became the season's idol." Storey said that Price practiced starts in the Wembley carpark until late into the night before the big meeting, and his win was "a brilliant achievement."

While he was hugely popular at Wembley, Tommy was not a universal fans' favourite and was often regarded as being too ruthless. He also lacked the glamour of some of his rivals, earning him an unfair tag of being an 'unfashionable' rider, and in some quarters it was suggested that Tommy would not have been crowned champion had the final been held at a track other than his home circuit.

The rivalry between Wembley and Wimbledon was very strong, and he was regularly booed at Plough Lane, particularly after an incident in the 1950 London Cup Final at Plough Lane. He fell out with Wimbledon promoter Ronnie Greene after his new car was attacked by some Wimbledon fans at Plough Lane and Greene refused to pay for the damage.

Freddie Williams said that Price was nice and supportive off the track, but was "ruthless and hard" on it. Price himself said that he had "ferocious determination" and told John Chaplin that "If you wanted to succeed at being a speedway rider, you had to be hard."

Tommy did not tour Australia with the test sides, preferring to remain at home in the winter, and was not always classed as a regular for England in domestic international matches, often finding himself in and out of the side. His best season for England came in the 1950 series against Australia when he top scored with 55 points from the five test matches and had the distinction of scoring double figures in each meeting. However, a fractured skull later in the season threatened to end his career and it was a sign of his courage and enthusiasm that he was back in the saddle in 1951. The last of his 23 appearances for his country came at the age of 44 when he was selected for the side to face Sweden at Wembley in 1956 – Tommy's last season in the sport. Ranking as one of Wembley's finest ever riders, he scored over 3,000 points in all competitions in the 11 post-war years he spent with the club, and holds the club records for point scoring and appearances in that era.

When West Ham returned to the sport in 1964, he was appointed team manager at Custom House, and managed the England team that faced Russia at Wembley that year. He managed the great West Ham team which won three trophies in 1965; but was never that popular with the Hammers fans, who remembered him as a hard-riding opponent from when he rode for the Lions.

Away from the track, he was a short-wave radio enthusiast. In the War he had lectured the troops on this subject, along with his regular job in an aircraft factory. In 1949, he did not stay for the post-World Final dinner because he wanted to get home to contact his radio friends.

Tommy emigrated to Perth, Australia, later in life and passed away in January 1998.

(Includes information from article by John Chaplin in *Classic Speedway*, Issue 30)

Year	Club	Division	M	R	P	BP	TP	CMA	FM	PM
1946	Wembley	NL	24	102	249	5	254	9.96	6	2
		ACU Cup	10	50	122	4	126	10.08	2	
		London Cup	4	23	49	2	51	8.87		
1947	Wembley	NL1	30	131	310	10	320	9.77	5	-
		British Speedway Cup	12	56	131	4	135	9.64	2	1
		London Cup	4	23	41	4	45	7.83		
1948	Wembley	NL1	27	114	220.5	14	234.5	8.23	2	2
		Anniversary Cup	12	55	106	3	109	7.93		
		London Cup	4	21	34	4	38	7.24		
1949	Wembley	NL1	43	175	378	23	401	9.17	10	2
		London Cup	4	23	56	2	58	10.09		
1950	Wembley	NL1	31	125	277	17	294	9.41	8	-
		London Cup	2	12	23	1	24	8.00		
1951	Wembley	NL1	34	142	263	18	281	7.92	5	-
		London Cup	6	34	63	8	71	8.35		
1952	Wembley	NL1	38	156	330	19	349	8.95	4	2
		London Cup	2	11	16	1	17	6.18		
1953	Wembley	NL1	22	98	216	11	227	9.27	1	-
		Coronation Cup	14	56	113	1	114	8.14	1	
		London Cup	2	10	15	1	16	6.40		
1954	Wembley	NL1	34	135	212.5	34.5	247	7.32	1	1
		RAC Cup	6	22	26	2	28	5.09		
1955	Wembley	NL1	29	145	234	24	258	7.12	-	-
1956	Wembley	NL1	26	106	177	13	190	7.17	2	2
		Totals	**420**	**1825**	**3662**	**225.5**	**3887.5**			

Individual Honours: World Champion 1949, World Finalist 1938 (12th), 1950 (5th), 1954 (11th), British Rider's Champion 1946, Finalist 1947 (10th).

International Honours: England international – 23 caps, 181 points.

Team Honours: National League Championship winner 1946, National League Division One Championship winner 1947, 1949, 1950, 1951, 1952, 1953, National Trophy winner 1948, 1954. London Cup: Winner 1946, 1948, 1949, 1950, 1951, 1954, runner-up 1947.

Trevor John Redmond
Born: 16 June 1927, Christchurch, New Zealand.
Died: September 1997.

One of the most prominent figures in the sport, particularly in the 1950s and 1960s, Trevor was an energetic character who was not only a fine rider but an enterprising promoter, always willing to take a risk in the opening of a new track. He had been impressive in Christchurch in the winter of 1949–50 and came to Britain for the new season to look for a track in the National League. He was signed by new Division Three side, Aldershot, and proved to be a huge hit, averaging over nine points per match in an excellent spearhead with Basil Harris. Despite being in the top five riders in the league, Trevor stayed on for a second season with the Shots and his superb scoring resulted in a scramble for his signature by the teams in Division One. For a fee of £1,500 Trevor linked up with Wembley despite competition from tracks such as Norwich and Bristol, with rumblings of discontent that one of the world's most promising riders was joining the strongest team in the country.

Starting the 1952 season as reserve at the Empire Stadium, Trevor had a great year with an average of 7.50 points per match and a place in the World Final, albeit as a non-riding reserve. A poor season in 1953 was followed by his best ever year as he claimed a World Final berth following an excellent league campaign which saw him supporting the heat leader trio of Brian Crutcher and the Williams brothers. This year saw the end of Wembley's domination of the league title as they handed over the baton to Wimbledon and Trevor's riding career was soon to follow a similar slide as he became more and more involved in business matters, both in the UK and abroad. This included being heavily concerned with the promotion of the sport in South Africa and he spent so many of his winters there that he was granted permission to race for the test side against visiting touring teams in international matches.

On the closure of Wembley early in 1957, Trevor drifted into a semi-retirement, having a few outings for Bradford and Swindon over the next few years and racing occasionally on the Continent, but turned more to the promoting side of the sport. He re-introduced racing to Plymouth and St Austell in open licence events and made a regular track return with Bristol in 1960 on the creation of the Provincial League. The new league had not really been designed for riders like Trevor but, as clubs strove to strengthen their teams, he proved to be a fantastic tutor to the less experienced members of the side as well as leading the Bulldogs to a cup triumph and winning the inaugural Provincial League Riders Championship. Trevor promoted and rode with distinction at various Provincial League centres until 1964, but quit as he became more and more involved in the administrative side of the sport. He was closely concerned in the reopening of Glasgow and also was one of the key people behind the return of the Lions to league racing in 1970. He became sole promoter in 1971, and in 1974 promoted a couple of stock car meetings at the stadium.

Year	Club	Division	M	R	P	BP	TP	CMA	FM	PM
1952	Wembley	NL1	40	159	251	47	298	7.50	1	1
		London Cup	2	10	11	1	12	4.80		
1953	Wembley	NL1	18	56	68	18	86	6.14	-	-
		Coronation Cup	16	56	68	17	85	6.07		1
		London Cup	2	9	8	3	11	4.89		
1954	Wembley	NL1	34	140	228	47	275	7.86	-	4
		RAC Cup	6	22	14	5	19	3.45		

1955	Wembley	NL1	29	138	177	32	209	6.06	-	-
1956	Wembley	NL1	25	92	120	20	140	6.09	-	2
		Totals	172	682	945	190	1135			

Individual Honours: World finalist 1954 (13th), South African Champion 1955, Provincial League Riders Champion 1960, Division Three Match Race Champion May 1951 to September 1951.

International Honours: New Zealand international – 17 caps, 63 points, South African international – 11 caps, 122.5 points.

Team Honours: National League Division One Championship winner 1952, 1953, National Trophy winner 1954, Provincial League Knock-Out Cup winner 1960. London Cup: Winner 1954.

George Henry Saunders

Born: 13 March 1910, Bristol, Avon, England.
Died: December 1987.

George started his career in the 1930s and rode for West Ham in 1933 under the guidance of Hammers star Tommy Croombs. He also rode for Bristol and Hackney before the war, winning league titles with both clubs, and returned to the sport in 1946 after being selected by Wimbledon from the pool of riders. Combining his racing with the running of a restaurant at Surbiton in Surrey, he showed his experience in that initial post-war season to turn in some useful performances from a second string role, including two paid maximums in an average of 5.79.

As new and younger riders began to emerge, George's average dropped and he lost his team place at Plough Lane early in the 1948 season. His absence from the sport was short lived, however, because he was signed by Wembley as cover for their injured skipper, Bill Kitchen. He remained with the Lions in 1949, but struggled badly and quit the sport after a torrid five match run with Birmingham. George was heavily involved in the opening of the Aldershot track for the 1950 season and had a spell as team manager at the Tongham circuit.

Year	Club	Division	M	R	P	BP	TP	CMA	FM	PM
1948	Wembley	NL1	22	55	47	10	57	4.15	-	-
		Anniversary Cup	12	41	51	7	58	5.66		
		London Cup	4	8	9	1	10	5.00		
1949	Wembley	NL1	9	18	6	3	9	2.00	-	-
1949	Birmingham	NL1	5	15	4	0	4	1.07	-	-
	Wembley	Totals	47	122	113	21	134			

Team Honours: National League Division One Championship winner 1949, Provincial League Championship winner 1937, National League Division Two Championship winner 1938. London Cup: Winner 1948.

Rune Bertil Leopold Sörmander
Born: 29 November 1929, Vaxjo, Sweden.

One of Sweden's greatest speedway riders, Rune was one of the new breed of Scandinavian stars who burst onto the speedway scene in the 1950s. Wembley fans got a brief look at this classy stylist in June 1953 when he was called into the side as cover for the injured George Wilks. He was the first Swede to ride for the Lions.

He made a perfect start, with an unbeaten performance from two rides from the reserve berth. However, around this time New Cross closed their doors and the Lions were allocated Eric French, ending Rune's association with the Empire Stadium club. The experience gained on the track was to help Rune as he qualified for the World Final later that year and finished in 11th place with a creditable five points.

He had another short spell with Belle Vue in 1954, but he was mainly occupied with riding in the Swedish League and appearing regularly for Sweden. He was tempted back into the National League by Leicester in 1957 as they embarked on their first season in the top flight and was a popular member of the side although his regular absences due to his Continental commitments often caused frustration. That season also saw Rune qualify for the World Final for a second time and he became a regular finalist, reaching the big night for six consecutive years between 1957 and 1962. Fifth place in the 1957 final at Wembley was the closest he came to becoming champion, but he made up for any disappointment by winning the World Team Cup with Sweden four times, including the inaugural event at Gothenburg in 1960 when he dropped only a single point. Three times his national champion, Rune was not seen in league action in Britain again after his spell at Leicester in 1957, but remained a leading figure in Swedish speedway, scoring an 18 point maximum for his country against England in the second test at Norwich in 1958 and was still a force to be reckoned with until injury ended his career in 1965.

Year	Club	Division	M	R	P	BP	TP	CMA	FM	PM
1953	Wembley	NL1	1	2	5	1	6	12.00		
		Coronation Cup	1	2	4	0	4	8.00		
		London Cup	2	5	3	0	3	2.40		
		Totals	4	9	12	1	13			

Individual Honours: World finalist 1953 (11th), 1957 (5th), 1958 (13th), 1959 (11th), 1960 (12th), 1961 (8th), 1962 (11th), Swedish Champion 1955, 1958, 1959.
International Honours: World Team Cup winner 1960, 1962, 1963, 1964, World Team Cup finalist 1961, Swedish international – 66 caps, 711 points.

Squire Francis (Split) Waterman
Born: 27 July 1923, New Malden, Surrey, England.

During the War, Split Waterman served in the Army in North Africa, Italy, Palestine and Germany. He recalls in his foreword to *Warzone Speedway* that "Army speedway racing with its crude bikes and rough tracks was a welcome diversion and relaxation from the ravages of war." Many post-war riders were motorcyclists in the Army, and Split was probably the best to come from this wartime background.

Shrapnel wounds saw him transferred away from front-line duties. His transfer to REME, where he was in a workshop led to him first involved in grass track racing, and then move onto speedway. Opponents included future Wembley team mates Bronco Wilson and Bill Kemp. His nickname, 'Split' came from this time. He fell in one meeting and split his leathers up the back. His fellow soldiers called him "Split Arse", but Sir Arthur Elvin said that he could not put that in the Wembley programme, so shortened it to the more acceptable 'Split'.

His commanding officer, Major Bill Fearnley, who later became manager of the SCB, recommended him to Alec Jackson, and he had a trial with Wembley in 1946, managing to get home from Germany to perform at Rye House. The Major helped him get back to his Army base in time as well. He was discharged from the Army early in 1947, having survived the attack on the King David Hotel in Jerusalem in 1946, when 91 people were killed.

Spilt was an overnight sensation when he joined Wembley in 1947 and recorded a superb average of over seven and a half points per match in his debut season. He claimed a league winner's medal and was one of the few riders to beat the great Vic Duggan that year, a fine achievement for a first year rider. The following season saw him develop further into a heat leader role, challenging Jack Parker for the British Match Race Championship in August and winning the prestigious London Riders Championship. His ready smile and infectious personality made him one of the most popular riders in the sport, but he had the rare ability of combining the jokes and high jinks with superb performances on the track.

After three years at the Empire Stadium he moved across London to Harringay for a world record £3,000 fee and he had his best spell of his career at Green Lanes. This move gave him the chance to shine, rather than just be one of the galaxy of stars at Wembley. Interviewed by John Chaplin in *Classic Speedway* (Issue 21), Waterman said that all the top stars at Wembley were on special deals, such as double money for winning races, and he could get the same as the top man at Harringay. He could also clean up in the second halves, as the leading riders had done at Wembley. It should be pointed out that the double payments would have broken the speedway regulations at the time, and cannot be confirmed from any other source so long after the event.

Although Spilt rarely achieved the consistency of some of his peers during the regular racing season, he often reserved his best performances for individual events and twice came within a whisker of winning the ultimate prize in speedway – the World Championship. In the famous final of 1951 Spilt finished behind Jack Young and ahead of Jack Biggs after a three man run-off and was one of the favourites for the 1952 crown but was forced to ride under the handicap of a broken knee cap, sustained just prior to the final. The injury was so bad that his wife Avril had to persuade the surgeon not to amputate his leg. The injury still troubles him today. That season had seen him become England's undisputed number one and he held the British Match Race Championship before injury forced him to forfeit the title.

In 1953 he was on the verge of becoming World Champion as he won his first four rides but, in his last outing he finished third, behind eventual winner Freddie Williams and the Swede Olle Nygren, and had to settle for another silver medal. It was also a successful season for the Racers. They won the National Trophy and Coronation Cup, and came close to beating the Lions for the league title. An injury to Split undermined their chances.

After Harringay closed at the end of the 1954 season, Spilt moved to West Ham for a year before they also closed. He found himself back at Wembley, and was still of heat leader class, although not the force he had been in the early 1950s at his peak with Harringay. In a profile of Split in the *Star* in October 1956, Dan Flynn commented that "... as the season progressed so the old Waterman fire returned and by the season's end he was again among the top 10 performers in the country."

He developed into something of a speedway nomad for the remaining years of his career, seeming to lose interest in the sport on several occasions and rarely spending any length of time at a particular track. He eventually retired at the age of 39 after a spell at Belle Vue, and the career of one of speedway's most flamboyant riders had finally come to an end.

He told John Chaplin that "...I often regret, in a way, that I left Wembley, because of Wembley's name. I mean Harringay was a good name but, in my opinion, it was just another stadium on the other side of town. There was a magic about Wembley."

Split is now retired and lives in Spain with his wife Avril. He had a long career in business, which he started when he was riding speedway. He was nearly 24 when he made his debut for the Lions in 1947, and obviously realised the importance of not relying on speedway for a living. In the late 1960s he was arrested for smuggling gold and firearms offences. He was sent to prison for four years and Avril was sentenced to six months. They got married in April 1970. But his later misdemeanours should not detract from the fact that he was one of the leading British riders in the sport's first decade after the War, and came so close to being World Champion.

Year	Club	Division	M	R	P	BP	TP	CMA	FM	PM
1947	Wembley	NL1	29	109	167	40	207	7.60	-	-
		British Speedway Cup	12	50	64	16	80	6.40		
		London Cup	4	20	32	4	36	7.20		
1948	Wembley	NL1	29	121	224	28	252	8.33	-	-
		Anniversary Cup	12	57	123	8	131	9.19		
		London Cup	4	20	19	8	27	5.40		
1949	Wembley	NL1	33	132	246.5	26	272.5	8.26	-	2
		London Cup	4	18	26	5	31	6.89		
1956	Wembley	NL1	26	105	162	31	193	7.35	-	2
		Totals	**153**	**632**	**1063.5**	**166**	**1229.5**			

Individual Honours: World Finalist 1950 (7th), 1951 (2nd), 1952 (12th), 1953 (2nd), 1954 (5th). British Riders Championship: Finalist 1948 (5th). British Match Race Champion July 1951 – April 1952. London Riders Championship: Winner 1948.
International Honours: England international – 32 caps, 268 points.
Team Honours: National League Division One Championship winner 1947, 1949, National Trophy winner 1948, 1952. London Cup: Winner 1948, 1949, runner-up 1947.

Robert (Bob) Wells
Born: 26 December 1915, Bushey Heath, Hertfordshire, England.

Bob started out at the Barnet track in 1936 with his friend Archie Windmill, who later rode for Wimbledon, and did well enough to be signed by Wembley, although he spent most of the time leading up to the war out on loan at various tracks, including Lea Bridge and Middlesbrough. After being captured at Dunkirk early in the war, Bob was held prisoner by the Germans in Poland for five years before being rescued by the American Army.

Undaunted, he returned to the Empire Stadium and resumed his speedway career in 1946. In a team laden with stars, Bob's scoring rarely hit the headlines but he was a fine lower order rider and played an essential role in helping to bring the Division One title to Wembley on five occasions between 1946 and 1951. After the third title triumph in 1949, Bob's scoring began to decline and he joined Swindon in 1952 where he proved to be a solid scorer and mentor to the club's younger riders, putting all his experience to good use. His career ended with a spell at Oxford. He retired in 1955 when he was aged almost 40.

Year	Club	Division	M	R	P	BP	TP	CMA	FM	PM
1946	Wembley	NL	24	85	101	20	121	5.69	-	1
		ACU Cup	10	31	48.5	7.5	56	7.23		
		London Cup	4	14	14	1	15	4.29		
1947	Wembley	NL1	28	86	84	21	105	4.88	-	-
		British Speedway Cup	12	37	60	16	76	8.22	1(3)	2 (3)
		London Cup	4	11	20	2	22	8.00		
1948	Wembley	NL1	29	75	90	17	107	5.71	-	-
		Anniversary Cup	12	44	48	8	56	5.09		
		London Cup	4	8	12	0	12	6.00		
1949	Wembley	NL1	39	136	187	37	224	6.59	1	-
		London Cup	4	10	15	1	16	6.40		
1950	Wembley	NL1	11	27	21	4	25	3.70	-	-
1950	Birmingham	NL1	13	50	35	4	39	3.12	-	-
1951	Wembley	NL1	16	34	17	10	27	3.18	-	-
		London Cup	4	8	13	2	15	7.50		
	Wembley	**Totals**	**201**	**606**	**730.5**	**146.5**	**877**			

Team Honours: National League Championship winner 1946, National League Division One Championship winner 1947, 1949, 1950, 1951, National Trophy winner 1948. London Cup: Winner 1946, 1948, 1949, runner-up 1947.

George Wilks
Born: 23 February 1911, Boxmoor, Hertfordshire, England.
Died: 1982.

A former TT and grass track rider, George was spotted racing at Barnet in 1934 and joined Harringay before moving to Hackney during the 1935 season. After spending three years at Waterden Road, George was signed by Wembley in 1938 for a £350 fee, progressed into an England international that same year and a rider of some repute until the war interrupted the sport in 1939. In 1938 he averaged 6.91 and in 1939 6.74.

George was selected by the Lions from the rider pool at the start of the 1946 season after serving in the RAF, and immediately resumed his role as one of England's leading competitors. Basil Storey said in 1946 that he was "a very useful chap to have around during the present transitional period in speedway racing. He is a product of the old school and learned the trade the hard way." (Reprinted in *Speedway Favourites*, 1947)

In a team full of stars, George was perhaps something of an unsung hero, being initially overshadowed at the Empire Stadium by Bill Kitchen and Tommy Price and later by Freddie

Williams and Brian Crutcher, but a look at his statistics in the years immediately following the war reveals his undoubted quality. He assisted the club to the league title in the first two post-war seasons and in 1948 he was in the form of his life, but a broken leg caused him to miss the last five months of the season and played a large part in the Lions relinquishing the league crown to New Cross.

At the end of that season he was ranked fourth in the Division One averages behind Vic Duggan, Ron Johnson and Wilbur Lamoreaux, but when he was fit to resume he was loaned to West Ham as a replacement for the injured Eric Chitty. He never settled at Custom House and was back at Wembley by the end of the year, although he was never able to quite recapture his pre-injury form.

George did, however, maintain a solid level of scoring and was able to play a large part in the Lions league successes in 1950, 1951 and 1952. Surprisingly, George was never really fancied by the England selectors and made only nine appearances for his country. In 1947, he was chosen at reserve for England against Australia at West Ham. With England losing, he was brought in and won three races out of four to save the test for England and finish as their second highest scorer.

Wilks would surely have reached a World Final had the competition been held at the height of his career. He did ride in the British Riders Championship Final in 1947, and finished fifth with nine points.

Year	Club	Division	M	R	P	BP	TP	CMA	FM	PM
1946	Wembley	NL	24	100	221	3	224	8.96	1	1
		ACU Cup	10	50	99	7	106	8.48		
		London Cup	4	22	46	7	53	9.64		
1947	Wembley	NL1	30	129	283	8	291	9.02	2	2
		British Speedway Cup	12	51	125	5	130	10.20		2
		London Cup	4	11	20	2	22	8.00		
1948	Wembley	NL1	12	46	111	0	111	9.65	3	-
1949	West Ham	NL1	35	140	219	17	236	6.74	2	1
1949	Wembley	NL1	5	20	25	4	29	5.80	-	-
		London Cup	4	21	43	4	47	8.95		
1950	Wembley	NL1	34	139	262	24	286	8.23	1	2
		London Cup	4	21	35	6	41	7.81		
1951	Wembley	NL1	35	141	217	47	264	7.49	-	1
		London Cup	6	31	43	13	56	7.23		1
1952	Wembley	NL1	38	146	212	51	263	7.21	-	2
		London Cup	2	11	17	2	19	6.91		
1953	Wembley	NL1	5	9	10	4	14	6.22	-	-
		Coronation Cup	12	35	42.5	11.5	54	6.17		
1954	Wembley	NL1	7	14	7	2	9	2.57	-	-
	Wembley	**Totals**	**248**	**997**	**1818.5**	**200.5**	**2019**			

Individual honours: British Riders Championship Final 1947 (5th)
International Honours: England international – 9 caps, 45 points.
Team Honours: National League Championship winner 1946, National League Division One Championship winner 1947, 1950, 1951, 1952. London Cup: Winner: 1946, 1949, 1950, 1951, runner-up 1947.

William Eric Williams
Born: 17 November 1927, Port Talbot, West Glamorgan, Wales.
Died: 24 July 2009

Eric Williams was born in Port Talbot. At the age of 14, he became an apprentice in the Army Technical College, but after some health problems was discharged as 'medically unfit'.

The younger brother of Freddie Williams, Eric was taken on by Wembley as a novice and was allowed to join Birmingham on loan in order to gain experience of league racing. His career started in an unfortunate manner as he suffered a broken thigh only three matches into his spell with the Brummies, with the injury causing him to miss the rest of the season. When he was fit to resume in 1949 he lined up with Cradley Heath in a similar deal and his form at Dudley Wood was outstanding as he rattled up a succession of high scores. This was a superb feat in light of such limited experience and the fact that he was recovering from a serious injury. Eleven maximums and an end of season run which put him among the best in the Second Division meant an inevitable call up to the Lions in 1950 and he added strength to a team that was already the best in the country.

With Eric in the side, Wembley almost won as they pleased and he claimed four championship winning medals between 1950 and 1953. In those seasons Eric achieved international standard. He made his debut in the final test of the 1951 series against Australia. He had toured Australia with Jack Parker's 'unofficial' England team in 1950–51.

Two years later, his 15 point score was instrumental in England's first win against the Kangaroos at Wembley for 14 years, and he went on to make 23 appearances in a time when the side were labelled England, but was selected from all the home nations. He reached three World Finals during his career, his best effort coming in 1955 when he finished fourth after a three man run-off for the runners-up position. However, the year had proved to be his worst domestic season since linking up with the Lions. This was the season that the Lions only rode one set of home league fixtures, with the management preferring to stage open meetings in an attempt to attract better crowds. This did not go down well with some of the riders, and Eric asked for a transfer. The Lions put a fee on his head similar to that they had paid for Brian Crutcher in 1953. Given the decline afflicting speedway at this time, and the financial problems many teams faced, there were no takers.

Prior to 1955, for three seasons he had been a real force for the Lions, and was one of the team's key riders as the older stars gradually retired. In 1954 his average was higher than his brother Freddie's. He also took part in the Match Race Championship that season, being beaten by Bradford's Arthur Forrest.

At the end of that year Eric, who had enjoyed previous trips to New Zealand, told Wembley that he was settling there and would not return for 1956. It was a major shock to the club and a blow to the national side who had seen him as a rider to rely on for years to come. After four seasons away from the sport, Eric was finally tempted back in 1960 when he signed for New Cross on their return to league racing. He looked as good as ever and averaged more than nine points a match and reclaiming his place in the international set up. He continued to ride with distinction for two further seasons, bowing out after a year at Norwich in 1962 and returning to New Zealand.

He died from cancer, aged 81, in New Zealand. At his cremation, his white coffin was decorated with red and white flowers, the Wembley colours.

(Some information from tribute by John Chaplin in *Classic Speedway* Issue 6)

Year	Club	Division	M	R	P	BP	TP	CMA	FM	PM
1948	Birmingham	NL2	3	7	4	0	4	2.29	-	-
1949	Cradley Heath	NL2	52	212	399	43	442	8.34	5	6
1950	Wembley	NL1	26	98	153	29	182	7.43	-	1
		London Cup	2	5	6	0	6	4.80		
1951	Wembley	NL1	38	149	257	30	287	7.70	1	3
		London Cup	6	32	54	6	60	7.50		
1952	Wembley	NL1	40	160	282	46	328	8.20	1	3
		London Cup	2	10	15	4	19	7.60		
1953	Wembley	NL1	22	97	202.5	20.5	223	9.20	2	3
		Coronation Cup	16	64	125.5	11.5	137	8.56		
		London Cup	2	11	16	1	17	6.18		
1954	Wembley	NL1	34	145	315	26	341	9.41	7	4
		RAC Cup	6	24	42	4	46	7.67		
		London Cup	4	23	55	4	59	10.26		
1955	Wembley	NL1	30	154	234	34	268	6.96	-	1
	Wembley	**Totals**	**228**	**972**	**1757**	**259**	**1973**			

Individual Honours: World finalist 1951 (12th), 1953 (13th), 1955 (4th).
International Honours: England international – 23 caps, 171 points.
Team Honours: National League Division One Championship winner 1950, 1951, 1952, 1953, National Trophy winner 1954. London Cup: Winner 1950, 1951, 1954.

Frederick Owen (Freddie) Williams

Born: 12 March 1926, Port Talbot, West Glamorgan, Wales.
Died: 20 January 2013.

From novice to World Champion in just three years was the sensational story of Freddie Williams, Wales' finest ever speedway product and one of Britain's all-time great riders. His brothers Eric and Ian both became professional speedway riders. Eric was Freddie's team mate with the Lions for some years, while Ian spent most of his career with Swindon.

He was born in Port Talbot, and, during the War, had an early ambition to be a fighter pilot. His uncle had been awarded the Military Cross as a pilot. He became an apprentice at Portsmouth Naval Dockyard, and was also in the Home Guard, where he was a despatch rider. He bought a motorbike to get to and from his home in Wales, but never watched speedway as a boy. He saw an advert in a motorcycle magazine that aspiring riders should write to Wembley Stadium, and was given a trial by Alec Jackson. By then he had some grass track experience.

Freddie began riding at Rye House in 1946 but he suffered a broken ankle in a grass track meeting and his league debut had to wait until the following season. He recalled the training at Rye House as "carnage". Bill Kitchen was one of the instructors, and Freddie stayed with him at his home; Kitchen became his mentor. His ankle injury was serious, and he had severed the tendons. He was in hospital in Southampton, and a visiting Czech surgeon used the new technique of stitching the tendons back together.

The Wembley promoter, Alec Jackson, had seen that Freddie was a fine prospect, but a quiet start to his career saw him score just one point from his only match that year. He recalled walking through the stadium from the changing rooms to the pits at the other end in front of 50,000 people. In his first ride at Wembley he looped at the gate, but never did that again.

He was given a place in the Lions starting line-up in 1948 and a series of impressive and consistent scores saw him cement his place in the main body of the team. Freddie progressed well over the next couple of years as the Lions dominated the league scene and he made his international debut for England on his home track in 1949. He recalled that "Wembley had to be winners" and were expected to win the league.

He said that the riders were very well supported by Wembley, with their bikes being maintained by a team of mechanics, and taken to away meetings on a lorry. Williams' mechanic was initially Jock Hamilton but then he was looked after by the head mechanic, Cyril Spinks. If a rider was injured, they were well cared for at Wembley Hospital. Williams believes that the hospital were given complimentary tickets by the Wembley management. The riders' fitness was supported by Tommy Barnett, their trainer, who went to every meetings. Williams did not take advantage of the gym facilities, riding almost every other night kept him fit.

He qualified for his debut World Final in 1950 and, despite the meeting being held on his home track and the fact that Freddie had the beating of most around the Empire Stadium, it was still a major surprise when the young Welshman took home the title and catapulted himself into the world's elite. He recalled that he was not affected by the size of the crowd – riding in front of a huge crowd was nothing new for Wembley. He had said in Port Talbot the day before the final that he thought he could win it. His dad suggested that he put down a marker by breaking the track record in his first ride, which he did. His parents came to watch the meeting. Afterwards, elated at having won, his dad criticised him for "Letting Jack Parker beat you". He took the trophy to Wales and was given the 'Freedom of Port Talbot'. He spent most of his winnings on a new car, at Alec Jackson's suggestion. Later he realised that buying a house may have been more sensible.

This was the first of four consecutive final appearances and a disappointing ninth place in 1951 was followed by the silver medal as he finished as runner-up to Jack Young in 1952. A second World title on a rain soaked Wembley track in 1953, when he adapted himself superbly to the conditions to snatch the crown from under the nose of Split Waterman, confirmed his place in the history books as the first British rider to win two World titles, a feat matched only by Peter Craven in the years of one-off World Finals.

He went to Australia in 1949–50 with England, but made little impact in a series which England lost 6–1. He also rode in South Africa several times in the winter in the 1950s.

Despite his World title triumphs, Freddie did not dominate the sport like some others who wore the crown and he only once finished in the top five of the league averages. However, the title was there to be won on the night and, although he may not have had the same success had there been a modern style Grand Prix system in place, Freddie remains one of the greatest British riders of all time. His success with Wembley was equally as impressive, winning five consecutive league titles between 1949 and 1953, and he continued to ride for the club until June 1956 when he quit following a poor run of scores and his increasing business commitments. He sold his bike and leathers to a young rider in a café the riders used in St Albans. He did later regret his hasty decision, but did have a family to take care of, all of whom later became involved in sport.

In 1970, he returned to the Lions as team manager, an unpaid post which he held for the two years that the Lions ran in their new era. He recalled that it was nice to meet the riders and visit tracks all over the country. Trevor Redmond was one of his closest friends in the sport. He was involved in the Veteran Speedway Riders Association, and usually attended the Grand Prix meeting in Cardiff; in 2011 and 2012 as guest of honour.

His former team mate, Brian Crutcher, one of the few Lions from Freddie's time still alive, and Bert Harkins, who read the eulogy, attended his funeral in January 2013. He had died after having a stroke. Wembley's anthem, *Entry of the Gladiators*, was played as the coffin was carried into the church. A red and white Number 1 body colour belonging to Bert Harkins was draped over the coffin. The *Pathe News* commentary on his 1950 World Final victory was played as the coffin was carried out of the church. A fitting tribute to a famous Wembley Lion and a speedway legend.

(Freddie Williams' recollections from *In conversation with Freddie Williams* – DVD produced by Retro Speedway. Report of his funeral by Tony McDonald in *Classic Speedway* Issue 20)

Year	Club	Division	M	R	P	BP	TP	CMA	FM	PM
1947	Wembley	NL1	1	2	1	0	1	2.00		
		British Speedway Cup	1	3	2	0	2	2.67		
1948	Wembley	NL1	30	124	155	36	191	6.16		
		Anniversary Cup	12	48	50	15	65	5.42		
		London Cup	4	20	26	2	28	5.60		
1949	Wembley	NL1	35	140	232	27	259	7.40	1	1
		London Cup	2	10	6	1	7	2.80		
1950	Wembley	NL1	34	139	276	19	295	8.49	4	2
		London Cup	4	23	47	5	52	9.04		
1951	Wembley	NL1	37	155	340	29	369	9.52	2	7
		London Cup	6	34	70	5	75	8.82		
1952	Wembley	NL1	40	166	379	15	394	9.49	7	4
		London Cup	2	11	16	4	20	7.27		
1953	Wembley	NL1	22	95	222.5	6	228.5	9.62	4	2
		Coronation Cup	16	64	138	5	143	8.94	2	
		London Cup	2	12	27	0	27	9.00		
1954	Wembley	NL1	34	144	295	25	320	8.89		2
		RAC Cup	6	24	43	5	48	8.00		
		London Cup	4	23	54	5	59	10.26		
1955	Wembley	NL1	30	144	229	14	243	6.75	1	1
1956	Wembley	NL1	10	35	38	7	45	5.14		
		Totals	332	1416	2646.5	225	2871.5			

Individual Honours: World Champion 1950, 1953, World finalist 1951 (9th), 1952 (2nd).

International Honours: England international – 28 caps, 222 points.

Team Honours: National League Division One Championship winner 1949, 1950, 1951, 1952, 1953, National Trophy winner 1948, 1954. London Cup: Winner 1948, 1949, 1950, 1951, 1954.

Horatio Nelson (Bronco) Wilson
Born: 1920, Gateshead, Tyne & Wear, England.
Died: 16 August 1947.

At six feet tall and weighing in at a reputed 14 stones, Bronco was one of the largest riders in the sport. He served during the war in North Africa and as a despatch rider in Italy, where he rode speedway for the first time in Naples. He was spotted by Wembley supremo, Alec Jackson, during trials at Rye House. Jackson plunged the former solider into a reserve berth at the Empire Stadium and Bronco proved to be hugely popular with the legion of Wembley fans, recording a first season average of 5.83 in the championship winning side. In 1947 he increased his average slightly and looked set for a long and successful career in the sport. It was a huge blow to the club when he was killed in a track crash at Harringay on 15 August 1947, aged 26. He touched a rival's rear wheel and was thrown off his bike. Leonard Sandys wrote that he was "considered one of the most improved riders on the track."

Interviewed by Rick Eldon for his *Speedway Souvenir*, which was published just after his fatal crash at Harringay, Bronco recalled that he had "quite expected to be hanging around one of the little local tracks for the first two or three years, yet here I am riding for Wembley while I'm still a learner. ... But I'm learning with the right man. Who? Why Bill Kitchen of course. He does everything but ride the bike for me." Eldon does note that Bill Kitchen did not agree with this. Bronco also said that "I go to the gate full of instructions and good intentions, and tapes go up and then – the next thing I remember is that I'm on my way back to the pits, sometimes walking, sometimes riding." Eldon had introduced the piece saying that Bronco Wilson was the "new tearaway idol of the Wembley thousands." Bill Kitchen rated him as one of the best novices at Wembley in 1947, along with Split Waterman.

In both their post-war eras, Bronco Wilson was the only rider to be killed while riding for the Lions, and the club's tribute to him is elsewhere in this book.

Year	Club	Division	M	R	P	BP	TP	CMA	FM	PM
1946	Wembley	NL	11	24	29	6	35	5.83		
		ACU Cup	5	6	7	1	8	5.33		
		London Cup	1	2	1	1	2	4.00		
1947	Wembley	NL1	17	61	73	17	90	5.90		
		British Speedway Cup	10	40	45	12	57	5.70		
		London Cup	1	2	4	0	4	8.00		
		Totals	45	135	159	37	196			

Team Honours: National League Championship winner 1946, National League Division One Championship winner 1947 (posthumous).

25. The Lions' riders 1970 and 1971

Bengt Andersson (1970)
Steve Bast (1970)
Wayne Briggs (1970)
Tim Bungay (1970 and 1971)
Tony Clarke (1971)
Brian Collins (1970 and 1971)
Reidar Eide (1970)
Ove Fundin (1970)
Bert Harkins (1970 and 1971)
Sverre Harrfeldt (1971)
Tommy Jansson (1971)
Dave Jessup (1970 and 1971)
Brian Leonard (1970 and 1971)
Des Lukehurst (1970)
Gote Nordin (1971)
Peter Prinsloo (1971)
Christer Sjosten (1971)

All riders who rode in at least three official meetings for the Lions are included in this chapter.

Bengt Andersson

Bengt Andersson was signed from Exeter in September 1970 to replace Steve Bast. He had averaged 5.26 in 18 meetings in the First Division for the Falcons, but made little impact in his time with the Lions, and was released at the end of the season. He joined Cradley Heath in 1971, but scored even worse than his time at Wembley.

Year	M	R	P	BP	TP	CMA	FM	PM
1970	9	28	14	3	17	2.43	0	0

Steven Roger Bast
Born: 25 December 1951
Died: 2007

Steve Bast was the second American rider to ride in the British League competition after Dwayne Keeter who had been at Leicester in 1969. He was not, of course, the first American to ride for the Lions, Wilbur Lamoreaux had been a team member in 1948. He was signed in August 1970 to try to fill the heat leader slot left vacant after Ove Fundin's departure. However, he found the British tracks and conditions very different from what he was used to, and flew home, a homesick and disillusioned 19-year old, after a couple of weeks.

In his own country he was national champion in 1969 and 1974, and according to Peter Oakes and Ivan Mauger in their *Who's who of World Speedway* was "Undoubtedly one of America's all-time greats in the new era of speedway." He rode for the USA against the Rest of the World on various occasions.

Bert Harkins knew Bast well, and said when he died "...who knows what heights he could have reached if he had persevered in British league a little longer? At his peak, he was every bit as good as Bruce Penhall, Greg Hancock or Sam Ermalenko." (*Backtrack* Issue 23).

When he died he was living as a semi-recluse, and had not gone for treatment for what turned out to be pneumonia. He had been working in a local hardware store, and his family felt that things were improving for him. His younger brother Mike was also a leading American rider in the same period as Steve.

Year	M	R	P	BP	TP	CMA	FM	PM
1970	2	5	2	1	3	2.40	0	0

Wayne Briggs
Born: 24 June 1944

Wayne Briggs came to Great Britain in 1961, aged 16, to join his brother Barry. There was a 10 year age gap between them. He was offered a trial by Johnnie Hoskins at New Cross, who were then in the National League. Hoskins loaned him to Edinburgh, and it was in the Scottish capital where he rode for the first half of his career.

By 1962, he finished with an average of 8.35, but a serious accident at Newport saw him out of action for almost a year. He only rode six meetings in 1965 before his injury problems returned. He rode for Poole in 1966, and a move to Exeter saw him regain his heat-leader role. After another successful season in the south west he returned to Scotland to join Coatbridge. In 1969 he averaged 6.39, and this score dropped slightly when he moved to

Wembley. He scored a maximum in the Lions first meeting, a challenge match at Newport, but did not continue that form. After a year with the Lions, mainly as a second string, his average had fallen slightly from his last season with Coatbridge. He asked for a move and rejoined Exeter, but a shoulder injury meant he did not ride after August, and he retired at the end of the 1971 season. At his best, he was heat-leader class, but injuries prevented him fulfilling his potential. After running a haulage business, he moved to live in Spain with his wife Teresa.

Year	M	R	P	BP	TP	CMA	FM	PM
1970	32	117	146	25	171	5.85	0	0

Tim Bungay

Tim Bungay made his debut for the Lions at Coventry on 11 April 1970. His career started in the Provincial League with Poole in 1961. He stayed with Poole until 1964, and also rode for Exeter that year. In the British League era he rode for Cradley Heath, had three spells at Exeter, rode for Newport in 1966, Oxford and 1967 and then was back at Poole in 1968. His best averages were 6.00 at Exeter in 1965 and 5.54 for Newport in 1966. He was signed to try to strengthen the team in the reserve slots, but with his average of 3.26, did not really manage this. He retired after three meetings for the Lions in 1971. Trevor Redmond did comment on his loyalty to the Lions and did not criticise him for retiring so suddenly.

Year	M	R	P	BP	TP	CMA	FM	PM
1970	28	86	61	9	70	3.26	0	0
1971	3	7	2	1	3	1.71	0	0
Totals	31	93	63	10	73			

Anthony Brian (Tony) Clarke
Born: 6 July 1940
Died: 2 May 2014

Tony Clarke's first experience of the Wembley Lions was as a young supporter in the late 1940s. With his dad, he would stand next to the pits. He did not actually ride in speedway until he went to a training school at Ipswich in the 1962-63 winter. He bought a bike and started having second half rides in 1965 at West Ham, who were managed by Tommy Price. Known as the 'Wembley Wild Man' in the West Ham programme, he made his debut in a memorable Cup win at Wimbledon in 1965.

He kept his team place at West Ham, in a side that included Brian Leonard and Sverre Harrfeldt which won the British League, Knock out Cup and London Cup. A move to Oxford for a year followed, where he didn't like the track and struggled, but he returned to the east London track in 1967 and by 1969 was an established heat leader and number one in the Hammers' side. His average increased to 9.36 in 1970, but he became disillusioned with West Ham, and joined the Lions in 1971. He was one of four rides with West Ham links in the memorable 1971 Lions team.

After the Lions withdrew from the 1972 season, he was allocated to Newport, which he was not happy about, and was relieved to return to London for the 1973 season with Wimbledon. He was released by the Dons, and after a two month break joined

Wolverhampton. However, he was convicted of handling stolen goods, following the theft of bikes and other speedway equipment from six Russian riders in London in 1972. His sentence saw him miss the 1974 season, but he returned to ride for Wolverhampton in 1975 before retiring.

On the international scene, he rode for England and Great Britain, and was a Lions tourist to Australia and New Zealand in 1969–70. He had strokes in 2010 and 2013 before being diagnosed with cancer; and he died in May 2014, aged 73. Wembley fans will remember his spectacular riding and the contribution he made to the team's second season.

(Based on interviews in *Classic Speedway* (Issue 12), *Backtrack* (Issue 43) and obituary in *Backtrack* (Issue 62)

Year	M	R	P	BP	TP	CMA	FM	PM
1971	35	146	234	30	264	7.23	1	0

Brian John Collins
Born: 13 May 1948

Brian Collins was the youngest of the four riders who joined Wembley in 1970 from Coatbridge. He played ice hockey and rode cycle speedway before graduating to speedway. He first rode at the Cowdenbeath training track before moving to Meadowbank in 1965 to join the Edinburgh Monarchs. Interviewed by Mike Hunter in *Backtrack* (issue 1), he recalled how he won his first two races at reserve for the Monarchs in 1966, and was briefly top of the speedway averages.

He broke his leg at Hackney in 1967, but returned at the end of the season to win the Scottish Junior Championship. He stayed with the team for the move to Coatbridge, and was the team's number 7. In 1968, he was reserve for Scotland against England, but ended up with 14 points. His average for his last season with the Monarchs was 5.93, including a paid maximum, and he was an established second string when he moved to London. Angus Kix said of his 1969 performance: "... he's come on a ton and likely to come on even further. Good rider, good team man, good prospect. It's all on for this lad..."

He was just 22 when he moved to London to join Wembley. The Lions programme said that he was a "member of last year's Coatbridge squad whose value to the team cannot be put too highly... A very welcome member of the Lions."

The Lions paid for him to have digs in Wembley with a local family, but in the *Backtrack* interview he recalled that "I didn't settle. I actually only lasted a week and I was set for coming home. I had no one to turn to and no one to help me." He moved to Poole to stay with Norman Strachan's family, initially for a weekend and stayed four years. This gave him the support he needed, and his career continued to develop. He commented that: "The track at Wembley really suited me. I was partnered with Fundin at one time which was a great experience. Although the stadium wasn't full, there was a great atmosphere." He also found that Trevor Redmond could criticise "but he knew what he was talking about".

He finished the 1970 season with a 6.20 average, up on 1969, and was the top second-string for the Lions. His average dropped marginally in 1971, to 5.99, but he was the top bonus point scorer with the Lions on 33. Danny Carter said in his review of the Lions 1971 campaign that he had expected Brian to 'make it big' in 1971, but an early season injury had held him back. His form was more consistent in the second half of the season. His best scores were a 10(+1) from four rides at home to Swindon, and 12(+2) from six rides against Coventry. In the winter of 1971 he rode in Rhodesia, and won the Rhodesian Championship.

When he returned home, the Lions were homeless, and he joined Poole, initially for the 1972 season. He stayed there for two years, but then returned to Scotland to rejoin Coatbridge in the Second Division. He had met his wife Brenda while at Poole, and was also starting a garage business.

In 1978 he joined Edinburgh, and then rode for Berwick and Glasgow before retiring in 1984. He says that Wembley was one of his favourite tracks, and remembers winning the Lions Pairs meeting riding with Bert Harkins in 1971.

He rode regularly for Scotland, both in internationals and the British qualifying round for the World Team Cup. According to Edinburgh speedway historian Mike Hunter, he had "one of the finest Scottish careers of the second half of the last [twentieth] century." He also made the most appearances in league and cup meetings with the Lions in the modern era; his 71 meetings being four ahead of Bert Harkins' 67.

Year	M	R	P	BP	TP	CMA	FM	PM
1970	36	149	200	31	231	6.20	0	0
1971	35	143	181	33	214	5.99	0	0
Totals	71	292	381	64	445			

Reidar Eide
Born: 6 November 1940
Died: February 1999

Year	M	R	P	BP	TP	CMA	FM	PM
1970*	37	163	354	17	371	9.10	3	1

* Ever present. Also top of the Lions averages.

Reidar Eide was an established British League number one when he joined the Lions from Coatbridge in 1970. He was also the only Lions rider in 1970 or 1971 to ride a full season and have an average of over nine points. Although his form in 1970 was uneven, with some very good periods and some less successful ones, he played an important role in establishing the Lions in the First Division. For a time he was almost unbeatable at Wembley.

He was aged 26, and established in Norwegian speedway before he signed for the Edinburgh Monarchs in 1966. Two themes seem to follow his career in British speedway – clashes with promoters over money and his popularity with the fans. Ian Hoskins, his promoter at Edinburgh and then Coatbridge for four years, outlines in his book details of clashes he had with Eide over payments. Bob Radford, in a feature on Eide in *Backtrack* (issue 32) recalls Eide instructing Roger Johns, his mechanic, to not warm up his bike for the meeting before he had seen Trevor Redmond privately, to ask for more money.

His first season with the Monarchs ended prematurely, according to Mike Hunter, because of a financial dispute with Hoskins. But in 1967, he improved his average from 5.83 in his first season to just under nine. For his two seasons at Coatbridge, he was established as a genuine number one. Bu then, following Sverre Harrfeldt's accident, he was also the leading Norwegian rider. He won the Norwegian title every year from 1967 to 1971. He rode in his only World Final in 1968, but finished 13th with just three points.

After his one season with the Lions, he was at Poole for a year, then Sheffield and then had three seasons at Newport. Two years at Leicester followed, then a season with Exeter. In 1979 he joined Reading, and in 1980 rode for them, Wolverhampton, Swindon and one meeting for Eastbourne before retiring from British speedway aged 39.

He was also a top class skier. In retirement he married a Thai woman, and took up pig farming. But he caught Brucellosis, and died at the comparatively young age of 58. Mike Hunter says that he "gave good service to all his clubs but never quite seemed to fulfil the promise he showed in the late 1960s." He also recalls Eide as a "real fan pleaser" on the track in his time riding for the Monarchs.

Ove Fundin
Born: 23 May 1933

Ove Fundin was undoubtedly, along with Barry Briggs and Ronnie Moore, one of the great speedway riders of the 1950s and 1960s. He won five World Championships; the first in 1956 and the last in 1967. Only Ivan Mauger and Tony Rickardsson, at the time of writing, have won more world titles. From 1956 to 1965, he was on the rostrum (i.e. in the top three) every year in the World Final. Add to that six World Team Cup wins with Sweden, a World Best Pairs win in 1968 and four European Championships and there is a remarkable record of consistency at the very top level of the sport.

Ove rode regularly for Sweden, was Swedish champion nine times between 1956 and 1970, and rode for almost 20 years in the Swedish League. In British speedway, he rode for Norwich from 1955 to 1964, when the track closed due to being sold for development. In 147 matches, he scored 57 maximums, and was undoubtedly one of the main reasons that the team survived for so long. He is still fondly remembered in East Anglia.

He had brief spells at long Eaton in 1966 and Belle Vue in 1967 before returning to British speedway with the Lions in 1970. The details of his return – and departure – have been covered elsewhere in this book. The recruitment of Fundin was important in establishing the Lions as a serious team in the First Division. When many people had doubts about Wembley's return, it gave the promotion credibility. Even as a veteran he was still a draw.

He continued to ride occasionally for a few years after 1970. He now lives in France, and maintains an interest in the sport. He was president of the Veteran Speedway Riders Association in Britain in 1993, and still attends some of the Grand Prix meetings. In 2006 he was made a Freeman of Norwich, only the second non-English person to receive this honour, and over 40 years after he had finished riding for the Stars.

Year	M	R	P	BP	TP	CMA	FM	PM
1970	14	59	115	2	117	7.93	0	0

Robert Pearson (Bert) Harkins
Born: 15 April 1940

One of the four riders who joined the Lions from Coatbridge, Bert Harkins was one of the most popular riders with the Wembley fans. He captained the side after Ove Fundin's departure until the end of the 1971 season.

Bert was born in Glasgow, and was a cycle speedway star in his youth. He participated in road racing before switching to speedway in 1961, when he was working as a lawn mower mechanic for the Glasgow Parks department. He first rode at the Stepps Stadium Trotting track in Glasgow, and also rode in second halves at Edinburgh. He rode to Edinburgh from Glasgow on his motorbike, with his speedway bike in the sidecar. He first rode for the Monarchs in 1963, but did not win a regular team place until 1964. He gradually developed from reserve to second string to heat leader in 1969. He was also one of the few speedway riders to wear glasses while racing.

His average dropped slightly in his first season with the Lions. Becoming familiar with a new home track that was never easy to ride, and regularly commuting from Glasgow probably didn't help. But, in 1971, he achieved the best average of his career, despite missing some meetings in the first half of the season with a series of injuries. He also reached the Nordic-British final in the World Championship. Riding at Hampden Park, he was handicapped by a recently broken collarbone and only scored three points. Had he been full fit, he could have qualified for the European Final, which was held at Wembley. Home advantage could have helped him reach a World Final.

When Wembley did not reopen in 1972, he joined Sheffield for a year, before returning to London to join Wimbledon in 1973. He suffered a serious back injury towards the end of the 1974 season, but returned to ride in 1975. A season in America followed, with the Bakersfield Bandits. On his return to the UK in 1977, he rode for Edinburgh when the Monarchs reopened in the National League for the 1977, 1978 and 1979 seasons. He finished his career with Milton Keynes in 1980.

On the international scene, he finished fifth, with Jim McMillan, in the 1970 Best Pairs. This was also the best international honour achieved by a Wembley rider in the modern era. He rode for the British Lions in Australia in 1971–72, Great Britain, the Rest of the World, and Scotland on many occasions. Over the years, he also rode in New Zealand, South Africa, Ireland, Germany, Austria, Italy and Israel.

Bert also wrote regularly in the speedway press, and still contributes to *Backtrack* and *Classic Speedway*. He also wrote about his experience with the Lions in *Wembley – Stadium of Legends* by Peter Tomsett and Chris Brand.

After retiring from speedway, Bert ran a motorbike / speedway parts business. He has also been heavily involved with the World Speedway Riders Association, and regularly attends their events and speedway meetings. A set of his leathers and other items of his can be seen on display in the Speedway Museum.

Bert's motorcycling days are by no means over since he retired from speedway. In 2015, he rode with Ove Fundin (aged almost 82) from Ove's home in the south of France to visit 91-year-old Split Waterman at his home in Spain. Bert rode his 990cc KTM Supermoto bike, while Ove was on his BMW F800. They made it to Spain, spent time with Split and his wife Avril and made it back to Ove's home. A round trip of over 2,000 miles. And those three would have made some heat leader trio for the Lions!

Year	M	R	P	BP	TP	CMA	FM	PM
1970*	37	157	262	25	287	7.31	1	0
1971**	30	130	238	31	269	8.28	1	3
Totals	67	287	500	56	556			

* Ever present. ** Top of the Lions averages.

Sverre Harrfeldt
Born: 23 November 1937

The young speedway fans who were watching the sport for the first time as Wembley Lions fans (such as the author of this section) had little idea of the status or history of the team's new recruit who made his debut at Swindon on 15 May 1971. He scored one point (plus a bonus point) in two races. An inauspicious start to his season with the Lions.

Sverre's early years in speedway were spent riding in Norway. But fourth place in the World Championship Nordic Final in 1963, when he was aged 25, brought him to Wimbledon's attention. He was signed as cover for Ronnie Moore, who had broken an ankle. Thirteen matches in the National League saw him produce an impressive average of over eight points a match. In his debut World Final, he finished sixth with 10 points, the same as future Lions team-mate Gote Nordin. He broke his collarbone in 1964 in the Nordic final, and in 1965 missed out when he arrived a day late for the European Final – having been given the wrong date by the Norwegian speedway officials.

By then he had left Plough Lane for West Ham, as part of the rider moves that created the British League. At club level, he had his best season as part of the treble-winning 1965 West Ham team. An average of over 11 did not seem him top the score charts – Ken McKinlay was a quarter of a point better, but his all action style endeared him to the Hammers fans. In 1966, his average fell by just over a point, but he finished as runner-up in the World Final, a point behind Barry Briggs, who beat him in heat nine. In an interview with Tony McDonald in *Classic Speedway* (issue 8) Sverre recalls that his best season was 1967. He won the London Riders Championship, and scored 15 maximums in the league (14 full, one paid). Bike problems saw him eliminated at the European Final stage of the World Championship.

In 1968, his championship ambitions ended at the same stage, but this time in a horrific accident in heat 12. He broke his right thigh, left ankle and fractured his pelvis. He came close to having his left foot amputated. His recovery saw him miss the 1969 season. He returned to Custom House in 1970, and broke his arm in May. He planned to go on the trip to Holland that resulted in the Lokeren accident, but a medical appointment meant he fortunately missed being involved in speedway's blackest day.

He made little impact on the track in 1970, and a falling-out with West Ham saw him join the Lions. He gradually recovered his form, and his final average with the Lions of nearly eight points was a good return for his efforts. He recalled in *Classic Speedway* that "In my mind I could still do some good things –I beat Barry Briggs at Wembley one night –but I knew I'd never be as good as I was before my big crash."

Sverre retired – to his wife's relief who had not been keen upon his return to action with Wembley – at the end of the 1971 season. When he retired he ran a car sales business in Norway, and lives near his brother Henry, who rode for Edinburgh in the 1960s. Given that he did not ride in Britain until the age of 25, one wonders what he could have achieved if he had started to ride earlier in Britain and remained injury free. But to the Lions fans of 1971 he will always be a hero.

Year	M	R	P	BP	TP	CMA	FM	PM
1971	33	121	216	20	236	7.80	1	0

Per Tommy Jansson
Born: 2 October 1952
Died: 20 May 1976

Tommy Jansson rode three away meetings for the Lions at the start of the 1971 season, aged just 19, but was then released. Given that he reached the World Final, where he finished 14th with one point, there must be some debate over whether such a hasty decision was correct.

He made his debut for Smederna in the Swedish League in 1969. He returned to London to continue his British career in 1972, when he joined Wimbledon. His average improved from 7.45 that year to 9.20 in 1973 and 10.06 in 1975. He represented Sweden both in the World Team Cup and in international matches, and with Anders Michanek won the World Best Pairs in 1973. His older brother, Bo Joel Jansson, also became a speedway rider. His father, Joel Jansson had also ridden for Sweden.

It was a great shock to everyone in speedway when Tommy Jansson was killed in a track accident in May 1976 at the Swedish Final. He was aged just 23, and was one of the most exciting riders of the 1970s. His best years were clearly ahead of him. He was the last holder of the Golden Helmet, and the helmet was given to his family, and not competed for again.

Year	M	R	P	BP	TP	CMA	FM	PM
1971	3	11	11	0	11	4.00	0	0

Dave Jessup
Born: 7 March 1953

The recruitment of Dave Jessup from Eastbourne by Wembley in 1970 was reminiscent of the signing of Brian Crutcher by the Lions in 1953. Jessup was aged just 17 when he joined the Lions – he passed his driving test during his first season – whereas Crutcher was 18 when he was signed. However, both were the outstanding young English rider of their generation, and both went onto challenge for the sport's top honours. Jessup's career lasted longer than Crutcher's; and he was a speedway rider for almost 20 years.

Jessup continued to ride for Eastbourne in 1970 after joining the Lions, and won the Second Division Riders Championship. He strengthened the Lions' tail when he arrived, but was soon challenging for a full team place. Interviewed by Tony McDonald in *Backtrack* (Issue 20), he recalled that "It was a thrill to be riding at Wembley every week – we got crowds of about 10,000 and just walking into the dressing rooms and knowing the history of the place was a great experience." He also revealed that Hackney had been interested in buying him, but that Len Silver wouldn't pay Eastbourne the "four or five hundred quid they wanted for me." He also remembered not being happy with Ove Fundin insisting on having the inside gate if they rode together. The management solved that problem by paying him more if he was on the outside gate.

In the Lions' second season, he finished the season in the third heat leader position, with an average marginally better than Tony Clarke's. It was a remarkable achievement for a rider in only his second season in the First Division. He had also benefitted from two seasons riding in Rhodesia in the winter. But before it was announced that the Lions would not run in 1972, he had asked for a move, wanting more meetings than Wembley, with their shorter home season, could offer. In 1975 he won the London Riders Championship, despite riding for the

Leicester Lions. The basis of him being invited was that he was a former Wembley rider, and therefore he could claim to be the last Wembley rider to win a trophy.

He remained a Lion by joining Leicester. He subsequently rode for Reading, Wimbledon and King's Lynn before finishing his career with Mildenhall. He was undoubtedly one of the great English riders of his generation, at a time when English speedway was very strong. He retired in 1987, apart from a one-off comeback for Mildenhall in a cup match at Wimbledon in 1988.

He represented England over 100 times, and in 1980 won the World best Pairs with Peter Collins and then was part of the England team that won the World Team Cup. He had previously been part of World Team Cup winning squads in 1974 and 1977. He captained England, and was later the England team manager.

In 1980 he achieved his best World Final result, when he was runner-up to Michael Lee. But in 1978 at Wembley, his bike packed up on the last bend of his first heat when he was winning. Four subsequent wins could not even bring third place, when he was beaten by Scott Autrey in a run-off. Two engine failures in the 1981 final, the last at Wembley, also saw him miss out on at least a rostrum spot.

In retirement he plays golf to a very high standard, and was selected for the seniors England team in 2008. He can reflect on a very successful career in the speedway, with only the World title eluding him.

Year	M	R	P	BP	TP	CMA	FM	PM
1970	19	71	73.5	11	84.5	4.76	0	0
1971	28	120	202	21	223	7.43	0	0
Totals	**47**	**191**	**275.5**	**32**	**307.5**			

Brian Leonard
Born: 19 February 1946

Brian Leonard made his debut for the Lions in a 41–37 win over Wimbledon at home on 4 July 1970. He was signed after Des Lukehurst had – temporarily – retired. He won his first race for the Lions, and his 5–1 with Tim Bungay in heat two was, arguably, decisive in Wembley's win.

His speedway career started with the Poole Pirates in 1962 as a 16-year-old. In 1965 he joined West ham and was part of the team that won the treble, along with future Wembley team-mates Sverre Harrfeldt and Tony Clarke. His best season was in 1967; his average was over seven for the first time in his career, the Hammers came close to winning the league again and reached the Knock out Cup final. After a poor spell at West Ham in 1969, he joined Hackney where things improved. But a return to Custom House in 1970 did not work out. He recalls, in an interview in *Backtrack* with Rob Peasley (Issue 64) that he had bike problems at the time. He joined Newport, but did not like the track, and was close to taking up car racing when he was signed by the Lions.

His time at Wembley overlapped with Ove Fundin's last few meetings for the Lions, and Leonard found himself partnering his hero: "I had idolised him. There was something about his style. I guess I'd tried to copy I, although I'm not sure how successfully." He ended that first season with the Lions with an average of just over four, and improved by 1.5 points in 1971. Then, he was riding with former West Ham colleague Sverre Harrfeldt. He told Rob Peasley that "Who could turn down the chance to ride for Wembley? It was an incredible feeling riding there every week." He was supported by Mike Erskine, who tuned his bikes, and he believes that Erskine contacted Trevor Redmond to suggest that he could strengthen the Lions' tail.

After Wembley closed he joined Swindon for three years. This saw him in the same team as former Wembley Lion from the 1950s, Mike Broadbank. Leonard blamed Broadbank for a crash that resulted in him breaking an ankle in 1967. For a long time he did not speak to Broadbank, and always aimed to beat him. Broadbank apologised when Leonard joined Swindon and the matter was resolved. At Swindon he rode with Barry Briggs, another of his heroes.

Then followed a short spell with Leicester which did not work out. He returned to speedway in 1976 with Oxford in the National League, and rode for them until early in 1978. Then an injury, and his marriage break-up and custody of his son ended his riding career at the age of 32. In 1987, he returned to active participation in the sport as team manager and co-promoter at Reading. But after a year he sold his share of the company. He subsequently was involved in moto-cross and when interviewed by *Backtrack* in 2014 was helping out in go-kart racing.

He was a popular rider at Wembley, who could have developed further with the Lions had the team kept racing after 1971.

Year	M	R	P	BP	TP	CMA	FM	PM
1970	20	71	66	8	74	4.17	0	0
1971	37	132	163	28	191	5.72	0	0
Totals	57	203	229	36	265			

Des Lukehurst
Born: 3 October 1937

Des Lukehurst rode for the Lions in the first half of the 1970 season. In the British League era he had been a second string for Exeter, Oxford and Hackney before going into the Second Division with Romford in 1969. He was signed by the Lions, and made his debut in the team' first outing at Newport, winning his first race in heat two. He rode regularly for a couple of months, including in the opening meeting against Hackney. Various problems, including a couple of car crashes, saw him temporarily retire at the end of June.

He returned to the sport in early August, but by then Wembley had signed Dave Jessup and Brian Leonard. He expected to be given a chance by West Ham, who were short of rides after the Lokeren disaster, but instead returned to Romford. He retired at the end of the season.

Year	M	R	P	BP	TP	CMA	FM	PM
1970	8	22	17	4	21	3.82	0	0

Gote Nordin
Born: 2 July 1935

Hasse Holmqvist was expected to join the Lions in 1971. But for family reasons he never made it, so Trevor Redmond signed Gote Nordin, who by then was almost 36 years old, on a short-term deal for June and July. He made his debut in the Lions first home meeting against Poole. He won twice and fell twice, but after that rode consistently well to average just over nine points. Wembley knew he would leave at the end of July to complete a course he was doing for work in Sweden. He was available on Saturdays, but Redmond felt that he did not want a 'part-time' rider, although in retrospect, with the inexperience of and then injury to Christer Sjosten, the team may have done better with Nordin. The Wembley programme (19 June 1971) said he was "rated by the experts as the best rider never to have won a world title."

In his last meeting, against Exeter on 31 July, when he scored 13 from five rides, the programme said: "A massive vote of thanks is due to Gote Nordin, who this week finishes his all too brief stint with the Lions... Nordin stepped into the breach and in no time at all has become a great favourite. Unfortunately he has to go home to resume a course of studies. He told us all about it before he came over. In no way is he letting us down. ... So we bid him farewell – and wish him all the best. His style and sportsmanship will guarantee him a huge welcome any time he can come back. Thanks, Gote."

He first rode in Britain in 1960, for Belle Vue. His first World Final appearance was in 1961. It was the first World Final not staged at Wembley. In Malmo the Swedes took the top three places. Fundin won it, but only Nordin beat him. In a run-off with Bjorn Knutson and Barry Briggs, who had all finished on 12 points, Nordin beat Briggs for third place overall. He rode in three more finals, 1962, 1963 and 1966, scoring 9, 10 and 9 points – close to the rostrum but not quite there. He was also non-riding reserve in the 1964 and 1971 finals.

Despite his high standing in the sport, he did not ride regularly in Britain. He rode for Wimbledon prior to the formation of the British League, and returned to Plough Lane as a Newport rider in 1966 to win the Internationale. He retained the trophy as a Poole rider in 1967, but early in the 1968 season, aged 32, returned to Sweden to study business engineering. A short spell with Coventry in 1969 followed before he joined Wembley in 1971. In 1972 he had a similar short spell with Halifax, and at the age of 37 retired from the sport.

In an interview in *Vintage Speedway Magazine* (Issue 51) by Bob Radford, he recalled that "I got a call from Trevor Redmond. What a character he was! Obviously it [Wembley] was a very special place to ride, so that was great fun and a very enjoyable experience."

In retirement he was involved in the construction business for many years.

Year	M	R	P	BP	TP	CMA	FM	PM
1971	11	46	101	3	104	9.04	0	0

Pietrus Johannes (Peter) Prinsloo
Born: 29 August 1949

Peter Prinsloo was spotted by Trevor Redmond riding in Zimbabwe in 1970-71. He was signed for the Lions, but was loaned out to Ipswich, then in the Second Division, to gain more experience. After the Lions did not ride in 1972, he continued to ride in Rhodesia, and won the national championship every year from 1971 to 1974. He also won the South African championship in 1974 and 1975, and rode for Rhodesia against South Africa.

He returned to British League racing in 1976 with Exeter. The Falcons persevered with him after a first season average of 3.54. He achieved second string / third heat leader status in his next three seasons with the Falcons, and then joined Poole in 1980. He rode for the Pirates until 1982. In South Africa, he rode for their Wembley Lions in the 1977–78 season. His brother Chris also rode in Rhodesia and South Africa.

Year	M	R	P	BP	TP	CMA	FM	PM
1971	11	24	7	1	8	1.33	0	0

Christer Sjosten
Born: 2 September 1948
Died: 9 December 1979

Christer Sjosten made his debut for the Lions at Reading at the beginning of August following the departure of Gote Nordin. The younger brother of Soren Sjosten, a star heat-leader at Belle Vue, the young Swede was clearly not ready for a heat leader role. After a handful of meetings for the Lions, he was injured and the team used rider-replacement for him on several occasions. He did return to action at the end of the season, and a 12 point maximum for the Lions at Hackney in a Silver Dollar Handicap meeting showed the potential he had.

In 1972 he rode a handful of meetings for Exeter. He joined Coatbridge in 1973, and Poole the following year. By now he was regularly reaching the third heat leader mark which the Lions had looked for in 1971. He stayed with Poole for the rest of his career. Sadly, he died in December 1979 eight days after a track accident in Brisbane. Poole staged a memorial meeting for him in 1980, which was won by Bob Kilby.

Year	M	R	P	BP	TP	CMA	FM	PM
1971	6	19	16	4	20	4.21	0	0

Other riders for Wembley:	Guest riders:
1970:	**1970:**
Graham Banks	Reg Wilson
George Barclay	Arnie Haley
Brian Davies	Dave Younghusband
Brian Foote	Colin Pratt
Tony Hall	Reg Luckhurst
Richard May	
Cec Platt	**1971:**
Stan Stevens	Ken McKinlay (2)
	Cliff Emms
1971:	Oyvind Berg
Trevor Geer	Charlie Monk (2)
Roger Johns	Bob Paulson
John Louis	Bob Andrews
Bobby McNeil	Garry Middleton
Norman Strachan	Malcolm Simmons
Reg Trott	Pete Smith

Appendix 1: Statistics and records

Trophies won by the Wembley Lions

1929 to 1939:

Southern League: 1930, 1931.
National League: 1932.
National Trophy: 1931, 1932.
London Cup: 1930, 1932, 1933.

1946 to 1956:

National League & National League Division 1: 1946, 1947, 1949, 1950, 1951, 1952, 1953.
National Trophy: 1948, 1954.
London Cup: 1946, 1948, 1949, 1950, 1951, 1954.
British Speedway Cup: 1947.

League record

1929 to 1939:

Year	Comp	Played	Won	Drawn	Lost	For	Against	Pts	Place
1929	SL	20	11	0	9	580	571	22	5
1930	**SL**	**24**	**20**	**1**	**3**	**768**	**496**	**41**	**1**
1931	**SL**	**38**	**29**	**1**	**8**	**1149.5**	**822.5**	**59**	**1**
1932	**NL**	**16**	**13**	**0**	**3**	**495**	**358**	**26**	**1**
1933	NL	36	19	1	16	1184	1057	39	6
1934	NL	32	26	0	6	980	731	52	2
1935	NL	24	11	0	13	855	852	22	4
1936	NL	24	15	0	9	891	826	30	2
1937	NL	24	16	0	8	1054	943	32	2
1938	NL	24	13	1	10	1043	953	27	3
1939	*NL*	*19*	*11*	*1*	*7*	*874*	*716*	*23*	*3*

SL: Southern League. NL: National League. 1939 results from when the league was abandoned due to the outbreak of the Second World War.

1946 to 1956:

Year	Comp	Played	Won	Drawn	Lost	For	Against	Pts	Place
1946	**NL**	**20**	**18**	**0**	**2**	**940**	**721**	**36**	**1**
1947	**NLD1**	**24**	**19**	**0**	**5**	**1153**	**846**	**38**	**1**
1948	NLD1	24	12	1	11	1040.5	966.5	25	4
1949	**NLD1**	**42**	**28**	**1**	**13**	**1902.5**	**1620.5**	**57**	**1**
1950	**NLD1**	**32**	**24**	**0**	**8**	**1503**	**1173**	**48**	**1**
1951	**NLD1**	**32**	**25**	**0**	**7**	**1535**	**1146**	**50**	**1**
1952	**NLD1**	**36**	**28**	**1**	**7**	**1751**	**1260**	**57**	**1**
1953	**NLD1**	**16**	**11**	**1**	**4**	**772.5**	**567.5**	**23**	**1**
1954	NLD1	28	20	0	8	1363	985	40	2
1955	NLD1	24	11	1	12	1181	1119	23	3
1956	NLD1	24	14	1	9	1063	946	29	2

Bold: League champions

1970 and 1971

Year	Comp	Played	Won	Drawn	Lost	For	Against	Pts	Place
1970	BLD1	36	15	2	19	1327.5	1474.5	32	14
1971	BLD1	36	17	3	16	1433	1372	37	9

World Champions

1936: Lionel Van Praag
1949: Tommy Price
1950: Freddie Williams
1953: Freddie Williams

British Riders Champion

1946: Tommy Price

Golden Helmet Match Race Championship

1946: Bill Kitchen nominated as Champion. Beat Ron Johnson, lost to Jack Parker.
Tommy Price lost to Jack Parker.
1947: Vic Duggan beat Bill Kitchen
1948: Jack Parker beat Split Waterman
Jack Parker beat Wilbur Lamoreaux
1949: Jack Parker beat Tommy Price
1950: Jack Parker beat Tommy Price
1951: Aub Lawson beat Freddie Williams
Jack Parker beat Bob Oakley
1952: Jack Young beat Freddie Williams
1953: Jack Young beat Freddie Williams
1954: Arthur Forrest beat Freddie Williams
1956: Brian Crutcher beat Ronnie Moore, Barry Briggs, Alan Hunt, Barry Briggs, lost to Peter Craven.

London Riders Championship

1930: Jack Ormston
1948: Split Waterman
1956: Brian Crutcher (at Wembley)

Appendix 2: Wembley Lions results

1929

Home team score given first

Southern League

Opponents	Home	Away
Birmingham	42–21	30–33
Coventry	37–26	27–14
Crystal Palace	23–40	42–21
Harringay	30–33	24–38
Lea Bridge	41–21	30–33
Southampton	22–40	43–20
Stamford Bridge	16–26	33–9
West Ham	29–12	31–32
White City	39–24	25–17
Wimbledon	48–15	27–36

1930

Southern League

Opponents	Home	Away
Coventry	39–14	0–36
Crystal Palace	31–22	30–23
Hall Green	28.5–24.5	19–35
Harringay	33–20	23–31
High Beech	37–16	21–32
Lea Bridge	40–14	23–31
Leicester	34–20	25–29
Nottingham	37–17	22–31
Southampton	35–19	26.5–26.5
Stamford Bridge	24–29	29–24
West Ham	36–18	21–33
Wimbledon	30–22	21–32

London Cup

First round:
Wembley 71 High Beech 25
High Beech 52 [77] Wembley 44 [115]

Semi-final:
Wembley 52 Wimbledon 44
Wimbledon 39 [83] Wembley 56 [108]

Final:
Wembley 59 Stamford Bridge 37
Stamford Bridge 49 [86] Wembley 46 [105]

1931

Southern League

Opponents	Home	Away
Belle Vue	37–16	28–26
	30–22	16–36
Coventry	37–17	29–25
Crystal Palace	41–12	16–36
	34–19	30–23
High Beech	43–11	30–24
	31–23	20–33
Lea Bridge	34–20	18–36
	34–18	22–32
Leicester	Not raced	22–31
Nottingham	37–16	26–28
Southampton	31–23	31–23
	32–22	30–24
Stamford Bridge	31–22	23–30
	34–19	32–21
West Ham	32–22	24–29
	29.5–24.5	20–32
Wimbledon	31–22	22–30
	27–27	28–25

NB Leicester withdrew from the League. Nottingham did not complete their fixtures, but their results are included in the final table.

National Trophy

Second round
Wembley 56 West Ham 37
West Ham 44 [81] Wembley 52 [108]

Third round
Wembley 70 Sheffield 25
Sheffield 41 [66] Wembley 55 [125]

Semi-final
Wembley 48 Wimbledon 47
Wimbledon 46 [93] Wembley 49 [93]

Final
Wembley 71 Stamford Bridge 24
Stamford Bridge 45 [69] Wembley 49 [120]

London Cup

First round
Wembley 49 Wimbledon 45
Wimbledon 46 [91] Wembley 50 [99]

Semi-final
Wembley 53.5 Stamford Bridge 41.5
Stamford Bridge 50 [91.5] Wembley 44 [97.5]

Final
Crystal Palace 59 Wembley 36
Wembley 40 [76] Crystal Palace 55 [114]

1932

National League

Opponent	Home	Away
Belle Vue	41–13	29–25
Clapton	33–20	20–34
Coventry	30–24	22–29
Crystal Palace	29–25	30–24
Plymouth	27–24	16–35
Stamford Bridge	30–24	29–25
West Ham	33–20	14–40
Wimbledon	29–25	23–31

National Trophy

Second round
Wembley 54 Stamford Bridge 42
Stamford Bridge 46 [88] Wembley 45 [99]

Semi-final
Wembley 63 Coventry 33
Coventry 38 [71] Wembley 56 [119]

National Association Trophy

Opponent	Home	Away
Belle Vue	28–25	29–25
Coventry	33–20	20–34
Crystal Palace	32–22	27–26
Plymouth	36–16	15–36
Sheffield	41–11	20–34
Southampton	37–16	24–29
Stamford Bridge	31–21	37–17
West Ham	31–23	25–29
Wimbledon	28–24	28–26

London Cup

Semi-final
Wembley 65 Crystal Palace 30
Crystal Palace 56 [86] Wembley 37 [102]

Final
Wembley 52 Stamford Bridge 44
Stamford Bridge 48 [92] Wembley 47 [99]

1933

National League

Opponent	Home	Away
Belle Vue	38–23	32–30
	21–42	32–31
Clapton	49.5–13.5	44–18
	31–31	34–28
Coventry	44–15	27–34
	35–28	42–21
Crystal Palace	34–29	39–23
	35–27	42–21
Nottingham	45–16	24–35
	46–17	25–37
Plymouth	46–17	34–29
	48–15	35–27
Sheffield	37–26	25–38
	51–12	33–30
West Ham	38–24	46.5–16.5
	28–35	36–27
Wimbledon	25–37	25–38
	24–38	30–32

National Trophy

First round
Wembley 103 Nottingham 22
Nottingham 44 [66] Wembley 79 [182]

Semi-final
Wembley 77 Crystal Palace 48
Crystal Palace 62 [110] Wembley 63 [140]

Final
Wembley 54 Belle Vue 72
Belle Vue 92 [164] Wembley 33 [87]

London Cup

Semi-final
Wembley 77 West Ham 46
West Ham 60 [106] Wembley 66 [143]

Final
Wembley 69 Wimbledon 56
Wimbledon 53 [109] Wembley 71 [140]

1934

National League

Opponent	Home	Away
Belle Vue	23–31	26–28
	23–31	35–19
Birmingham	35–19	20–34
	36–17	22–32
Harringay	23–31	26–28
	22–30	22–32
Lea Bridge / Walthamstow	35–17	23–31
	32–21	22–32
New Cross	33–20	24–29
	28–25	28–26
Plymouth	40–14	23–30
	41–12	22–32
West Ham	35–17	24–30
	36–18	23–31
Wimbledon	31–23	21–32
	29–24	20–32

National Trophy

Second round
Wembley 59 Harringay 49
Harringay 33 [82] Wembley 74 [133]

Semi-final
Wembley 67.5 New Cross 40.5
New Cross 42 [82.5] Wembley 62 [129.5]

Final
Belle Vue 71 Wembley 36
Wembley 34 [70] Belle Vue 74 [145]

London Cup

First round
Wembley 60 Wimbledon 47
Wimbledon 48 [95] Wembley 57 [117]

Semi-final
West Ham 62 Wembley 46
Wembley 57 [113] West Ham 51 [113]

ACU Cup

First round
Birmingham 49 Wembley 59

Second round
Belle Vue 79 Wembley 29

1935

National League

Opponent	Home	Away
Belle Vue	37–34	46–25
	30–42	49–23
Hackney	42–28	43–28
	45–26	40–32
Harringay	41–31	41–30
	32–39	43–28
New Cross	38–34	34–38
	50–22	40–31
West Ham	28–42	40–31
	45–25	41–31
Wimbledon	35–36	29–41
	48–22	25–46

ACU Cup

Opponent	Home	Away
Belle Vue	57–50	74–34
Wimbledon	72–35	43–62

National Trophy

First round
West Ham 67 Wembley 41
Wembley 55 [96] West Ham 52 [119]

London Cup

Semi-final
Harringay 66 Wembley 41
Wembley 50 [91] Harringay 55 [121]

1936

National League

Opponent	Home	Away
Belle Vue	32–40	41–30
	37–34	45–27
Hackney	43–29	30–42
	28–44	30–42
Harringay	44–28	39–33
	43–29	45–26
New Cross	47–25	28–43
	36–35	42–30
West Ham	43–28	27–45
	43–28	34–37
Wimbledon	33–38	34–37
	33–38	35–36

ACU Cup

Opponent	Home	Away
New Cross	59–37	37–59
	54–42	42–54
Wimbledon	59–37	37–59
	49–45	45–49

National Trophy

Quarter-final
Wembley 61 Wimbledon 47
Wimbledon 42 [89] Wembley 65 [126]

Semi-final
Belle Vue 78 Wembley 30
Wembley 54 [84] Belle Vue 53 [131]

London Cup

Semi-final
Harringay 63 Wembley 44
Wembley 60 [104] Harringay 47 [110]

1937

National League

Opponent	Home	Away
Belle Vue	43–40	48–36
	50–34	52–31
Hackney	44–40	38–46
	45–39	34–49
Harringay	48–36	46–36
	53–28	43–41
New Cross	52–31	49–35
	47–36	42–41
West Ham	52–30	68–16
	44–40	49–34
Wimbledon	56–28	31–49
	55–28	33–51

ACU Cup

Opponent	Home	Away
Harringay	53–42	44–52
New Cross	54.5–41.5	47–48
Wimbledon	58–38	42–54

Final
Belle Vue 61 Wembley 35
Wembley 49 [84] Belle Vue 45 [106]

National Trophy

Quarter-final:
Wembley won 44–40 at Southampton. Wembley were awarded a walkover.

Semi-final
New Cross 59 Wembley 48
Wembley 50 [98] New Cross 58 [117]

London Cup

First round
Wembley 58 Harringay 49
Harringay 46 [95] Wembley 61 [119]
Semi-final
New Cross 62 Wembley 46
Wembley 50 [96] New Cross 56 [118]

1938

National League

Opponent	Home	Away
Belle Vue	54–30	48–36
	47–36	43–41
Bristol	57–27	37–47
	54–28	32–50
Harringay	50–34	38–45
	49–35	47–37
New Cross	37–46	45–39
	35–48	45–39
West Ham	44–40	40–34
	48–35	50–34
Wimbledon	43–41	42–42
	45–39	47–36

ACU Cup

Opponent	Home	Away
Belle Vue	67–40	71–36
Bristol	61–47	44–64
Wimbledon	54–54	54–53

National Trophy

Quarter-final
Wembley 61 Belle Vue 47
Belle Vue 60 [107] Wembley 48 [109]

Semi-final
Wembley 38 Norwich 15
Norwich 53 [68] Wembley 55 [93]

Final
Wimbledon 58 Wembley 49
Wembley 43 [92] Wimbledon 65 [123]

London Cup

First round
Wembley 60 Harringay 44
Harringay 59 [103] Wembley 49 [109]

Semi-final
Wimbledon 66 Wembley 42
Wembley 47 [89] Wimbledon 61 [127]

1939

National League

Opponent	Home	Away
Belle Vue	50–34	57–27
	43–41	
Harringay	42–42	36–48
New Cross	52–31	42–40
	59–24	
Southampton	57–27	46–38
	61–22	
West Ham	55–29	
	58–26	
Wimbledon	53–30	48–36
	39–45	

Season abandoned when War declared.

National Trophy

Quarter-final
Wembley 63 West Ham 45
West Ham 62 [107] Wembley 46 [109]

Semi-final
Wembley 74 Southampton 33
Southampton 62 [95] Wembley 46 [120]
Final against Belle Vue not held

London Cup

Semi-final
Wimbledon 59 Wembley 49
Wembley 55 [104] Wimbledon 52 [111]

1946

Date	Home	Away	Type of fixture	Attendance
Friday 19 April 1946	West Ham 41	Wembley 42	Ch	57,000
Thursday 2 May 1946	Wimbledon & New Cross 47	Wembley 34	Ch @ Wimbledon	
Saturday 4 May 1946	Belle Vue 34	Wembley 49	NL	
Thursday 9 May 1946	**Wembley 50**	**Belle Vue 32**	**NL**	**50,000**
Saturday 11 May 1946	Bradford 52	Wembley 32	NL	28,000
Monday 13 May 1946	Wimbledon 41	Wembley 43	NL	
Thursday 16 May 1946	**Wembley 48**	**Wimbledon 35**	**NL**	**43,000**
Wednesday 22 May 1946	New Cross 36	Wembley 48	NL	
Thursday 23 May 1946	**Wembley 54**	**New Cross 24**	**NL**	**65,000**
Tuesday 28 May 1946	West Ham 33	Wembley 49	NL	
Thursday 30 May 1946	**Wembley 47**	**West Ham 36**	**NL**	**70,000**
Saturday 1 June 1946	Wembley 41	The Rest 42	Ch @ Odsal	
Thursday 6 June 1946	**Wembley 47**	**Bradford 37**	**NL**	**71,000**
Monday 10 June 1946	Belle Vue 53	Wembley 43	ACU Cup	
Thursday 13 June 1946	**Wembley 80**	**Birmingham 27**	**NT**	**72,000**
Thursday 20 June 1946	**Wembley 43**	**Belle Vue 39**	**NL**	**76,000**
Saturday 22 June 1946	Birmingham 31 [58]	Wembley 77 [157]	NT	
Tuesday 25 June 1946	West Ham 50	Wembley 46	ACU Cup	61,000
Thursday 27 June 1946	**Wembley 53**	**West Ham 42**	**ACU Cup**	**85,000**
Thursday 4 July 1946	**Wembley 57**	**New Cross 37**	**ACU Cup**	**67,000**
Tuesday 9 July 1946	West Ham 62	Wembley 46	LC SF	62,000
Thursday 11 July 1946	**Wembley 65 [109]**	**W Ham 43 [105]**	**LC SF**	**85,000**
Saturday 13 July 1946	Belle Vue 60	Wembley 48	NT	
Monday 15 July 1946	Wimbledon 38	Wembley 45	NL	
Thursday 18 July 1946	**Wembley 46**	**Wimbledon 36**	**NL**	
Thursday 25 July 1946	**Wembley 50 [98]**	**B Vue 57 [117]**	**NT**	**80,000**
Saturday 27 July 1946	Belle Vue 51	Wembley 33	NL	
Thursday 1 August 1946	**BRCQR**	**Jack Parker 15**	**BRCQR**	**67,000**
Thursday 8 August 1946	**Wembley 68**	**Bradford 27**	**ACU Cup**	**65,000**
Saturday 10 August 1946	Bradford 48	Wembley 48	ACU Cup	17,000
Wednesday 14 August 1946	New Cross 39	Wembley 55	ACU Cup	
Thursday 15 Aug 1946	**Wembley 46**	**Belle Vue 50**	**ACU Cup**	**75,000**
Thursday 22 Aug 1946	**BRCQR**	**Eric Langton 15**	**BRCQR**	**60,000**
Monday 26 August 1946	Wimbledon 53	Wembley 55	LC F	
Thursday 29 Aug 1946	**Wembley 66 [111]**	**Wimbledon 42 [95]**	**LC F**	**78,000**
Saturday 31 August 1946	Norwich 38	Wembley 34	Ch	
Wednesday 4 Sept 1946	New Cross 37	Wembley 47	NL	
Thursday 5 September 1946	**Wembley 53**	**New Cross 30**	**NL**	**65,000**
Thursday 12 Sept 1946	**BRCF**	**Tommy Price 15**	**BRC F**	
Saturday 14 Sept 1946	Bradford 38	Wembley 46	NL	25,000
Thursday 19 Sept 1946	**Wembley 52**	**Bradford 32**	**NL**	**50,000+**
Tuesday 24 Sept 1946	West Ham 36	Wembley 48	NL	
Thursday 26 Sept 1946	**Wembley 59**	**West Ham 24**	**NL**	
Saturday 28 Sept 1946	Bradford 43	Wembley 41	Ch	40,000
Thursday 3 Oct 1946	**Wembley 58**	**Wimbledon 38**	**ACU Cup**	**85,000**
Monday 7 October 1946	Wimbledon 47	Wembley 48	ACU Cup	
Monday 14 October 1946	Newcastle 40	Wembley 40	Ch	
Wednesday 16 Oct 1946	Glasgow 38	Wembley 43	Ch	
Thursday 17 October 1946	Middlesbrough 34	Wembley 50	Ch	
Thursday 21 October 1946	Wimbledon 40	Wembley 44	Ch	30,000+
Saturday 26 October 1946	Birmingham 38	Wembley 46	Ch	

NL: National League
NT: National Trophy
LC: London Cup
Ch: Challenge
BRC: British Riders Championship

1947

Date	Home	Away	Type of fixture
Friday 4 April 1947	Harringay 20	Wembley 16	Reserves @ Harringay
Friday 11 April 1947	Harringay & W Ham 42	Wembley 65	Ch @ Harringay
Monday 14 April 1947	Wimbledon 43	Wembley 39	NLD1
Saturday 19 April 1947	Belle Vue 35	Wembley 49	NLD1
Tuesday 29 April 1947	West Ham 42	Wembley 41	NLD1
Saturday 3 May 1947	Bradford 50	Wembley 33	NLD1
Thursday 8 May 1947	**Wembley 41**	**Wimbledon 42**	**NLD1**
Wednesday 14 May 1947	New Cross 33	Wembley 51	NLD1
Thursday 15 May 1947	**Wembley 50**	**New Cross 34**	**NLD1**
Thursday 22 May 1947	**Wembley 52**	**Harringay 32**	**NLD1**
Friday 23 May 1947	Harringay 34	Wembley 46	NLD1
Thursday 29 May 1947	**Wembley 53**	**Bradford 43**	**BSC**
Saturday 31 May 1947	Belle Vue 47	Wembley 49	BSC
Wednesday 4 June 1947	New Cross 45	Wembley 47	BSC
Thursday 5 June 1947	**Wembley 47**	**Wimbledon 35**	**NLD1**
Thursday 12 June 1947	**Wembley 60**	**West Ham 24**	**NLD1**
Friday 13 June 1947	Harringay 38	Wembley 46	NLD1
Thursday 19 June 1947	**Wembley 54**	**Belle Vue 30**	**NLD1**
Thursday 26 June 1947	**Wembley 52**	**Bradford 31**	**NLD1**
Monday 30 June 1947	Wimbledon 42	Wembley 54	BSC
Thursday 3 July 1947	**Wembley 60**	**New Cross 36**	**BSC**
Thursday 10 July 1947	**Wembley 65**	**Harringay 31**	**BSC**
Tuesday 15 July 1947	West Ham 40	Wembley 52	BSC
Thursday 17 July 1947	**Wembley 76**	**West Ham 20**	**BSC**
Thursday 24 July 1947	**Wembley 62**	**Belle Vue 31**	**BSC**
Saturday 26 July 1947	Belle Vue 49	Wembley 35	NLD1
Thursday 31 July 1947	**BRCQR**	**Vic Duggan 15**	**BRCQR**
Monday 4 August 1947	**Wembley 69**	**West Ham 38**	**LC SF**
Thursday 7 August 1947	**Wembley 61**	**Harringay 45**	**NT**
Saturday 9 August 1947	Bradford 44	Wembley 52	BSC
Thursday 14 August 1947	**England 49**	**Australia 57**	**Test**
Friday 15 August 1947	Harringay 47 [92]	Wembley 58 [119]	NT
Thursday 21 August 1947	**Wembley 54**	**Wimbledon 41**	**BSC**
Tuesday 26 August 1947	W Ham 57 [95]	Wembley 51 [120]	LC SF
Wednesday 27 August 1947	New Cross 39	Wembley 45	NLD1
Thursday 28 August 1947	**Wembley 57**	**Harringay 26**	**NLD1**
Tuesday 2 September 1947	West Ham 55	Wembley 51	NT SF
Thursday 4 September 1947	**Wembley 68 [119]**	**West Ham 40 [95]**	**NT SF**
Thursday 11 Sept 1947	**BRC F**	**Jack Parker 14**	**BRC F**
Thursday 11 September 1947	Wembley 44	North of England 39	Ch @ Middlesbrough
Monday 15 September 1947	Wimbledon 38	Wembley 46	NLD1
Wednesday 17 September 1947	New Cross 49	Wembley 58	LC F
Thursday 18 Sept 1947	**Wembley 47 [105]**	**N Cross 61 [110]**	**LC F**
Friday 19 September 1947	Harringay 32	Wembley 64	BSC
Tuesday 23 September 1947	West Ham 40	Wembley 42	NLD1
Thursday 25 Sept 1947	**Wembley 55**	**West Ham 27**	**NLD1**
Thursday 2 October 1947	**Wembley 57**	**New Cross 27**	**NLD1**
Saturday 4 October 1947	Bradford 38	Wembley 46	NLD1
Thursday 9 October 1947	**Wembley 55**	**Belle Vue 53**	**NT F**
Saturday 11 October 1947	Belle Vue 63 [116]	Wembley 45 [100]	NT F
Thursday 16 October 1947	**Wembley 49**	**Belle Vue 35**	**NLD1**
Thursday 23 October 1947	**Wembley 60**	**Bradford 24**	**NLD1**

NLD1: National League Division One
BSC: British Speedway Cup

1948

Date	Home	Away	Type of fixture	Attendance
Thursday 25 March 1948	Wimbledon 30	Wembley 52	Ch	
Friday 26 March 1948	West Ham 49	Wembley 35	Ch	
Friday 9 April 1948	Harringay 39	Wembley 45	NLD1	
Tuesday 13 April 1948	West Ham 54	Wembley 30	NLD1	
Wednesday 21 April 1948	New Cross 56	Wembley 27	NLD1	
Saturday 24 April 1948	Bradford 38	Wembley 46	NLD1	
Thursday 29 April 1948	***Wembley 52**	**Belle Vue 31**	**NLD1**	
Saturday 1 May 1948	Belle Vue 42	Wembley 42	NLD1	
Thursday 6 May 1948	***Wembley 44**	**Wimbledon 39**	**NLD1**	
Thursday 13 May 1948	***Wembley 51**	**Bradford 33**	**NLD1**	
Monday 17 May 1948	Wimbledon 27	Wembley 57	NLD1	
Thursday 20 May 1948	***Wembley 40.5**	**New Cross 43.5**	**NLD1**	
Wednesday 26 May 1948	New Cross 46	Wembley 38	NLD1	
Thursday 27 May 1948	***Wembley 31**	**Harringay 50**	**NLD1**	
Saturday 29 May 1948	Belle Vue 53	Wembley 43	AC	
Thursday 3 June 1948	***Wembley 40**	**West Ham 44**	**NLD1**	
Saturday 5 June 1948	Bradford 66	Wembley 30	AC	
Thursday 10 June 1948	***Wembley 45**	**Belle Vue 51**	**AC**	
Tuesday 15 June 1948	West Ham 49	Wembley 47	AC	
Thursday 17 June 1948	***Wembley 47**	**Harringay 49**	**AC**	
Friday 18 June 1948	Harringay 59	Wembley 36	AC	
Wednesday 23 June 1948	New Cross 49	Wembley 46	AC	
Thursday 24 June 1948	***Wembley 49**	**New Cross 47**	**AC**	
Monday 28 June 1948	Wimbledon 40	Wembley 56	AC	
Thursday 1 July 1948	***Wembley 60**	**West Ham 36**	**AC**	
Thursday 8 July 1948	***Wembley 60**	**Wimbledon 35**	**AC**	
Thursday15 July1948	***Wembley 61**	**Bradford 35**	**AC**	
Thursday 22 July 1948	***Wembley 59**	**Belle Vue 25**	**NLD1**	
Thursday 29 July 1948	***Wembley 35**	**Harringay 49**	**NLD1**	
Friday 30 July 1948	Harringay 53	Wembley 28	NLD1	
Saturday 31 July 1948	The Rest 39	Wembley 45	Ch @ Birmingham	16,000
Thursday 5 August 1948	***Wembley 57**	**Bradford 27**	**NLD1**	
Thursday 12 August 1948	***Wembley 39**	**West Ham 45**	**NLD1**	
Thursday 19 August 1948	**BRCQR**	**Wilbur Lamoreaux 15**	**BRCQR**	
Saturday 21 August 1948	*Belle Vue*	*Wembley*	*NT Rain off*	
Monday 23 August 1948	Wimbledon 35	Wembley 49	NLD1	
Thursday 26 August 1948	***Wembley 64**	**Belle Vue 42**	**NT**	
Saturday 28 August 1948	Bradford 37	Wembley 47	NLD1	30,321
Tuesday 31 August 1948	West Ham 61	Wembley 46	LC SF	
Thursday 2 September 1948	**Wembley 67 [113]**	**West Ham 40 [101]**	**LC SF**	
Saturday 4 September 1948	Belle Vue 64 [106]	Wembley 44 [108]	NT	
Thursday 9 September 1948	**Wembley 73**	**Harringay 35**	**NT SF**	
Friday 10 September 1948	Harringay 52 [87]	Wembley 56 [133]	NT SF	
Thursday 16 Sept 1948	**BRC Final**	**Vic Duggan 14**	**BRC F**	**90,000+**
Saturday 18 Sept 1948	Belle Vue 48	Wembley 36	NLD1	
Thursday 23 Sept 1948	**Wembley 65**	**New Cross 40**	**LC F**	
Friday 24 September 1948	New Cross 58 [98]	Wembley 50 [115]	LC F	
Monday 27 Sept 1948	Wimbledon & Wembley 48	New Cross & West Ham 36	Ch @ Wimbledon	
Thursday 30 Sept 1948	**Wembley 60**	**Wimbledon 24**	**NLD1**	
Tuesday 5 October 1948	West Ham 38	Wembley 46	NLD1	40,000
Thursday 7 October 1948	**Wembley 64**	**New Cross 44**	**NT F**	
Friday 8 October 1948	New Cross 52 [96]	Wembley 56 [120]	NT F	
Thursday 14 October 1948	**Wembley 41**	**New Cross 43**	**NLD1**	**70,000**
Saturday 16 October 1948	Wembley 45	West Ham 39	Ch @ Norwich	10,000

Lions 'home' matches at Wimbledon*.
AC: Anniversary Cup

1949

Date	Home	Away	Type of fixture	Attendance
Friday 8 April 1949	Harringay 31	Wembley 53	NLD1	
Friday 15 April 1949	West Ham 44	Wembley 40	NLD1	
Saturday 16 April 1949	Belle Vue 45	Wembley 39	NLD1	
Monday 18 April 1949	Wimbledon 42	Wembley 42	NLD1	
Saturday 23 April 1949	Birmingham 54.5	Wembley 29.5	NLD1	35,000+
Saturday 30 April 1949	Bradford 51	Wembley 32	NLD1	
Friday 6 May 1949	New Cross 40	Wembley 44	NLD1	
Thursday 12 May 1949	**Wembley 53**	**New Cross 31**	**NLD1**	
Thursday 19 May 1949	**Wembley 54**	**Bradford 30**	**NLD1**	
Saturday 21 May 1949	Birmingham 34	Wembley 49	NLD1	
Thursday 26 May 1949	**England 41**	**Australia 67**	**Test**	**70,000**
Friday 27 May 1949	Harringay 37	Wembley 47	NLD1	
Thursday 2 June 1949	**Wembley 49**	**Wimbledon 35**	**NLD1**	
Friday 3 June 1949	New Cross 48	Wembley 36	NLD1	
Monday 6 June 1949	Wimbledon 39	Wembley 45	NLD1	
Thursday 9 June 1949	**Wembley 40**	**Harringay 44**	**NLD1**	
Thursday 16 June 1949	**Wembley 58**	**West Ham 28**	**NLD1**	
Thursday 23 June 1949	**Wembley 53**	**New Cross 31**	**NLD1**	
Saturday 25 June 1949	Bradford 34	Wembley 50	NLD1	
Tuesday 28 June 1949	West Ham 39	Wembley 45	NLD1	
Thursday 30 June 1949	**Wembley 47**	**Belle Vue 37**	**NLD1**	
Saturday 2 July 1949	Belle Vue 52	Wembley 32	NLD1	
Thursday 7 July 1949	**Wembley 62**	**Birmingham 22**	**NLD1**	
Thursday 14 July 1949	**Wembley 58**	**Wimbledon 26**	**NLD1**	
Friday 15 July 1949	Harringay 30	Wembley 53	NLD1	
Thursday 21 July 1949	**Wembley 65**	**Harringay 19**	**NLD1**	
Monday 25 July 1949	Wimbledon 40	Wembley 44	NLD1	20,000+
Tuesday 26 July 1949	**Wembley 45**	**Bradford 39**	**NLD1 DH**	**40,000+**
Tuesday 26 July 1949	**Wembley 48**	**Belle Vue 36**	**NLD1 DH**	
Thursday 28 July 1949	**Wembley 49**	**Birmingham 35**	**NLD1**	
Thursday 4 August 1949	**Wembley 37**	**West Ham 47**	**NLD1**	
Saturday 6 August 1949	Belle Vue 59	Wembley 25	NLD1	
Thursday 11 Aug 1949	**Wembley 43**	**Bradford 41**	**NLD1**	
Tuesday 16 August 1949	West Ham 64	Wembley 44	NT	
Thursday 18 Aug 1949	**Wembley 56 [100]**	**West Ham 52 [116]**	**NT**	
Tuesday 23 August 1949	**Wembley 54**	**Harringay 30**	**NLD1**	
Tuesday 23 August 1949	**Wembley 41**	**Birmingham 43**	**NLD1**	
Thursday 25 August 1949	**WCQR**	**Wilbur Lamoreaux 15**	**WCQR**	
Wednesday 31 August 1949	New Cross 38	Wembley 46	NLD1	
Thursday 1 Sept 1949	**Wembley 45**	**Belle Vue 39**	**NLD1**	55,000
Saturday 3 September 1949	Wembley & Harringay 42.5	West Ham & New Cross 64.5	Ch @Norwich	14,000
Monday 5 September 1949	Wimbledon 48	Wembley 36	Ch	
Thursday 8 Sept 1949	**Wembley 47**	**Wimbledon 37**	**NLD1**	
Thursday 15 Sept 1949	**Wembley 65**	**Harringay 43**	**LC SF**	
Friday 16 September 1949	Harringay 51 [94]	Wembley 57 [122]	LC SF	
Thursday 22 Sept 1949	**WCF**	**Tommy Price 15**	**WCF**	**93,000**
Thursday 29 Sept 1949	**Wembley 52**	**New Cross 32**	**NLD1**	
Saturday 1 October 1949	Odsal 50	Wembley 33	NLD1	
Thursday 6 October 1949	**Wembley 58**	**West Ham 50**	**LC F**	
Tuesday 11 October 1949	West Ham 42 [92]	Wembley 66 [124]	LC F	
Thursday 13 Oct 1949	**Wembley 47**	**West Ham 36**	**NLD1**	**66,000**
Saturday 15 October 1949	Birmingham 50	Wembley 34	NLD1	

WC: World Championship
DH: Double Header

1950

Date	Home	Away	Type of fixture	Attendance
Wednesday 29 March 1950	New Cross 49	Wembley 70	Ch	
Friday 31 March 1950	Bristol 50	Wembley 70	Ch	19,000
Friday 7 April 1950	West Ham 38	Wembley 46	Ch	58,000
Saturday 8 April 1950	Wimbledon 44	Wembley 76	Ch	
Monday 17 April 1950	Edinburgh 38	Wembley 46	Ch	
Tuesday 2 May 1950	West Ham 33	Wembley 51	NLD1	
Friday 5 May 1950	Bristol 43	Wembley 40	NLD1	15,000
Saturday 6 May 1950	Birmingham 35	Wembley 49	Ch	18,000
Thursday 11 May 1950	**Wembley 43**	**New Cross 41**	**NLD1**	**66,000**
Friday 12 May 1950	Harringay 29	Wembley 55	Ch	
Wednesday 17 May 1950	New Cross 36	Wembley 48	NLD1	
Thursday 18 May 1950	**Wembley 46**	**Wimbledon 38**	**NLD1**	**60,000**
Monday 22 May 1950	Cradley Heath 36	Wembley 48	Ch	
Thursday 25 May 1950	**Wembley 48**	**Belle Vue 36**	**NLD1**	
Saturday 27 May 1950	Belle Vue 45	Wembley 39	NLD1	
Monday 29 May 1950	Harringay 36	Wembley 48	Ch @ Coventry	
Thursday 1 June 1950	**Wembley 58**	**Bristol 26**	**NLD1**	**35,000**
Saturday 3 June 1950	Bradford 41	Wembley 43	NLD1	
Thursday 8 June 1950	**Wembley 51**	**Harringay 33**	**NLD1**	
Monday 12 June 1950	Wimbledon 34	Wembley 50	NLD1	
Thursday 15 June 1950	**Wembley 60**	**Birmingham 24**	**NLD1**	
Thursday 22 June 1950	**Wembley 60**	**West Ham 24**	**NLD1**	
Friday 23 June 1950	Harringay 31	Wembley 52	NLD1	
Thursday 29 June 1950	**Wembley 59**	**Bradford 25**	**NLD1**	
Saturday 1 July 1950	Birmingham 39	Wembley 45	NLD1	
Thursday 6 July 1950	**Wembley 45**	**New Cross 36**	**NLD1**	
Friday 7 July 1950	Bristol 48	Wembley 35	NLD1	
Thursday 13 July 1950	Wembley 33	Wimbledon 48	NLD1	
Tuesday 18 July 1950	West Ham 51	Wembley 32	NLD1	
Thursday 20 July 1950	**Wembley 39**	**Belle Vue 45**	**NLD1**	
Thursday 27 July 1950	**Wembley 54**	**Bristol 29**	**NLD1**	
Saturday 29 July 1950	Bradford 52	Wembley 32	NLD1	
Thursday 3 August 1950	**Wembley 59**	**West Ham 25**	**NLD1**	
Saturday 5 August 1950	Birmingham 79	Wembley 29	NT	
Monday 7 August 1950	Wimbledon 52	Wembley and New Cross 32	Ch	
Thursday 10 August 1950	**Wembley 53 [82]**	**Birmingham 51 [130]**	**NT**	
Thursday 17 August 1950	**Wembley 58**	**Harringay 50**	**LC SF**	
Friday 18 August 1950	Harringay 56 [106]	Wembley 51 [109]	LC SF	
Thursday 24 August 1950	**WCQR**	**Aub Lawson 15**	**WCQR**	
Thursday 31 August 1950	**England 53**	**Australia 55**	**Test**	**54,000**
Thursday 7 September 1950	**Wembley 56**	**Wimbledon 51**	**LC F**	
Monday 11 September 1950	Wimbledon 56 [107]	Wembley 52 [108]	LC F	
Thursday 14 September 1950	**Wembley 53**	**Second Division Stars 30**	**Ch**	
Thursday 21 September 1950	**WCF**	**Freddie Williams 14**	**WCF**	
Wednesday 27 September 1950	New Cross 39	Wembley 45	NLD1	
Thursday 28 September 1950	**Wembley 59**	**Birmingham 25**	**NLD1**	
Saturday 30 September 1950	Belle Vue 40	Wembley 44	NLD1	
Thursday 5 October 1950	**Wembley 52**	**Bradford 32**	**NLD1**	
Friday 6 October 1950	Harringay 36	Wembley 48	NLD1	
Monday 9 October 1950	Wimbledon 41	Wembley 43	NLD1	
Wednesday 11 October 1950	Birmingham 47	Wembley 37	NLD1	
Thursday 12 October 1950	**Wembley 54**	**Harringay 30**	**NLD1**	

1951

Friday March 23 1951	West Ham 44	Wembley 40	Ch	
Monday 2 April 1951	Wimbledon 33	Wembley 51	Ch	
Saturday 14 April 1951	Belle Vue 43	Wembley 41	NLD1	
Monday 16 April 1951	Edinburgh 49	Wembley 35	Ch	
Tuesday 17 April 1951	West Ham 37	Wembley 47	NLD1	
Friday 20 April 1951	Bristol 48	Wembley 35	NLD1	>10,000
Saturday 21 April 1951	Wembley 40	Harringay 44	Ch@ Norwich	
Wednesday 25 April 1951	New Cross 31	Wembley 51	Ch	
Friday 27 April 1951	Harringay 25	Wembley 17	Second Half Ch	
Sunday 2 May 1951	Chapelizod 42	Wembley 42	Ch @ Dublin	
Monday 7 May 1951	Walthamstow 45	Wembley 39	Challenge	
Saturday 12 May 1951	Bradford 25	Wembley 59	NLD1	
Monday 14 May 1951	Wimbledon 47	Wembley 37	NLD1	
Thursday 17 May 1951	**Wembley 49**	**Wimbledon 35**	**NLD1**	**47.000**
Thursday 24 May 1951	**Wembley 60**	**Bradford 24**	**NLD1**	
Saturday 26 May1951	Birmingham 41	Wembley 43	NLD1	
Thursday 31 May 1951	**Wembley 56**	**Bristol 28**	**NLD1**	
Thursday 7 June 1951	**Wembley 55**	**Harringay 29**	**NLD1**	
Saturday 9 June 1951	Bradford 40	Wembley 44	NLD1	
Thursday 14 June 1951	**Wembley 49**	**Wimbledon 35**	**NLD1**	
Friday 15 June 1951	Bristol 37	Wembley 47	NLD1	7,910
Thursday 21 June 1951	**Wembley 44**	**West Ham 40**	**NLD1**	
Tuesday 26 June 1951	West Ham 39	Wembley 44	NLD1	
Thursday 28 June 1951	**Wembley 57**	**Belle Vue 27**	**NLD1**	
Wednesday 4 July 1951	New Cross 29	Wembley 53	NLD1	
Thursday 5 July 1951	**Wembley 43**	**Birmingham 41**	**NLD1**	
Saturday 7 July 1951	Belle Vue 45	Wembley 39	NLD1	
Monday 9 July 1951	Wimbledon & Bristol 37	Wembley 17	Second Half Ch	
Thursday 12 July 1951	*Wembley 30*	*Harringay 18*	*NLD1 Abandoned*	
Thursday 19 July 1951	**England 49**	**Australia 58**	**Test**	
Friday 20 July 1951	Harringay 47	Wembley 36	NLD1	
Monday 23 July 1951	Wimbledon 55	Wembley 51	LC	14,100
Thursday 26 July 1951	**Wembley 64 [115]**	**Wimbledon 44 [99]**	**LC**	**62,000**
Wednesday 1 August 1951	New Cross 45	Wembley 63	LC SF	
Thursday 2 August 1951	**Wembley 70 [133]**	**New Cross 38 [83]**	**LC SF**	
Friday 3 August 1951	Bristol 42	Wembley 42	Ch	
Thursday 9 August 1951	**Wembley 52**	**Belle Vue 55**	**NT**	
Thursday 16 August 1951	**WCQR**	**Freddie Williams 11**	**WCQR**	
Thursday 23 August 1951	**Wembley 43**	**Harringay 41**	**NLD1 DH**	
Thursday 23 August 1951	**Wembley 50**	**Bradford 34**	**NLD1 DH**	
Thursday 30 August 1951	**Wembley 53**	**Bristol 31**	**NLD1 DH**	
Thursday 30 August 1951	**Wembley 55**	**New Cross 28**	**NLD1 DH**	
Saturday 1 September 1951	Birmingham 45	Wembley 39	NLD1	
Wednesday 5 September 1951	Belle Vue 46 [101]	Wembley 62 [114]	NT	
Thursday 6 September 1951	**Wembley 38**	**West Ham 45**	**NLD1**	
Wednesday 12 September 1951	New Cross 35	Wembley 49	NLD1	
Thursday 13 September 1951	**Wembley 59**	**Harringay 49**	**LC F**	
Friday 14 September 1951	Harringay 49 [98]	Wembley 59 [118]	LC F	
Monday 17 September 1951	Wimbledon 36	Wembley 48	NLD1	
Thursday 20 September 1951	**WCF**	**Jack Young 12**	**WCF**	
Friday 21 September 1951	Harringay 35	Wembley 49	NLD1	
Tuesday 25 September 1951	**Wembley 61**	**Belle Vue 23**	**NLD1 DH**	
Tuesday 25 September 1951	**Wembley 55**	**Birmingham 29**	**NLD1 DH**	
Thursday 27 September 1951	*Wembley*	*New Cross*	*NLD1 Rain off*	
Wednesday 26 September 1951	New Cross 53	Wembley 55	NT SF	
Monday 1 October 1951	Wimbledon 61	Wembley 47	Ch	
Thursday 4 October 1951	**Wembley 78 [133]**	**New Cross 29 [82]**	**NT SF**	
Monday 8 October 1951	Wimbledon 58	Wembley 50	NT F	20,000+
Thursday 11 October 1951	**Wembley 41 [91]**	**Wimbledon 67 [125]**	**NT F**	
Monday 15 October 1951	Exeter 42	Wembley 42	Ch	14,000
Thursday 18 October 1951	**Wembley 57**	**New Cross 27**	**NLD1**	

1952

Date	Home	Away	Type of fixture	Attendance
Friday 11 April 1952	Harringay 43	Wembley 41	Middlesex Cup	>40,000
Saturday 12 April 1952	Birmingham 47	Wembley 37	Ch	23,000
Monday 21 April 1952	Wimbledon 28	Wembley and Bristol 26	Ch SH	
Saturday 26 April 1952	Belle Vue 37	Wembley 47	NLD1	
Monday 28 April 1952	Wimbledon 29	Wembley 54	NLD1	
Saturday 3 May 1952	Bradford 45	Wembley 38	NLD1	
Thursday 8 May 1952	**Wembley 62**	**Norwich 21**	**NLD1**	
Saturday 10 May	Norwich 37	Wembley 47	NLD1	
Wednesday 14 May 1952	New Cross 40	Wembley 42	NLD1	
Thursday 15 May 1952	**Wembley 43**	**Wimbledon 41**	**NLD1**	
Saturday 17 May 1952	Stoke 40	Wembley 42	Ch	19,500
Tuesday 20 May 1952	West Ham 48	Wembley 33	NLD1	
Thursday 22 May 1952	**Wembley 55**	**Belle Vue 29**	**NLD1**	
Friday 23 May 1952	Bristol 44	Wembley 39	NLD1	
Thursday 29 May 1952	**Wembley 51**	**New Cross 33**	**NLD1**	
Saturday 31 May 1952	Birmingham 53	Wembley 31	NLD1	
Thursday 5 June 1952	**Wembley 47**	**Birmingham 37**	**NLD1**	
Thursday 12 June 1952	**Wembley 49**	**Wimbledon 59**	**LC**	
Saturday 14 June 1952	Norwich 48	Wembley 35	NLD1	
Monday 16 June 1952	Wimbledon 55 [114]	Wembley 53 [102]	LC	22,000
Thursday 19 June 1952	**Wembley 52**	**Bradford 32**	**NLD1**	
Friday 20 June 1952	Harringay 42	Wembley 42	NLD1	
Thursday 26 June 1952	**England 52**	**Australia 56**	**Test**	36,000
Saturday 28 June 1952	Belle Vue 41	Wembley 43	NLD1	
Monday 30 June 1952	Wimbledon 43	Wembley 41	Ch	
Thursday 3 July 1952	**Wembley 60**	**West Ham 24**	**NLD1**	
Saturday 5 July 1952	Edinburgh 36	Wembley 48	Ch	
Thursday 10 July 1952	**Wembley 61**	**Harringay 23**	**NLD1**	
Wednesday 16 July 1952	New Cross 41	Wembley 43	NLD1	
Thursday 17 July 1952	**Wembley 66**	**Bradford 41**	**NT**	
Thursday 24 July 1952	**Wembley 62**	**Bristol 22**	**NLD1**	
Saturday 26 July 1952	Bradford 58 [99]	Wembley 50 [116]	NT	
Thursday 31 July 1952	**Wembley 52**	**Wimbledon 32**	**NLD1**	
Saturday 2 August 1952	Birmingham 55	Wembley 29	NLD1	
Thursday 7 August 1952	**Wembley 53**	**Birmingham 29**	**NLD1**	
Friday 8 August 1952	*Bristol*	*Wembley*	*NLD1 Rain off*	
Thursday 14 August 1952	**WCQR**	**Jeff Lloyd 14**	**WCQR**	
Saturday 16 August 1952	Birmingham 69	Wembley 39	NT	
Tuesday 19 August 1952	West Ham 21	Wembley 63	NLD1	
Thursday 21 August 1952	**Wembley 59 [98]**	**Birmingham 49 [118]**	**NT**	
Thursday 28 August 1952	**Wembley 63**	**Norwich 21**	**NLD1 DH**	
Thursday 28 August 1952	**Wembley 45**	**New Cross 39**	**NLD1 DH**	
Saturday 30 August 1952	Bradford 35	Wembley 49	NLD1	
Thursday 4 September 1952	**Wembley 40**	**Harringay 44**	**NLD1**	
Thursday 11 Sept 1952	**Wembley 56**	**Bristol 28**	**NLD1 DH**	
Thursday 11 September 1952	*Wembley 17*	*West Ham 7*	*NLD1 DH Abandoned*	
Monday 15 September 1952	Wimbledon 35	Wembley 49	NLD1	
Thursday 18 September 1952	**WCF**	**Jack Young 14**	**WCF**	
Saturday 20 September 1952	Belle Vue 45	Wembley 26	Ch	
Thursday 25 September 1952	**Wembley 58**	**West Ham 25**	**NLD1 DH**	
Thursday 25 September 1952	**Wembley 62**	**Bradford 22**	**NLD1 DH**	
Friday 26 September 1952	Bristol 37	Wembley 47	NLD1	
Thursday 2 October 1952	**Wembley 50**	**Belle Vue 34**	**NLD1**	
Friday 3 October 1952	Harringay 36	Wembley 48	NLD1	
Thursday 9 October 1952	**Wembley 33**	**Second Division Stars 21**	**Ch**	

1953

Date	Home	Away	Type of fixture	Attendance
Friday 3 April 1953	Harringay 52	Wembley 31	Middlesex Cup	
Monday 6 April 1953	Birmingham 37	Wembley 47	Ch	
Thursday 9 April 1953	**Wembley 48**	**Norwich 36**	**CC @ Wimbledon**	
Thursday 16 April 1953	**Wembley 39**	**Bradford 45**	**CC @ Wimbledon**	
Saturday 18 April 1950	Birmingham 34	Wembley 50	CC	
Wednesday 22 April 1953	New Cross 49	Wembley 35	CC	
Thursday 23 April 1953	**Wembley 40**	**Belle Vue 44**	**CC @ Wimbledon**	
Saturday 25 April 1953	Bradford 55	Wembley 29	CC	
Saturday 2 May 1953	Norwich 47	Wembley 37	CC	
Thursday 7 May 1953	**Wembley 38**	**Harringay 46**	**CC**	
Thursday 14 May 1953	**Wembley 51**	**Wimbledon 33**	**CC**	
Thursday 21 May 1953	**Wembley 54**	**Birmingham 30**	**CC**	
Friday 22 May 1953	*Bristol*	*Wembley*	*NLD1 Rain off*	
Monday 25 May 1953	Wimbledon 61	Wembley 46	LC	
Thursday 28 May 1953	**Wembley 52 [98]**	**Wimbledon 56 [117]**	**LC**	
Saturday 30 May 1953	Belle Vue 46	Wembley 38	Ch	
Thursday 4 June 1953	**Wembley 51**	**Belle Vue 33**	**NLD1**	
Saturday 6 June 1953	West Ham 40	Wembley 44	CC	
Monday 8 June 1953	Wimbledon 47	Wembley 37	CC	
Thursday 11 June 1953	*Wembley*	*West Ham*	*CC Rain off*	
Thursday 18 June 1953	**Wembley 49**	**West Ham 35**	**CC**	
Friday 19 June 1953	Bristol 36	Wembley 48	CC	
Thursday 26 June 1953	**Wembley 59**	**Bristol 25**	**CC**	
Saturday 27 June 1953	Belle Vue 38	Wembley 46	CC	
Thursday 2 July 1953	**Wembley 59**	**Norwich 25**	**NLD1**	
Saturday 4 July 1953	Bradford 40	Wembley 43	NLD1	
Thursday 9 July 1953	**Wembley 57**	**Birmingham 27**	**NLD1**	
Thursday 16 July 1953	**Wembley 60**	**Harringay 48**	**NT**	
Saturday 18 July 1953	Harringay 40[88]	Wembley 68 [128]	NT	
Thursday 23 July 1953	**Wembley 39.5**	**West Ham 44.5**	**NLD1**	
Friday 24 July 1953	Leicester 28	Wembley 56	Ch	
Thursday 30 July 1953	**Wembley 59**	**Bradford 25**	**NLD1 DH**	
Thursday 30 July 1953	**Wembley 51**	**Bristol 33**	**NLD1 DH**	
Saturday 1 August 1953	Norwich 44	Wembley 39	NLD1	
Monday 3 August 1953	Wimbledon 42	Wembley 41	NLD1	
Thursday 6 August 1953	**Wembley 78**	**Birmingham 29**	**NT SF**	
Saturday 8 August 1953	Birmingham 62.5 [91.5]	Wembley 45.5 [123.5]	NT SF	
Thursday 13 August 1953	**England 57**	**Australasia 51**	**Test**	
Thursday 20 August 1953	**WCQR**	**Jack Biggs 14**	**WCQR**	
Saturday 22 August 1953	Harringay 52	Wembley 32	CC	
Thursday 27 August 1953	**Wembley 58**	**Wimbledon 26**	**NLD1**	
Thursday 3 September 1953	**Wembley 50**	**Harringay 34**	**NLD1**	
Saturday 5 September 1953	Harringay 33	Wembley 51	NLD1	
Monday 7 September 1953	Wimbledon 68	Wembley 40	NT F	
Thursday 10 September 1953	**Wembley 66 [106]**	**Wimbledon 42 [110]**	**NT F**	40,000
Saturday 12 September 1953	Belle Vue 42	Wembley 42	NLD1	
Tuesday 15 September 1953	West Ham 33	Wembley 51	NLD1	
Thursday 17 September 1953	**WCF**	**Freddie Williams 14**	**WCF**	90,000
Friday 18 September 1953	Bristol 40	Wembley 43	NLD1	
Saturday 26 September 1953	Birmingham 46	Wembley 38	NLD1	

CC: Coronation Cup

1954

Date	Home	Away	Type of fixture	Attendance
Monday 5 April 1954	Wimbledon 25 W. Ham 21.5	Wembley 9.5 Harringay 22	4 Team	
Friday 9 April 1954	Harringay 41	Wembley 43	Middlesex Cup	
Friday 16 April 1954	West Ham 48	Wembley 36	RAC Cup	
Monday 19 April 1954	Wimbledon 58	Wembley 50	Ch	
Saturday 24 April 1954	Norwich 37	Wembley 46	RAC Cup	
Saturday 1 May 1954	Birmingham 44	Wembley 40	RAC Cup	
Wednesday 5 May 1954	Harringay 27	Wembley 57	NLD1	
Thursday 6 May 1954	**Wembley 45**	**Harringay 39**	**NLD1**	
Saturday 8 May 1954	Norwich 47	Wembley 36	RAC Cup	
Monday 10 May 1954	Wimbledon 43	Wembley 40	NLD1	
Tuesday 11 May 1954	West Ham 48	Wembley 35	RAC Cup	
Thursday 13 May 1954	**Wembley 33**	**Wimbledon 51**	**NLD1**	
Thursday 20 May 1954	**Wembley 53**	**Bradford 31**	**NLD1**	
Saturday 22 May 1954	Birmingham 38	Wembley 46	RAC Cup	
Thursday 27 May 1954	**Wembley 65**	**Birmingham 19**	**NLD1**	
Wednesday 2 June 1954	Harringay 44	Wembley 63	LC SF	
Thursday 3 June 1954	**Wembley 60 [123]**	**Harringay 48 [92]**	**LC SF**	
Saturday 5 June 1954	Bradford 45	Wembley 39	NLD1	11,000
Thursday 10 June 1954	**Wembley 50**	**Norwich 34**	**NLD1**	
Saturday 12 June 1954	Norwich 33	Wembley 51	NLD1	
Tuesday 15 June 1954	West Ham 46	Wembley 38	NLD1	
Thursday 17 June 1954	**Wembley 54**	**West Ham 30**	**NLD1**	
Thursday 24 June 1954	**Wembley 67**	**Belle Vue 17**	**NLD1**	
Saturday 26 June 1954	Belle Vue 37	Wembley 46	NLD1	
Thursday 1 July 1954	**Wembley 44**	**Norwich 40**	**NLD1**	
Sunday 4 July 1954	Shelbourne Tigers 36	Wembley 42	Ch @ Dublin	
Wednesday 7 July 1954	Harringay 30	Wembley 54	NLD1	
Thursday 8 July 1954	**Wembley 53**	**Harringay 31**	**NLD1**	
Thursday 15 July 1954	**Wembley 64**	**Birmingham 20**	**NLD1**	
Saturday 17 July 1954	Belle Vue 25	Wembley 59	NLD1	
Tuesday 20 July 1954	West Ham 50	Wembley 58	NT	
Thursday 22 July 1954	**Wembley 70 [128]**	**West Ham 37 [87]**	**NT**	
Thursday 29 July 1954	**Wembley 36**	**Wimbledon 48**	**NLD1**	
Saturday 31 July 1954	Norwich 47	Wembley 37	NLD1	
Monday 2 August 1954	Wimbledon 43	Wembley 41	NLD1	
Thursday 5 August 1954	**Wembley 63**	**Bradford 44**	**NT SF**	
Thursday 12 August 1954	**Wembley 49**	**West Ham 35**	**NLD1**	
Thursday 19 August 1954	**Wembley 69**	**Wimbledon 38**	**LC F**	
Saturday 21 August 1954	Birmingham 31	Wembley 52	NLD1	
Thursday 26 August 1954	**WCQR**	**Eddie Rigg 14**	**WCQR**	
Saturday 28 August 1954	Bradford 63 [107]	Wembley 45 [108]	NT SF	
Monday 30 August 1954	Wimbledon 47 [85]	Wembley 61 [130]	LC F	
Thursday 2 September 1954	**Wembley 51**	**Bradford 33**	**NLD1 DH**	
Thursday 2 September 1954	**Wembley 50**	**Belle Vue 34**	**NLD1 DH**	
Thursday 9 September 1954	**Wembley 61**	**Norwich 46**	**NT F**	
Saturday 11 September 1954	Norwich 46 [92]	Wembley 62 [123]	NT F	
Thursday 16 September 1954	**WCF**	**Ronnie Moore 15**	**WCF**	
Saturday 18 September 1954	Birmingham 32	Wembley 52	NLD1	
Tuesday 21 September 1954	West Ham 32	Wembley 51	NLD1	
Saturday 2 October 1954	Bradford 52	Wembley 32	NLD1	
Monday 4 October 1954	Wimbledon 31	Wembley 39	Ch Abandoned	

1955

Date	Home	Away	Type of fixture	Attendance
Friday 8 April 1955	West Ham 43	Wembley 53	Ch	17,000
Saturday 9 April 1955	Belle Vue 49	Wembley 47	Ch	
Monday 11 April 1955	Wimbledon 48	Wembley 48	Ch	
Monday 25 April 1955	Wimbledon 49	Wembley 46	NLD1	
Saturday 7 May 1955	Belle Vue 57	Wembley 39	NLD1	
Monday 9 May 1955	Wimbledon 32 Bradford 6 West Ham 20	Wembley 17 Birmingham 15	Inter-track	
Tuesday 10 May 1955	West Ham 46	Wembley 50	NLD1	
Saturday 14 May 1955	Bradford 46	Wembley 50	NLD1	
Saturday 21 May 1955	Birmingham 50	Wembley 45	NLD1	
Thursday 26 May 1955	**Wembley 49**	**Wimbledon 47**	**NLD1**	
Monday 30 May 1955	Wimbledon 51	Wembley 45	NLD1	
Thursday 2 June 1955	**Wembley 66**	**Norwich 30**	**NLD1**	
Saturday 4 June 1955	Norwich 46	Wembley 50	NLD1	
Thursday 9 June 1955	**Wembley Open**	**Barry Briggs**	**Individual**	
Saturday 11 June 1955	Bradford 55	Wembley 41	NLD1	
Thursday 16 June 1955	**Wembley 66**	**Belle Vue 30**	**NLD1**	
Saturday 18 June 1955	Birmingham 55	Wembley 41	NLD1	
Tuesday 21 June 1955	West Ham 48	Wembley 48	NLD1	
Thursday 23 June 1955	**England 67**	**Australasia 41**	**Test**	
Thursday 30 June 1955	**Wembley 68**	**Birmingham 28**	**NLD1**	
Saturday 2 July 1955	Belle Vue 53	Wembley 43	NLD1	
Monday 4 July 1954	Wimbledon 30, Bradford 17, West Ham 17,	Wembley 16, Norwich 10	Inter Track Ch	
Thursday 7 July 1955	**All Star Trophy**	**Jack Young**	**Individual**	
Thursday 14 July 1955	**Wembley 67**	**Belle Vue 41**	**NT**	
Saturday 16 July 1955	Belle Vue 61 [102]	Wembley 47 [114]	NT	
Thursday 21 July	**Empire Trophy**	**Ronnie Moore**	**Individual**	
Tuesday 26 July 1955	West Ham 50	Wembley 46	NLD1*	
Thursday 28 July 1955	**Wembley 50**	**West Ham 46**	**NLD1**	
Saturday 30 July 1955	Bradford 45	Wembley 51	NLD1	
Monday 1 August 1955	Wimbledon 49	Wembley 46	NLD1*	
Thursday 4 August 1955	**Wembley 63 [109]**	**Wimbledon 45 [94]**	**NT SF**	
Saturday 6 August 1955	Rayleigh 41	Wembley 55	Ch	
Thursday 11 August 1955	**WCQR**	**Brian Crutcher 14**	**WC**	
Saturday 13 August 1955	Norwich 51	Wembley 45	NLD1	
Monday 15 August 1955	Wimbledon 61	Wembley 47	NT SF	
Thursday 18 August 1955	**Handicap Trophy**	**Gerald Jackson 13**	**Individual**	
Tuesday 23 August 1955	West Ham 58	Wembley 38	Ch	
Thursday 25 August 1955	**Wembley 61**	**Bradford 35**	**NLD1**	
Thursday 1 September 1955	**Wembley 67**	**Wimbledon 40**	**Ch**	
Saturday 3 September 1955	Belle Vue 57	Wembley 38	NLD1*	
Thursday 8 September 1955	**Wembley 43**	**Norwich 64**	**NT F**	
Saturday 10 September 1955	Birmingham 53	Wembley 43	NLD1*	
Monday 12 September 1955	Wimbledon 77	Wembley 31	Ch	
Thursday 15 September 1955	**WCF**	**Peter Craven 13**	**WCF**	60,000
Saturday 17 September 1955	Norwich 45 [109]	Wembley 63 [106]	NT F	
Saturday 24 September 1955	Norwich 42	Wembley 54	NLD1*	
Saturday 1 October 1955	Swindon 29	Wembley 67	Ch	

* Wembley home league fixtures moved to opponent's track.

1956

Date	Home	Away	Type of fixture	Attendance
Saturday 31 March 1956	Belle Vue 45	Wembley 39	Ch	
Monday 2 April 1956	Wimbledon 61.5	Wembley 46.5	Ch	
Saturday 14 April 1956	Norwich 42	Wembley 42	NLD1	
Saturday 28 April 1956	Odsal 32	Wembley 52	NLD1	7,000
Saturday 5 May 1956	Birmingham 33	Wembley 50	NLD1	
Monday 15 May 1956	Poole 55	Wembley 29	NLD1	
Monday 21 May 1956	Wimbledon 48	Wembley 36	NLD1	
Thursday 17 May 1956	**Wembley 38**	**Wimbledon 46**	**NLD1**	
Thursday 24 May 1956	**Wembley 50**	**Birmingham 33**	**NLD1**	
Thursday 31 May 1956	**Wembley 61**	**Belle Vue 23**	**NLD1**	
Thursday 7 June 1956	**Wembley 57**	**Odsal 27**	**NLD1**	
Saturday 9 June 1956	Belle Vue 54	Wembley 30	NLD1	
Thursday 14 June 1956	**Wembley 45**	**Poole 39**	**NLD1**	
Monday 18 June 1956	Poole 61	Wembley 47	Ch	
Thursday 21 June 1956	**Wembley 48**	**Norwich 35**	**NLD1**	
Saturday 23 June 1956	Birmingham 50	Wembley 32	NLD1	
Monday 25 June 1956	Wimbledon 49	Wembley 35	NLD1	
Thursday 28 June 1956	**England 49**	**Sweden 59**	**Test**	
Thursday 5 July 1956	**Wembley 63**	**Odsal 20**	**NLD1**	
Saturday 7 July 1956	Odsal 35	Wembley 49	NLD1	
Thursday 12 July 1956	**Wembley 44**	**Wimbledon 44**	**NLD1**	
Saturday 21 July 1956	Birmingham 61	Wembley 47	NT	
Thursday 26 July 1956	**Wembley 60**	**Birmingham 47**	**NT**	
Saturday 28 July 1956	Belle Vue 37	Wembley 47	NLD1	
Thursday 2 August 1956	**Wembley 51**	**Poole 32**	**NLD1**	
Monday 6 August 1956	Poole 55	Wembley 29	NLD1	
Thursday 9 August 1956	**Wembley 46**	**Birmingham 38**	**NLD1**	
Thursday 16 August 1956	**Wembley 54**	**Belle Vue 30**	**NLD1**	
Thursday 23 August 1956	**WCQR**	**Brian Crutcher 15**	**WC**	
Thursday 30 August 1956	**Wembley 41**	**Norwich 43**	**NLD1**	
Monday 3rd September 1956	Wimbledon 53	Wembley 31	Ch	
Thursday 6 September 1956	**London Riders Champ**	**Brian Crutcher 14**	**LRC**	
Saturday 8 September 1956	Norwich 52	Wembley 32	NLD1	
Thursday 13 September 1956	**Wembley 44**	**Wimbledon 40**	**Ch**	
Saturday 22 September 1956	**World Final**	**Ove Fundin 13**	**WCF**	65,000

1970

Date	Home	Away	Type of fixture	Attendance
Friday 27 March 1970	Newport 40	Wembley 38	Ch	
Wednesday 1 April 1970	Poole 37	Wembley 41	BLD1	
Saturday 4 April 1970	Swindon 48	Wembley 29	BLD1	
Saturday 11 April 1970	Coventry 47	Wembley 31	BLD1	
Saturday 18 April 1970	King's Lynn 49	Wembley 29	BLD1	
Thursday 23 April 1970	Oxford 45	Wembley 33	Ch	
Friday 24 April 1970	Newport	Wembley	BLD1 Rain off	
Saturday 9 May 1970	Cradley Heath 37	Wembley 40	BLD1	
Thursday 14 May 1970	Sheffield 43	Wembley 35	BLD1	
Friday 22 May 1970	Glasgow 43	Wembley 35	BLD1	
Saturday 23 May 1970	Halifax 46	Wembley 32	Ch	
Saturday 30 May 1970	**Wembley 41**	**Hackney 37**	**BLD1**	21,000
Monday 1 June 1970	Newcastle 41	Wembley 37	KOC2	
Friday 5 June 1970	Wolverhampton 45	Wembley 33	BLD1	
Saturday 6 June 1970	**Wembley 38**	**Sheffield 39**	**BLD1**	
Friday 12 June 1970	Hackney 52	Wembley 26	BLD1	
Saturday 13 June 1970	**Wembley 47**	**West Ham 31**	**BLD1**	18,000+
Thursday 18 June 1970	Wimbledon 43	Wembley 34	BLD1	
Saturday 20 June 1970	**Wembley 41**	**Swindon 37**	**BLD1**	10,700
Tuesday 23 June 1970	Leicester 45	Wembley 33	BLD1	
Saturday 27 June 1970	Belle Vue 48	Wembley 28	BLD1	
Saturday 27 June 1970	**Hackney 32, Scotland 26**	**Overseas 20, British Lions 18**	**Ch - 4TT**	
Saturday 4 July 1070	**Wembley 41**	**Wimbledon 37**	**BLD1**	15,000
Saturday 11 July 1970	**Wembley 42**	**Glasgow 36**	**BLD1**	
Tuesday 14 July 1970	West Ham	Wembley	BLD1 Postponed	
Saturday 18 July 1970	**Wembley 39**	**Belle Vue 39**	**BLD1**	
Saturday 25 July 1970	**Wembley 45**	**Newport 33**	**BLD1**	
Saturday 1 August 1970	**Wembley 45**	**Exeter 33**	**BLD1**	
Saturday 8 August 1970	**SRC QR**	**Reidar Eide 15**	**SRC**	
Thursday 13 August 1970	Oxford 42	Wembley 36	BLD1	
Saturday 15 August 1970	**Wembley 40**	**Poole 38**	**BLD1**	
Tuesday 18 August 1970	West Ham 18	Wembley 6	BLD1 Abandoned	
Saturday 22 August 1970	**Wembley 37**	**Leicester 41**	**BLD1**	
Saturday 29 August 1970	**Wembley 39**	**Wolverhampton 39**	**BLD1**	
Friday 4 September 1970	Hackney 44	Wembley 34	NLC	
Saturday 5 September 1970	**Wembley 41**	**Coventry 37**	**BLD1**	
Monday 7 September 1970	Newcastle 42	Wembley 36	BLD1	
Wednesday 9 September 1970	**Wembley 40**	**Halifax 38**	**BLD1**	
Thursday 10 September 1970	Wimbledon 41	Wembley 37	Ch	
Saturday 12 September 1970	**Wembley 42**	**Oxford 36**	**BLD1**	
Saturday 19 September 1970	**Sweden 42 Great Britain 31**	**Poland 20 Czechoslovakia 3**	**WTC**	40,000
Monday 21 September 1970	Halifax 47.5	Wembley 30.5	BLD1	
Wednesday 23 September 1970	**Wembley 42**	**Cradley Heath 36**	**BLD1**	
Friday 25 September 1970	Newport 45	Wembley 33	BLD1	
Saturday 26 September 1970	**Wembley 40**	**Newcastle 38**	**BLD1**	
Monday 28 September 1970	Exeter 47	Wembley 31	BLD1	
Wednesday 30 September 1970	**Wembley 38**	**King's Lynn 40**	**BLD1**	
Saturday 3 October 1970	**Wembley 36**	**European Stars 42**	**Ch**	12,500
Tuesday 13 October 1971	West Ham 47	Wembley 31	BLD1	
Friday 16 October 1970	Wimbledon 28 Wembley 26	Hackney 21 West Ham 21	London Fours	

BLD1: British League Division One
NLC: North London Cup. The second leg was raced in a second-half at Wembley
SRC: Southern Riders Championship
WTC: World Team Cup

1971

Date	Home	Away	Type of fixture	Attendance
Friday 9 April 1971	Wolverhampton 44	Wembley 32	BLD1	
Saturday 10 April 1971	Belle Vue 59	Wembley 19	BLD1*	
Friday 16 April 1971	**Wembley 30**	**Belle Vue 48**	**BLD1 @ Newport****	
Saturday 8 May 1971	Coventry 45	Wembley 33	BLD1	
Saturday 15 May 1971	Swindon 43	Wembley 34	BLD1	
Saturday 22 May 1971	Cradley Heath 39	Wembley 39	BLD1	
Friday 28 May 1971	Hackney 39	Wembley 40	BLD1	
Thursday 3 June 1971	Wimbledon 45	Wembley 33	BLD1	
Saturday 5 June 1971	**Wembley 37**	**Poole 41**	**BLD1**	**10,500**
Thursday 10 June 1971	Sheffield 48	Wembley 30	KOC2	
Saturday 12 June 1971	**Wembley 45**	**Sheffield 33**	**BLD1**	**8,000**
Wednesday 16 June 1971	Poole 44	Wembley 34	BLD1	
Saturday 19 June 1971	**Wembley 49**	**West Ham 29**	**BLD1**	**Nearly 10,000**
Saturday 26 June 1971	**Wembley 46**	**Reading 32**	**BLD1**	
Wednesday 30 June 1971	**Wembley 52**	**Halifax 26**	**BLD1**	
Tuesday 6 July 1971	West Ham 32	Wembley 46	BLD1	
Saturday 10 July 1971	**Wembley 51**	**Cradley Heath 27**	**BLD1**	
Saturday 17 July 1971	**Wembley 43**	**Swindon 35**	**BLD1**	**14,000**
Thursday 22 July 1971	Sheffield 44	Wembley 34	BLD1	
Saturday 24 July 1971	**Wembley 48**	**Wolverhampton 30**	**BLD1**	**12,000+**
Saturday 31 July 1971	Wembley 54	Exeter 24	BLD1	
Monday 2 August 1971	Reading 40	Wembley 38	BLD1	
Saturday 7 August 1971	**Wembley 37**	**Coventry 41**	**BLD1**	
Monday 9 August 1971	Exeter 47	Wembley 31	BLD1	
Saturday 14 August 1971	**Wembley 50**	**Hackney 28**	**BLD1**	
Friday 20 August 1971	Newport 40	Wembley 38	BLD1	
Saturday 21 August 1971	**WC European Final**	**Ivan Mauger 14**	**WCEF**	
Tuesday 24 August 1971	Leicester 39	Wembley 39	BLD1	
Wednesday 25 August 1971	**Wembley 47**	**King's Lynn 31**	**BLD1**	
Saturday 28 August 1971	**Wembley 45**	**Newport 33**	**BLD1**	
Thursday 2 September 1971	Oxford 38	Wembley 40	BLD1	
Saturday 4 Sept 1971	**Wembley 39**	**Leicester 39**	**BLD1**	
Saturday 11 Sept 1971	**Wembley 44**	**Oxford 34**	**BLD1**	
Monday 13 September 1971	Halifax 48	Wembley 30	BLD1	
Thursday 16 September 1971	Wimbledon 39	Wembley 39	Ch	
Saturday 18 Sept 1971	**Wembley 44**	**Glasgow 34**	**BLD1**	
Saturday 25 Sept 1971	**Wembley 49**	**Wimbledon 29**	**BLD1**	
Friday 1 October 1971	Glasgow 45	Wembley 33	BLD1	
Saturday 2 October 1971	**Best Pairs**	**Bert Harkins 13 & Brian Collins 9: 22**	**Pairs**	**14,000**
Saturday 9 October 1971	King's Lynn 48	Wembley 30	BLD1	
Friday 15 October 1971	Hackney 32 Wimbledon 24	West Ham 23 Wembley 17	London Fours	
Friday 22 October 1971	Hackney 38	Wembley 40	Silver Dollar Handicap	

* Corrected from 58–20 on the night
** Corrected from 31-47 on the night

Bibliography

Books

Bamford, Robert & Shailes, Glyn *A History of the World Speedway Championship* (Tempus, 2002)
Belton, Brian *Hammerin' Round* (Tempus, 2002)
Chaplin, John *Ove Fundin – Speedway Superstar* (Tempus, 2006)
Dalling, Philip *The Golden Age of Speedway* (The History Press, 2011)
Davies, Trevor *Warzone Speedway* (Trevor Davies Publishing, 2008)
Eldon, Rick *Speedway Souvenir* (Linden Lewis 1947)
Foster, Peter *A History of the Speedway Ashes* (Tempus, 2005)
Hawthorn, Fred H & Price, Ronald *The Soulless Stadium* (3-2 Books, 2001)
Higgins, Lawrence *The First Book of British Speedway* (Bonar Books, 1950)
Hoskins, Ian *History of the Speedway Hoskins* (First Edition Ltd, 2005)
Inglis, Simon *Played in London*, (English Heritage, 2014)
Jacobs, Norman & Broadbent, Chris *Speedway's Classic Meetings* (Tempus, 2005)
Jacobs, Norman & Lipscombe, Peter *Wembley Speedway – The pre-War Years* (Tempus, 2005)
Jacobs, Norman *Speedway in London* (Tempus, 2001)
Low, AM *Wonderful Wembley* (Stanley Paul, 1953)
McDonald, Tony *British Speedway Memories* (Retro Speedway 2013)
Oakes, Peter & Mauger, Ivan (Eds) *Who's Who of World Speedway*, (Studio Publications, 1976)
Oakes, Peter (Ed) *The Complete History of the British League* (Front Page Books, 1991)
Parish, Paul *Webster's Speedway Mirror 1971*, (Webster's Publications 1971)
Parish, Paul *Webster's Speedway Mirror 1972*, (Webster's Publications 1972)
Price, Tommy *Tommy Price's Speedway Mixture* (Atomic Press, 1950)
Sandys, Leonard *Broadside to Fame!* (The Argus Press 1948)
Sportsword, *Wembley 1923–1973* (1973)
Stenner, Jim & Stenner, Tom (Eds) *Stenner's Speedway Annuals* 1946 to 1954 (Stenner Printing & Publishing)
Stenner, Tom *Sport for the Million* (Sportsman's Book Club, 1959)
Storey, Basil *Speedway Favourites* (Speedway Gazette, 1947)
Tomsett, Pete & Brand, Chris *Wembley – Stadium of Legends* (Dewi Lewis Media Ltd, 2007)
Wareham, Tom *Brian Crutcher – The authorised biography* (Stadia, 2008)
Wick, John *Coming Speedway Stars* 1952 & 1953 editions (Fairfax Publications)

Magazines, Journals and Newspapers

Backtrack
Classic Speedway
Speedway Express
Speedway Gazette
Speedway News
Speedway Star

Speedway Star & News
The Sports Historian
Wembley News (1970 and 1971)
Wembley Observer
Willesden Chronicle (1970 and 1971)

Programmes

Wembley Lions home and away match programmes, including World Championship Finals and international matches staged at Wembley

Websites

Speedway Researcher

DVDs

In conversation with Freddie Williams (Retro Speedway)
Memories of Wembley Speedway (Retro Speedway)

THE JOHN SOMERVILLE
COLLECTION

The most extensive photographic history of speedway in the world
IS NOW AVAILABLE ONLINE AT

www.skidmarks1928.com

Browse and purchase iconic photos taken over many decades by the sport's best-known photographers, including Alf Weedon, Wright Wood, Mike Patrick, Trevor Meeks and many others.
From junior novices to world champions, portraits, action and team groups, etc, . . . there are thousands to evoke fond memories of days gone by.
All images on the website have been personally scanned by John himself from his base in Scotland. However, the quality of the original sources vary.